Peasant Maids—
City Women

Peasant Maids—
City Women

From the European Countryside to Urban America

Christiane Harzig
Deirdre Mageean
Margareta Matovic
Maria Anna Knothe
Monika Blaschke

Edited by Christiane Harzig

Cornell University Press

ITHACA AND LONDON

11479108

Learning Resources
Centre

Cornell University Press gratefully acknowledges a grant from the University of Bremen, Germany, which helped bring this book to publication.

First published 1997 by Cornell University Press.

Printed in the United States of America.

Library of Congress Cataloging-in-Publication Data

Peasant maids—city women : from the European countryside to urban
  America / edited by Christiane Harzig.
     p. cm.
    Includes index.
    ISBN 0-8014-3273-1 (cloth : alk. paper), ISBN 0-8014-8395-6 (paperback : alk. paper)
    1. Women immigrants—Illinois—Chicago. 2. Women—Europe,
Northern—Social conditions. 3. Europe—Rural conditions—19th
century. 4. Europe, Northern—Emigration and immigration.
  I. Harzig, Christiane.
  HQ1439.C47P43 1997
  305.48′8′00977311—dc21   97-5368

Contents

◆

Illustrations, Maps, and Tables

Preface

Throughout the nineteenth and early twentieth centuries, immigrants from Europe came to America in search of a better life for themselves and their offspring—or just for better wages in order to maintain their family life. These immigrants made up three-fourths of the population in many urban centers and were largely responsible for the industrialization and urbanization that created the modern United States. About 30 to 50 percent—the exact number varies by ethnic group—were women. *Peasant Maids—City Women* examines where these women came from, analyzes their place in the societies they left behind, and shows how their lives changed and how they participated in building urban America.

The book focuses on the four largest ethnic groups in Chicago around the turn of the century: Germans, Irish, Swedes, and Poles. It begins its story in the respective home countries. Because of the vast regional variations in nineteenth-century Europe, however, we did not look at nation-states but chose regions that sent many migrants to Chicago. The first part of the book presents concise social histories of four seemingly different European rural cultures, with an emphasis on gender rarely found in European historical scholarship. At the end of each chapter we know why some women wanted to emigrate. The stories continue in Chicago, where we examine how the women organized their lives in the city's ethnic neighborhoods.

Each chapter follows a similar outline. After a brief description of the national historical framework, the regions are introduced with basic information on geographical, social, and political structures. Then follows in-depth analysis of the life-course experience of women, their functions and roles in rural society, their work as well as their prospects. Chapters in the second part describe the neighborhoods and parishes that provided living space for the four ethnic groups. We obtained demographic information on family formation and family change. The statistical skeletons were fleshed out with information on family crises and family culture. The broader picture of community formation and ethnic women's organizations introduces an ethnic women's movement that has hitherto gone unnoticed in historical writing. In the end we assess the change that took place in immigrant women's lives, and also the degree to which these women participated in constructing modern Chicago.

This research design was accomplished through close cooperation among five scholars from the four ethnic groups involved: Deirdre Mageean from Ireland, now living in Maine; Margareta Matovic from Sweden, living in Stockholm; Maria Anna Knothe from Warsaw, Poland; and Monika Blaschke and Christiane Harzig, both living in Bremen, Germany. This multiethnic research team allowed for extensive use of original sources and language material, and each scholar brought with her firm knowledge and understanding of national histories and historical discourses. We nevertheless followed a joint research agenda, agreeing on major research questions, interpretative framework, and chapter outlines. The chapters are comparable and specific at the same time—the scholars represented not only four languages and four national academic traditions but also three academic disciplines (history, sociology, and anthropology).

Something else became apparent throughout the work: a three-month stay in Chicago, living together and cooperating in research and also in housekeeping, provided us with a delicious variety of ethnic cooking and also gave us the chance to get to know each other. We realized how much our personalities shaped and influenced our academic research. With the days of historicism and the search for a positivistic, value-free objectivity long past, historians have become aware of the limitations imposed and opportunities offered by the personality a researcher brings to the job. We know how much the facts we collect, the sources we consult, what we decide to include and to leave out, shape the way we organize our storyline and influence our interpretations. Very rarely, however, do we have the chance to experience these processes at work. The sensitive reader will grasp the different personalities behind the various chapters, and we are convinced the book is better for it.

Without the generous financial support of the Volkwagen Foundation, the project would have not been possible. We especially thank Helga Junkers and Ingrid Frommer for their unbureaucratic and efficient cooperation. Additional funding from the University of Bremen helped to put the finishing touches on the book. Jürgen Timm, rector of the University, and Rosemarie Goerke smoothed the way.

The Newberry Library in Chicago granted the project members the status of research fellows. The staff of the library, especially Richard Brown, David Thackeray, and Ruth Hamilton—respectively academic vice president, curator of local and family history, and assistant director, research and education—offered us working facilities and advice and made our research stay not only productive but also very pleasant. Archie Motley, curator of manuscripts at the Chicago Historical Society, contributed greatly in locating materials.

For the German chapters we appreciate the assistance of the late Lothar Elsner, professor of history at the University of Rostock, who made cooperation possible long before the walls came tumbling down. For guidance through the archives of Mecklenburg we owe thanks to Axel Lubinski and particularly to Heike Müns from the Institut für Volkskunde, Wossidlo Archiv, whose knowledge of Mecklenburg folk culture was invaluable to us. In Chicago, Tom Gora from the German-American Heritage Institute as well as John Jentz and Ursula Blix opened up new sources. The archives at Concordia Historical Institute in St. Louis and at Special Collections, University of Illinois, Chicago Circle, provided valuable information. Many thanks to the staff.

Research on Irish immigrant women was greatly aided by the staff of the Public Record Office of Northern Ireland, the National Library of Ireland, and the Folklore Commission of Ireland. The staff of the Archdiocesan Archives of Chicago, particularly Tim Slavin, helped us identify the contours of the Irish community. We are most grateful to Ellen Skerett for sharing her wealth of knowledge on parish histories and to Janet Nolan of Loyola University for her useful comments.

The Swedish part profited from the comments of Lars-Göran Tedebrand at the University of Umeå and of Ann-Sofie Ohlander, University of Uppsala, who gave advice and suggestions. Ulf Beijbom from the Emigrant Institute in Växjö and Kerstin Söderling and Bengt Åkermalm at the library of the Arbetslivscentrum helped in the process of historical discovery. Heartfelt thanks go to the many people in Dalsland, especially Roland Olsson and Monika Antonsson, who provided personal insights into Swedish emigration. On the other side, special thanks go to Stina Hirsch and Marie Carlson in Evanston, who helped us understand Swedish maids. The support and generous help of Anita Olson at the Scandinavian Section of North Park College and Selma Jacobson at the Swedish-American Museum brought the Swedish-American community in Chicago to life for us.

Work on the Polish chapters was inspired by Anna Reczyńska and Marta Trembecka from the Polonia Research Institute at Jagiellonian University in Kraków, and aided by John and Regina Kulszycki, Dominik Pacyga, and Kathleen Alaimo, scholars and friends in Chicago. C. Frank Phillips, Felix S. Miliskiewicz, Edward Janas, and Dolores Glowinski at St. John Cantius Parish, and Jan Kiełbasa from Zaborów parish were very helpful in archival searches. Walerlia Noiszewska gave us a wonderful woman's perspective on historical processes of migration. Anna Kuczyńska from Warsaw University helped with translations and offered much useful advice. Dorota and Michaeł Praszałowicz were always at the right place at the right time.

We gratefully acknowledge comments from Mary Cygan, Hasia Diner, Tamara Hareven, Ewa Morawska, and all the women and men who shared their ideas with us during a conference on women in the migration process in Worpswede, Germany, in 1990 and who helped in focusing our concepts. In particular, Kathy Conzen, Donna Gabaccia, and Dirk Hoerder have provided constant encouragement, supportive criticism, and valuable insights at all stages of planning, research, and writing.

Thomas Kozak applied his superior language skills to our text, and Roger Haydon put much more than usual effort into turning a sometimes untidy manuscript into a book. Thank you.

CHRISTIANE HARZIG

Bremen

Peasant Maids—
City Women

INTRODUCTION

Women Move from the European Countryside to Urban America

Christiane Harzig

This book is about women who left rural Europe to help build Chicago. From the 1850s to the 1920s 30 to 50 percent of the migrants who came to the United States were women. Far from an undifferentiated mass, they varied in their ethnicity, regional origin, class, education, work experience, religion, age, and family role. Their reasons for leaving and their hopes and dreams for the future were as numerous as the people themselves.

Our work has been guided by two major hypotheses: women experience migration and subsequent acculturation differently from men; and among women the process differs according to cultural background.

Our first aim is to examine how migration affected women's lives. During the second half of the nineteenth century, migration was the central reality for many. Europeans migrated themselves, their kin and neighbors migrated, they were part of migration networks, and they had to accommodate changes brought about by migration. To understand these changes we have to show where women migrants came from, what defined their place in the old and the new society, and what structured and organized their lives before and after migration.

Our second aim is to identify the part ethnicity and culture played in the migration experience by comparing four separate places of origin. Mecklenburg in Germany, Munster in Ireland, Dalsland in

1

Sweden, and Zaborów in Polish Galicia had their own specific tradi-tions at the same time that they participated in different courses of national development. Thus we examine how rural cultures differed, how these differences affected the migrants' lives, and also what these cultures had in common.

Contributing to a broad understanding of the process of urban-ization is another of our central aims. Focusing on the roles of gen-der and ethnicity in the creation of an urban culture, we show how these immigrant women built their neighborhoods and communi-ties. They shaped social relations in an urban American environ-ment, affected gender relations, and helped to create a social net-work and charity system in which they both gave and received assistance.

Last but not least this book offers a nuanced account of accul-turation. Immigrant women, we find, neither became full-fledged Americans in one sweeping stroke nor remained stuck in traditional enclaves. They had to organize their lives in an American city so as to ensure immediate survival and to shape the future. These women kept from their former lives what had value and discarded what did not work as they learned to function in their new situation. The book provides a gendered understanding of how two powerful processes of American history, acculturation and urbanization, inter-acted.

Over the last twenty-five years feminist research has demon-strated that the male-dominated recording of the past presents only a fraction of the complex system of gendered relationships and de-velopments which we call history. The exclusion of women distorts and impoverishes our understanding of the past, and attempts to remedy this situation have led to far-reaching changes in historical analysis.[1]

Historiographical interest specifically in immigrant women has undergone several phases. First there was the search for the excep-tional experience, the outstanding immigrant woman.[2] Then came an emphasis on immigrant women as laborers who slaved in textile

---

[1]See Sydney Stahl Weinberg, "The Treatment of Women in Immigration History: A Call for a Change," *Journal of American Ethnic History* 11/4 (1992): 25–46.

[2]See Maxine Seller, "Beyond the Stereotype: A New Look at the Immigrant Woman, 1880–1924," *Journal of Ethnic Studies* 3 (1975): 59–70.

industries or as family members who provided stability and continuity but lost out during modernization. In a third phase, the analysis became complex and more revealing as immigrant women of particular ethnic groups were studied in depth.

Research filled in blank spots and eventually changed our analytical models for grasping historical reality. Hasia Diner's analysis of Irish immigrant women challenged the stereotype of passive rural European women who faithfully followed their husbands into a future over which they had no control.[3] Varpu Lindström-Best made us aware of the rebellious nature of single working women in the Finnish-Canadian community and how the "unbalanced sex ratios" (in lumber camps and mining towns) shaped gender relations. The focus on daughters and mother-daughter relationships provided by Susan Glenn and Sydney Weinberg shifted our attention to the concept of "generation" and made us sensitive to gender as an aspect in acculturation. Christiane Harzig's account of German women volunteer work in Chicago revealed that women's charity activities were not only essential in immigrants' acculturation but also shaped later concepts of social work.[4]

The overall results of the research are a re-evaluation of the role of the family, an understanding that what structures the family is gender hierarchy and generational interest, and the realization that the relevance of neighborhood and community is equal to that of political forces and work experiences. These changes in interpretation have affected how immigration historians pose their questions. Now migrations have to be considered as complex processes in which labor and marriage markets, the division of labor and migration traditions, family networks, the family economy, prospects for family formation, and gender all interact. The process affects cultures of origin and receiving cultures, as well as individuals.

To gain a better understanding of women's experience of migration, we have borrowed from family and women's history as well as

[3] For example, Hasia Diner, *Erin's Daughters in America: Irish Immigrant Women in the Nineteenth Century* (Baltimore, 1983); Sydney Stahl Weinberg, *The World of Our Mothers: Lives of Jewish Immigrant Women* (Chapel Hill, N.C., 1988).

[4] Varpu Lindström-Best, *Defiant Sisters: A Social History of Finnish Immigrant Women in Canada* (Toronto, 1988); Susan Glenn, *Daughters of the Shtetl: Life and Labor in the Immigrant Generation* (Ithaca, N.Y., 1990); Christiane Harzig, *Familie, Arbeit und weibliche Öffentlichkeit in einer Einwanderungsstadt: Deutschamerikanerinnen in Chicago um die Jahrhundertwende* (St. Katharinen, 1991).

from anthropology. We place the woman at center stage and view events from a woman's perspective. We follow women from childhood to old age and relate tasks specific to their life course inside and outside the family to the larger structure of the community. Women's rites of passage and status changes serve as points of comparison across the four cultures. Feminist historians often use anthropology's concept of networks to re-evaluate power structures and the relationship between the public and private spheres. We have also used anthropological "thick description" to capture a sense of everyday culture and women's place in it. Our life-course analysis shows how women's lives in rural Europe were dominated by the agricultural cycle and by agrarian social and economic structures. We thus examine the habits of mind and the everyday routines that dominated their lives.

Emigration offered many new opportunities for women to determine their own fates. Women emigrated to escape gender constraints, to enhance their chances in the marriage market, and to fulfill family obligations. And emigrating required that they overcome a variety of personal and social obstacles, including cultural conditioning.

For an understanding of women's migration experience, a "systems approach" is more revealing than a push-pull one in which analysis is confined to whether migrants are pushed out of their country by unfavorable circumstances or pulled toward another country by greater opportunity. Migration is, we believe, a complex process through which the contexts of the immigrants' destinations and their places of origin are closely linked.[5] Therefore, we emphasize the structural and cultural determinants of the migration experience. Our attention to "antiquarian details" shows how social networks, the life course, religion, and local politics shape migration. Migration changes the rural gender system in that it introduces additional elements of choice, legitimate alternatives for women.

The book is concerned with migration as it related to ethnicity, gender, and urbanization; we take the analytical concept of class as a starting point. Rural Europe of the nineteenth century was unmistakably stratified. Monika Blaschke (Chapter 1) explores how migration

---

[5]Cf. James Jackson and Leslie P. Moch, "Migration and the Social History of Modern Europe," *Historical Methods* 22 (1989): 27–36.

affected one particular group of the rural poor in Mecklenburg society, the farm hands and maids, who constituted the majority of emigrants to Chicago. Deirdre Mageean and Margareta Matovic (Chapters 2 and 3) show how changes in social relations—a growing distance between classes, the landed and landless, and the employers and servants in rural Munster and Dalsland—triggered out-migration. And Maria Anna Knothe's smallholders in Zaborów (Chapter 4), though a landed class, all had to migrate when they wanted to form families and needed money to buy more scarce and thus expensive land.

In Chicago, class relationships became more complex and the social structure of the city was in constant flux. The occupational categories of husbands and fathers, which are usually used to classify social stratification, have proved to be inadequate indicators of social position when applied to women. Many other factors—family economy, time of arrival, neighborhood, family structure and coherence, religious and charity activities—determined everyday life and tell us about individual aspirations and about how the migration process worked for families and affected their social position.

When Mecklenburgers arrived in Chicago in the 1860s they became part of the laboring class. However, in organizing their families and households they participated in the creation of an urban culture, which shared many elements across class and ethnic lines. The cult of domesticity for women, educational aspirations for children, participation in the semi-public sphere of churches and clubs, and housework in a consumer society were elements of everyday life which most women shared. This is not to say that class differences were not important. The poor German woman who petitioned the German Aid Society in 1895 and the bourgeois German woman who listened to a lecture at the Columbia Damen Club in the same year lived in distinctly different class cultures though they shared ethnicity and gender. On the other hand, consider a poor young Irish woman who joined a religious order and later became a teacher in the parochial school: What is her class affiliation? Or the Swedish domestic servant—a working-class occupation—who saved her money for a respectable dowry, postponed marriage till she found a suitable husband, and then moved to middle-class Lake View to give her children a healthy, clean environment to grow up in. She became a member of the modern urban bourgeoisie.

Gender, Migration, and Rural Life

In his influential study of changes in rural Europe from the French Revolution to World War I, Jerome Blum outlines social development from order to class.[6] Key factors in this transition are demographic changes (e.g., population growth), political developments (peasant emancipation), technological innovations (improved farming methods), and changes in attitude (from group consciousness to individualism). Although these factors are interrelated, population growth had the most far-reaching consequences. It led to a growing pressure on land, which for most Europeans remained the main source of income throughout the century. Increasing subdivisions of land and industry's growing demand for labor prompted many people to consider migration.

Mass emigration from Germany began in the 1830s and continued through the 1950s. By then, about seven million people had left the country, mainly for the United States. Starting in the southwestern regions of Baden and Württemberg, emigration fever reached the midlands of Hesse and Westphalia in the 1850s and 1860s. In the 1880s, people from East Elbia (the agricultural provinces east of the river Elbe) joined the move for better pay and working conditions.

Mecklenburg was socially and economically part of East Elbia, and experienced migration in the 1850s, reaching its peak in 1854. Even though in absolute numbers migration from the two provinces of Mecklenburg (Schwerin and Strelitz) was rather small, as a percentage of population the provinces had the highest rates of outmigration among German states. As a result, this region experienced a population decline from 1865 to 1885.[7]

The sex ratio among German emigrants bound for the United States was almost equal from the 1830s to 1914: the proportion of females averaged 40–42 percent, ranging from 24 percent in 1833 to 45 percent in 1885.[8] For the years 1855–1870, the average was 40 percent.[9]

---

[6]Jerome Blum, *The End of the Old Order in Rural Europe* (Princeton, N.J., 1978).

[7]The two heaviest periods of decline were 1867–1875 and 1880–1885. See Wilhelm Mönckmeier, *Deutsche überseeische Auswanderung* (Jena, 1912), 175.

[8]Walter F. Willcox and Imre Ferenczi, eds., *International Migrations*, vol. 1, *Statistics* (New York, 1929), Table 10, 432–443.

[9]Peter Marschalck, *Deutsche Überseewanderung im 19. Jahrhundert* (Stuttgart, 1973), 173.

From the very beginning, women were part of the mass exodus from Mecklenburg. They made up 45.7 percent of people leaving the Grand Duchy of Mecklenburg-Schwerin in 1855 and in 1856, for example. The proportion of females remained high and reached 52.8 percent in 1874.[10] Their large numbers refute the notion of male pioneer migration. Moreover, during 1846–1914, a fourth of the women who emigrated from Mecklenburg-Strelitz were heads of family households, and 18.6 percent were "single" women.[11]

In Ireland, emigration has been a fact of life since the middle of the nineteenth century. Between 1851 and 1900, nearly four million Irish women and men emigrated to the United States. More than 1.75 million people left Ireland in response to the years of potato blight, 1846–1848, but the Great Famine only intensified a process begun much earlier. The Famine was nonetheless of particular importance in triggering emigration from the province of Munster, because it coincided with an abrupt increase in literacy, which caused people to raise their sights. A total of 1.46 million people left the province between 1851 and 1911; in 1851 alone, 434,000 people emigrated. During the 1851–1911 period, an average of 48.9 percent of Munster emigrants were female, the years 1891–1901 exhibiting an especially high percentage of 52.8. Reduced transatlantic fares and increased remittances sent back by friends and relatives who had left earlier helped poorer women and men to leave the country in the second half of the century. Landlord-assisted emigration to British North America, though insignificant for the entire country, was a special feature of some counties in Munster.

Much as with Germans, Swedes emigrated to North America in concentrated numbers between 1845 to 1930. The emigration can be divided into five periods: the pioneer period (1845–54), the famine years (1868–73), the peak years (1879–93), pre–World War I emigration (1900–1914), and postwar emigration. Between 1851 and 1930, 1.2 million people left; 97 percent of them went to United States.[12]

---

[10] For Mecklenburg-Strelitz, the percentages are similar. E. H. Dietzsch, *Die Bewegung der mecklenburgischen Bevölkerung von 1850–1910* (Schwerin, 1918), 12–16.

[11] For a detailed discussion of emigration from Mecklenburg-Strelitz, see Axel Lubinski, "Die überseeische Auswanderung aus dem Großherzogtum Mecklenburg-Strelitz im 19. Jahrhundert" (Ph.D. thesis, Universität Rostock/Oldenburg, fall 1992).

[12] For an overview of Swedish emigration, see Sten Carlsson, "Chronology and Composition of Swedish Emigration to America," in Harald Runblom and Hans Norman, eds., *From Sweden to America: A History of the Migration* (Minneapolis, 1976), 114–148.

Emigration from Dalsland began shortly before the famine years, and from 1862 to 1930 about 33,000 people left. The province became the second largest area of out-migration in Sweden and also experienced population decline between 1880 and 1910. Twenty-five percent of the emigrants returned, however, which undermines the notions that migration in the nineteenth century was a one-way path and that return migration was a peculiarity of southern and eastern Europeans.

The proportion of females among Swedish emigrants during the peak years was a little lower than for the Germans and somewhat higher than for the Poles. It averaged 35 percent, ranging from 32 percent in 1880 to 53 percent in 1897.[13] Existing migration traditions, a distinctive youth culture with a sense of independence and self-reliance, and growing economic problems that dampened the prospects for marriage were catalysts for emigration. Crop failures in the late 1860s, cheap American grain imports in the 1880s, and growing kinship networks between Dalsland and the United States also caused people to move. Economic necessity was always the main incentive, but toward the turn of the century, wanderlust became an element of youth culture. Young women were just as affected by wanderlust as young men were. Emigrants from Dalsland tended to be young and single. Some were sons and daughters of farmers; others were farm servants with no immediate prospects for starting a family. In some Dalsland parishes during the 1890s, women (especially servants), were the first to emigrate.

Whether Swedish women emigrated as part of a family unit—such were a minority in the case of Dalsland—or as single women, they had experienced the same restraints that had caused men to emigrate. As Chapter 7 shows, they knew what the urban (female) labor market had to offer with regard to working conditions and wages. More than any other group of women in this book, they acted rationally on the basis of this knowledge, attempting to sell their labor to best advantage.

Because Poland was divided among three different power structures and cultural systems (Prussian, Russian, and Austro-Hungarian),

---

[13]The statistics given by Willcox and Ferenczi, *International Migrations*, Table 10, do not differentiate among Scandinavians.

distinctive migration patterns emerged in the three parts of the country. In the Prussian-dominated areas, modernization in agriculture was leading to overpopulation and surplus labor in the 1850s. These factors, along with poor crops and infertile land, were the main reasons for out-migration. In addition to overseas emigration, there was intra-European migration to newly industrialized areas in Germany and France. And there was seasonal migration to fill labor shortages in agriculture (for example, in Mecklenburg). Migration to the United States from this Prussian-dominated part peaked in the 1880s, with 235,000 emigrants leaving during the years 1875–1890.

Emigration from Russian-dominated parts of Poland did not begin until later, but it had greater momentum: 680,000 people left between 1899 and 1914 (Jews were 45 percent of emigrants). During the 1890s, emigration to overseas destinations to countries such as Brazil became popular (40,000 in 1890–1891). By and large, emigrants were the poorest people, landless peasants, and rural workers, all of whom wanted to become independent landowners.

Migration from Galicia, the Austrian-dominated part of Poland, also included Jews and Ukrainians as well as those of Polish descent. The emigrants' destinations were primarily to the United States, Brazil, Canada, and Argentina. Emigration began in the 1880s and reached its peak at the turn of the century (1899–1914), when 600,000 Poles and more than 200,000 Ukrainians left for the United States. In addition, there was significant seasonal migration to Germany and northern Europe, and some emigration to Russia. More than three million people emigrated, the majority of whom had been agricultural workers in Germany.[14]

The sex ratio for Polish immigration to the United States for the years 1899–1914 varied from 27 percent female in 1907 to 41 percent female in 1911; the median range was 32–35 percent.[15] From 1910 onward, more than 40 percent of Polish immigrants were women, and in the first few years after World War I, women actually became the majority.

---

[14]See Krzysztof Groniowski, "The Socio-economic Base of Polish Emigration to North America," in Frank Renkiewicz, ed., *The Polish Presence in Canada and America* (Toronto, 1982), 1–10. See also A. Pilch, ed., *Emigracja z ziem polskich w czasach nowozytnych i najnowszych (XVIII–XXw)* (Warsaw, 1984).

[15]Willcox and Ferenczi, *International Migrations*, Table 10.

By the 1850s, when the story of this book begins to unfold, the paths of social and economic change in rural Europe were well established. The reorganization of social relationships in the villages and the countryside and the city, as well as between the old and the new worlds, were well under way. From the middle of the century until 1914, people adjusted their lives accordingly. Change did not entail sudden ruptures but involved a slow-moving evolution. Our snapshot of people's—especially women's—lives in four different rural provinces helps us understand what change meant to individuals. Many women rightfully became concerned about their futures, especially about their ability to start families. And they acted on their concerns. "Jane" from Munster, for example, refuses to be matched to some man for the price of two cows; she heads for the harbor and finds her way to Chicago. "Hedwig" from Zaborów in Galicia decides to enhance her chances for marriage by earning cash in Chicago for her dowry. "Liza" from Dalsland returns from Chicago a mature, well-to-do woman, to marry an older widower. And "Dorothea," a former maid from Mecklenburg, rejects the manorial landlord's decision to prohibit her marrying. She takes her fiancé and her "illegitimate" children and leaves—and stays away.

Migration, Ethnicity, and Culture

Looking for migration experiences specific to women involves a claim that women and men experienced migration differently. The underlying assumption is that women have in common something that cuts across such analytical categories as class, religion, culture, and ethnicity. Rita Simon and Caroline Brettell claim that attention to gender makes it possible to identify individual motives for emigration that are quite apart from social factors.[16] Donna Gabaccia, on the other hand, shows the structural similarities in male and female migration.[17] But patterns and trends that emerge from the overly

---

[16]Rita J. Simon and Caroline Brettell, eds., *International Migration and the Female Experience* (Totowa, N.J., 1985).

[17]Donna Gabaccia, "Women of the Mass Migration: From Minority to Majority, 1820–1930," in Dirk Hoerder and Leslie P. Moch, eds., *European Migrants: Global and Local Perspectives* (Boston, 1996), 90–114.

broad perspective of surveys need to be supplemented by more detailed analysis, including the role of gender.

As is apparent from the picture painted by Blaschke (Chapter 1) of Mecklenburg, it is not at all surprising that women as much as men felt the desire to leave their home countries. Although there was gender-specific work in agriculture, females and males were subject to the same socioeconomic forces and cultural patterns. During early and middle childhood, they were expected to work within the family. When they reached adolescence, they were sent out to work on larger estates as maids and farm laborers. Once these workers married, they performed grueling work not only for their employers on the estates but also for their own households. The oppressive social and economic conditions of late-nineteenth-century Mecklenburg gave neither women nor men hope for a better future.

Post-Famine adjustments in Ireland included impartial inheritance, high marriage age, reduced marriage rate, and a decline of the textile industry. These factors, as Deirdre Mageean points out (Chapter 2) produced a social and economic situation in which Irish women were particularly vulnerable. Only women with a dowry had a reasonable chance to marry. And with reduced prospects for finding industrial employment, women's status and security deteriorated considerably. Women were marginalized in the post-Famine economy and became more dependent on male support. Mageean also shows how another post-Famine adjustment, new educational opportunities intended to qualify women for work in agriculture and domestic production, also served as an incentive for emigration. When women who had household training heard encouraging reports from abroad, they realized the potential value of their labor.

Most women from Dalsland, one of the most rural provinces in Sweden, experienced a severe decline in living conditions and their future prospects during the second half of the nineteenth century. Customarily, young single women in this part of Sweden worked to earn their keep. Daughters of poorer or landless farmers usually became maids on larger estates and were often treated as part of the family. With growing social differentiation in Swedish peasant society and with middle-class values permeating the wealthier peasant households, however, the distinction between the daughter of a landowning farmer and a servant maid became sharper. As a result, the working conditions for maids deteriorated considerably. Emigration was an escape from—and protest against—exploitative working conditions. In addition, prospects for marriage became worse: women lacked both dowries and suitable marriage partners, and fewer acres of profitably arable land were available. Young women left with the consent and support of their parents and with the help of an extended network of friends and neighbors. Many of them would return.

When Polish women from Galicia began to migrate overseas, they had experience of the systems and traditions of seasonal migration to rely on. For decades, almost every family had sent one or two members to work in German agriculture (who brought back cash needed to survive the winter). Family formation was becoming more difficult because the growing population had made land scarce, and agriculture was the main way to earn a living. Abroad, women could earn the cash needed for a dowry or to help in the partition of the family inheritance. They could also hope to find husbands abroad. As Knothe makes clear (Chapter 4), Polish peasant society had absolutely no place for single people—women in particular. The need to find a husband was foremost, and emigration became the single most important means to this end.

Different as the four rural societies may seem at first glance, there are striking similarities in the context of female emigration. Historians agree that socioeconomic factors, such as changes in agriculture and inheritance patterns, were the most important stimuli of emigration. Our studies, emphasizing gender and using a life-course approach, show how these factors affected family formation. Whether partial or impartial inheritance prevailed, or a landlord decided the people's fates, economic considerations shaped the decision to form a new family. Scarcity of land, inability to find a house to live in, failure to find an appropriate spouse, inadequate dowry or no money at all—any of these could trigger a decision to emigrate.

Women reacted to socioeconomic limitations on family formation in ways that varied according to culture. Women and men from Mecklenburg—often couples who had been engaged for many years—left their country, legalized their relationship (thereby legitimizing their children), and started life anew in the United States. Irish women, on the other hand, might choose relative independence over an "economically sound" relationship. They tended to rely on their own resources, selling their labor or seeking the protected status of a nun to pursue a career. For them, marriage was just one of many options and not always the most attractive. The same is true of women from Sweden. They, too, realized that family formation had become more difficult and that they had other options. Married or single, they could employ their talents and labor to sustain themselves in Dalsland's rural economy, or they could emigrate. For Polish women, on the other hand, no such alternatives existed: they directed their emigration efforts to the single goal of forming their own families.

The distinctive adolescent culture that evolved from domestic service was also crucial to the migration experience of women. Domestic service, work in a house but outside the parental home, prepared women for migration. It trained women in housework skills and, more important, allowed them to mature in a peer group independent of parental supervision. In sum, it prepared them for separation from the family. In both Mecklenburg and Dalsland, young girls and boys went into service on nearby farms. Munster girls, in contrast, left the countryside to work as servants in urban households, often in Britain. Some young Galician women worked on nearby estates, but others left their village every year to work on German estates for the harvest season.

Gender-specific analysis reveals surprising patterns within migration. Men long have been regarded as pioneers in migration who established patterns and made decisions that women would later emulate. Our analyses show that women were subject to the same social and economic pressures—and showed the same disposition to act. Single women had the same incentives to leave as men. Beyond the underlying trends and broad socioeconomic patterns, however, there were differences in the way women approached their migration and what they expected to get out of it.

Feminizing and Ethnicizing Urbanization

Chicago is considered at once prototypical and exceptional for U.S. urban development. A prairie village as late as the 1830s, in eighty years it developed into a metropolis of more than two million inhabitants. It became a center of trade, commerce and industry second only to New York City. European men and women made this growth possible. At the turn of the century, first- and second-generation immigrants made up 77 percent of the total population, with Germans (24.5 percent), Irish (12.7 percent), Poles (6.5 percent) and Swedes (5.9 percent) the largest groups. Most others came from central and northern Europe, primarily Bohemia, Hungary, Italy, and Russia.

Employment opportunities—rapidly growing industry, neighborhood-based crafts and trades, and an ever-present demand for services—attracted immigrants. Also appealing to immigrants were the open social structures of a developing city that permitted ethnic communities to thrive. Most immigrant men worked in manufacturing and mechanical pursuits and in trade and transportation (as unskilled laborers). Immigrant women were servants in private households and restaurants and workers in textile sweatshops. The neighborhood trades provided room for self-employment and the ability to work with fellow countrymen and countrywomen.

From the beginning Chicago was organized by immigrant neighborhoods—so much so, in fact, that the concept of neighborhood and community gave rise to the theories prominent in the newly developing Chicago School of Sociology.[18] For immigrants, ethnic communities offered a sheltered, if not always healthy, environment that assisted acculturation. Immigrant life focused on churches, turner halls, saloons, grocery stores, bookshops, and streetcorners. Ethnic identity became visible in foreign language newspapers, associations, and public festivities expressing pride in Old World traditions. Together these elements composed the ethnic communities that contributed to the historical narrative of urban life in the United States.[19]

An urban environment affected the content and meaning of work and influenced family. City life also brought new family crises, such as desertion and prostitution, and it increased the incidence of

---

[18]Stow Persons, *Ethnic Studies at Chicago, 1905–45* (Urbana, Ill., 1987).

[19]See Bessie Louise Pierce, *A History of Chicago*, 3 vols. ([1938] New York, 1957); John M. Allswang, *A House for All Peoples, 1890–1936* (Lexington, Ky., 1971); Lizabeth Cohen, *Making a New Deal: Industrial Workers in Chicago, 1919–1939* (Cambridge, Mass., 1990); Joanne J. Meyerowitz, *Women Adrift: Independent Wage Earners in Chicago, 1880–1930* (Chicago, 1988).

not-so-new crises such as alcoholism, beating, and unwanted pregnancies. On the positive side, the city introduced new elements of choice and control, and it acquainted immigrant women with new forms of leisure and pleasure (including dress codes that were more fun to follow). Finally, in the city there was not only room, but also the need, for a female public sphere.

Work and Family Roles

The large variety of work tasks, the predictability of the seasonal cycle, and centuries of tradition dominated women's work in rural society. For children, too, responsibilities within the family economy were well defined, whether in Polish families or within the peer group cultures of maids and farm hands in Mecklenburg and Dalsland. How did these cultural traditions change in the city?

When women moved to Chicago, they had to discard much of what had structured their lives; it was no longer of use in a capitalist industrial economy. Women who had worked on the land and who had managed an extended household were reduced to life in a tenement apartment or a city house—to a household governed by the demands of factory workers who brought in cash for them to spend in the neighborhood stores. Women and their families thus were abruptly introduced to the work cycle of a capitalist economy, unemployment, layoffs, underemployment, long working hours, and work-related accidents. Their lives were organized around factory employment, the consumer economy, and neighborhood life. Work in and for the household was a reclusive activity, and they could no longer rely on an extended family.

The idea of the husband being the sole provider notwithstanding, the husband's income was seldom sufficient, and women found means to augment the family economy. Taking in boarders was popular, though it was less common among Irish and German families than it was among Swedish and Polish ones. In family crises arriving from alcohol abuse, illness, or desertion, women had to assume responsibility for the family's income. The women took in washing, cleaned offices, collected rags, or convinced the charity agent that aid was appropriate. (This may have been easier for an Irish woman confronting a Catholic charity than for a German woman facing the German Aid Society, whose credo was the Protestant work ethic.) Thus in managing the family economy, women were often torn between dominant ideology and reality.

In Poland and Ireland, the opportunity to marry had been constrained by overpopulation and diminishing chances for obtaining a farm. Marrying and starting a family in Munster and Zaborów became almost impossible. In Mecklenburg tight marriage restriction prevailed. Women who had moved away from overpopulated areas would probably be sensitive about marriage and fertility. After they emigrated did they opt for smaller families?

After immigrants had lived for a while in an American city, their outlooks on marriage and family changed. Immigrants began to marry earlier out of choice, but they also began to have smaller and sometimes better spaced families. City life everywhere seemed to lead to such changes: migration from rural to urban areas in Europe produced the same results.

We believe that cities in North America gave rise to strong forces fostering modernization and acculturation. In all pre-migration cultures, women were recognized as adult members of society only through marriage. Marriage was an economic contract, affected by property holdings, inheritance rights, dowry provisions, and social status. The urban environment did not erase these matters but altered their meaning. A new wage-earning ability made women more able to control their own fates. This is not to say, however, that the immigrant became an "emancipated" woman because she participated in the labor market, as Marxist feminists used to argue. Experience in the labor market was too circumscribed to launch anyone into liberated womanhood. Nevertheless, access to cash allowed some degree of self-determination, and it changed gender relations. Women who postponed marriage to work as domestics either were considered spoiled for married life, as men in the Swedish community believed, or their experience was regarded as good training for marriage as was sometimes argued in the German press.[20]

Adult status in the urban environment was more related to money-earning capacity than to marriage. A woman's own effort

---

[20]See Christiane Harzig, "The Role of German Women in the German-American Working-Class Movement in Late Nineteenth Century New York," *Journal of American Ethnic History* 8 (1989): 87–108.

could influence the amount of dowry: land holdings in her native country were no longer fixed but could be increased, altered, or transferred by cash earned in Chicago. A woman could even become independent of a land dowry altogether by establishing a new existence as an urban worker. In addition, potential marriage partners, some of whom had left behind a tight marriage market, were looking for wives in Chicago. Finally, because every sibling had access to cash, there were no restrictions as to who was to get married (though immigrant families in Chicago could still have considered the order in which they "married daughters off").

Now marriage and family formation were subject to a different set of rules: factors such as age, religion, and ethnicity gained prominence, sometimes unintentionally. Romantic love had been a marginal, if not downright alien, concept to peasant cultures, but it became important in urban culture.[21] Greater selection from among potential mates was also novel for the immigrants. The chance of marrying somebody from a different religious or ethnic group had been almost nonexistent in rural Europe because of limited social contacts. Very few first-generation immigrants made use of this wider marriage market, however.

In surveying the effects of migration and urbanization on women of four ethnic groups, we discern no neat pattern but a tangled skein. Marriage age, for example, dropped considerably among Germans and Poles, but it followed different patterns. For the Germans, marriage age exhibited an initial steep drop, followed by a smaller second drop a few years later. For the Poles, the initial drop was even greater, but the marriage age rose again after some years. For the Irish and the Swedes, marriage age was less affected by migration: it remained high (it has been argued that this was owing to women's reluctance to rush into marriage). For Polish and Swedish women an increased tendency toward peer group marriages was a marked change; German and Swedish women tried to keep their families small; Irish and Polish women continued to have high fertility rates.

All groups continued to have a high rate of endogamy, but it took various forms. Irish women, if they did not marry Irish men,

---

[21]Cf. Kathy Peiss, *Cheap Amusements: Working Women and Leisure in Turn-of-the-Century New York* (Philadelphia, 1986).

preferred English-speaking partners over Catholics. Swedes could choose from among other Scandinavians, crossing national frontiers but preferring neighbors (Dalsland women often married Norwegians from just across the border). Mecklenburgers always married other Germans but chose partners from other states in Germany, especially Protestants from the North. But Zaborowian women married Poles only—all from within a ten-kilometer radius around Zaborów parish.

Each of these groups reacted to the modernizing influence of a multiethnic urban society in the same basic way. The marriage age and fertility rate dropped, but marriage partners continued to come from the same culture. At what age women chose to marry was influenced by individual experiences with the marriage market, changing female roles, and expectations about marriage and family life derived from the old culture.

Activities in the Public Sphere

By 1900, each of our four ethnic groups had developed extensive networks of female activities in the public sphere. The existence of an ethnic women's culture went unnoticed by contemporary women activists, as it has by most present-day historians of immigrant women. Historians' focus on emancipatory participation in the labor force on the one hand, and an implicit rejection of middle-class women's organizations and charity work on the other, may account for this omission.[22] However, the existence of this female ethnic public sphere in fact contributed substantially to the fabric of city life.

In all four ethnic groups, women played crucial roles in building the community. They performed valuable charity work, which was particularly important at a time when many immigrants had lost the benefits of having an extended family. (Government social programs did not exist yet, and all aid came from private individuals or organizations.) The women's fund-raising activities brought people together and got them involved beyond particular group interests. The skills entailed in publicizing causes, organizing people, and raising

---

[22]See Donna Gabaccia, "Immigrant Women Nowhere at Home," *Journal of American Ethnic History* 11 (1991): 61–87.

money among their own ethnic groups prepared them for larger public responsibilities.

With few exceptions, women's groups remained within their ethnic communities. Only the English-speaking Irish could cross ethnic boundaries, using religion as a vehicle. As a rule, however, immigrant women took no notice of the Anglo-American women's movement, which in turn ignored them. The two movements pursued different agendas. Suffrage and temperance had little attraction for ethnic women, whereas Old World nationalisms and the maintenance of ethnic identity did not attract Anglo-American women. They could have cooperated in charity work, but cultural and language barriers resulted in mutual disregard.

Acculturation

Throughout this book we use, often interchangeably, the concepts of acculturation and assimilation. Whether *assimilation* is used, as in the Polish context, or *acculturation,* as in the German, we all write from the assumption that significant social changes occurred during emigration and that these changes affected the receiving culture as much as the people who arrived in it. Immigrants had to adjust to city life and an industrial consumer society. The city also adjusted. The neighborhoods that immigrants created became the foundation of American urban culture, and the products they sold and bought shaped the consumer society. Our research confirms the conclusions of other researchers: the city was the primary agent of assimilation.[23]

During the past forty years, immigration researchers have offered new paradigms. We have left "the uprooted" behind and substituted "the transplanted." Oscar Handlin, from the old school of thought, observed in 1951: "Emigration took these people out of traditional

---

[23]Cf. Paul F. Cressey, "Population Succession," in James F. Short, ed., *The Social Fabric of the Metropolis: Contributions of the Chicago School of Urban Sociology* (Chicago, 1971), 59–69; Kathleen N. Conzen, "Ethnic Patterns in American Cities: Historiographical Trends," in Ulf Beijbom, ed., *Swedes in America: Intercultural and Interethnic Perspectives on Contemporary Research* (Växjö, 1993), 24–32.

accustomed environments and replanted them in strange ground, among strangers, where strange manners prevailed. The customary mode of behavior was no longer adequate, for the problems of life were new and different. With old ties snapped, men faced the enormous compulsion of working out new relationships, new meanings to their lives, often under harsh and hostile circumstances."[24] But a subsequent generation of scholars discovered ethnic pride in many urban (and some rural) ethnic communities, where an Old World heritage had been maintained. They stressed continuity rather than breakdown and they looked for active, responsible people who were subjects of their own lives rather than objects of historical processes. John Bodnar, for example, became interested in seeing "not only how they adapted to it all but what, if anything, endured in their lives and brought it order and stability."[25]

The idea of the melting pot was replaced by the concept of distinct ethnic communities whose members tried to maintain a home culture in an American environment. Some immigration historians now reject the notion of the melting pot and emphasize ethnic persistence. They argue that these immigrants not only resisted change but also changed American society. Instead of immigrants who wanted to become as American as baseball and apple pie, transplanted Europeans lived in strongly ethnic communities whose influence extended deeply into American urban culture.

In *Peasant Maids—City Women*, we take a closer look at these conceptual transitions. Emigrants from the European countryside to Chicago had to accept tremendous changes in their lives. Urban life itself was the most difficult, the most encompassing change they had to confront. By imposing urban demands on the migrants' lives, the city served as a forceful adaptor—we are tempted to say "melting pot."[26]

We do not, however, see migration as a process of alienation and uprootedness. The women in our book left Europe voluntarily; they had reasons to leave and goals to pursue. They knew what they were doing and what lay ahead of them. They had the benefit of knowing

---

[24]Oscar Handlin, *The Uprooted: The Epic Story of the Great Migrations That Made the American People* (New York, 1951), 5.

[25]John Bodnar, *The Transplanted* (Bloomington, Ind., 1985), 20.

[26]A similar position is taken by Robert F. Harney, "Ethnicity and Neighborhoods," in Harney, ed., *Gathering Places: Peoples and Neighbourhoods of Toronto, 1934–1945* (Toronto, 1985), 1–24.

what the previous generations of emigrants had encountered, and more often than not, the help of relatives and neighbors. By the end of the nineteenth century, the culture of migration had become an integral element of European rural life. Migration networks had made emigration a predictable experience.

Life in America for the new women immigrants, and the urban Americans they interacted with, involved a three-phase assimilation process. In the initial phase, adaptation, fulfilling basic needs (work, food, shelter) demanded a tremendous amount of effort from the immigrants. The extent of adjustment can be deduced only by juxtaposing the culture of origin and the receiving urban culture, in this case Chicago's.

Life in its ethnic communities initiates the second phase, acculturation, in which immigrant women were significantly influenced by—and influenced—urban culture. These ethnic communities offered experience already far removed from the rural cultures of origin. It was here that Mecklenburgers became Germans and Zaborowians turned into Poles. "Americanization," the third step in the process, took place when people began to move out of these ethnic communities into encompassing urban America.

The comparative approach and focus on women of *Peasant Maids—City Women* does not alter the major narrative of emigration, but it adds to the complexity. This historical and anthropological analysis of premigration cultures underscores the enormous adjustments that had to be made. Cross-regional comparison illuminates the great similarities that existed among women—their rural lifestyles and gender roles, their reasons for emigration, and their modes of adaptation to an urban environment. Ethnicity cannot be disregarded as a factor in women's emigration experience, nor should it be disregarded. Urban living arrangements and ethnic patterns interacted to produce a resilient American pattern.

Our historical research for this book has made us admire the courage and fortitude of these pioneer immigrant women. The women's determination to improve their lives and the lives of those around them left an indelible mark on urban America.

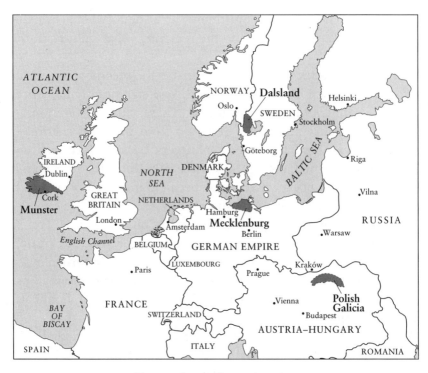

Europe: Areas of outmigration

PART I

Rural Life

1

No Way but Out: German Women in Mecklenburg

Monika Blaschke

To break with the past and to achieve freedom in social relations, thousands of people left the German state of Mecklenburg in the nineteenth and early twentieth centuries.[1] Between 1848 and 1900, the state lost more than 150,000 people to migration overseas. An additional 100,000 moved to the western parts of Germany. By 1900, an equivalent of one-third of Mecklenburg's population lived outside the state.[2] Emigration peaked in the 1850s and 1860s, when almost three percent of the local population boarded ships for America. At that time, Mecklenburg's emigration rates surpassed those of most other German states.

Mecklenburg in the Nineteenth Century

Because of the state's land redistribution policies in the eighteenth and nineteenth centuries and the power of political elites, few peasants had been able to obtain land of their own. Instead, a majority of the peasant population was forced to work on the large manorial or

---

[1]G. J. Bock, *Gedanken über die Ursachen der Entvölkerung Mecklenburgs und Ideen zur Abhilfe derselben* (Rostock, 1865), 4.

[2]Friedrich Mager, *Geschichte des Bauerntums und der Bodenkultur im Lande Mecklenburg* (Berlin, 1955), 417.

governmental estates. Overpopulation, a lack of suitable jobs and housing, and the rulers' general indifference to popular rights (especially their linking of the right of domicile to the right to marry) forced large numbers of the rural population to go abroad. Even more important, however, was an overall climate of inflexibility and stagnation that left little or no room for the local population to take control of their own lives. Both men and women were subject to these political forces. Gender roles were particularly constrained, and little deviation was allowed.

Economic and Political Structures

Mecklenburg is situated in the northeast of Germany, where it is bordered by the Baltic Sea to the north; the provinces of Schleswig-Holstein and the Hanseatic cities of Lübeck and Hamburg to the west; the province of Brandenburg to the south; and the province of Pomerania to the east. As late as 1895, agriculture was the only source of income for 46 percent of the state's population, a higher percentage than in most other German states. The widespread success of agriculture in Mecklenburg can be attributed to a change at the turn of the eighteenth century, when the local peasants and manorial lords adopted convertible husbandry (*Koppelwirtschaft*). With this method, farmers alternated fields used for grazing and grain cultivation, instead of using the traditional three-field rotation system, in which one field of three was left fallow for a growing season. Fallow land almost disappeared, and agricultural productivity increased accordingly. A new crop rotation was introduced; wheat acreage expanded and pushed buckwheat, millet, and lentils into the background; and the raising of livestock grew.[3]

When, later in the century, cheap American wheat lowered prices, competition on world markets became intense, and landowners promoted the intensification of agriculture and rapid mechanization. After 1865, there was increased use of agricultural machines, fertilizer, and seasonal labor. The cultivation of root crops such as sugar beets was expanded, reducing fallow land even further. And

---

[3]See Ulrich Bentzien, "Das Eindringen der Technik in die Lebenswelt der mecklenburgischen Landbevölkerung" (Ph.D. diss., Berlin, 1961), 84.

the new practice of feeding livestock in stalls made possible an intensive use of the soil for crops.[4]

Politically, Mecklenburg was a corporate state (*Ständestaat*) dominated by feudalistic land ownership. It was divided into the two states of Mecklenburg-Schwerin (four-fifths of the total) and Mecklenburg-Strelitz (one-fifth) and was represented politically by the dukes of Schwerin and Strelitz and a common representative assembly (*Landtag*). Together, the two dukes owned roughly 40 percent of the state's land, the so-called *Domänen*. The estates of monasteries and county towns accounted for another 16 percent. The remainder of land was divided among approximately 650 nobles owning a total of more than 1,000 estates. And although the dukes held absolute power in the government estates, they held only constitutional power in the manorial estates.

The apportionment of land and power between nobles and dukes occurred in the seventeenth century, when the dukes asked the nobles for financial support. In exchange, the nobles won the right to jurisdiction and governmental administration on their estates and began to take peasant land at will. They either moved the peasants to other inferior holdings (*Umlegen*) or reduced them to landless laborers (*Niederlegen*), thereby eliminating all peasant farms in their realm. By the end of the eighteenth century, the nobles had achieved a position of strength unequaled elsewhere, and they managed to hold on to it until the early twentieth century. The representative assembly, for instance, was made up of nobles and a few representatives from the county towns, with the dukes having no say at all.

Nineteenth-century attempts to bring about fundamental changes proved to be short-lived. Deep in debt after the Napoleonic wars, many nobles had been forced to sell out to commoners from outside Mecklenburg. These bourgeois owners adopted a more liberal stand on political and social issues and thus came into conflict with the noble delegates, who clung to conservative traditions. In 1844, the bourgeois group gained a majority of seats in the assembly and in 1847 pressed for the introduction of a liberal constitution (ratified on October 10, 1849). Under pressure from Prussia and Austria, this revolution fell

---

[4]See Hans Joachim Ulrich, "Die mecklenburgische Landwirtschaft," in Richard Crull, ed., *Mecklenburg—Werden und Sein eines Gaus* (Bielefeld, Leipzig, 1938), 150–153.

apart. In 1851, the *Ständestaat* was re-established, and Mecklenburg was left without a constitution until after World War I. It was to be the last German state to repeal the corporative system.

Mecklenburg had also been the last German state to abolish the system of serfdom, which it did in 1820. The abolition did little, however, to improve the peasants' situation, liberating them only de jure but not de facto. There was no new division of land. On the contrary, the practice of evicting peasant holders gained new momentum on the nobles' estates. Plans put forward by administrators on the government estates to grant peasant farmers full ownership of their holdings were met with strong opposition by the nobles. In 1822, the government estates introduced hereditary tenure (entitlement) in an attempt to consolidate the state's finances, and hereditary tenure became general law on all government estates in 1867. Although such tenure was far less desirable than ownership, at least the peasant farmers were protected from eviction. Tenant farmers on government estates could thus aspire to a limited degree of independence, whereas their fellows on the nobles' estates continued to suffer from arbitrary eviction.[5] Moreover, large individual land holdings continued to dominate and were more common in Mecklenburg than anywhere else in Germany.[6]

Equally conservative in its politics and theology was the Lutheran Church, the predominant church in Mecklenburg. During the revolutionary uprisings in mid-century, the church hierarchy saw its main function as keeping "the people" under control and liberal elements excluded. Any attempts to give the parishes and their parishioners some autonomy and control over their own affairs failed mainly because of the very influential and extremely conservative *Oberkirchenrat*, the head of the regional church organization. Many parishioners, disappointed by the revolutionary aftermath—

---

[5]The temporary prohibition of eviction that had been ratified in 1849 was nullified in 1852.

[6]As of 1895, large estates covering an average of more than 100 hectares (one hectare equals 2.47 acres) made up 59.5 percent of the total land in agricultural use in Mecklenburg, as compared to 24 percent for Germany as a whole; large estates comprised up to 80 percent of northwestern Mecklenburg. Another 28 percent of the state's acreage was composed of farms ranging from 20–100 hectares. This left a total of 12.5 percent for peasant-held farms (as compared to 46 percent in all of Germany), with 4 percent in use by day laborers (less than 2 hectares), 2.5 percent for small farmers (2–5 hectares), and 6 percent in the intermediate size range (5–10 hectares). Sebaldt Schwarz, *Landeskunde der Großherzogtümer Mecklenburg und der Freien und Hansestadt Lübeck* (Leipzig, 1910), 61.

including many pastors who had supported the people in their demands for greater democracy at the local level—left for the United States. The church, however, had no need to worry about the exodus. The Duke of Mecklenburg-Schwerin was pious and gave freely in support of new church buildings, the pastors were politically loyal and well educated in the correct spirit, and the nobles helped in the reconstruction of a tightly organized church structure. In the second half of the nineteenth century, people who had propagated reform and charity work to help the poor had left the Mecklenburg church.[7]

The People

An overwhelming majority of the state's population was forced to seek work on the large government or nobles' estates. There were three groups of workers: day laborers and their families, male and female servants, and so-called free workers. Day laborers and their families and farm hands and maids constituted the majority of emigrants.

Servants made up between one-third and one-half of the rural work force. They were bound by one-year contracts starting on November 11th (St. Martin's Day). Notice of termination was given at Easter.[8] They worked for bed and board, a fixed annual payment, and some special compensation in kind. Mostly unmarried and in their teens and twenties, live-in farm hands and maids had a variety of fixed positions, such as horse grooms and dairy maids. In the normal course of events, they would settle as day laborers and wives after a couple of years, but circumstances sometimes worked against that, leaving the workers little alternative but to continue in their old positions for a prolonged period of time.[9]

The day laborers (*Tagelöhner*) and their families made up another one-third to one-half of the agricultural population. An estate of 500 hectares employed an average of twenty day laborers, along

[7]Karl Schmalz, *Kirchengeschichte Meckenburgs*, vol. 3 (Berlin, 1952), 392–395.

[8]After 1852, June 24 and October 24 were added as termination dates.

[9]Ulrich Hintze, "Die Lage der ländlichen Arbeiter in Mecklenburg" (Ph.D. diss., Rostock, 1894), 21; Dr. Heike Müns, interview by Monika Blaschke and Christiane Harzig, Wossidlo Archiv, Rostock, 28 November 1988.

with their families.[10] Husband, wife, children, and possibly grand-parents lived in small, crowded estate-owned huts, which they often shared with other families. Working was a family business, and men and women performed equally important tasks. A work week ran from Monday to Saturday, and a typical workday started at sunrise and continued until sunset. The workday lasted at minimum from 6 A.M. to 8 P.M., with an hour-and-a-half lunch break and half-hour breaks at breakfast and supper.[11] Men worked for daily wages. Wives worked mostly for a set range of allowances or considerably lower wages. What little income the families had was spent on rent, fuel, military and church taxes, and so on. In exchange for the women's work on the estate (constituting approximately 200 days a year), the families were allotted a garden plot where they could grow grain, potatoes, and flax, along with land for a cow or two, a pig, or possibly sheep and geese. Other allowances included some coffee, straw, and hay. In times of illness, the lord supplied medical treatment.[12]

For many years, a fixed share of grain accounted for the largest amount of their annual income. During threshing season in winter (up to 150 days), men—supported by at least one additional helper from the family (often women)—received a fixed share of grain, but no other payment. The grain was partly consumed within the family and partly exchanged for cash. After the 1850s and especially after 1870, however, the increased use of threshing machines severely re-duced this source of income. The machine symbolized the growing capitalization of agriculture. It not only led to a decline in the num-ber of day laborers working on an estate but also decreased the la-borers' payments in kind. In later years, mowing and binding ma-chines affected the laborers in similar ways. At the same time, the families' traditional sources of additional income were curtailed when cheaper manufactured goods flooded rural markets. Eco-nomic insecurity became a constant part of life.

---

[10]Ulrich Bentzien, *Landbevölkerung und agrartechnischer Fortschritt in Mecklenburg vom Ende des 18. bis zum Anfang des 20. Jhdts. Eine volkskundliche Untersuchung* (Berlin, 1983), 95.

[11]Max Weber, *Die Verhältnisse der Landarbeiter im ostelbischen Deutschland*, Schriften des Vereins für Sozialpolitik 55 (Leipzig, 1892), 703–715.

[12]K. F. Deiters, *Auswanderung, Arbeitslohn und Bodenwert. Nach Mecklenburgischen Thatsachen* (Frankfurt, 1866), 73.

In the second half of the nineteenth century, free workers supplemented the rural workforce. Hired temporarily as seasonal labor only, they were at the bottom of the social hierarchy. They included small peasants who held land (*Erbpächter* or *Büdner*), others who lived independently in small houses with an adjacent garden and some land for agricultural use (*Häusler*), and those with no land at their disposal (*Einlieger*), who rented lodging from day laborers or small peasants. Not given the security of labor contracts, free laborers had to put up with frequent changes of work places and cyclic unemployment. In addition, there were contract laborers (*Hofgänger*) hired by the day laborers. Working for women's—that is, very low—wages with an occasional extra, the contract laborers assisted with the daily chores imposed on the family and were also expected to work at least an additional 120 days in exchange for cash.[13] When emigration started to take its toll, day laborers often had to rely on out-of-state agencies for a continuous supply of contract laborers.[14] In later years, migrant workers from the east (especially Poland) significantly altered the social structure of the rural population.

Rural Life in Mecklenburg: Not a Matter of Individual Choices

Economic options to improve one's lot were rather limited. In addition, relations between rulers and subjects were strained. General living conditions were affected by a set of patrimonial rules governing the people's daily lives. The manorial lords wielded both police and patrimonial jurisdictional power. They could sentence villagers to up to eight days in jail, and the nobles had the right to personally

---

[13]Deiters, *Auswanderung, Arbeitslohn und Bodenwert*, 34, 72–76; bill ratified by the Mecklenburg *Schiedskommission* regulating day laborers' contracts, 15 May 1848; Ingeborg Müller, "Damshagen—aus dem Alltagsleben der Tagelöhnerfrauen," *Deutsches Jahrbuch für Volkskunde und Kulturgeschichte* 20 (1977): 90.

[14]One contract laborer, a former factory worker from Berlin, provided a vivid description of the contract laborer's daily fight against huge workloads, bad food, and low status in the rural community. See "A City Man on a Farm," in Alfred Kelly, ed., *The German Worker: Working-Class Autobiographies from the Age of Industrialization* (Berkeley, 1987), 204–229; originally published by the Social Democratic Vorwärts Verlag in 1896. See also Fritz Lindig, "Entwicklung und gegenwärtiger Zustand des Auswanderungswesens im Großherzogtum Mecklenburg," in E. von Philippovich, ed., *Auswanderung und Auswanderungspolitik in Deutschland*, Schriften des Vereins für Sozialpolitik 52 (Leipzig, 1892), 305–315, and Hintze, "Die Lage der ländlichen Arbeiter," 47.

apply corporal punishment. Only in 1879 did the legal reform of the German empire finally abolish patrimonial jurisdiction.

The repressive laws made life unbearable for many. The villagers likely suffered most from the statute linking the right of domicile, the right to receive poor relief, and the right to marry. Poor relief was granted to day laborers after two years of continuous residence, and to farm hands and maids living on the estate only after fifteen years of residence. Thus it was in the interest of the manorial land-lords to restrict the number of people who became dependent on them, and this statute helped to keep the number of people work-ing and living on one estate at a constantly low level. Widows, chil-dren, and injured, old, or rebellious people were pushed off the es-tate. Furthermore, although Mecklenburg's population had been increasing, there were no new positions for day laborers. Growing numbers had to take occasional jobs as free laborers to survive. Moreover, the housing shortage was severe, and renting out space was usually forbidden. Both the lack of housing and manorial re-strictions in granting the right of domicile kept the laborer depen-dent on his superiors' goodwill. To make things worse, couples ask-ing to be married had to supply proof that they had a legitimate domicile. Victims of the manorial lords' policy to keep the number of resident laborers to an absolute minimum, couples sometimes had to wait until another laborer's death before they could marry. Deferred marriages and illegitimate births became virtually the rule.

The rigid separation of government and nobles' estates made it almost impossible for people born on one estate to resettle anywhere other than the place where they had acquired the right of domicile. The situation was at its worst on the nobles' estates, where any in-habitant had practically no chance to move beyond his or her tradi-tional sphere, and depended fully on the lord's goodwill. The labor-ers remained in total political and social subordination to the nobles' interests, with no right to appeal.[15] Moving to one of the county towns was no alternative, as the rigid guild system left no room for newcomers in the cities.

---

[15]Martin Stammer, "Die Anfänge des Mecklenburgischen Liberalismus bis zum Jahr 1848," in Helge Bei der Wieden, ed., *Schriften zur Mecklenburgischen Geschichte* (Cologne, 1980), 5–6.

To paraphrase Fritz Reuter—the state's most famous popular nineteenth-century writer—the laborers' efforts yielded neither property, nor rights, nor money, but only a bunch of children.[16] Sociologist Max Weber, on the other hand, found the laborers' situation in Mecklenburg to be clearly better than living conditions in other areas east of the Elbe River.[17] Older historiography generally holds that it was less material need than a lack of prospects to improve one's situation that triggered mass migration.[18] Historiographers point to the noncash portion of the servants' and day-laborers' wages, such as room and board and other payments in kind to support their argument. This view has been challenged, however. Evidence clearly indicates that, although contracts specified payments in kind, the manorial lords often did not fulfill them. And employees faced with termination of their contracts generally fared the worst: left homeless, the only choices left to them were odd jobs, the poor men's huts, the rural laborers' home, or emigration.

Life Taking Its Course

Childhood

Childhood was believed to be little more than the physical inability to participate fully in agricultural labor. As anthropologist Ingeborg Weber-Kellermann suggests, growing up meant first of all an increase in skill and fitness for work.[19] Not considered personalities in their own right, small children were only spectators in the adult world. And although boys and girls each had to fulfil a number of tasks to gain legitimacy in the adult world, their paths were separate from the very beginning. As a popular saying went, if it was a boy, the parents celebrated with a bottle of drink—half a bottle would do for a baby girl. According to a source in the Wossidlo Archive, Rostock, boys were considered real children, while girls were just a

---

[16]Quoted in Karl Schomaker, "Die Auswanderung aus Mecklenburg," *Archiv für Sippenforschung und alle verwandten Gebiete* 28 (1962): 260–266.

[17]Weber, *Die Verhältnisse der Landarbeiter*, 762.

[18]Mager, *Geschichte des Bauerntums*, 395.

[19]Ingeborg Weber-Kellermann, *Landleben im 19. Jahrhundert* (München, 1987), 245.

bunch of "brats." Too many children, whether boys or girls, would be harmful to the family: in that case, so the saying went, only prayers would help. Unfortunately, no detailed statistics on fertility in Mecklenburg are available.

In a day laborer's family, the grandmother or an older girl often took care of the children. At times, the mother would drag the children along to the fields; at other times she would lock them inside the family home and simply hope for the best. The father left in the dark of early morning and did not return before late evening, when the children were already asleep. Seeing their father only rarely, children often were wary of him. From a very early age, local rituals took on a significant role in the children's socialization. Fairy tales and rhymes not only enlivened the day but also often took on the role of direct instruction. Listening to a story or joining in a song, the children learned to identify their place in the world.[20]

Children started to work at a young age, in gender-specific tasks. Starting at the age of seven, girls were hired out and charged with looking after younger children. Girls were fed at work and sometimes given a small present but received no other payment. They had to assist with all household chores, especially when the mother was sick, pregnant, or otherwise unable to keep up with her work. Boys were hired out to mind geese and pigs, to cut fodder for cattle, and to collect weeds. To supplement the family income, both girls and boys picked berries in the forests, collected herbs for tea and medicines in the fields, and gathered fir cones to burn in the fireplace.[21] In late summer, all boys older than ten or twelve years of age were put to work in the potato harvest. Working at a piece rate for up to eight hours, they received only minimal payment, such as, a basketful of potatoes. With the increased cultivation of sugar beets after the 1870s, young boys often spent long days pulling beets in the fields. Girls the same age were sent away from home to peasants' farms or other estates to work as small maids. Other boys and girls took over their mother's, or *Hofgänger's*, work on the estate. There was little time for play, and whatever few toys the children had they usually had made themselves.

[20]Müns, interview. See also Weber-Kellermann, *Landleben*, 248.

[21]See Marie Wegner, *Die Lage der Landarbeiterinnen* (Leipzig, 1905), 8; Müller, "Damshagen," 98; Mager, *Geschichte des Bauerntums*, 523; Weber-Kellermann, *Landleben*, 248, 258.

School was just an interlude for the majority of children. They were crammed into damp, unheated schoolrooms with 40, 50, or 100 other children and instructed by a teacher without much of an education himself. According to one estimate, three-quarters of all children never learned arithmetic. In 1866, another observer estimated that only 15 percent of all military recruits in Mecklenburg had acquired a basic education.[22] The situation was especially troublesome on the nobles' estates, where the teachers were poorly paid and depended on supplementary sources of income for survival. Here, school was usually held during winter only. Access to school was also poor on the government estates. Moreover, many parents were eager to send their children to work to earn extra income. Parents asked for and were given the right to keep their children away from school.[23]

Maids

At the end of October, adolescent girls packed their personal belongings to start working as maids on one of the larger estates or with an individual peasant farmer. The girls likely knew in advance about the long working hours, the large number of tasks to carry out, and the meager rewards. The employment plan was for a one-year contract, followed by an extension of the contract or a switch to another employer. Eventual marriage to a farm hand was expected.

Leaving home early to seek employment as maids on agricultural farms was a common phenomenon across Europe. Many young Swedish or Polish girls, for example, even crossed borders to neighboring countries, where higher wages were paid. Life as a maid brought childhood to a close. Once on her new job, a young maid would join with others the same age and would become in the process part of a distinctively adolescent culture. Not yet bearing full responsibility for family and household, a maid had a sphere of action considerably larger than that of a married woman. From this

---

[22]Heike Müns, "Jahresbrauchtum im mecklenburgischen Dorf während der Übergangsperiode vom Feudalismus zum Kapitalismus (ca. 1800–1870). Eine volkskundliche Untersuchung" (Ph.D. diss., Berlin, 1983), 94.

[23]Müller, "Damshagen," 98. This permission was called "Frieschien," referring to the paper on which it was written.

stage of relative independence, many took the opportunity to determine their own lives more actively. For a considerable number, employment as maids was only a prelude to emigration.

A new maid took up her position among more experienced servants. In general, a peasant's farm had two maids (one 12 to 14 years old and the other 15 to 18 years old) and two farm hands, while the manorial estates required additional helpers. Regulations for servants were strict, and all newcomers were expected to submit to the hierarchical order. Among the servants, it was generally accepted that the longer the individual servants had been with the household or the more experienced they were, the higher up the order they would move.[24] The lack of solidarity among servants very often made collective action impossible—for example, to improve working conditions. Nor did gender necessarily prove to be a unifying factor. Only on rare occasions did the maids develop a group spirit that set them apart from farm hands and superiors.[25]

Work was long and exhausting. It began early in the morning and lasted—with the exception of two or three one-hour breaks for meals—until 8 P.M. Thus, a fifteen-hour workday was typical. With only an occasional Sunday or Thursday afternoon off, maids usually worked 360 days a year. On a typical day, a maid rose around 4 A.M. to milk the cows (usually fifteen cows per maid); feed pigs, horses, and cows; make butter (usually a duty performed by the older, more experienced maids); clean the dung out of the pigpen; and spread manure on the fields. Indoors, household chores had to be taken care of: the potatoes peeled, the green beans hulled, the plums stoned, the house cleaned up, the washing done, and the meals prepared. Depending on the season of the year, fruit had to be picked, potatoes gathered, or grain harvested. Last but not least, there were various special tasks in the threshing, flax breaking, and harvesting seasons, all of which required intensive effort.

Spinning of wool (in the summer) and of flax (during winter) formed another important part of the maid's workload. Flax dominated her workday routine during the winter months, beginning be-

---

[24]Priester, *Arbeits- und Lebensverhältnisse der Frauen in der Landwirtschaft in Mecklenburg* (Jena, 1913), 49–56.
[25]See Weber-Kellermann, *Landleben*, 172–175, for examples of rituals related to flax breaking.

tween late September and early November and lasting until Christmas, February, March, or Easter. To reach the goal of 25 pounds of flax she had to deliver by early spring, every available moment had to be used. Sometimes she started long before sunrise and then, between other chores, often sat spinning until 11 P.M. That schedule left her only five hours of sleep before it was time to get up once again and milk the cows. Many maids suffered from fatigue, and the younger ones especially would fall asleep during monotonous routines. Contemporary reports noted repeated complaints about milking, stable work, and harvesting, which the maids found too strenuous.[26]

Once the working year had come to a close, a big dinner given for maids and farm hands on October 24th concluded the contract year and offered one last chance to get together before some of them left to take up work someplace else. On their three days off, their only such leisure during the year, the maids usually spent time shopping in a nearby town, visiting with their parents, and fixing up their belongings. On the night of the 26th, it was once again time to begin work.

What did they get in return? For servants working on either estates or peasant farms, both lodging and meals were supplied as part of their contracts. Maids enjoyed the relative luxury of sleeping in small rooms in the attic of the main building or in an adjacent house, whereas farm hands were given rooms in the barns. In most cases, two maids or two farm hands shared one bed. According to one observer, this was a safeguard against immorality.[27] According to other sources, however, it was merely the lord's effort to save room. A separate day room for farm hands and maids offered additional space, where the group took its meals or got together on a regular basis and where the maids spun into the night. Farm hands and maids often enjoyed a greater variety of foods and greater quantities than day laborers' families as well. For example, they received a sufficient amount of bread, whereas the poorer day laborers' families often ate thickened pea soup.[28]

---

[26]Priester, *Arbeits- und Lebensverhältnisse,* 5, 107–109.

[27]Karl Borromäus Breinlinger, "Die Landarbeiter in Pommern und Mecklenburg dargestellt nach den Erhebungen des Evangelisch-sozialen Kongresses" (Ph.D. diss., Heidelberg, 1903), 141.

[28]See Müller, "Damshagen," 99.

In addition to free lodging and meals and free (but minimal) medical treatment, the maids received for one year's labor both a lump sum of money and a number of special payments in kind, such as aprons, scarves, a skirt or two for Christmas, flax, wool, a bale of cloth, and sometimes a penny for the local dance. In the 1870s, the maids' wages amounted to only about two-thirds of the farm hands' income.[29] This was no fortune to be sure, yet if prudent with their income the maids could save a substantial part. Maids more often than farm hands saved their annual payment.[30] Lubinski observes that saving was an integral part of that life stage, which was to provide for married life.[31] Savings could also be used for transportation out of the area, whether to larger cities or overseas.

Local Rituals: A Guide to Understanding Adolescent Roles

An analysis of local rituals sheds light on interpersonal behavior and the roles of adolescent girls. Heike Müns has identified three functions of social customs in nineteenth-century Mecklenburg: transmitters of experience, practice in behavioral norms, and confirmation of membership in a specific group (by age, gender, or ownership).[32] Customs thus expressed the participant's social background and position in the social hierarchy. Seasonal and working festivities created a rhythm of productivity and conviviality. Most customs were related to Christian holidays, seasonal working activities, or recurrent events in people's life cycles. Acted out either within one social group or between groups, customs also mirrored social distinctions between manorial and peasant villages. Far from being static, rituals took on different forms over time. They were subject to

---

[29]See Axel Lubinski, "Die überseeische Auswanderung aus dem Großherzogtum Mecklenburg-Strelitz in der zweiten Hälfte des 19. Jahrhunderts" (Ph.D. diss., Universität Osnabrück, 1992), 168. See also Dr. Theodor Freiherr von der Goltz, *Die Lage der ländlichen Arbeiter im Deutschen Reich* (Berlin, 1875), 453.

[30]Weber, *Die Verhältnisse der Landarbeiter,* 716–717; *Mecklenburgisches Wörterbuch* (Berlin, 1957), 292; Priester, *Arbeits- und Lebensverhältnisse,* 54 ff. See also Breinlinger, "Die Landarbeiter in Pommern und Mecklenburg," 144.

[31]Lubinski, "Die überseeische Auswanderung aus dem Großherzogtum Mecklenburg-Strelitz," 196.

[32]Müns, "Jahresbrauchtum im mecklenburgischen Dorf."

changes in political structure, legal status, social hierarchies, and relations among the region's inhabitants.

Unmarried maids and farm hands were the most active transmitters of rural rituals because of their relative independence from family obligations. Functioning as living calendars, they kept others aware of special occasions and cultural life within the community. The rituals they followed acted as a safety valve, making possible actions that were otherwise constrained by rules governing relations between superiors and servants. Emotions suppressed by marriage restrictions found an outlet in rituals that had sexual overtones. Thus anything stimulating the senses was especially favored.

Harvest activities had an abundance of rituals and festivities. Starting at the end of July with the gathering of rye, followed by wheat and oats, and lasting until August 24th, harvesting required everyone's full efforts. Bringing to a climax the year's working activities, harvest was the festive high point of the year as well. A variety of rituals sprang from the cooperation between male mower and female binder during harvest. In the course of preparation for work in the fields, the mower gave a rake to the binder girl, and sometimes she gave him a bouquet of flowers in return. If the two were romantically involved, the exchange of a handmade, richly decorated rake and a carefully picked bouquet took on special meaning, marking man and woman as a couple bound not only by work but by love as well. More often, however, and especially during the rye harvest (when each mower was followed by two binder girls), the exchange of goods served to make the work less burdensome and to encourage smooth technical cooperation. Working together as a team, men and women performed work of equal value.

In the manorial villages, everyone partook of the festivities, including the laborers' families. After the festive parade, a chosen maid handed over the harvest crown to the manorial lord and thus opened the evening program. At the evening dance, the manorial lord might even dance with one of the maids, a gesture of goodwill but clearly understood to be an exception to the rule by every person involved. Such attentions did not always stop at that point, however; sexual assaults on young maids by both nobles and administrators were not uncommon. Contemporary observers noticed that though "immoral relationships" between superiors and maids were rare, a number of landlords or inspectors considered maids as well as day laborers' wives and daughters their property.[33]

Minor household rituals were used to maintain social hierarchy among the workers. During most of the first half of the nineteenth century, for example, who dined when and where in the peasant household was not only indicative of individuals' rank within the patriarchal community but was gender specific as well. Men shared the privileged bench along the window and sat according to their specific tasks, with the farmer sitting on the left and the young boy who herded the cattle on the far right. Similarly, the women's bench next to the wall reflected social distinctions, with the oldest maid sitting next to the farmer's wife, and so on. Toward the end of the nineteenth century, separate tables and separate eating rooms for peasants and servants became the rule, following the example long set by the larger estates. The servants continued to sit on benches, and the farmer's dining room emulated urban styles, with chairs, plates, and silverware.

Marriage Restrictions and Illegitimacy

Most European cultures regarded unmarried females not as individuals but as mere parts of the family structure. Only marriage would bestow full adult status on women; it was, therefore, a highly desirable goal. Marriage options depended on cultural attitudes, social patterns, economic restraints, and legal options. In Mecklenburg, the timing was clearly not a matter of free choice. Although Napoleon's civil code (1804) had granted freedom of marriage to all citizens and repealed marriage restrictions, fear of pauperism reversed the trend it had set in motion. With the exception of Prussia and Saxony, all German states enforced marriage restrictions after the 1830s as a way of limiting the increase in the poor population. In the state of Mecklenburg, restrictions were especially severe, since they linked the right of domicile and permission to marry. This left it basically up to the manorial lord to decide on his laborers' marital status.

Moreover, marriage restrictions were imposed over a prolonged period of time. During the 1850s, government authorities feared a

---

[33]Breinlinger, "Die Landarbeiter in Pommern und Mecklenburg," 174.

mass exodus and recommended a more liberal interpretation of marriage rights, but to no avail.[34] Nor did Mecklenburg's entry into the *Norddeutsche Bund* (North German Confederation) in 1866–1867 mean the end of marriage restrictions. Although the *Bund* granted freedom of marriage to all its citizens after July 1, 1869, restrictions continued to be imposed in Mecklenburg. Simply by limiting the number of houses available for families, the nobles continued to exercise control throughout the 1890s. Not until 1919 did a national law establish a uniform legal right to marriage for all Germany residents.[35]

But marriage restrictions fell short of achieving their original goal to curtail the number of births. All over Germany, illegitimate birth rates grew in proportion to the severity of the restrictions imposed and fell only after marriage restrictions had been repealed. In Mecklenburg, illegitimate births peaked in 1850, when 20.9 percent of all babies were born out of wedlock.[36] Between 1845 and 1867, illegitimate births never constituted less than 17 percent of all births. According to another estimate, illegitimate births exceeded 30 percent in 260 villages and 50 percent in 209 villages. What is more, nothing but illegitimate births were reported in 79 villages (54 on nobles' estates, 20 on government estates, and 5 on estates belonging to monasteries).[37]

Such high rates of illegitimacy amply demonstrate that premarital relationships were widespread. Reporting on female laborers in rural Germany in 1905, Marie Wegner found premarital sex to be common, especially in the state of Mecklenburg. One observer talked about premarital rather than illegitimate births. Similarly, Karl Breinlinger concluded that girls gave in to premarital sex after their parents had given them permission to marry.[38] Estate owners

---

[34]As can be seen in pamphlets issued by the Geheime- und Staatsarchiv, Schwerin (Lindig, "Entwicklung und gegenwärtiger Zustand des Auswanderungswesens," 308); Max Wiegandt, "Auswanderung aus Mecklenburg nach Übersee," *Deutschtum im Ausland* 25 (1942), 170; see also Friedrich Thudicum, *Über unzulässige Beschränkungen des Rechts auf Verehelichung* (Tübingen, 1866), 123.

[35]John Knodel, "Law, Marriage, and Illegitimacy in Nineteenth Century Germany," *Population Studies* 20 (March, 1967): 282.

[36]E. H. Dietzsch, *Die Bewegung der mecklenburgischen Bevölkerung von 1850–1910* (Schwerin, 1918); see especially tables on 33.

[37]Wiegandt, "Auswanderung aus Mecklenburg nach Übersee," 178.

[38]Breinlinger, "Die Landarbeiter in Pommern und Mecklenburg," 168. See also Wegner, *Die Lage der Landarbeiterinnen*, 14. Wegner argues that an attempt to test one's prospective partner was an important factor.

and peasants actually preferred a maid's illegitimate children to those of a day laborer's family, considering the children cheap and readily available labor.[39] Although illegitimacy appears to have been widely accepted as a fact of life, we can only guess at the consequences it bore for individual maids. Not only did the maid have to take full responsibility for what had happened, but she was also put at the mercy of her superiors. Moreover, the maid may have suffered from a combination of ostracism from the other maids and the pressure to conform to Protestant morality.

Some farm hands argued that the lack of housing made it impossible for them to marry the maids in question. Other farm hands chose to live with the maids outside the convention of marriage. In any case, there is ample reason to believe that marriage restrictions and the dilemma of bearing an illegitimate child prompted emigration.

Marriage

Throughout the 1850s, 1860s, and 1870s, marriage rates remained relatively low. Only in the 1880s, when marriage restrictions had been lifted, did the number of marriages slowly increase. Between 1853 and 1880, the average marriage age was 30.8 years for males and 26.6 years for females.[40] But once the manorial lords finally gave their consent, weddings were among the most important events of the year. Festivities started on a Friday, when bride and groom were met by the villagers and led to church, and lasted until Sunday, when all energy and food were exhausted. Contrary to myth, the manorial lords had no first right to the bride on the wedding night.[41] It was customary for the bride to be led to the fireside of her new home by her future mother-in-law, to take symbolic possession of fire and ashes. This, according to popular belief, would make her the real mistress of the home. Legally, however, she had practically no rights.

---

[39]Wegner, *Die Lage der Landarbeiterinnen,* 14.

[40]"Die Heiratsaussichten der Mecklenburgischen Bevölkerung," *Beiträge zur Geschichte Mecklenburgs* (1885): 55–56. The average age at first marriage in 1880 was 24.5 years for females and 28 for males.

[41]See Hanno Kühnert, " 'Ein Herrenrecht' entpuppt sich als Juristenwitz: Wie ein Studiendirektor dem 'Jus Primae Noctis,' dem Recht der ersten Nacht, auf die Spur kam," *Frankfurter Rundschau,* 15 July 1988, 10.

No married woman could hold any property, enter into any legal contract, or claim any rights over her children.

Once the festivities had come to an end, the workaday routine started again. A day laborer's wife worked on the estate and also at her own home, where she took care of the household, children, cattle, and garden. She also took on additional jobs to make ends meet. Her workday was typically eighteen hours long. Women's contributions to the family economy were especially important, and her work was indispensable to the family's well-being.

The day laborers' wives were obliged to work on the estate for 40 days each during summer and winter (for no payment) and an additional 100 to 120 days during the harvest and threshing season (for women's wages). It became general practice after 1848 to hire a contract laborer, and this left only the additional 100 days as a compulsory requirement. At the same time, men's wages (wages only, not remunerations in kind) increased, with one day laborer in Mecklenburg earning as much as husband and wife together in Silesia or other states east of the Elbe.[42] Many contemporaries praised the addition of a contract laborer, because it allowed women to remain at home.[43] But after the 1890s, when attempts to attract contract laborers from outside Mecklenburg became increasingly unsuccessful, many women had to assume their full workload on the estate again—as they did when the contract laborer fell ill or was otherwise unable to perform the women's duties. Women continued to assist with work in the manorial garden, with laundry and cleaning, and with other "women's duties," such as slaughtering and the shearing of sheep. During threshing season, women were required to assist their husbands in threshing for no extra payment. With work starting at 2 or 3 A.M. every morning and lasting for up to 120 days, threshing season put an especially heavy burden on the women.

Furthermore, they had to deliver eight to nine pounds of flax and a fixed amount of thread and number of geese by early spring. Women received extra payment for work in the beet and potato fields, for cleaning out dung, and for various tasks in the harvest of hay and grain—but the work kept them away from home for weeks

---

[42]Deiters, *Auswanderung, Arbeitslohn und Bodenwert*, 73.

[43]Hintze, "Die Lage der ländlichen Arbeiter," 39.

at a time, and they had only one day off per week, leaving little time for family life. Extra shearing was paid by the piece in cash and some wool, which the women used for knitting socks and gloves at home. In exchange for a small amount of cash, some of the women helped with milking twice a day. Before the turn of the century, milking could turn into a well-respected yet demanding business for a few, since most estates hired women to supervise the milking. This opportunity was lost when centrifuges and the growth of dairy cooperatives started to centralize the dairying process in the 1880s.

Day laborers lived in small villages of approximately ten farmhouses, shared by two, three, or four families each. In general, each family had one main room (16–20 square meters), one or two small and unheated bedrooms (8–10 square meters each), a kitchen, sometimes a cellar or pantry, a barn, and a smokehouse (used jointly by all the families in one building).[44] Managing the family's meager wages and finding supplemental income were considered the women's domain. An examination of some typical tasks shows the extent to which the women's productive labor was vital for family consumption. Although the family cow, for example, was kept with all other cows in the estate's barn, the milking remained the individual woman's responsibility. The milk was drunk, used for cooking, or made into butter and cottage cheese as a side product.[45] Taking care of the family's pigs was even more time-consuming. The wives had to feed pigs three times a day, prepare the feed from potatoes and grain, and clean out the dung. Quite often day laborer's wives spent more time feeding the swine than preparing the families' meals, since the family's well-being depended on the best possible care of the pigs. One of the day laborers slaughtered the village pigs, but the women prepared the meat for storage in the families' smokehouses. As a result of their labor, smoked sausage, bacon, and ham lasted all year, and no additional meat needed to be bought. Aside from pigs, the women kept chicken and geese, and they grew fruit, potatoes, vegetables, and herbs.

---

[44]"A City Man on a Farm," 208.
[45]After the turn of the century, most milk was brought to the central dairy cooperatives, which converted it into ready-to-use products such as butter and cheese for public sale. Müller, "Damshagen," 94. Bentzien, "Landarbeiter," in *Mecklenburgische Volkskunde* (1988), 155.

Transforming raw materials into items the family could con-
sume was never ending. By making such tasks occasions for socializing, however, the women established some control over their lives.
For example, bread baking was a joint effort. Every two weeks, on
Saturday evenings, the women met to prepare and form the heavy
loaves at one of the women's homes, marking them with the respective family's emblem. Early the next morning, around 3 A.M., one of
the men came to fire the village's local bake house, and the first
woman started to bake. By the following evening the women had
produced up to 150 loaves of bread, each averaging twelve to fourteen pounds, which were baked and ready to be stored. Subse-
quently, fruit and vegetables were dried in the oven; other vegetables
were salted to preserve them for the winter. Homemade candles lit
the family rooms on winter nights when the wives sat up spinning
flax. Earlier that season, the women had jointly prepared the flax in
the local bakehouse, celebrating the completion of the day's work
with a communal meal. Flax was given to the local weaver, whereas
clothes, quilts, and the like had to be sewn by the women at home or
during spare moments in the fields. Only after 1900 did ready-made
clothes become the rule.

Despite the women's efforts, however, total self-sufficiency could
not be achieved. In 1894, sugar, coffee, salt, herring, rice, and buckwheat for the kitchen; petroleum, soap, liquor, and tobacco for the
men; and clothes, household utensils, taxes, insurance fees, and payment of a contract laborer required external income.[46] Although
men's wages supplied the largest share of the family's income,
women also contributed cash. They sold eggs, sausage and ham, or
fruit and vegetables to local traders, who in turn sold the products in
Lübeck and Hamburg. Other traditional female means of income,
such as spinning, were reduced when changes in agriculture and
worldwide competition rendered homemade products less profitable. The loss of income sometimes threatened the family's economic survival.

Women's contributions to the family savings played a significant
role. One historian found the family's annual savings to amount to

---

[46]Hintze, "Die Lage der ländlichen Arbeiter," 35; Deiters, *Auswanderung, Arbeitslohn und Bodenwert*, 36–41.

more than 50 marks in the early 1890s.[47] Women also decided what items the families should acquire.[48] We do not know whether it was a joint decision to spend the family's savings on tickets to go overseas, but surely the wife at least contributed to the decision.

Married women's lives were marked by frequent births. Childbirth interrupted seasonal work and added a heavy burden. Medical services were totally insufficient, and there was little time for convalescence. At first, sympathy for the mother seemed to prevail. Even the manorial lords welcomed the first child of a day laborer's family by sending a pewter bowl, engraved with a little stork inside. Such apparent manorial benevolence, however, has been unmasked as pure hypocrisy. Not only did the day laborers' families have to pay for the midwife's fees, but the women also had to make up for any time lost in confinement or during illness. The women usually rushed back to work as soon as their strength allowed. Of a sample of 15 women studied in 1913, 13 resumed household tasks within a fortnight, and 10 were back on the estate after four weeks. Infant mortality remained high throughout the nineteenth century; some women died in childbirth; and others suffered in old age from pregnancy-related diseases such as varicose veins as a result of the premature resumption of work.

It clearly appears, then, that the day laborers' wives bore multiple burdens, and technical improvements did little to ease the burden on them. Increasing mechanization alleviated much of the agricultural labor but left most of the women's domains untouched. Women often had to double their efforts when the capitalization of agriculture reduced both the couple's payments in kind and their supplementary sources of income.

Moreover, women were caught in a patriarchal society. Insufficient education, physical overexertion, little spare time, and lack of communication with the outside world combined to place women at

---

[47]Hintze ("Die Lage der ländlichen Arbeiter," 37) sets the day laborer's family average income at 1,181 marks and estimates their annual expenditures at 1,134 marks.

[48]Elly zu Putlitz, *Arbeits- und Lebensverhältnisse der Frauen in der Landwirtschaft in Brandenburg* (Jena, 1914), quoted in Ute Frevert, "Tradition und Veränderung im Geschlechterverhältnis," *Funkkolleg Jahrhundertwende* 22 (1988/89): 71. Legal control given by the German civil code, ratified 18 August 1896; see Gottlieb Planck, *Die rechtliche Stellung der Frau nach dem bürgerlichen Gesetzbuch* (Göttingen, 1899); Ute Gerhard, *Verhältnisse und Verhinderungen. Frauenarbeit, Familie und Rechte der Frauen im 19. Jahrhundert* (Frankfurt, 1978), 162–167.

the bottom of the social ladder. Analyzing the role of female labor in agricultural Germany, Weber-Kellermann pointed out the women's dependence on both husband and manorial lord.[49] However difficult the position of a day laborer's wife, life posed even greater hardships for landless laborers' wives, seasonal (Polish) female migrants, or women in regions further to the east.

The Aged and Widowed

Advancing age brought not only a decline in health and strength but financial insecurity as well. In fact, few lived to old age, and those who did entertained little hope of living in comfort. The inability to earn a sufficient income usually marked the beginning of old age. Most day laborers continued to be employed on the estate as long as their physical condition allowed, but had to content themselves with lower wages. In return for a lifetime's work, they were provided with free lodging (though not usually in homes of their own), fuel, six bushels of rye, three bushels of barley, a pig, and a piece of potato land in old age. The majority lived in their children's homes. In Schwerin in 1882, for example, out of a total of 7,661 old people, 5,073 were living with close relatives. In general, the day laborers' families were compensated by the estate for taking in widowed grandparents unable to maintain themselves. Deiters reported in 1866 that the day laborers' wives were granted five days off during winter work for the duration of the old people's stay.[50] Crowded living conditions no doubt must have put remarkable strains on the families. In Damshagen, for example, grandparents slept in the family's pantry, which was usually used for eating (summer) and storing potatoes (winter). On the other hand, the grandparents' presence at home could offer some advantages as well, especially if they could take care of the children. If the elderly people's offspring had emigrated, remained unmarried, or were otherwise unable to take them in, the elderly had to live in special old people's huts that were generally in poor condition.

---

[49]Weber-Kellermann, *Landleben*, 152.

[50]Weber, *Die Verhältnisse der Landarbeiter*, 725–742; Breinlinger, "Die Landarbeiter in Pommern und Mecklenburg," 171; Deiters, *Auswanderung, Arbeitslohn und Bodenwert*, 72.

Widows seeking to eke out a living after the deaths of their husbands were particularly pitiable. These women often lacked the very necessities of life. Remarriage was an alternative for a limited few, with chances to marry declining when women reached their mid-thirties.[51] For elderly widows, working on the estate or at the local inn or making brooms hardly sufficed to make a living. As a last resort, many took to spinning flax to survive. Old-age allowances were gender specific. Men received a piece of potato-growing land plus other provisions (as mentioned previously). Widows received only three bushels of grain. On the nobles' estates, teachers' widows in particular suffered from poverty and social disgrace. Although teachers' pensions were low, they at least provided a small safety net. Teachers' widows, however, were not entitled to the pensions and were dependent on public charity. Fear of old age contributed to mass migration.

Emigration

There were two distinct phases of migration from Mecklenburg. The first, starting in the early 1850s, instantly made Mecklenburg one of the most important German areas of emigration. In the second phase, after 1865, increasing social stratification changed the emigration stream: the proportion of day laborers going abroad expanded significantly. At the same time, internal migration became a more feasible option for single young women and men. When domestic service in the cities of Hamburg or Schwerin became a realistic opportunity, many opted for that strategy instead.

Migration before 1865

Emigration from Mecklenburg is reported as early as the eighteenth century, when people boarded ships for Petersburg in Russia; others migrated to Poland in later years.[52] But it was not before the aboli-

---

[51]"Die Heiratsaussichten der Junggesellen und Jungfrauen im Großherzogtum Mecklenburg-Schwerin," *Beiträge zur Statistik Mecklenburgs* 10 (1886): 38–56, 52, 55.

[52]See Lubinski, "Die überseeische Auswanderung." Emigration to eastern states was prohibited by Mecklenburg law in 1760, 1763, 1766, and 1770, followed by an edict that forbade emigration to the United States in 1792.

tion of serfdom in 1820 that migration began to expand. For the next thirty years, the migrant stream was fed mostly by laborers dislocated from their farms or driven from the estates where they had been employed. Migration remained limited, partly because poor transportation made the move a difficult (and expensive) one and return unlikely. A total of 27,503 people (from the Grand-Duchy of Schwerin) left Mecklenburg between 1834 and 1842. In the 1850s, however, migration figures exploded.[53] The relative figures for Mecklenburg surpassed those of all other German states, ranking third after Ireland and Galicia. Out-migration led to a decline in population and a resulting lack of laborers. In absolute numbers, a peak was reached in 1854, with a total of 8,750 emigrants. Altogether, 67,779 people left for destinations overseas between 1853 and 1870.[54]

At home, overpopulation, inequitable land distribution, guild restrictions, patrimonial jurisdiction, and rigid marriage restrictions offered nothing but misery and social disgrace. America, in contrast, seemed to promise a golden future. There, land was still available: the Homestead Act of 1862 would offer 160 acres of land free after five years of settlement. Gold in California stirred the more adventurous souls. Letters, journals, newspaper and magazine articles, and pamphlets praised America—its physical beauty, system of social equality, and rewards for hard labor. In particular, however, it was the pioneer migrants' letters home that kindled enthusiasm to pack and go. Jürn Jakob Swehn, for example, an emigrant from Mecklenburg, wrote his family and friends back home:

> Had I stayed at home, I would have been a day laborer for the rest of my life, and prospects for my children would have been the same. Here, we had to work hard, much harder than in the old country, that's a matter of fact. But consider the rewards! Here, I became a free man. I work on my own field, not for some peasant. Being a free man is worth a couple of buckets of sweat.

---

[53]When migration first hit the local regions in the 1850s, anger and desperation among the nobles prevailed. Some offered to pay for the families' return passage, to obtain much-needed labor. It was considered unwise, however, to import American customs as well, and therefore only families gone for less than a year were welcomed back. *Archiv für Landeskunde* (1857), 353–55.

[54]Dietzsch, *Die Bewegung der mecklenburgischen Bevölkerung*, 23: figures for Schwerin only; add another 10–25 percent for emigration figures including Strelitz.

> Am **Montag**, den 23. October, von Vor=
> mittags 10 Uhr an, sollen in meiner Wohnung
> wegen Auswanderung folgende Gegenstände un=
> ter an Ort und Stelle näher bekannt zu ma=
> chenden Bedingungen meistbietend gegen gleich
> baare Zahlung verkauft werden, als:
>   1 junge Kuh, 2 Koffer, 1 Tisch, 1 Schrank,
>   1 Bettstelle, 4 Brettstühle, 1 Wanduhr, 1
>   kupf. Kessel, 3 Grapen, 1 Pfanne, 3 Eimer
>   1 Häcksellade mit Messer, 1 Schiebkarre,
>   Heu, ca. 20 Sack Kartoffeln, Ackerwirthschafts=
>   und Küchengeräth und was sich sonst noch
>   findet.
> Trebs bei Lübtheen.
>   **Joh. Daudt**, Arbeiter.

Auction handbill, 1882.
*"On Monday, 23 October, at 10 o'clock in the morning in my flat, due to
emigration, the following objects will be auctioned off to the highest bidder,
immediate cash necessary: 1 young cow, 2 suitcases, 1 table, 1 closet, 1 bedstool,
4 chairs, 1 (wall) clock, 1 copper kettle, 3 cauldrons, 1 pan, 3 buckets, 1 chaff-
cutter with blade, 1 wheelbarrow, hay, ca. 20 sacks of potatoes, field and
kitchen tools, and everything else.*

Tales of life in seeming luxury also held a special appeal:

> When the people in my village heard of white bread, sugar, and
> syrup and of cheaply available land, they asked a lot of questions
> and said: "How can such a country exist? Why didn't we know
> anything about it?" And they got moving and followed overseas.[55]

Although American attractions and local troubles account for
people's interest in going abroad, the desire to emigrate was not
sufficient. Family and local connections played a decisive role. Interactions among maids or between maids and farm hands, and com-

---

[55]Theodor Gillhoff, *Jürn Jakob Swehn, der Amerikafahrer* ([1917] Dreieich, 1987), 40, 44.

munication between the day laborers' wives and families, created opportunities to discuss issues of mutual importance. Similarly, spontaneous get-togethers or celebrations of seasonal festivities probably encouraged social communication between the day laborers' families. Most important, once emigration was under way, relatives living in America sent prepaid tickets, and fellow countrymen offered support when the immigrants arrived.[56]

By necessity and by choice, then, thousands of women and men crossed Mecklenburg's borders in the 1850s and subsequent decades. Rural servants and the families of day laborers made up the bulk of the emigrant stream. Rural artisans formed the second largest group. To take emigration from Mecklenburg-Schwerin in 1856 as an example, 11.4 percent were city residents, 30.4 percent came from government estates, and 58.4 percent came from the nobles' estates.[57] Considering the remarkable strains that had been endured by the latter group, the high number comes as no surprise. Riding the recently (1847) built rails from Schwerin to Hagenau, the states' emigrants caught the train going from Berlin to Hamburg and embarked there for America. Costs for overseas transportation amounted to a substantial 30–50 Taler per person in the 1850s with children's fees slightly lower. Farm hands and maids were able to finance the voyage overseas by accumulating one to three years' savings. The day laborers' families, on the other hand, though having less cash on hand than the rural servants, could sell most of their household belongings (including the family's cow, pig, furniture, and so on) to pay for transportation and additional expenditures.

State regulation of the emigration business required official permission for all subjects' departures. After 1847, passports to leave the country could be obtained readily unless there were objections. In 1857, another law made the procedures stricter: potential migrants now had to ask for their dismissal from state obligations and rights, in particular giving up their right to domicile or poor relief in case of return. A permit to emigrate (*Auswanderungskonsens*) was issued if the following conditions were fulfilled: age of majority and legal independence established, military duties absolved, and proof that

---

[56]See for example ibid., 40, 66, 137; Staatsarchiv Schwerin, various Emigration Consents.

[57]Dietzsch, *Die Bewegung der mecklenburgischen Bevölkerung*, 12–15. These figures include only those using local emigration agents; the actual number of emigrants would be even higher.

there were no unmet obligations to individuals provided. Women, not considered legal persons, needed their parents' or relatives' consent as well. Furthermore, transportation had to be booked with a local agent authorized by the state. Applicants had to have 50 Taler in ready cash, in addition to the money needed to pay for transportation. Finally, a small fee had to be paid, which was often waived or reduced in the case of widows or almshouse dependents.[58] On February 13, 1864, for instance, Catherine Marie Dorothea Koch, 30 years old, was given permission to emigrate together with her three small sons. She left to join her foster parents and her older brother, who had already settled abroad. The estate's manorial lord agreed to support her financially, probably considering it to be a final payment before getting rid of the unwanted group.[59]

Women comprised approximately 46 percent of emigrants in the 1850s, with figures rising slightly in the following years and at times even surpassing male emigration.[60] Among the female migrants, single and widowed women were prominent. According to figures available for Mecklenburg-Strelitz for the second half of the nineteenth century, this group constituted a remarkable 23–29 percent, thus highlighting the myriads of difficulties experienced by women of this rural society. The number of widowed women was almost five times higher than that of widowed men. Moreover, single women (25 percent) were more likely than single men (8 percent) to bring their children or other family members along. In 1863, 30-year-old Sophie Catharine Dorothea Griese (from Wüstenmark in the district of Grevesmühlen), took her five-year-old son along.[61] In another case, 20-year-old Auguste Maibohm, (from the district of Schwerin) applied for an emigration permit for herself and two sons—twins only six months old.[62] Single maids often used their relative state of independence to escape the drudgery of dead end, hard work. Some

---

[58]It has been speculated that more than 70 percent of all migrants actually complied. In spite of more flexible federal and national emigration laws, Mecklenburg officials continued to demand emigration permits until the mid-1880s. For further information on German policies, see Ingrid Schöberl, "Emigration Policy in Germany and Immigration Policy in the United States," in Günter Moltmann, ed., *Germans to America: 300 Years of Immigration 1683–1983* (Stuttgart, 1982), 36–43.

[59]Staatsarchiv Schwerin, Ministerium des Inneren (MdI), 10866, Emigration Consent, 1864.

[60]Wiegandt, "Auswanderung aus Mecklenburg nach Übersee," 248.

[61]Staatsarchiv Schwerin, MdI 10866, Emigration Consent, 17 November 1863.

[62]Staatsarchiv Schwerin, MdI 10866, p. 671; MdI 11010, 24 May 1872.

bypassed marriage restrictions or followed their families or future husbands; others hoped to find mates abroad. Often a combination of these motives accounted for women's departures. Thirty-year-old Sophie Pann from Glarna, for example, accompanied her father, retired shoemaker Johann Pann, to join her two siblings abroad.[63] Johann Pann represented yet another group, that of parents grown old and finding their last accommodation at their children's new American homes.

Unmarried couples were allowed to legalize their quasi-marital relationships by obtaining an emigration permit and thus agreeing to cede claims to alms' pensions. This allowed them to circumvent marriage restrictions, albeit for the price of leaving their home behind.[64] Joachim Friedrich Schumacher and Sophie Catharine Dorothea Lindemann, parents of two-year-old twin boys, applied for a marriage license two weeks before leaving the country in 1857. They claimed that they had not been able to earn a living at home. Transportation payments amounted to 130 Taler for all, leaving the family with 50 Taler in cash. That same year, 26-year-old farm hand Johann Heinrich Friedrich Möller (son of a day laborer in Mölln in the district of Kritzkow), planned to marry the mother (daughter of a small landowner from the neighborhood) of the couple's nine-month-old son.[65] Altogether 547 couples, with and without children, applied for marriage licenses between 1854 and 1863. For the majority of those years, more than 50 percent of the couples came from nobles' estates.[66] Others got married on board the ships taking them to the U.S. or at the port of departure (usually Hamburg).

Migration after 1865

The gradual transition from a feudal to a capitalist economy left its mark on rural society in a variety of ways. Technological changes (such as mowing and threshing machines) influenced traditional lifestyles. Hereditary tenure raised the peasants' position within the

---

[63]Ibid., 8 February 1864.

[64]State laws issued 3 February 1854 and 4 February 1859; MdI 10829/43, 10829/47.

[65]Staatsarchiv Schwerin, MdI 10829/44; MdI 10829/44, 2 June 1857.

[66]Ibid., MdI 10829/43, "Trauung von Auswanderern. Statistische Übersicht über die in den Jahren 1854–1863 erteilten Dispensationen und Beibringung des Domizialscheins zur Trauung und Auswanderung."

community, and patriarchal relationships increasingly gave way to social stratification—putting owners of land above members of the rural workforce. Although the rural community had never acted as a single entity, social class stratification increased remarkably in the second half of the nineteenth century. With rural communities losing their coherent character, migration both within Germany and to America became an easier option to take. In addition, because new forms of cultivation and technical advances eliminated traditional means of earning supplementary income, economic and social conditions deteriorated. The advance of the threshing machine after the mid-1860s was followed by a marked increase in the proportion of day laborers' families emigrating overseas. Whereas the ratio of emigrating day laborers to servants had been 6.3:10 in 1859–1869, in 1873–1874 twice as many day laborers as servants left for overseas.

The rapid rise of German industry redirected migration into the German cities, greatly reducing the migration overseas. Starting in the 1870s and accelerating after the depression years 1880–1885, German industry boomed. By 1900, almost a quarter of a million Mecklenburg residents had moved elsewhere. Of these, more than 50,000 lived in Hamburg and almost 10,000 in Berlin.

At the same time, the rise of an urban middle class offered positions for servants, cooks, and housekeepers, thus promoting female migration in particular. In Hamburg in 1873, for example, a total of 2,820 servants from the state of Mecklenburg accounted for 11 percent of all servants (2,303 females and 517 males) in that city. Mecklenburg thus ranked fourth among regions supplying servants to Hamburg.[67] In later years, health spas along the Baltic coast attracted others, again females rather than males and daughters rather than mothers. Drawn by higher wages and better working conditions, many worked as servants and cooks in private households or restaurants. Some came to marry, others to learn a trade. According to contemporary observers, the search for amusement appears to have been yet another factor. Guided largely by their quest for improvement, the maids hoped to escape the drudgery of rural married life,

[67]Dagmar Müller-Staats, "Klagen über Dienstboten. Eine Untersuchung zum Verhältnis von Herrschaften und Dienstboten, mit besonderer Berücksichtigung Hamburgs im 19. Jahrhundert" (Ph.D. diss., Berlin, 1986), Graph 11, p. 288.

Fritz Paulsen (Schwerin 1838–1898 Berlin), Bei der Stellenvermittlung
*[Employment agency for domestics], 1881. This painting probably
shows Mecklenberg maids in Berlin.*

Photograph, Deutsches Historisches Museum, Berlin.

the heavy workload, the meager rewards, and rural isolation. Had
they been given a chance to learn a trade such as dressmaking, some
might have chosen to stay. Once accustomed to life in a foreign environment, some migrated even farther, embarking on a ship to the
United States or South America. For example, Anna Beckmann (born
in Lübtheen in the district of Schwerin), came to Hamburg in 1881 to
work as a servant and emigrated three years later to the United States,
together with her servant friend Wilhelmine Wiebusch. Generally,
higher wages, more spare time, and a good chance to find suitable husbands were foremost among the servants' reasons for emigration.[68]

When a severe depression crippled the German economy during
the early 1880s, migration from Mecklenburg rose one last time (before later dropping down to a few hundred per year). The situation

---

[68]See *Peter Tütt: Erlebnisse eines Schleswig-Holsteinischen Offiziers in Nordamerika 1851–1861* (Al-
tona, 1861), a novel by Graf Adalbert Baudissin, on Mecklenburg maids in the United States. See
also Walter D. Kamphoefner, Wolfgang Helbich, and Ulrike Sommer, eds., *News from the Land of
Freedom: German Immigrants Write Home* (Ithaca, N.Y., 1991).

abroad served to strengthen migration. A young American West was courting new settlers, and the whole country was experiencing an upswing of industry. The United States was in desperate need of workers. A vigorous campaign was underway not only by Western states but also by railroad companies to recruit workers for urban industries. Once again, thousands of Mecklenburg residents boarded the emigrant ships. Many were lured by a dream of earning enough money to buy their own farms. Most immigrants ended up as urban workers, however, and return to Germany became a more likely option.

The picture that emerges when discussing emigration from Mecklenburg is one of determined women and men taking their lives into their own hands. They were unwilling to submit to manorial pressures and unwilling to give up personal hopes for independent lives. Living away from home was part of the young people's lives, be it departing for work on larger estates or crossing borders. Young women from Mecklenburg were accustomed to finding employment away from home; mobility seems to have been an integral part of their lives. With it came a flexibility that made it easier to endure the enormous personal hardships involved in emigration and to adjust to the very different environment of the American city.

2

To Be Matched or to Move: Irish Women's Prospects in Munster

Deirdre Mageean

Emigration has been one of the key formative factors in the lives of Irish women and men—shaping not only those who left but also those who remained behind. Remarkably large numbers of women left Ireland in the second half of the nineteenth and the early twentieth centuries. Particularly after the Great Famine of 1845–1851, emigration became an expected part of the life cycle among women. Emigration was always a young person's game, and women braved emigration even earlier than did their male counterparts.[1]

The period of heavy emigration after the Famine contrasts sharply with the period between 1815 and 1844, when comparatively few women left Ireland. To explain this phenomenon better, we need to understand the demographic, economic and social forces at play in Irish society both before and after the Famine. I focus on three topics: changes in the economic environment and how these affected wage-earning opportunities for women; changes in inheritance, marriage, and fertility patterns; and changes in the social status of women. Tens of thousands of women who left Ireland were products of a traditional rural society that had shaped their daily lives. They had been socialized by a society very different from the world they were about to enter. Yet they were willing to face the uncertainties of life in a new country to escape the known insecurities of the country they were leaving behind.

---

[1] See David Fitzpatrick, *Irish Emigration 1801–1921* (Dundalk, 1984), 8.

I concentrate on the province of Munster in the southwest of Ireland, which contains the counties of Cork, Kerry, Limerick, Clare, Tipperary, and Waterford. The province covers slightly more than a quarter of the area of Ireland (29.3 percent), and in 1840 it had 2,386,373 inhabitants—almost a quarter of the country's population. By 1900, the population had dropped to 1,076,188, a decline of 55 percent. Most of the loss can be attributed to emigration. During the period 1851–1901, 1,349,129 people (691,059 males and 658,070 females) left the province for destinations overseas.[2]

Politics, Economics, and Population in Post-famine Munster

The major city of the province was, and is, Cork. Like Munster's two other major cities, Waterford and Limerick, Cork served as a trading center with primary links to small market towns. It was also a major emigration port. In the mid-nineteenth century approximately 18 percent of Munster's population lived in towns of 2,000 people and over. By the turn of the century, the figure had risen to just over 25 percent. The western counties of Clare and Kerry, however, had a much smaller percentage of their population living in towns and villages.[3] Villages were rather rare. More common were *clachans,* small kin-settlements or groups of homesteads.[4] Most of the small towns were market centers that served a rural hinterland and were frequently the focus of social life such as fairs. Each county had a major center in terms of both municipal administration and market economy.

Towns grew in importance after the Famine, but the urban population remained low compared to the rest of Europe. In 1861, for example only 19.4 percent of the country's, and 21 percent of Munster's, population lived in towns. Opportunities for internal migra-

---

[2]W. E. Vaughan and A. J. Fitzpatrick, *Irish Historical Statistics, 1821–1971* (Dublin, 1978), 16, 346–348.

[3]T. W. Freeman notes that many of the towns in Munster by mid-century included large numbers of poor and destitute people. *Pre-Famine Ireland* (Manchester, 1957), 203–204.

[4]A village is here defined as a cluster of twenty houses or more.

tion were severely restricted, and by 1911, the urban population in Ireland had grown only to 33.5 percent.[5]

The best farmland lay in eastern Tipperary and Waterford, northern Cork and Limerick, and eastern Clare. Poor soil and bogland predominated in much of the western portions of west Cork, Kerry, and Clare. In these areas, small farms were common. For both large and small farmers in Munster, tillage was an important part of the pre-Famine farm economy. Potatoes were the staple food crop, and grain was a cash crop grown to pay the rent. Pigs, which were cheaply fed on potatoes and household scraps, were important for many households. Slaughtering was carried out at home, and the preserved meat (smoked or salted hams and bacon) was often the only meat eaten by the family. In the latter half of the nineteenth century, Cork was the main producer of cereals, largely wheat and barley, in the province. Oats were grown throughout the area. Potato cultivation declined but remained a mainstay on farms for home consumption. Sheep and lamb production was extensive, as were cattle raising and the related dairy industry. In Limerick and parts of Kerry, pig production was most important.

Population pressure and land hunger were endemic during the nineteenth century and frequently resulted in agrarian strife. Violence was often directed against a farmer who attempted to take over a vacant farm against the wishes of the local people. After the Famine, when some landlords tried to clear their estates of the poorest of tenants, the landlord's agent became the target of peasant protest.[6] Violence typically erupted when agricultural conditions were bad.

Political Structure and Economic Conditions

Ireland had been under the rule of the British government since 1800. Catholics were denied the vote until 1829, when they gained limited suffrage. Thereafter an "Irish party" sought various reforms. In the first half of the nineteenth century, political control was centralized. Elected parliamentary representatives for the area legislated from Westminster, London and, until Ireland achieved independence

---

[5]Vaughan and Fitzpatrick, *Irish Historical Statistics*, 27.
[6]Louis M. Cullen, *Six Generations: Life and Work in Ireland from 1790* (Cork, 1986), 37–38.

in 1921, all laws governing Ireland emanated from that parliament. Local government was weak, and local political affairs were dominated by wealthy landowners and aristocrats. The Secret Ballot Act of 1872, however, destroyed the influence of landlords in parliamentary elections, and the establishment of elected county councils in 1898 took away their control of local government. Also in that year, women with certain property qualifications were granted a vote in local government. By the end of the century, 85 women were serving as poor-law guardians and rural and urban district councilors. But they were still denied parliamentary franchise (the right to vote in national elections).[7] This franchise was primarily property based (i.e., certain minimum property qualifications were necessary to vote), but property holders or not, all women were excluded.

The political events of the last quarter of the nineteenth century were dominated by agrarian interests and discontent, most notably the tenant-rights movement. The Land League, formed in 1879, encouraged tenant farmers to refuse payment of exorbitant rents and helped those who were evicted for nonpayment. The demand for peasant proprietorship, expressed by the league, drew broad support from farmers, the Catholic Church, and many Irish in America, who sent funds to support the campaign. In Munster, where there were many tenant farmers with little security, the league was active and strong. The political efforts of these groups resulted in land acts that, over the period 1870–1916, transferred ownership of land from landlords to farmers.

For most of the century, land ownership was essentially feudal. In the pre-Famine economy, the system of stratification comprised landlords, middlemen, independent farmers, tenant farmers, and, at the base of the social and economic pyramid, the class of landless laborers, cottiers, and day laborers.[8] Most of Munster was organized

---

[7] Rosemary Cullen Owens, *Smashing Times: A History of the Irish Women's Suffrage Movement, 1889–1922* (Dublin, 1984), 30–31. Unpaid Poor Law guardians were elected by the ratepayers; see Gerald O'Brien, "The New Poor Law in Pre-Famine Ireland: A Case History," *Irish Economic and Social History* 12 (1985): 33–49.

[8] In the agreement between landlords and cottiers, the farmer provided a house and one-half to one acre on which to grow potatoes. He also permitted the cottier to keep a couple of sheep on the farm and provided some cutting of peat for fuel and some land on which to grow flax. In return, the cottier paid with his labor. Agricultural laborers paid rents for cabins and potato gardens and were obliged to work for farmers whenever they were called.

into estates that varied considerably in size and organization, from the large estates of the Duke of Devonshire (61,000 statute acres in Counties Cork and Waterford)[9] to small estates of a few hundred acres. Many were hopelessly mismanaged by disinterested and absentee landlords. The most common system of estate management split the estates into tracts of from 100 to 1,000 acres and rented them to middlemen through long leases. The middlemen frequently sublet to tenant farmers. These tenant farmers subdivided their holdings, sometimes to provide their children with settlements at marriage and other times to rent to poor cottiers. The system was pernicious. Tenants scraped a bare existence out of tiny plots of land, depending heavily on the potato crop, and many of the people lived on the verge of starvation.

By 1841 in the county of Cork, almost 65 percent of holdings were less than 15 acres.[10] In the province, 35 percent of the farms were of one to five acres.[11] As the numbers of laborers and cottiers grew, the condition of these workers deteriorated. Since subdivision produced smaller and smaller farms, the need for hired labor decreased, and farmers' families were more often able to provide all the necessary labor. The ranks of unemployed laborers were further swelled by those displaced by de-industrialization and the collapse of handloom weaving. More and more were forced to work for pitiful wages. Depending on geographical location and type of farmer, the wages of unbound laborers in County Cork, for example, ranged from 4d. (four pence) to 8d. per day in ordinary times, with an increase to 10d. or 1s.2d. at the harvest and during potato planting and digging. The laborers were poorly paid, poorly housed, poorly fed, and often hungry in the lean months between potato crops. They were the most vulnerable of all groups when the Great Famine occurred.

Female labor was vitally important on these small, semi-subsistence farms. Women were employed at 3d. or 4d. per day in digging

[9]See Lindsay Proudfoot, "The Management of a Great Estate: Patronage, Income, and Expenditure on the Duke of Devonshire's Irish Property," Irish Economic and Social History 13 (1986): 32–55.

[10]Great Britain, Parliamentary Papers, Report from the commissioners appointed to take the census of Ireland for the year 1841 No. [504] 24 (1843), 454–457.

[11]Freeman, Pre-Famine Ireland, 54.

or picking stones from pasture and meadow land, and in weeding potato plots; at busy times, they occasionally earned 5d. or 6d. by planting or gathering potatoes and binding grain.[12] These examples suggest the division of labor between the sexes in the pre-Famine economy.

Fewer than 5 percent of householders in Munster owned any land up until 1870. Farm size increased after the Famine through consolidation, but land was still largely rented. The series of land acts from 1860 onward helped first to convert feudal relations into a contract agreement, then to offer some protection and security to tenants in terms of compensation for improvements and, finally, to guarantee fair rent, fixity of tenure, and freedom of sale. Landlordism was virtually gone by the 1920s.

Throughout the early 1800s, the fundamental problem in Munster was growing poverty. For those evicted or otherwise driven from the land, there was little alternative employment. Some migrated to the towns, and others swelled the ranks of the already overabundant class of servants and laborers. Several land reclamation schemes were undertaken but none were sufficient to meet the demand for land. Fishing was carried out along the coast, but the number of full-time fishermen was low. In 1836, a witness to the Devon Commission noted that "five or six dispossessed families would congregate in a single house, living in utter misery and only able to support a life at all by the begging of the women folk."[13]

In 1800, domestic textile industries had been strong, and spinning had been carried out in many homes, particularly in the poorer districts where the income helped pay the rent or buy a few luxuries such as salt, tobacco, or drink. Spinning was women's work, although in poor families children also learned to spin.[14] On fine days, the wheels were carried outdoors, and often three generations of

---

[12]James S. Donnelly, *The Land and People of Nineteenth Century Cork* (London, 1975), 21.

[13]Freeman, *Pre-Famine Ireland*, 206. The number of dispossessed families recorded for the province was 3,569, of whom half were in Cork.

[14]W. Tighe, in his 1802 *Statistical Survey of County Kilkenny*, calculated that a laborer could not support a wife and three children on his wages alone. The balance came from the earnings of his wife and children. Women and children were mainly employed during the busy period between May and November. Their earning power was low, however, and as witnesses to the Poor Inquiry of 1836 testified, there was a scarcity of remunerative work for women and children throughout the country (see *First Report of Inquiry into the Condition of the Poorer Classes in Ireland*, App. C [35], 30, 84–92).

Three women, one seated, outside a cottage.
Photograph, Cooper Collection, Public Record Office, Northern Ireland.

women—mother, grandmother, and some of the older daughters—
would work together. The spinning of worsted yarn from wool was
widespread in Cork and parts of Tipperary. As the century wore
on, domestic production of textiles declined, although some survived. The 1841 census, for example, records 76,317 spinners—almost
all women. Only a very small proportion worked in factories in
towns.

Industry consisted mainly of processing agricultural products.
Larger towns had flour mills, a brewery or distillery, and occasionally
a wool mill. Bacon curing was important in the cities of Cork and
Limerick and the town of Tralee. Cork had become the largest butter
market in the British Isles. Scattered throughout the rest of the
province were some localized industries such as paper mills and iron
foundries. Overall, however, only the three major ports had a significant export trade, and most industry served local markets and was
oriented toward marketing rather than manufacturing. Opportunities

for growth and employment were therefore limited. What industry existed could not absorb the growing surplus of people on the land.

Agriculture in post-Famine Ireland was marked by consolidation of land and a shift from tillage to pasture. The combination of mortality, emigration, and clearances led to a dramatic fall in the numbers of those working on the land. The decimation of the cottier class and the reduction through high mortality and emigration of the poorer classes in general were important because women had contributed most heavily to the economic viability of these groups. The increase in the average size of a farm allowed for economies of scale and the introduction of innovations. Notable demographic changes included a shift in inheritance practices from partible to impartible inheritance and an increase in the age at marriage, along with a reduction in the marriage rate. Because of these changes, the period 1854–1876 has been called one of "post-Famine adjustment."[15] These changes, along with steady economic improvement, meant increased prosperity for many of the province's inhabitants and improvements in housing, diet, and education. Partible inheritance, low age at and high rate of marriage, small farms, and dense population remained prevalent in the remote and mountainous parts of Kerry and Clare for decades after the Famine. By the turn of the century, however, these trends had died out.

Industry continued to be of minor importance and was mainly concentrated in the cities of Cork, Limerick, and the town of Waterford. It remained agricultural or artisan in nature, and the province did not develop a manufacturing industry on any significant scale. The percentage of the labor force in industry in Muster rose from 23.7 in 1821 to only 24.3 in 1881. As a consequence, internal migration remained low. Those seeking industrial employment followed the path of emigration to Britain or North America.

Population

Ireland's population growth in the nineteenth century looks like a classic Malthusian story. High rates of marriage and high fertility within marriage gave rise to rapid population growth, and eventually

---

[15]Cormac O'Gráda, *Ireland before and after the Famine* (Manchester, 1988), 128–129.

population was dramatically reduced by Famine mortality. Similarly, Irish demographic behavior after the Famine was characterized by low rates of marriage and high rates of both celibacy and emigration and thus fits the description of Malthusian "preventive checks." Debate continues among historians, but certain facts are incontrovertible. Between 1808 and the mid-1840s, the population of Ireland increased by 50 percent, although the census figures indicate that population growth was slowing.[16] Population pressure was intense throughout the island, particularly in the poorer counties. The demand for labor lessened, while the population grew.

The result was too many people and too little land. The areas of densest population were the remote coastal areas. Subdivision of land was extreme in poor areas, but there is evidence that partible inheritance was practiced in the more affluent parts of the country as well. By 1841, marriage was almost universal: only 10 percent of the men and 12 percent of the women ages 46–55 were single.[17] Infant mortality figures are unreliable, but they seem to suggest light mortality.

The Great Famine struck hard in the province of Munster. It was truly a watershed in the region's history. The long-term effects were registered in changing marriage patterns, social and economic relations, changes in the division of labor among the sexes, and people's expectations about their lives and futures. The first signs of potato blight appeared in gardens near Cork city in 1845, but the full impact was not felt until the successive failures of the 1846 and 1847 crops. Starvation and disease on a massive scale followed. The people of Munster suffered high mortality.[18] Some of the most horrifying accounts of suffering and distress come from remote towns such as Skibereen and Skull in West Cork.[19] Many small towns were literally invaded by paupers and the sick and dying who had fled the countryside. Desperate cottiers and laborers not only migrated in large numbers to towns but also engaged in food riots and food stealing. The

---

[16]Ibid., 6. The figures for Munster record a change of +15.06 percent between the years 1821 and 1831 and a change of +7.59 percent between the years 1831 and 1841.

[17]Freeman, Pre-Famine Ireland, 16.

[18]Joel Mokyr, Why Ireland Starved (London, 1983), 266–267.

[19]It is estimated that Skibereen suffered a population loss of more than 36 percent between 1841 and 1851—heavier than any poor-law union in the country. See Donnelly, The Land and People, 124.

classes of laborers and smallholders bore the brunt of the death, disease, and loss of land. Even farmers with holdings between 15 and 30 acres suffered heavy losses. On the other hand, farmers with 30 acres or more often improved their situations through the consolidation of land previously rented by those who had since died or been evicted. The immediate consequences for the province were a drastic decline in smallholdings and a sharp fall in the remaining population, primarily from emigration. Even in 1845–51, however, the majority of emigrants were not laborers but farmers with medium-size holdings who were responding to a decline or anticipated decline in their standards of living. The tenants of estates whose landlords offered assisted passages were also able to leave. Numerically insignificant in the countryside, the proportion of people who emigrated in this manner was highest in counties Clare, Limerick, and Kerry.[20] After 1851, emigration continued at a significant level, peaking in certain years of agricultural depression. The resultant loss of population can be seen in Table 2.1.

TABLE 2.1

Population of Munster, 1821–1911

Year	Males	Females	Total	Percent change
1821	960,119	975,493	1,935,612	
1831	1,093,411	1,133,741	2,227,152	+15.06
1841	1,186,190	1,209,971	2,396,161	+7.59
1851	904,979	952,757	1,857,736	−22.47
1861	744,682	768,876	1,513,558	−18.53
1871	686,106	707,379	1,393,485	−7.93
1881	659,994	671,121	1,331,115	−4.48
1891	587,611	584,791	1,172,402	−11.92
1901	540,970	535,218	1,076,188	−8.21
1911	526,130	509,365	1,035,495	−3.78

Source: W. E. Vaughan and A. J. Fitzpatrick, *Irish Historical Statistics, 1821–1971* (Dublin, 1978), 16.

[20]Between the years 1829 and 1845, 309,872 Irish migrants landed in the ports of Quebec and Montreal. It is estimated that the majority of these went on to the United States; see William Forbes Adams, *Ireland and Irish Emigration to the New World* (Baltimore, 1980), 415.

The sheer loss of numbers, however, made less difference in people's lives than the changes in behavior and farming practices. In agriculture, the cultivation of potatoes declined, and subsistence farming gave way to more commercial farming. The social structure of the province had been altered radically, and post-Famine Ireland became a land of impartible inheritance, a low rate of marriage, late marriages, and a culture where economics dominated one's choice of spouse.

Material Culture

Irish women who left rural Munster had to adapt to a great number of changes with regard to their daily activities. They had to adjust to life in an urban tenement, and the notion of home—which in Munster was the center of life—had to be filled with a new meaning. What did these women leave behind?

Housing

In the first half of the century, many people in the poorer regions of the province lived in one-room cottages or cabins, frequently sharing their accommodation with animals. From the small cottages of the laborers to the comfortable homes of substantial farmers, most homes were made from local materials.

The heart of the interior was the turf fire. At the side of the fire, in the chimney corner, the man of the house had a seat.[21] Over the fire, there were hooks and a crane to hold the pots and kitchen utensils. The crane could be lifted or lowered or swung outward when lifting heavy pots. On one of the walls hung a "clevy," or miniature dresser, of three or four shelves that held ornamental pieces of ware or any crockery not in use. It also housed any fancy painted jugs or pottery and perhaps some pewter or tin. The main dresser held rows of plates (some wooden), shiny jugs, and china jugs for tea. Frequently there was a "settle bed" that could be used as a seat during the day. Other furniture was a press, in which food items were kept,

---

[21]Cullen, *Six Generations*, 17.

and a table. In some areas the room or loft above the hearth was used for sleeping because it was warm; in others it was used for storing goods that needed to be kept dry.

Churning was generally done in the kitchen, although on more prosperous farms the work was carried out in an adjacent dairy. On larger farms, two or three dairy maids were employed under the supervision of the housewife. On the small farms, the equipment was kept in the house:

> Approximately centreways along the wall were placed the churn, the butter firkin and towards the center, opposite the entrance door, were placed buckets, some filled with cream and others just in the process of being filled. Above the cream bucket were built two shelves on which were arranged the milk pans setting and waiting for the removal of the cream.[22]

The 1841 census divided the houses of the country into four classes. The fourth, and worst, consisted of one-room mud cabins. The next class up consisted of cottages built of mud but having two to four rooms and windows. Class-two houses were those with five to nine rooms and windows; class-one houses were those exceeding these standards. Classes three and four accounted for the overwhelming majority of houses in the rural areas. The proportion varied according to the richness of the land, however. In counties Waterford, Cork, and Tipperary, one-fifth to one-quarter of the houses were in the top two classes. But in the poorer counties of Limerick, Kerry, and Clare, these better homes constituted only between one-seventh and one-tenth of the total houses. With the drastic reduction in the population of cottiers and the poorest laborers, much of the worst housing disappeared. Although the dwellings of agricultural laborers still left a lot to be desired, there was a general improvement in housing standards. In County Cork, for instance, more than 80 percent of the class-four houses had disappeared by 1861, and of those still classified as such, many were made of brick or stone. By 1891, they comprised only 3 percent of all houses in County Cork.[23]

---

[22]Liam Kelly, *Blennerville: Gateway to Tralee's Past* (Tralee, 1989), 46; account of Maurice Williams, an elderly resident of Blennerville, County Kerry.

[23]Donnelly, *The Land and People*, 242–243.

Three women doing needlework.
Photograph, Cooper Collection, Public Record Office, Northern Ireland.

The virtual elimination of these cabins was part of an overall improvement in living standards in the decades following the Famine. The growth in floor space and rooms also reflected shifts in morality. Privacy became socially desirable, especially the separation of unmarried males and females in the sleeping arrangements.

Diet

The diet of laborers before the Famine was notoriously bland, but generally nutritious. The ordinary diet consisted of potatoes and salt fish (usually herring), along with milk, when available. Eggs and fish played a larger part in the daily diet in some areas. Meat was rarely eaten, mainly on feast days and on celebrations such as weddings or christenings. The problem was not the diet's nutritional value but the reliability of the staple food. During the periodic potato famines and the lean months between crops, there was significant hunger and starvation.

After the Famine, diet improved or at least became more varied. The potato, though still widely consumed, lost its dominance in the peasants' diet. What took its place was grain or "meal," which became available from the 1850s onward, when cheap foreign grain was imported on a major scale. "Yellow male," as it was known, was the staple food for three to six months in the year. It was usually served in the form of "stirabout"—a mixture of grain and sour milk. More affluent small farmers were able to substitute the more nutritious oatmeal; for fairly prosperous farmers, wheaten bread was a regular item in the daily diet, and meat was no longer an item restricted to feasts and celebrations. As breads of various grains became more popular, butter consumption rose. Tea became an increasingly popular drink, and milk, of varying quality, was consumed with meals.

Drink of a stronger nature was always popular. Drinking was mainly a male activity, and men of all classes drank heavily. Drink was an integral part of births, weddings, and wakes, as well as fairs. The cheapness of beer and wine probably contributed to heavy consumption, but so did the culture; as an old saying suggests, "Drink is a disease without shame." Whiskey was also a popular drink, and in the poorer parts of the countryside, it was replaced with poteen, an illicit home-distilled liquor. A temperance campaign begun in the late 1830s apparently reduced consumption, but other economic factors may have played a role. With the gradual transfer of land from landlord to peasant, the responsibilities of ownership may have induced a greater sobriety. Witness the saying, "Once a man becomes the owner of land, he drinks far less."

Clothing

The standard of clothing also improved in the latter half of the nineteenth century, partly because the Famine greatly reduced the numbers of the poorest. At mid-century, a woman's outfit consisted of a cloak, dress, petticoat, shift, cap, and apron. As the century wore on, the cloak gave way to a shawl, under which women wore a skirt, usually of red flannel, and a bodice. Women and children in poor families often went barefoot. Although the wives of small farmers owned shoes, it seems that they only wore them when going to mass, market, or fairs. Even then, they would carry their shoes until they were near the church or town and then put them on. As cheaply manufactured cotton clothes became more available, the appearance of women's clothes improved, although the quality was frequently poor and offered insufficient protection against inclement weather. "Much of the clothing was bought secondhand at fairs and markets or from pawn brokers and quite an amount of it appears to have been brought over to Ireland from dealers in London and Liverpool."[24]

No national or regional costume was worn by peasant women. A combination of poverty and suppression of Irish culture during the Penal times seems to have prevented the evolution of the type of costume prevalent in other European peasant societies.[25] Instead, as women gradually became more aware of fashions through newspapers, and as small retailing businesses spread, the shawl and flannel skirt gave way to versions of English urban styles. Provincial stores increasingly stocked fashionable attire for the wives and daughters of farmers, and "shop clothes" gradually replaced homemade attire. Photographs and letters from those who had emigrated must have played some part in influencing ideas about clothes. As one commentator in 1910 said:

> It is these photographs [that] do all the mischief with her remaining sisters. The girl who was remembered without a hat, with bare feet, with short red petticoat, is seen as a duchess in her American transformation. She stands transfigured in the picture before her breathless, admiring friends. Is this fashionably attired lady the Bridget they knew? Ballybog never provided hats like that, never pictured such elegance in its wildest dreams. And could that be little Nora who looks out under a picture hat like a queen? One after

---

[24]T. P. O'Neill, "Rural Life," in R. B. McDowell, ed., *Social Life In Ireland 1800–45* (Dublin, 1973), 50.

[25]The Penal Laws were designed to suppress the culture, religion, and economic and political status of the native Catholic population and to maintain the "Protestant ascendancy." See Kerby Miller, *Emigrants and Exiles: Ireland and the Irish Exodus to North America* (Oxford, 1985), 21–25, 86–89, 181–183.

one Ballybog's daughters have gone away. One after one in a couple of years they re-visit the glimpses of Ballybog in photographs, and they are all transfigured. Irish girlhood sees itself reflected in American photographs and trembles with longing and delight.[26]

Leisure, Feasts, and Festivities

The Irish rural landscape lacked the nucleated agricultural village. Many of the ordinary forms of entertainment took place not so much on the common as within the home. In the evenings, particularly the long winter evenings, people would gather in "rambling houses" for storytelling, card playing, music, singing, and dancing. In most communities, there was a local *seanachai* (storyteller) who would entertain the company with a tale. Frequently, too, someone who was literate, such as the schoolmaster, would read aloud from a national or local newspaper, or from a letter from someone who had emigrated.

Music and dancing were an integral part of festivities and celebrations such as weddings. Many districts had itinerant fiddlers and pipers who would travel from one wedding to another and to fairs and markets. Community dances were usually held at a crossroads. Other dances, such as Maypole dancing, were associated with seasonal festivities. Feast days and the marking of the seasons of the year were the main days for celebration and the occasion for scattered communities coming together.

The four "quarter days" of the years were celebrated: February 1st, *Lá Fheile Brighde* (literally "the day of the festival of [Saint] Bridget"); May 1st, *Lá Bealtaine;* August 1st, *Lá Lunasa;* and November 1st, *Lá Samhna.* Magical powers were believed to be at their greatest at these turning points of the year, during midwinter and midsummer, and at Halloween (when the souls of the dead visited their old homes and the fairies were given to stealing young women). May 1st and November 1st were regarded as the beginning and end of summer and were the dates of departure and return for seasonal migrants who left their home communities to work in Britain. May 1st

---

[26]Quotation from George W. Russell, in *Selections from the Contributions to "The Irish Homestead,"* ed. Henry Summerfield (London, 1978), 214.

was the day of the year when the power of the fairies was at its height, and precautions had to be taken not to anger them. In her account of May Eve in County Limerick, Sissy O'Brien remarks on the difference in belief between herself (convent educated) and the dairy maids who worked on the farm. The maids attended mass like everyone else, but they were more sensitive to fairies, banshees, and witches than to angels and saints:

> On that day the maids were apt to be uneasy and rather sullen, watching us suspiciously lest we might, through our unbelief, frustrate their precautions against danger. They strewed primroses on the threshold of front and back doors . . . and in the cow-byres they hung branches of rowan while the head dairywoman sprinkled holy water in mangers and stalls. The milkmaids, at the end of the evening milking, stood to make the sign of the cross with froth from the pails, signing themselves and making a cross in the air towards the cows.[27]

On the eve of the feast of St. Bridget, groups of men and women bearing an effigy of the saint moved from house to house in the locality. On November Eve, a cake of bread would be made and thrown at the door. This custom, initiated during the Famine, was reputed to keep hunger from the door for the coming year. Other important feasts were Christmas, St. Stephen's Day (December 26th), and Easter.

In the rites and celebrations associated with these various days, women played an important role. For most of the uneducated peasantry, the magical world was real and fraught with danger. "God be between us and harm" was a common phrase. The strength of the magical, pagan world and its connection to nature is particularly evident in the *Piseoga*, practical measures and folk beliefs known throughout Munster. For instance, a birth every year or so was expected in families and seen as a contribution of the wife to general well-being. Infertility was a terrible plight for two reasons: it not only deprived the family of future working hands but also sympathetically affected the fertility of herds and crops.

---

[27]Mary Carberry, *The Farm by Lough Gur* (Cork, 1982), 158.

Wakes for the dead similarly blended pagan and religious elements. The dead person was laid out, in a shroud or in the best clothes, on a big table in the middle of the room. A sixpenny bit would be put in a pocket to pay a fare to get away from earth. A plate of snuff and a plate of tobacco (for guests) were put on the corpse's stiff chest, and lit candles were placed around the table to keep the devils off. Female relations and neighbors would cry and lament and pray over the body. But the grieving did not take long, and the event, which would last through the night, was also marked by games, singing, and music. The merriment would stop frequently for another prayer to be said for the reposed soul, but in general, wakes were not sorrowful affairs. This gaiety distinguished them from the "live wake," which was the more somber farewell party held before a young person left for America.

Some historians see the Famine as a watershed in the history of old customs and beliefs, and one account remarks: "It didn't matter who was related to you, your friend was whoever would give you a bit to put in your mouth. Sport and pastimes disappeared. Poetry, music and dancing stopped. They lost and forgot them all and when the times improved in other respects, these things never returned as they had been. The Famine killed everything."[28]

Although this account is an overstatement, it is probably fair to say that customs did not hold quite as much sway in post-Famine Ireland as they had in the years before. The reasons are threefold. First, the Catholic Church that emerged in post-Famine Ireland was a revivalist church, anxious to get people back to regular church attendance and practices. It aimed to shift the peasantry to a more formal and orthodox practice. Second, the class in which these practices were most common—the illiterate and poor—was severely reduced in numbers by the ravages of the Famine. Third, the more restrictive social and economic climate of post-Famine Ireland did not provide the same opportunities for merrymaking. For rural women in particular, the loss of female-centered features of popular religion may have eroded their traditional status.[29]

---

[28]Mary E. Daly, *The Famine in Ireland* (Dublin, 1986), 124.
[29]Kerby A. Miller, "For Love and for Liberty: Irish Women, Emigration, and Domesticity in Ireland and America, 1815–1920" (paper presented at New York University, 5 November 1992), 4.

Women's Everyday Lives

• *Family*

Children in Munster were regarded as economic assets, as a source of labor on farms, and as a hedge against old age. They were also the necessary means of attaining generational continuity, of "keeping the name on the land." Because inheritance was based on patrilineal succession, male children were preferred. Generally, mothers believed their sons were physically more delicate and intellectually slower than female children. Hence there was more "coddling" of male children. They were nursed longer than girls, and fewer chores were assigned to them.

A child was baptized as soon as possible after birth, usually in a matter of days. (The Catholic faith taught that an unbaptized person could not enter heaven.) Baptism, apart from being a religious ceremony, was an important family and social event. The ceremony gave the child its name and godparents. Naming practices varied by locality. In some areas, the firstborn male was given the father's name, and in others he was named after the mother's father. The firstborn daughter was named after the father's mother. Sisters and brothers of the parents were chosen as godparents, and their role was generally ceremonial.

Infant mortality was higher among boys. Since boys were more valued (Estyn Evans refers to them as "another spade in the bog") special precautions were taken with male children. It was generally believed that male children were more attractive to fairies, who would often exchange them for one of their own ailing children. Occasionally, boys would be dressed in petticoats and long frocks to mislead thieving fairies. If a thriving, happy child became a whining brat, he was regarded as a "changeling."[30] Special precautions were taken to protect male children:

> Bits of coal or iron (invested with magical properties in Eire from
> pre-Christian times) or tongs opened in the sign of the cross were

[30]Estyn Evans, "Peasant Beliefs," in D. Casey and R. Rhodes, eds., *Views of the Irish Peasantry, 1800–1916* (Hamden, Conn., 1977), 42–43.

kept in the boy's cradle; red ribbons tied across his bed; or red thread sewn into the infant's underwear. Holy water was sprinkled over the child liberally. To ensure that the boy baby would not be abducted by the "little people," a mother was cautioned never to leave her son alone prior to his baptism.[31]

Neither the fairies nor envious neighbors were interested in little girls. Silence and passivity were admired qualities in young children of both sexes, and parental authority was strong. Sick, retarded, or physically handicapped children were often hidden from the prying eyes of neighbors. If they survived, they were found a place in the community, usually in an occupation that did not demand physical strength (such as music making). Children with mental disabilities were known in Irish as "God's Fair Innocents," and an "innocent" or a "natural" was under the protection of the heavens.

Various religious rites of passage demarcated age transition. Early childhood was seen as ending with First Communion (usually around age seven). This also marked the beginning of socialization into separate, gender-related work spheres. Boys were expected to give some help with farm chores, whereas girls, unlike servants in Mecklenburg, remained with their mother in the house. Starting at the age of ten, boys might be kept home from school when needed for farm work during busy times of the year. Confirmation marked the beginning of adolescence and responsibility. In her account of growing up on a farm in post-Famine County Limerick, Sissy O'Brien remarks: "After that day [her confirmation] I was put in charge of my three sisters. I had to see that they were neat and tidy, that they brushed their nails and their teeth and did not shirk their tubs. Their hair was my special duty. I brushed and combed the brown, the gold and the baby-flaxen heads until they shone—in spite of protest, wriggles and tears. Their tears were my own, shed over their waywardness and over my difficult duty."[32] At this stage, girls became integrated into domestic chores, whereas boys were expected to take on a full adult load of work after schooling was completed. Children were often hired out to large farms or exchanged to

---

[31]Nancy Scheper-Hughes, "Breeding breaks out in the eye of the cat: Sex Roles, Birth Order and the Irish Double-bind," *Journal of Comparative Family Studies* 10, no. 2 (1979): 214.

[32]Carberry, *The Farm by Lough Gur*, 93.

help with seasonal activity. Landless laborers and small farmers were more likely to send their adolescent children to more fertile parts of the province, where larger farms predominated, as "servant boys" and "servant girls."

It was only through marriage, and becoming head of a household, that an individual achieved full adulthood. Chronological age alone did not bring adult status. As Kevin Danaher notes, "A young married woman of twenty had all the independence, all the rights, all the privileges of a full member of the community while her unmarried aunt of fifty was still called a 'girl,' and, if she lived in the family home, was no more than a dependent, still subject to restriction and the head of the family."[33]

In pre-Famine Ireland, girls and boys could expect to marry young, perhaps in their late teens or early twenties. According to evidence given to a government commission, "Early marriages are universal; the usual age for contracting matrimony being about 20 on the part of the man, and from 16 to 20 on that of the woman, but more frequently 17."[34] It has been suggested that the reasons for this young age at marriage were (1) that economic conditions (reliance on the high-yielding potato crop and subdivision of land, discussed earlier) permitted them to do so and (2) that there was no real prospect of improving their conditions by delaying marriage.[35] It is clear that the evidence applied to "the lower classes;" i.e., those below the level of farmer. Although the children of laborers could marry whom they wanted when they wanted, the children of owners of small and large farms were generally more constricted in marriage choice. Among this class, the arranged marriage and dowry system, which was to become more widespread after the Famine, was already well established. Crucial to this system was the bride's dowry, which reflected both the status of her husband and that of the household she was entering. The system generally was less restrictive than after the Famine. There is also the suggestion that, unlike the post-Famine era, when only one child inherited the land

---

[33] Kevin Danaher, "Marriage in Irish Folk Tradition," in Art Cosgrove, ed., *Marriage in Ireland* (Dublin, 1985), 99.

[34] Great Britain, Parliamentary Papers, *First Report of His Majesty's Commissioners for Inquiring into the Condition of the Poorer Classes in Ireland*, HC (1835) (369), vol. 32, Part 1, 446.

[35] Kenneth Connell, *The Population of Ireland 1750–1845* (Oxford, 1950), 47–85.

and the other children faced the prospect of emigrating or remaining as a dependent, small farmers subdivided their land to allow their children to marry. Under this arrangement, separate households were set up while the fathers were still alive.

Throughout the nineteenth century, illegitimacy was rare in Ireland, and the rates remained among the lowest in Europe. The outlook for the mother and her illegitimate child was bleak. She was likely to be despised by the community and rejected by her own family. Sissy O'Brien tells the tale of Mary Dooley, who became pregnant while a single girl of seventeen: "[We] heard the maids talking and telling how Mary had been thrown out by her father and the door shut on her. Some days later Mary ventured home, but still the door was shut, so she crept into the pig-sty where her mother made up a bed for her. The baby, she said, had died. Then poor Mary developed rheumatic fever from living in the damp pig-sty, and when for shame of his own cruelty, Dick Dooley [her father] relented, she hobbled home almost helpless, crippled for life."[36] Many fled their native parishes and embarked on a life of begging and prostitution in the cities of Cork, Limerick, and Waterford and in the garrison towns and ports. There they probably bore subsequent illegitimate children. The authority on this aspect of peasant life remarks: "In a tolerant parish, by avoiding further lapses, by generally seemly behavior, she might, over the years, wear down her disgrace. But even the tolerant, drawn into a quarrel, always charge her with shame."[37]

Connell argues that harsh treatment acted as a major deterrent, and that this, combined with strict parental control, kept illegitimacy low. Among those outside parental control, such as farm and domestic servants, the rates were higher. In these cases, however, the girls were often treated more leniently, especially if it was considered that they had been "laid astray" by senior servants or, as in most cases, by their masters. Pressure was put on the father to face up to his responsibilities, and frequently he was offered an extra incentive in the form of an attractive dowry. For those girls who did not marry the fathers of their children, marriage to another man was highly unlikely. They were more likely to end up in the towns or, if they had

---

[36]Carberry, The Farm by Lough Gur, 49–50.
[37]Kenneth H. Connell, Irish Peasant Society (Oxford, 1968), 51–52.

the means, to emigrate. Andrea Ebel Brozyna asserts that, because of their marginal position in society, Irish women had to adopt various sexual strategies to ensure their economic security.[38] Many used premarital pregnancy to obtain the high status of a married woman. Marriages that occurred before the child was born conceal the true rate of premarital sexual activity in Irish society.

Both abortion and infanticide appear to have been rare, although the latter was probably more common simply because knowledge of abortive practices was minimal. One solution was to abandon an illegitimate child at a church or "big house." The one major institution in the province that cared for illegitimate children was the Cork Foundling Hospital. The hospital took in the children of prostitutes, other illegitimate children from that city, and children brought in from the surrounding countryside. As with so many foundling hospitals throughout Europe, the outlook for the inmates or for infants put out to wet nurses in the country was forlorn. For the years 1820–1833, mortality averaged 62 percent.[39] Occasionally, foundlings would be left at the parish church, whereupon the pastor would pay an older woman to take care of the child. Sometimes the child would be passed around to poor families, who would share with it their meager resources. As with the children in the hospital, the long-term chances for survival of the infant were slim.

However harshly unmarried mothers were treated in pre-Famine times as a means of discouraging illegitimacy, social control of marriage and inheritance was even tighter in the post-Famine period. A comparative study of fifteen countries conducted in the 1890s shows the percentage of illegitimate births to be the lowest in Ireland. As Connell remarked, "the incidence of extra-marital relations has been relatively low in Ireland—astonishingly low for a people marrying so little and late."[40] Post-Famine society was a world of tight control and restricted practices, of high rates of celibacy but high fertility within marriage. The post-Famine years were marked by a somewhat higher

---

[38] Andrea Ebel Brozyna, "Female Virtue and Chastity in Pre-Famine Ireland: Kenneth Hugh Connell Revisited" (paper presented at the annual meeting of the American Conference for Irish Studies, University of Wisconsin–Madison, April 1991).

[39] Connell, *Irish Peasant Society*, 74–75.

[40] The comparative study is quoted by Connell in "Catholicism and Marriage in the Century after the Famine" and cites a figure of 2.46 percent illegitimate births to total births. See Connell, *Irish Peasant Society*, 119.

age at marriage and a dramatic decline in the rate of marriage.[41] This was associated with the spread of impartible inheritance and "stem family" succession. The association between acquisition of property and acquisition of spouses (male land and female cash in the form of a dowry) became more restrictive. As a result, marriages were increasingly arranged and (in the eyes of contemporary commentators) loveless.

For men, the timing of marriage was linked to succession of the land. A spouse was sought after a man had inherited a farm from an aged or deceased father. For women, the timing was less restrictive but was usually linked to the aging of her parents. Daughters were encouraged to remain at home during their teens and early twenties, when they could work vigorously and contribute to the farm. When a farmer felt his daughter was of an age to marry or a man sought a wife following his succession to the farm, a "match" was normally sought and arranged. Crucial to the success of a match was the dowry or fortune that a woman brought to a marriage. The arranged marriage was the norm throughout rural Ireland and proceeded along well-recognized lines:

> What usually happened was that the boy or his parents sent some person to the girl's parents first to sound them out about the match and get their opinion. If the parents were satisfied, then the boy and the girl, and the parents, fathers anyway of the boy and girl respectively, would meet, and the man who started negotiations would be there too. They'd meet in some pub in some town.
>
> The discussion then took place about how much money the girl had and what land, stock, etc., the boy had. The boy's parents and brothers and sisters would be discussed also, whether they expected any of the fortune or not. . . . Fifty years ago, from £70 to £100 was a good dowry. The dowry was paid on the morning of the marriage before the ceremony took place.[42]

The dowry was usually a cash settlement, although it could be in land or in kind. When it came in cash, it was sometimes used to

---

[41]David Fitzpatrick, "Marriage in Post-Famine Ireland," in Cosgrove, *Marriage in Ireland*, notes that the mean marriage age for those born about 1851 was 30 for men and 26 for women (similar to ages in Germany, Belgium and Norway). The lowest rate of marriage (3.92 marriages per 1,000 population) was recorded in 1880. See Vaughan and Fitzpatrick, *Irish Historical Statistics*, 246.

[42]O'Gráda, *Ireland before and after the Famine*, 166.

compensate noninheriting siblings of the groom. The amounts of money were often very substantial—often equivalent to many years' rent or several years toward payment of a farm. Those with the most to offer had most leverage in their choice of partners. Those worst off were the men who had only a small patch of land or the girls who were one of many daughters on whom a dowry had to be bestowed. Women whose parents were too poor to afford a respectable, or any, dowry remained at home, unmarried, and always inferior to married women. Disputes over dowries were frequently bitter. In some areas, it was customary for part of the dowry to be paid before the wedding and part afterward. If the remainder of the money was not paid, violence broke out, and in some cases the wife was unceremoniously ejected from the marital home until the payment was made. For those who spurned the marital match, elopement was a way out. Literary evidence suggests that the usual route for such couples was to flee their parishes and emigrate.

The match was based on women's economic worth rather than their personal qualities. This fact is reflected in the advice given by an old sage to a young man who liked a young woman with only one cow as a fortune, compared to her rival who had two. "Take the gyurl wid the two cows. There isn't the difference of a cow, begorra, betune any two women in the wor-r-ld."[43] Matchmaking was usually carried out within parishes, and most people married within their own class. Hence marriage was truly endogamous. Men or women who married beneath their class faced being disinherited or left without a dowry. The economic imperative was to keep fortunes intact and children comfortably settled on the land. Given the importance of a dowry, some women may have planned to emigrate, accrue some money, and return in search of a husband. In fact, return migration by Irish emigrants was low, but stories from folklore archives refer to emigrant women who came home, ostensibly on holiday, but in reality to find a husband. These women with their money competed with local women for the hands of local men—competition resented by the local women.[44]

---

[43]Donnelly, *The Land and People,* 224. Evidence from the Irish Folklore Commission.

[44]Grace Neville, " 'She Never Then After That Forgot Him': Irish Women and Emigration to North America in Irish Folklore," *Mid-America: A Historical Review* 74 (October 1992): 283–284.

The most popular day for marriages in Munster was Shrove Tuesday, a day favored by Irish custom and the last day before Lent, during which the canon law prohibited marriages. The timing also made economic sense, since the day preceded the busy part of the agricultural year. Further, the emigration season did not begin until May, so that the chance that a potentially good match might fall through because of emigration was reduced.

The wife was weakest when the marriage was new and childless—that is, before succession had been ensured. Once there were children, her position was stronger because, even if her husband died, they would inherit the land. The rights of widows to control the farm became more generally recognized after the Famine. There is evidence, however, that, should a woman become a widow before the birth of any children, the collateral kin of her husband might attempt to oust her from the farm. Thus she would be left with only the cash equivalent of her dowry. Although the status of widows was fairly secure, widows' prospects for remarriage were bleak. There was reluctance among men to marry young widows who could still bear children, because of potential disputes over the property and inheritance rights of any future offspring. The deceased husband's family would have strongly opposed any transfer of property out of the family, thus making the widow a less attractive marriage partner.

Divorce was virtually unknown, although there were separations in which the partners went their own ways. English laws gradually liberalized the grounds for divorce, but these changes were never extended to Ireland. Separation without the right to remarriage could be granted by Catholic ecclesiastical courts, but the courts had no power to make decisions concerning property.[45] Divorce was not only unobtainable but dysfunctional in the social and economic structure of rural Ireland. If a marriage did break down, usually as a result of a dowry dispute or the failure of the wife to bear children, then the couple would separate and the wife would return to her parents' home. More frequently, couples at odds adopted habits that ensured minimal personal contact. Certainly the social relations of this period allowed for such arrangements. The worlds of husbands

---

[45]See D. Fitzpatrick, "Divorce and Separation in Modern Irish History," *Past and Present* 114 (1987): 174, 183.

and wives were quite distinct. Their labor was complementary rather than shared, and their social worlds separate.

Desertion was quite common before the Famine but declined afterward. Many abandoned wives and children ended up in the workhouses, and some desertions occurred as a result of male migration to the towns or to America. For instance, according to a poor-law inspector in Kerry in 1849, "A great many when they get out there [America] marry again; they forget that they have wives and children at home."[46] Other women and children were temporarily abandoned until their husbands sent for them.

In most cases, the marriage arranged by the match was, initially at least, loveless. It was often, too, one of hard work and continuous childbearing. Overall, the position of women deteriorated as they became more marginal to the post-Famine economy. The extent and severity of the effects of male dominance seem to have been reflected in the declining living standards and health of women. Robert Kennedy has shown how the female edge in life expectancy declined, particularly during the years 1890–1927.[47] Subordinate status meant neglect in the allocation of vital resources such as food (women ate only after men had finished), and women carried a heavier workload. A woman was expected to take a share of farm work, in addition to her normal duties as wife and mother. Chores in the farmyard were considered an extension of the work in the home.

Women who wanted to avoid that lifestyle either had to avoid marriage (which meant remaining subordinate) or improve their social status by emigrating. As David Fitzpatrick succinctly put it, "Twenty-year-olds in rural Ireland consciously confronted three alternative futures: to be matched, to be dismissed as unmatchable, or to emigrate."[48] Peig Sayers, who faced the choice of an arranged marriage or going into service either in Ireland or in the United States, chose marriage.[49] Increasingly, however, many chose to emigrate. Through letters and newspapers, young women were well

---

[46]Ibid., 181.

[47]Kennedy cites these figures as evidence of malnutrition and fatigue. Robert Kennedy, *The Irish: Emigration, Marriage and Fertility* (Berkeley, Calif., 1973), 51–65. In Ireland, the edge in longevity during the period 1890–1912 ranged from a mere 0.1 to 0.5 years.

[48]Fitzpatrick, "Marriage in Post-Famine Ireland," 120.

[49]See Peig Sayers, *An Old Woman's Reflections* (London, 1971), 124.

aware of the opportunities in America. The very option of emigration altered the mental outlook of women even before they left the country. More and more girls rejected Irish rural life in favor of modern urban life, and they dominated the migrant stream by the end of the nineteenth century. Marriage became a minority experience in Ireland.

Work

The declining status of women and their marginal economic position in rural post-Famine society cannot be attributed solely to changes in marriage patterns. In large measure, it was owing also to the changes in agriculture. Traditional domestic industries such as textiles and butter making, which had been the domain of women, were lost. In the pre-Famine peasant economy, all household members contributed to the family income. The income from women's labor was often essential to the family's survival; the loss of the woman's earnings could plunge the family into destitution.

Females contributed to the economy of laboring families in various ways. Some begged (on the roads or door to door) to support the family, and often took over the role of family breadwinner through begging.[50] In the heyday of the domestic textile industry, income from spinning regularly paid the rent. On the farm, women were responsible for the raising of pigs and poultry, both of which made a substantial contribution to the family's income. Rearing poultry for sale was a particularly important job for rural women in the late nineteenth century. Profits on small farms contributed to the purchase of essentials, and on moderately well-off small farms, they even paid for rent or purchase of the farm.[51]

Important as the poultry business was to individual households, it was nevertheless disorganized at a commercial level. Standards varied enormously, as did prices. Colleges were established to train women, and at the Munster Institute, Ireland's leading school for the

[50]Mary Cullen, "Breadwinners and Providers: Women in the Household Economy of Labouring Families 1835–36," in Maria Luddy and Cliona Murphy, eds., *Women Surviving: Studies in Irish Women's History in the 19th and 20th Centuries* (Dublin, 1990), 106–111.

[51]Joanna Bourke, "Women and Poultry in Ireland, 1891–1914," *Irish Historical Studies* 35, no. 99 (1987): 293–310.

Woman feeding chickens.
Photograph, Cooper Collection, Public Record Office, Northern Ireland.

training of women in rural domestic economy, classes in poultry-keeping and dairying were taught. The school trained women as instructors, who in turn would train women in rural areas. Some of the trained women, however, became domestic servants or emigrated. Indeed, numerous commentators were concerned that the education that the women received was simply providing them with the skills and confidence to emigrate.

The turn of the century witnessed increasing commercialization of agriculture in most of Ireland. One aspect particularly affected women: creameries were set up throughout Munster. Now butter was no longer produced at home; instead, milk was brought to the creameries (most of which were small local cooperatives). As the production of butter and other "women's" commodities was commercialized, the prestige attached to them grew, and men began to take over.

Outside of agriculture, the main area of employment for women was domestic service. Although the proportion of women employed as servants was low in Ireland (7 percent in 1861, 5 percent in 1901) compared to other European countries, it was an important occupation for young women, particularly in the richer dairy farming areas of Munster. Domestic service was common for many thousands of working-class girls and girls from orphanages, industrial schools, and reformatories. It was appealing to parents, because it offered board and lodgings as well as wages. Furthermore, in keeping with the ideology of the times, domestic work was seen as a "natural" occupation for women.

Mona Hearn points out: "The vast majority of Irish servants were children of small farmers, estate workers, the semi-skilled and the unskilled. The lack of alternative employment in Ireland was a crucial factor in limiting career choice for these girls; in fact the usual choice facing them was domestic service or migration."[52] Because employment opportunities were scarce, domestic service became the "automatic" choice. The proportion of women employed as domestics was particularly high in cities where there was little industry. Cork, for example, had 49 servants for every 1,000 of the population in 1908, whereas Belfast, where there were manufacturing jobs, had only 22 per 1,000. Although a domestic servant was still a dependent, wages were good compared to those in other industries.[53] For most of the rural women, becoming a servant involved migration to towns or cities, and for many it was their first experience of life outside their native community. Life in a middle- or upper-class home also introduced girls to a new social, cultural, and economic world. Hence it offered an escape from a dreary rural life and unpaid drudgery on the farm. The majority of servants were young and unmarried. Employers clearly preferred single girls, and conditions of service certainly did not provide many opportunities for meeting members of the opposite sex. Between 1881 and 1911, the numbers of domestic servants decreased steadily as competition for jobs in the retail, manufacturing, and clerical sectors grew. Although these jobs frequently did not pay as well as domestic service, they carried social status.

[52]Mona Hearn, "Life for Domestic Servants in Dublin, 1880–1920," in Luddy and Murphy, *Women Surviving*, 149.
[53]Wages in Cork and Limerick were lower than those in Dublin or Belfast, where there was competition from industry. See ibid., 157.

Girls in the retail trade were similar in many respects to those in domestic service. Often board and lodgings were provided on the premises. Most of the girls were daughters of tenant farmers and sent nearly all of their money home. One witness to a government report on the employment of women told how she received a wage of £30 a year (more than usual, because she lived with her aunt). Her relatives testified that "for ten years she had sent the whole of her money to her parents with the exception of a few shillings spent on necessary material for clothing."[54]

The majority of women employed outside the home were single. In the rural areas, a laborer's wife would sometimes work for a wage and do casual work on a neighboring farm for payment. Poor women in the larger towns often worked in the factories and mills as a matter of economic necessity, but medical officers were of the opinion that the health of mothers and infants suffered when young married women were employed. Since arrangements for child care were inadequate, many women "put out" their children. This practice attracted particular concern, since the infants were often poorly fed or given harmful substances. Witnesses who testified before a government commission attributed most of the injuries of children to cordials and sleeping drugs administered by women looking after them.[55] The same experience characterized the lives of women working in industries in England and other manufacturing regions of Europe.

Most of these opportunities for employment outside the home were for working-class girls. For most middle-class women, marriage and motherhood followed adulthood. Yet the advances made in education after the 1850s raised expectations, and some women began to seek a degree of autonomy that could not be found within marriage. An increasingly popular route was what, at first glance, seems unlikely: the religious life.

The number of nuns in Ireland increased eightfold between 1841 and 1901, at a time when the Catholic population was nearly halved. Convents were particularly widespread in Munster, where many had

---

[54]Great Britain Parliamentary Papers, *Report on the Conditions of Work in Various Industries in England, Wales, Scotland and Ireland* (1893–1894), Command C. 6894, vol. 27, part 1, 321–322.

[55]Ibid., 329.

been established even before the Famine. It was in the city of Cork that Nano Nagle had founded her Sisters of the Charitable Instruction of the Sacred Heart of Jesus as early as 1776. Her sisterhood taught in the schools, visited the sick and elderly, and performed other services that today would be described as social work. Indeed many of the new orders, such as the Sisters of Mercy founded by Catherine McAuley in Dublin in the 1820s, had specific social purposes. The order of the Sisters of Mercy, which, unlike other orders, was not centralized in organization, was particularly active. The order grew more than any other, and its practical work appeared to attract women. In Limerick, for instance, the order was the first to carry out nursing in the hospitals of the Poor Law Unions. This order and others, such as the Daughters of Charity, became dominant in those hospitals.[56]

Nuns shared many features of female life with other Irish women. The celibate life in itself was not significant, since many Irish women were spinsters. The difference lay in their organization, their autonomy, and their visibility. The opportunity to live and work together in an organization run by and for women was not found elsewhere. Irish women did not participate in trade unions (because of the isolated and nonindustrial nature of their work) and shared work identity was found almost exclusively in convents. Nuns' activities were also seen as traditionally female, nurturing, and caring. They experienced the same hard work as other women, however: "The nuns, like mothers of families and other unpaid domestic workers, were working for no personal gain and were working until they dropped."[57] They also had to contend with a patriarchal structure in the church. Still, the religious life offered opportunities that did not exist elsewhere.

Although the number of nuns rose, at a time of evangelism and revival in the Catholic Church (as did the number of priests), the popularity of the sisterhood probably owed as much to changes in family life and female aspirations. The growth of religious communities can also be seen as a response to economic change. During the

---

[56]Catriona Clear, "The Limits of Female Autonomy: Nuns in Nineteenth Century Ireland," in Luddy and Murphy, *Women Surviving*, 21–34.

[57]Ibid., 42–43.

course of the nineteenth century, nuns became the main social workers of the country, tending to the needs of the poor, the sick, and the disadvantaged, as well as running educational establishments and local government institutions. Most of the upper-echelon "choir sisters" were well educated and from middle-class backgrounds.[58] In their various institutions, these women held positions of authority as teachers, nurses, and administrators and were respected in the community. The religious life became the leading profession for women.

Education

In the eighteenth century, education in Ireland was a mixture of estate schools, open-air "hedge schools," and sessions conducted by traveling schoolmasters. Elementary education was made widely available by a National School system in 1831 and was supplemented by voluntary schools of religious orders. The state-supported system began to instill the basics of reading, writing, and arithmetic to a gradually growing number of children and to have an impact on illiteracy in rural areas. In the middle of the century, literacy rates were low in Munster, varying from 45 percent in Limerick to 30 percent in Kerry; rates were generally higher for males than females. Over the next few decades, the scene improved enormously. In rural County Cork, for instance, literacy increased from 34.4 percent in 1841 to 79.2 percent in 1891. Equally notable was the way in which the literacy rates of females increased, until by late century young women were more likely to be literate than males. The increase in national literacy levels reflected growing rates of school attendance. By 1880, adolescent girls had overtaken boys in school attendance. The influence of primary, and later secondary, education was to be felt in many areas of Irish life. Probably the impact was greatest on female status and mobility.

The superior performance of girls reflected, according to Fitzpatrick, "not only their stronger desire to better themselves, but also

---

[58]Women who entered convents brought a certain amount of money, or dowry, with them. These women entered the ranks of the "choir sisters." Women who entered with a very small or no dowry became lay sisters. The lay sisters usually were from a lower-class background and carried out the more menial tasks in the convent, such as kitchen chores.

their declining importance in the labor market."[59] As noted earlier, the economic contribution of females had diminished considerably, and the contraction of the domestic textile industry meant much-reduced employment opportunities for young women. As Fitzpatrick notes: "Abnormally high rates of school attendance and literacy were recorded for Munster and southern Leinster, where few children brought home wages. . . . In Limerick, where nine-tenths of girls were unoccupied, over two-thirds could read and write while half attended school during a mid-summer census week."[60]

As conditions for Irish women deteriorated in the second half of the nineteenth century, women availed themselves of two means of improving their condition: education and emigration. The promise of emigration generated interest in literary and domestic skills, all of which would be useful in obtaining employment in America. Simply put, girls exploited the training being offered in order to enhance their chances abroad. The education boards, believing they were imparting good domestic skills to the future wives and mothers of Ireland were, in reality, training the future domestic servants of New York, Boston, and Chicago. In Dublin, the Irish branch of the Society for Promoting the Employment of Educated Women (founded in 1861) taught classes in writing and reading as well as bookkeeping, law-copying (hand-copying legal documents), lithography, and etching. The Irish branch worked in conjunction with the London branch of the society (which operated an emigration agency) to find positions for women in the colonies.

Employment opportunities were extremely limited for women who remained in Ireland. For decades, the only routes for women who aspired beyond menial service or semiskilled labor were to become a nun or a schoolteacher. Formal training of teachers through training colleges began in 1870, and teaching became the number-one professional job for women. Revolutionary changes in access to education toward the end of the century also affected employment. In 1877, the Irish College of Physicians and Surgeons allowed women to pursue medical degrees. With the passing of the Intermediate Ed-

---

[59]David Fitzpatrick, "A Share of the Honeycomb: Education, Emigration and Irishwomen," *Continuity and Change* 1, no. 2 (1986):220.
[60]Ibid., 222–223.

ucation Act of 1878 and the Royal University Act of 1879, boys and girls began to compete on equal terms in the intermediate exams and entrance exams for universities. Some convent schools began preparing girls for these exams.[61]

By the turn of the century, clerical opportunities began to emerge, first in the post office system and in industries such as the Guinness brewery, and gradually in the civil service.[62] The high proportion of unmarried women in Ireland (48.26 percent of women ages 15 and over; 21.9 per cent of women ages 45–54 in 1901) meant that for many women, good permanent employment was a necessity. Education and skills became as important for those who remained behind as for those who departed.

Emigration

Mass migration from Munster was a nineteenth-century phenomenon, differing in this respect from the northern province of Ulster and parts of Leinster, which had experienced emigration from the

TABLE 2.2

Emigration from Munster, 1851–1911

Years	Males	Females	% females	Total
May 1, 1851–March 31, 1861	213,653	220,685	50.1	434,338
April 1, 1861–March 31, 1871	168,002	136,103	44.7	304,105
April 1, 1871–March 31, 1881	96,288	85,082	46.9	181,370
April 1, 1881–March 31, 1891	129,414	122,666	48.7	252,080
April 1, 1891–March 31, 1901	83,702	93,534	52.8	177,236
April 1, 1901–March 31, 1911	54,753	56,150	50.6	110,903
Total 1851–1911	745,812	714,220	48.9	1,460,032

Source: Adapted from W. E. Vaughan and A. J. Fitzpatrick, *Irish Historical Statistics, 1821–1971* (Dublin, 1978), 346–348.

[61]Owens, *Smashing Times*, 31.

[62]Anne V. O'Connor, "The Revolution in Girls' Secondary Education in Ireland 1860–1910," in Mary Cullen, ed., *Girls Don't Do Honours: Irish Women in Education in the 19th and 20th Centuries* (Dublin, 1987), 50–54.

eighteenth century onward. For the people of Munster, the economic and social dislocation arising from the Famine, was truly a watershed. The rate of emigration had been low, probably because landless laborers lacked the means to go. Although the population pressure on the land was intense, emigration was not evident on any great scale. The major exceptions were various schemes devised by landlords in the 1830s to clear tenants off lands that the landlords wished to consolidate. Landowners anxious to consolidate but fearful of outrage availed themselves of assisted passage schemes to Canada. (One example was the Earl of Kingston, who consolidated the holdings on his County Cork estate. Approximately 200 families were sent to Upper Canada in the "first emigration," before 1835.[63]) The majority of those who emigrated from Munster (most from southern Munster) sailed for Canada, mainly to Quebec but some to Saint John, New Brunswick. Of the 40,800 who sailed directly from Ireland to Quebec during 1833–1834, approximately 25 percent sailed from Cork and the other ports of Munster.[64] Canada remained the primary destination for Munster emigrants until 1848, the height of the Famine, when the United States became the destination of choice.

The sheer volume of emigrants during the Famine years brought about a change in destination patterns. Much of the emigrant traffic went through Liverpool to New York and other American ports. Further, American ships landing with supplies of maize carried Irish passengers on their return. Most important, America's rapid urban expansion and the concomitant growth of job opportunities at the middle of the century coincided with the heaviest influx from Ireland in these years.

Famine migration began as early as 1846, with total failure of the potato crop. Vessels in ports all around the province took on emigrants. As can be seen from Table 2.3, the numbers decreased somewhat in the years 1848–1850 before picking up again in 1851. Until the early 1900s, the emigration hemorrhage was unending. Those who left during the Famine years were not the most needy or desperate—

---

[63]Donnelly, The Land and People, 56.
[64]Cecil J. Houston and William J. Smyth, Irish Emigration and Canadian Settlement (Toronto, 1990), 32.

TABLE 2.3

Recorded emigration from the Port of Cork to foreign lands, 1845–1851

Year	United States	Canada	Australia	Others	Total
1845	358	4,473	—	—	4,831
1846	1,383	5,683	—	—	7,066
1847	4,360	13,159	—	—	17,519
1848	8,600	3,021	—	6	11,627
1849	7,846	1,869	—	6	9,721
1850	6,026	2,071	—	2	8,099
1851	7,753	4,709	—	—	12,462
Total	36,326	34,985	—	14	71,325

Source: James S. Donnelly, *The Land and the People of Nineteenth Century Cork* (London, 1975), 126.

the cottiers and the laborers—but middling, respectable farmers who had some capital and, therefore, the means to emigrate. As the *Cork Constitution* in April 1846 noted, "The large mass of emigrants are parties having the appearance of respectable farmers, all of whom are taking with them sums of money from £500 (down) to £10."[65] Likewise the *Kerry Evening Post* remarked in 1847, "Those that go now, and by their own enterprise and means are not of the class we would like to see leaving our shores, because they are carrying with them the capital and sinew of the country."[66] Those of the poorer classes who emigrated during this period were generally tenants who had been cleared off estates or were inmates of workhouses. These assisted passages were invariably directed to Quebec, although the Cork poor-law unions sent about 700 female orphans to Australia.

From the 1850s onward, the costs of transatlantic passage came down, and remittances from those who had emigrated earlier began to arrive in the countryside. The 1850s witnessed significant emigration of laborers and women. During the next 40 to 50 years, although the socioeconomic background of the migrants varied, the emigrant stream was always strong. Another large wave of emigration was to

[65]*Cork Constitution*, 2 April 1846.
[66]*Kerry Evening Post*, 14 April 1847.

occur in the 1880s, during an agricultural depression. Mostly it was the young and unattached who moved. Approximately equal numbers of men and women emigrated up until the last decades of the century, when women dominated. Heavy migration was experienced by most of Munster, and Cork experienced greater per capita emigration than any other Irish county. Some areas were much less affected, however. In parts of West Cork, Kerry, and Clare, in which early marriage and subdivision persisted, peasants clung fiercely to their patches of land. Only when agricultural crises occurred were there sudden bursts of emigration. The resistance to emigration was displayed when young people left: "In many other regions of Munster . . . the trains carrying emigrants to Queenstown moved off to the sounds of the fiddle and dancing feet on the station platform. But those bringing emigrants up to Cork City from Skibereen in 1882 still creaked out of the station amid 'the heart-rending wails of parents and friends.' "[67]

As the old practices gradually died out, emigration became more widespread, and significant population loss was experienced by all counties.

Remittances and letters from America were powerful forces in stimulating emigration. Although remittances from the Irish abroad were always considerable, immigrants seemed to respond particularly to crises, helping those who would otherwise be unable to go.[68] Remittances also were evidence of success in America. As the *Kerry Evening Post* of 1861 commented: "No man, or woman, boy or girl, of the laboring classes in Kerry, will refuse the offer of a free passage to America, when offered by friends already comfortably settled there, and anxiously and affectionately waiting to receive them."[69] Women, in particular, seem to have been dutiful in sending money home.

The amount of money sent by relatives and the speed at which it arrived may well have helped create the image that America was a land of plenty—an image probably further fostered by letters home. Advertising through posters and the work of local agents further spread the lure of America. Most of these agents were small retailers

---

[67]Donnelly, *The Land and People*, 230.
[68]Arnold Schrier, *Ireland and the American Emigration, 1850–1900* (Minneapolis, 1958), 167–168.
[69]Donnelly, *The Land and People*, 229.

and publicans who were paid on a commission basis and took bookings for emigrants.

Some mention has to be made of the "America Wake" because of its ritual importance. Because of the similarity between death and emigration (a loved one was departing, almost certainly never to be seen again), both events were marked by wakes. It is believed that the tradition began in the 1830s, when mass emigration commenced.

The wake would begin at night in the home of the emigrant and continue until the early hours. All who felt close to the intending emigrant attended. In the small farms and holdings, it was a sad event. The night would be spent in drinking, some music, and somber conversations and advice for the departing young person. In parts of Kerry, old women, known for their ability to keen (wail or lament), would deliver a eulogy in a high-pitched wail, extolling the virtues of the emigrant and the suffering and loss of his or her parents. By the end of the eulogy, the room would be full of keening women and crying men. Folklore evidence suggests that there were significant gender differences in the America Wake. Daughters were more lamented and missed than sons—perhaps because a dutiful daughter was so valuable to parents in their old age. Reflecting this attitude, parents were often extravagant in their gifts of clothes to daughters.[70]

In more affluent areas, the affair was somewhat merrier and accompanied by more music, food, and drink. But beneath the outward merriment would be sadness, often brought out by the singing of emigrant ballads. In the morning, the young person would take his or her final parting from family and friends and would set out by foot or horse cart for the nearest train station. "The last embraces were terrible to see; but worse were the kissing and clasping of hands during the long minutes that remained. . . . There it was, the pain and the passion: and the shrill united cry, when the [horse] car moved on, rings in our ears, and long will ring when we hear of emigration."[71]

Between 1851 and 1911, close to 1.5 million people from Munster made their departures from family and friends, the vast majority of them never to return. Most made homes in the United States; others

---

[70]Neville, " 'She Never Then After That Forgot Him': Irish Women and Emigration to North America in Irish Folklore," 275.

[71]Harriet Martineau, quoted in *Blennerville: Gateway to Tralee's Past*, 150.

settled in Australia, Britain, and Canada. Apart from the 1880s, when agricultural depression and disturbances stimulated heavy emigration, the numbers of people who emigrated never again matched the figures for the immediate Famine and post-Famine period.

As with so many aspects of Irish history, the Great Famine was a watershed in the history of women's emigration. In the period 1815–1844, about one-third of Irish emigrants were women (later, the proportion by gender became approximately equal). Demographic, economic, and social changes in Irish society produced by the Famine created an environment that marginalized women economically and reduced their status in society. The virtual ending of partible inheritance, the eradication of the poorer classes among whom female labor was particularly important, the spread of arranged marriages and the dowry system, and the reduced opportunities for female wage earning combined to spur emigration. These factors alone are not sufficient explanation, however, for the abrupt change in the gender balance in Irish emigration. The increase in female literacy and the increased opportunities for education were particularly important developments, especially since women eagerly pursued these to enhance their ability to move and to gain employment in America. The opportunities for female employment in the United States and the ability to get there, as a result either of remittances or the reduction in the transatlantic fares, made emigration a more viable option for women.

Certainly the status and economic position of women was better in the pre-Famine era than in the following years. Women's lives, however, were still filled with drudgery and hard work and should not be romanticized. Likewise, a generalization cannot be made about women's reasons for emigrating. Various post-Famine forces stimulated and facilitated emigration, but these worked in different ways for different women. Many women chose to remain. Either they were able to marry and accepted marriage or chose to join the ranks of the never-married in Irish society rather than risk the uncertainties of emigration. Theirs is a different story.[72] For the

---

[72]See Miller, "For Love and for Liberty"; Timothy Guinnane, "Re-thinking the Western European Marriage Pattern: The Decision to Marry in Ireland at the Turn of the Century" (paper presented at the annual meeting of the Population Association of America, 30 March–1 April 1989, Baltimore, Md.).

714,220 Munster women who did emigrate in the period 1851–1911, Ireland could not offer the economic and social opportunities they desired. Their destinies lay elsewhere, in the towns of England, the communities of Australia and, most commonly, the cities of the United States.

3

Maids in Motion: Swedish Women in Dalsland

Margareta Matovic

Dalsland, located in the western part of the country close to the border of Norway, is one of Sweden's smallest provinces. This chapter focuses on the Vedbo district in the north—more than 50 percent of the province.

As a border province, Dalsland has a history filled with warfare. Until the end of the nineteenth century, it was affected by the varying alliances and feuds between Denmark and Sweden; in 1905, on Norway's independence, the border was finally closed.[1] For Dalsland people, trade and economic exchanges that had occurred during the previous century suffered a setback; the labor market was severely affected, since it had traditionally involved migration. Many Dalslanders regarded Norway as a second homeland, and it was often the country they emigrated to first, before continuing on to North America.

Dalsland women of the second half of the nineteenth century lived in an environment affected by the forces of nature, by century-old traditions, and by socioeconomic change that made family formation more and more difficult and led to a widening social gap between landed and landless families. When women decided to emigrate, they uprooted themselves from the material aspects of

---

[1]Sven-Axel Hallbäck, *Dalsland* (Hälsingborg, 1982), 92–101. See also Sten Carlsson and Jerker Rosén, *Svensk Historia* II (Stockholm, 1964), 333–335, 584–585.

their culture. In the new city environments to which they moved, the forces that had shaped their lives—the forests, the fields, the work system, social relationships, history, and tradition—had to be modified and sometimes even abandoned. A detailed description of their lives indicates the extent to which the women had to adjust to life in the city. Some aspects of Dalsland culture, particularly the assertive and self-confident youth culture on the one hand and the close family networks on the other, facilitated women's adjustment.

Nature, Land, and the Family in Dalsland

Economy and Social Structure

In the nineteenth century, Dalsland, like most of Sweden, depended on agriculture. During the second half of the century the southern region came to be dominated by the cultivation of oats, which were exported mainly to England. When prices were high, both large and small landowners maintained good incomes. Potatoes also began to play an important role in the agrarian economy, becoming the staple food for tenant farmers' and cottagers' families. The price of oats on the world market collapsed in the early 1880s, and farmers faced ruin. The overpopulated Dalbo plain, Slätt Dal, was struck especially hard, because there were no sources of supplementary income.[2] In the forest region, Skogs Dal, the economy was more diverse, and cattle breeding was important. The forest was used for grazing and fodder gathering. Additional income came from timber, charcoal, and tarmaking.

The land-owning and tenant farmers of the Vedbo district could not rely solely on farming; they had to combine agricultural work with other economic activities. Lumber became a major export, and a tremendous economic upsurge in the lumber industry offered employment in paper and saw mills. The new industries of Vedbo were located close to the lake system and the Dalsland Canal, which opened in 1868. Farmers became less interested in agricultural work, and many sold off their land. By 1870, vast parts of Vedbo were con-

---

[2]Paul Noreen, "Emigrationen från Dalsland," in *Svenska Turistföreningens årsskrift* (1981), 298, 299.

trolled by lumber corporations and paper mills, and by 1900 only 849 tenant farms survived. In 1905, there were 1,124 industrial workers employed in the Vedbo district, mostly the sons of tenant farmers. About 100 women also worked in industry.[3]

Growing industrialization, however, could not compensate for the problems in agriculture. A crop failure in 1868 drove many people onto the roads as beggars. Grains were in such short supply that bread had to be made from tree bark. Large numbers of people died from starvation or disease. Population pressure forced men and women to migrate or to rely on industrial work or handicrafts for survival. During these years, the female handicraft of straw plaiting developed in Ärtemark parish. A report on the period 1886 to 1890 claimed that "the straw craft is a good source of income for nearly every home in the parish of Ärtemark,"[4] and according to some observers it even delayed emigration. As the story goes, 19-year-old Märta-Stina Gottman, was employed as a maid in Norway. During the summer of 1851, she met a sailor, who taught her how to plait and sew straw hats. She returned home to Ärtemark, married, and started to make hats for a living.[5] During the 1880s and 1890s, the straw craft developed into a domestic industry. It was the men's task to distribute the straw hats for sale, and many unpropertied or tenant farmers made their way to Norway, where the market for "Ärtemark hats" was large. When the union between Sweden and Norway was dissolved in 1905, however, duty restrictions were imposed, and the market declined.

Making pipes from clay was another craft and business managed by women. It was said that a Swedish woman had learned the skill in Kristiania (Oslo) and brought it home, where it was passed on. For many landless men and women, crafts and short-term emigration were means to avoid misery or starvation.

During the first half of the nineteenth century, Sweden, like the rest of Europe, had experienced accelerating population growth. This trend did not slow until the end of the century. Population growth was caused by decreasing mortality, the cultivation of new crops, the

[3]Ernst Lundholm, *Vedbo och Nordmarks härader* (Emigrationsutredningen, bil 8), Bygdeundersökningar (Stockholm, 1908), 39–40.

[4]"Elfsborgs län," *Bidrag til Sveriges officiella Statistik, 1886–1890* (BiSOS), Statistiska centralbyrån (SCB) (Stockholm, 1895), 56.

[5]Kristina Rosell, "Om halmflätning i Dalsland. HALM I," no. 1 in *Västgöta/Dal* (1985/86): 163–182, Länsmuseet i Vänersborg.

opening of new land, and intense subdivision of land. In Dalsland, the population increased by 106 percent, from 41,063 inhabitants in 1805 to 84,056 in 1865.[6] The highest figure was reached in 1868, just before famine caused a large wave of emigration. Thereafter, the population decreased continuously. In 1890, Dalsland had 74,482 inhabitants, and 40 years later the figure was 69,057 inhabitants.[7]

The Sweden of this period may be divided into three geographically connected demographic regions. The southwestern region was characterized by low marriage rates, high marital fertility, and low extramarital fertility, which contrasted with the low marital fertility and high extramarital fertility of central eastern Sweden.[8] The marriage rate of the county of Älvsborg, which included Dalsland and a part of Västergötland, decreased from 7.3 to 4.91 marriages per 1,000 inhabitants during the period 1840–1905.[9] However, since married women in the county gave birth to many children, there was a small birth surplus from 1890 to 1900. The tendency for Dalsland (as for the rest of Sweden) was, however, a declining marriage and birth rate, with an increasing age at first marriage for both men and women. In 1890, the average marriage age for men was 28.8 years and for women 26.8 years.[10]

The population explosion at the beginning of the nineteenth century affected the district of Vedbo as well; the population more

TABLE 3.1

Births and deaths in Dalsland, 1871–1910

Year	Births	Deaths	Population increase
1871–1880	23,521	13,385	10,136
1881–1890	20,101	12,199	7,902
1891–1900	16,896	11,234	5,662
1901–1910	15,169	11,158	4,011

Source: Kjell Sanne, *Dalslands befolkning i statistisk belysning* (Hembygden, Göteborg, 1929), Table 7, 73.

[6]For the whole of Sweden the increase was only 62 percent. Kjell Sanne, *Dalslands befolkning i statistisk belysning* (Hembygden, Göteborg, 1929), Table 6, p. 72.

[7]Ibid.

[8]BiSOS A I 1890, bihang Table A and pp. III–VI; *Emigrationsutredningen*, bil 5 (Stockholm, 1910), 4; *Swedish Population Census* 1900, 62:4, XX–XXI.

[9]Gustaf Sundbärg, *Ekonomisk statistisk Beskrifning öfver Sveriges olika Landsdelar* (Emigrationsutredningen, bil 5) (Stockholm, 1910), here: *Bygdestatistik* Table 31, 42.

[10]*Historisk Statistik för Sverige I, Befolkning 1720–1967* (Stockholm, 1969), Table 32, 103.

TABLE 3.2

Population of the Vedbo district, 1890–1910

Year	Total	Years	Emigrants	Immigrants
1890	24,533	1881–1890	3,970	629
1900	24,048	1891–1900	2,847	888
1910	23,151	1901–1910	2,806	1,116

Source: Kjell Sanne, *Dalslands befolkning i statistisk belysning* (Hembygden, Göteborg, 1929), Table 6, 72, and Table 8, 74.

than doubled, reaching its peak in 1868 with 25,924 inhabitants. After the famine of that year, the first wave of emigration started. The population gradually decreased, and in 1910 the district had only 23,151 inhabitants. According to the Swedish census of 1900, women outnumbered men.

The same year, 76 percent of the people in the Vedbo district were working in agriculture and forestry, 14.3 percent in industry, 4.4 percent in trade, and 5.3 percent in government service.[11]

Land ownership was traditionally the main source of wealth in rural Dalsland. Family holdings dominated, and farm families did

TABLE 3.3

Population composition in the Vedbo district, 1900

	N	%
Unmarried men	3,667	15.3
Unmarried women	3,779	15.7
Married men	3,666	15.3
Married women	3,723	15.5
Widowers	564	2.3
Widows	1,033	4.3
Boys (under 15)	3,854	16.0
Girls (under 15)	3,748	15.6
Total	24,034	100.0

Source: *Swedish Population Census* 1900, Table E, 10.

---

[11]*Swedish Population Census* 1900, Table E, 10.

most of their own work. Since arable land was scarce in Vedbo and forests dominated the landscape, most farmers lived on small holdings. Large landowners were few, and the social gap between landed and landless was not large. In the fertile plains of Slätt Dal, manors and large-scale farming were more common, and the social differences between landed and landless were larger.

At the beginning of the nineteenth century, land reforms resulted in larger parcels of land. Between 1827 and 1850, reform reduced the severe fragmentation of farms in Dalsland. The practice of dividing property among heirs continued unabated in many parts, however. This caused an increasing number of small holdings, and farmer's sons settled on land that was insufficient to support a family—but still sufficient for the farmer to be called a landowner. In 1865, about 40 percent of all holdings in Dalsland consisted of such small farms. In Vedbo, the numbers of landless were increasing: poor soil and backward agricultural methods, together with day-labor duties (which by the end of the nineteenth century had been transformed into cash payments), created a new agricultural proletariat.

The growing groups of tenant farmers and cottagers in Vedbo created new social problems. The tenant farmer was regarded as inferior to even the smallest farm owner, but the classes were dependent on each other: the tenant farmer worked seasonally for the farmer, who provided him with land and a house. The situation for cottagers was worse, because they lived on common land in miserable huts, wandering around to find temporary work as day laborers.[12] Cottagers were especially numerous in Slätt Dal, whereas the tenant farmers were dominant in Skogs Dal, where they often worked in the forest. The children of tenant farmers and cottagers were among the first to go into industries and cities or to emigrate. These rural proletarians combined many economic activities to survive: they developed occupational diversity, along with flexibility in family roles, in contrast to the landed farmers.[13]

---

[12]Unlike in the context of Mecklenburg society, the term "day laborer" refers to a peasant worker seeking employment on a daily basis.

[13]See Orvar Löfgren, "The Potato-People: Household Economy and Family Patterns among the Rural Proletariat in the 19th Century," in Sune Åkerman et al., eds., *Chance and Change: Social and Economic Studies in the Historical Demography in the Baltic Area* (Odense, 1978), 103.

Family Formation and Inheritance

In traditional Dalsland society, children were expected to enjoy the same land and proprietary status as their parents. Landed wealth belonged to the family. It could be partitioned within established custom, but the farm owner had to see that the land remained inside the family. Anyone who sold land outside the family was held in disgrace. Different strategies were used to avoid selling land: late marriages, cousin marriages, celibacy, temporary work migration, emigration to North America. Toward the end of the century, Dalsland had the lowest marriage rate in Sweden.

For the landed group in Dalsland, land and marriage were closely linked goals. No man could plan marriage without first securing the means to support wife and children. For the farmer's son, marriage could rarely precede the initial inheritance or acquisition of landed wealth. Many parents delayed their retirement, and their adult sons had to wait until their thirties or forties to receive the wherewithal to marry. Until then, they were dependent shareholders in the family farm. Sometimes a son married and brought his spouse into the parental home. This practice led to three-generation families in northwestern Dalsland (and in the Norwegian mountain districts). Such arrangements, however, were temporary adaptations rather than stable structures. For a woman, matrimony brought economic and social benefits, and she became a central figure in the newly created economic alliance between her own family and the family of her husband. Marriage gave her the right to a sexual life and to motherhood. She acquired status in the community as wife and household manager, even if she was under the control and guardianship of her husband. In times of stress and crisis, allied households frequently exchanged further marriage partners. Two or three children from one household might marry children in another, to keep the property and land intact. In some parishes, the practice of marriages between first cousins existed as well.

Who would inherit? Before 1845, the Swedish law of inheritance awarded sons double the share of daughters, but all children of the same sex were entitled to equal shares. Norwegian law, however, laid down explicit rules concerning primogeniture, and some parts of Dalsland were clearly influenced by the Norwegian model. Both impartible and partible inheritance systems existed side by side. When the oldest son inherited, his brothers and sisters received a portion of the farm's value in money or animals. For the daughters, inheritance normally took the form of a dowry. But in many cases, farms were divided equally among the heirs, who later sold their shares to other family members to keep the farm in the family.

A third variant existed in the Vedbo district: a farm could be taken over by adult unmarried sons and daughters living and working together, in a collective called *sambruk*. When conflicts arose, family members were often forced to sell the farm or to help by contributing money for tickets to America.

Tenant farmers, cottagers, soldiers, and day laborers had no reason to delay marriage. For them, family formation was based mainly on economic opportunities. Since there was no land to inherit, their main interest was to take a tenant farm as soon as possible; marriage followed soon after. A tenant farm was often kept in the same family, and for the tenant farmer the family provided a safeguard against the problems of old age. Tenant farms were hard to obtain, however, and adult children often had to leave home and find employment as farm hands, servant maids, lumberjacks, or industrial workers. There was discussion of what to do with the so-called irresponsible and quick family formation among the landless groups that resulted in overcrowded tenant farms and cottages.

Marriage in the Vedbo district at the beginning of the 1890s was affected by lack of economic opportunities and emigration. The average age at marriage was extremely high. In an 1892 case study of six parishes, the average age at marriage for men was 35.8 years and for women 30.2 years. Seventy-seven percent of the men and 60 percent of the women married after the age of 25. During the late nineteenth century in Dalsland, there were fewer opportunities for men to settle down and, consequently, fewer chances for women to get married. The slim prospects for marriage stimulated women to emigrate.

At the same time, the rate of illegitimate births in Sweden rose to about 10 percent in rural areas and 20 percent in urban areas. Dalsland, however, had a low rate of illegitimacy. In the county of Älvsborg, between 1891 and 1900 only 59 illegitimate children per 1,000 births were born each year, and the figure for the years 1900 to 1910 was still lower (this compared to 171 and 181 per 1,000 for the same

TABLE 3.4

Average marriage age in six parishes of the Vedbo district, 1892

Men	Average age	N	Women	Average age	N
Sons (living at home)	29	28	Daughters (living at home)	28.3	46
Land-owning farmers	46.2	17	Servant Maids	28	17
Crofters	42	2			
Workers	30.7	10	Workers	39	3
Artisans	28.3	3	Teachers	28.5	2
Other household members	57	2	Other household members	40	3
Soldiers	27.5	6			
Insufficient information		6	Insufficient information		3
Total		74			74

Source: Marriage records for 1892, including the following parishes: Ärtemark, Torrskog, Tisselskog, Vårvik, Laxarby, and Steneby. Microfiche at the Emigrant Register of Bengtsfors.

TABLE 3.5

Illegitimate births in six parishes of the Vedbo district, 1890–1897

Mothers	Births	Percent
Daughters	42	32.1
Servant maids	33	25.2
Farm owners' daughters	4	3.0
Crofters' daughters	2	1.5
Workers	15	11.5
Insufficient information	3	2.3
Unmarried females	7	5.3
In-living women	8	6.1
Betrothed women	15	11.5
Widows	1	0.8
Paupers	1	0.8
Total	131	100

Source: Birth records from the parishes: Ärtemark, Torrskog, Tisselskog, Vårvik, Laxarby, Steneby, 1890–1897. Microfiche at Emigrant Register of Bengtsfors.

two periods in the county of Gävleborg in the eastern part of Sweden).[14] Low extramarital fertility has been attributed to the influence of the Lutheran Church of Sweden. Margareta Larsson has shown that the less secularized districts in southwestern Sweden (the "Bible belt"), were characterized not only by family land holdings but also by a low extramarital fertility rate, a low proportion of married women, and high marital fertility.[15] These characteristics also held true for the Vedbo district. Between 1890 and 1897, only 131 illegitimate births occurred in a total of 2,200 births, or 5.9 percent. Most of the women who bore illegitimate children in Dalsland were from landless families, who were therefore less able to force the child's father into marriage. Thus, social and economic clout affected patterns of mating and family formation.

The dominant family type in Dalsland was the nuclear family, which transmits property through women as well as men. The French demographer and anthropologist Emmanuel Todd found a striking correlation between high female age at marriage and literacy, and he suggests that the educational power of a family system may well be determined by the strength of maternal authority.[16] Women who married late to men of the same age had a stronger position within the marriage, and the women's influence on their children's education was great. Todd's model is useful in explaining the Dalsland family structure, in which a sense of equality and self-reliance was passed from mothers to daughters.

Despite the general trend toward smaller households in Sweden, average household size in Dalsland and especially in Ärtemark parish remained fairly large. A case study of four villages in Ärtemark parish between 1891 and 1895 shows an average household size of 5.4 members. Although nuclear families were dominant, 13 percent of the households included three generations.

There were few one-person households: 47 percent had between two and five members, and 40 percent between six and ten members.

---

[14]Jonas Frykman, "Sexual Intercourse and Social Norms: A Study of Illegitimate Births 1831–1933," *Ethnologia Scandinavica* (1975): 110–150, Table 1, 123.

[15]Margareta Larsson, "Fruksamhetsmönster, Produktionsstruktur och Sekularisering," *Publication of the Department of Sociology,* University of Stockholm (Stockholm, 1984), 143.

[16]Emmanuel Todd, *The Cause of Progress: Culture, Authority, and Change* (Oxford, 1987), 15–17, 36–37.

*The Glimserud crofter household, Stenserud farm, parish of Håbol,
end of the 19th century.*

Photograph by Elis Persson. Courtesy Barbro Johansson.

TABLE 3.6

Family structure in four villages of Ärtemark parish, 1891–1895

Family type	N	Percent
Nuclear families	44	51.8
Incomplete nuclear families	24	28.2
Three-generation families	6	7.0
Incomplete three-generation families	5	5.8
Single households	6	7.0
Total	85	100

Source: Case study of the villages of Backen södra, Bön, Djupviken, and Dåverud in Ärtemark parish, based on household lists for the period 1891–1895. Microfiche at the Emigrant Register of Bengtsfors.

The average number of children in the families was 3.48; the ranks of the large households were not swollen by numerous children, but rather by relatives, servants, and paupers (who needed a place to live). In the three-generation households, there were usually retired fathers or mothers living with a married son or daughter, his or her unmarried brothers and sisters, and the grandchildren. The married couple was often quite young, about 20 to 25 years of age. Among the heads of households we find in this study were 44 landed farmers and 12 landless people, including tenant farmers.

The Female Life Course

Childhood and Adolescence

Pregnancy and childbirth were risky in Dalsland and were surrounded by many superstitions and rules. There were few certified midwives to assist women in labor.[17] There was a belief in the evil eye and in dangerous "powers" that could hurt the pregnant woman and, later, the baby. A pregnant woman was not to be frightened or to take part in hard work.[18] As in Irish folk culture, there were many rites and customs concerning childbirth. Irish fairies seem to have been interested only in boys; in Dalsland, however, male and female babies alike had to be saved from trolls and demons.

The mother was also in danger and had to be kept inside with all doors locked. Six weeks after giving birth, she was taken to the church. Before that, she was treated as a heathen and regarded as "unclean," someone who could damage crops and harvest work. Many farmers encouraged their wives to go through the church ceremony as soon as possible so that the wives could go back to work in the fields. When women emigrated to American cities, they quickly discarded or were forced to discard these superstitious rules. In doing so, however, they also lost the physical rest and protection so badly

---

[17]The county of Älvsborg had a total of 109 midwives, of whom 89 were certified. *Swedish Population Statistics* BiSOS H 1891–1895, Älvsborgs län, 25.

[18]Nils Andersson, "Folksed i helg och söcken," in Bertil Johansson, ed., *Brålanda II* (Uddevalla, 1984), 477.

needed following childbirth. It took the women's movement in the United States half a century of struggle to regain this protection, in the form of maternity leave.

Marital fertility was high in all of Dalsland, and there is no indication that birth control was practiced. Breast-feeding was widespread in western Sweden, and often children were breast-fed for two years and more—perhaps one reason for the relatively low child mortality in Dalsland.[19] The baby slept in a cradle and was wrapped in swaddling clothes from head to toe—a protection against the evil eye. The baby would continue wearing these clothes until it started to crawl or walk, at which time it graduated to a child's smock, which had the shape of a tunic. The smock was normally worn until the child was out of diapers.

Both paternal and maternal grandmothers (farmor and mormor) took an active part in the upbringing of their grandchildren. As in all other peasant cultures, frightening tales were used to teach children obedience. Hulda Olsson, born in Skoghem, Dalen, in Rölanda parish in 1882, recalled that her grandmother had seen both trolls (evil goblins) and tomtar (farmyard spirits). They were small, but "you had to treat them nicely, otherwise something bad could happen to you." Though she did not believe in such creatures herself, she said, older people often did; she recalled having seen many crosses, painted in tar or colored paints, on the doors of cow barns to frighten off the trolls.[20]

Sometimes Lutheran strictness and authority dominated child-rearing methods, and disobedient children were punished by spanking and slapping. Parents expected total obedience from their children.

Dalsland children started to work at a young age, and their labor was an integral part of running the household. Boys and girls were assigned tasks based on gender. A small girl had to look after her younger siblings and learn from her mother or grandmother how to clean the house and set the table, as well as do textile handicrafts. Young boys were responsible for chopping wood and helping to look after the horses. But girls and boys also shared many tasks, such as

---

[19]Christer Ahlberger and Christer Winberg, "Biologi, Medvetet handlande och Struktur," *Historisk Tidskrift* 3 (1987):360–365.

[20]Hulda Olsson from Skoghem, Dalen, in Rölanda, interviews by Karl-Erik Andersson in 1972 and 1975, tape recording.

carrying water and wood, running errands, helping with the potato crop, weeding, haymaking, gleaning grain after harvest, and leaf-fodder gathering.

From age seven or eight, children were of greatest use in animal husbandry. Olsson remembers that it was autumn 1889, when she was seven years old, that she began herding cows in the forest.[21]

Girls and boys were herders (*holingar*) all over Sweden, with girls preferred in western and northern Sweden. Sometimes they assisted an adult herder, but often they were on their own with the cattle in the forest. Several households could hire a girl or boy to look after the animals during summer months. Usually tenant farmers, cottagers, and day laborers were the ones who hired out their children as herders. The pay was low, and the children were often poorly fed and inadequately clothed. They did receive training, however, in how to take responsibility and care for themselves. Dalsland children were often kept out of school to herd animals, cart materials, work in the fields, or pick berries. They worked like adults, and girls and boys were treated equally.

Compulsory elementary school was introduced in Sweden in 1842, with obligatory attendance for six years and later for eight years. Those parents who did not send their children to school could expect trouble from the vicar and the local school administration. Attempts to promote literacy in Sweden in fact go as far back as 1686, when the parish members' ability to read and understand catechism was required by ecclesiastical law. The time of reckoning came at the *husförhör*, the yearly examination given in each household by the parish vicar. All household members, including *inhyse* ("in-house" or resident) paupers and servants, were required to be present to read and respond, under the watchful eye of the vicar, to questions on the Lutheran catechism. The head of the household was charged with the responsibility of making sure that all the children were adequately taught, though the actual teaching was usually done by mothers or grandmothers. Everyone had to know the catechism by heart and be able to read the Bible.[22] Literacy was widespread in Dal-

---

[21]Ibid.

[22]Anders Lignell, *Beskrifning öfver grefskapet Dal* (Stockholm, 1851), 407; and Emma Åttingsberg, *Seder och Språkbruk fran dalsländsk hembygd* (Uddevalla, 1986), 42–43.

sland, and the Catechism meetings remained a tradition. Swedish household lists were a byproduct of these meetings, since the vicar made note of who was present, their ages and household positions, the family relationships, and the members' knowledge of the Lutheran religion. These lists now enable scholars to arrive at a crude estimation of family size and a relatively accurate view of household structure.

A great event in every boy's or girl's life was the day of confirmation, which normally happened at age sixteen or seventeen. Thereafter the boy or girl was treated as an adult and was expected to support himself or herself. The church ceremony was preceded by eight months of preparation, with intensive teaching at the vicar's home; boys and girls were instructed in different rooms. Since Dalsland was less secularized than the rest of Sweden, Lutheranism was taught very rigorously. Ceremonies were marked by somberness and formality. On the big day of confirmation, everyone was dressed in black, and the girls wore their new long dresses, which nearly swept the floor.

For girls, entry into the labor market following confirmation usually meant becoming a servant. The girls' first employment as maids was often arranged by their parents, and the girls worked for people they were acquainted with. The time spent working as a servant maid was a training period for girls waiting for marriage. A distinction was made in the parish records, however, between *hemmadotter* (girls living at home) and *pigor* (girls working away from the family). Girls who lived at home emphasized their status as daughters of landed farmers. They could expect a dowry as a part of advanced inheritance and were prospective wives to other landed farmers. Otherwise, there was little social stratification between family members and servants, since the position of servant represented a transitory stage in life between confirmation and marriage. Landowning farmers augmented family labor by adding hired servants to their households.

During the nineteenth century, however, when landless groups were expanding, new patterns of social segregation appeared. The distance between employer and employee grew accordingly. There were also growing social differences in sex roles. These were enhanced by a cultural reorientation among landed farmers, whose wives and daughters began to pattern themselves after the urban bourgeoisie. Farmers' wives started to withdraw from field work, which was taken over by hired male and female servants. Also, more daughters of landed farmers remained home after confirmation and avoided employment as servant maids. Servanthood as a transitory stage of the life course for farmers' children came to an end. Work as a servant girl became more and more despised, but for a girl growing up in a landless family, there was no choice.

Dalsland farm owners were famously greedy[23] and it is little wonder that farmers' daughters tried to avoid this type of employment. One alternative was emigration. Kerstin Hesselgren, in her study of emigrating Swedish women in 1907, stated the differences between the landed farmers' daughters and the female servants: farmers' daughters were better-fed, taller, healthier, and more self-confident than the servant maids, who were often sickly, small, and thin.[24] The food for servants was of bad quality, and servant maids were subjected to harder work.

The daily routine was described by a 19-year-old servant maid before her departure to America in 1907.[25] She was one of seven children, and her father, who did not own the land he farmed, had problems providing a livelihood for his family. The children left home early, and the girl started to work as a *piga* when she was 15 years old. She found employment at a large dairy farm where she knew the people. Conditions were harsh. Three maids slept in the kitchen together with the farmer and his wife. Work began at five o'clock in the morning and lasted without any break until nine or ten o'clock in the evening. She stayed there for a year. Her next employment was at a smaller dairy farm, where she was the only female servant. She had to work in the cow barn and also helped with haymaking and the harvest, as well as indoor work. Her first milking of the cows was at six o'clock in the morning; usually the cows were milked three times

---

[23] Axel Brusewitz, *Sundals, Nordals och Valbo härader* (Emigrationsutredningen, bil 8. Bygdeundersökningar), (Stockholm, 1908), 58.

[24] Kerstin Hesselgren, *Reseberättelse* (Emigrationsutredningen. Utvandrarnas egna uppgifter, bil 7) (Stockholm, 1908), 23–24.

[25] She told her story to Kerstin Hesselgren, who conducted an investigation in Liverpool, contacting female emigrants going by boat to the United States. The young woman was born in the county of Älvsborg (she might have been a Dalsland maid) and had worked on two farms before 1907.

The harvest in August was a busy time. Work was traditionally sex-segregated, but women worked close to the men. 1910.
Photographer unknown.

a day. Her work went on nonstop until ten or eleven in the evening. In winter, her job was a little easier, and she could go to bed at nine o'clock. Although she had to sleep in the same room with the farmer, his wife, and their three children, she found this quite natural. She stayed on this farm three years. But the work was too hard for her, and she had to work seven days a week. The journey to America was suggested by her brother and her aunt, who lived in America and sent her a ticket. Her aunt had told her she could stay with her for as long she needed to learn the language properly. Then she would quickly find employment as a housemaid.[26]

Working conditions were based on the Servants Act of 1686, as revised in 1805, 1833, and 1858. The act gave the employer nearly total control over his servants. Work was contracted on a yearly basis, and servants could not quit before the last week of October, when they

---

[26]Hesselgren, *Reseberättelse,* 114–115.

got their only free week of the year and had to sign a new contract or move to another employer. By the end of the 1890s, wages had risen and included room and board and a piece of cloth for a dress. Sometimes servants also got a pair of shoes. The employer could, however, ask his servants to work both day and night, and many Dalsland maids were not even allowed to go to church on Sundays. Church was a welcome break for hardworking servants, and many took the chance to take a nap. These naps tended to be brief, however: the vicar employed a man who carried a stick long enough to wake up all who fell asleep.[27]

The work of servant maids was similar to the work done by their Mecklenburg sisters, and maids and farm hands shared a similar youth culture across the Baltic Sea. Everybody was expected to attend church, and for young people the long walk to church offered opportunities for amusement and getting to know one another. Food for picnics, along with alcoholic beverages, was hidden, on the way to church; after the service, boys and girls had their meal in the forest. Even if leisure time was nonexistent for a servant maid, there were still occasions like the Saturday night dances when young people could meet in a meadow, on the road, or in the barn. To tunes from the concertina, boys and girls could dance the hambo, mazurka, or German polka. Homemade brandy and beer were served, and nobody tried to enforce temperance promises.

The nearly total control by the employer was broken temporarily during the summer, when Dalsland maids lived far away from both parental control and their master. Work in the forest meant freedom in many senses—no authority, no punishment, no contempt. Cattle raising and dairy products were important for Dalsland households, and the servants were responsible for the safety of the animals during the summer months. The girl herders and servant maids followed the cattle to the *fäbod* settlement in the summer feeding grounds, where they spent the summer watching over the animals, taking care of the milking, and making butter and cheese. Every household maintained a *fäbod*, which consisted of a rather primitive timber house, containing a fireplace and a few beds, and a number of other small timber buildings for the cattle and the dairy

[27]Olsson interview.

work. A skilled dairy maid, who might be a farmer's daughter or a hired girl specially employed by the households of the village, was in charge of overseeing the work; she began her day at four o'clock in the morning by milking the cows and goats. Then the herders left with the cattle to work alone in different parts of the forest, which had been divided into a number of grazing areas. Predators were an ever-present danger. Wolves might grab a lamb or a lynx might jump on a calf. Herders also had to be on the lookout for the great brown bear *Nalle,* although he was not regarded as a major killer. Since the bear was afraid of noise and music, the girl herders had to learn how to shout and sing in dangerous situations. The girls always carried a horn made of the rowan tree, which was said to have the power to drive away all wild beasts. With the horn, which they often made themselves, the herders could also communicate, warning or informing each other. The female servants and girl herders spent the night in the cabins, often receiving visits from boyfriends or boy herders; often, tales were told about mysterious creatures of the forest. Through these gatherings, the girls also learned about herbal medicines and how to cure sick animals.[28]

Summer life in the forest offered possibilities for young women and half-grown girls and boys to organize their work on their own. Social background and patriarchal norms related to the Lutheran church were left behind in the village. The dairy maid, together with her company of servant maids and herders, comprised a small female ensemble that lived rather independently. In the forest region of Dalsland, a special youth culture existed where premarital contacts were collectively regulated by the village youth. On certain evenings, boys visited girls in their sleeping quarters (often hay barns), and sometimes these contacts developed into stable premarital relations. Everybody knew one another in the village and who was paired with whom, and relatively great freedom existed in the choice of marriage partners.

Courtship and Marriage

Sexual relations during the time between betrothal and marriage were widely accepted among Scandinavian peasants. Dalsland was

---

[28]David Skoog and Konrad Thedin, *Dalsland* (Uppsala, 1929), 324.

culturally influenced by Norway, and "night courting" traditionally occurred in the forest region; it was an old custom and regarded as preparation for marriage. The promise of marriage more or less authorized a sexual relationship, or the relationship itself was interpreted as a decision to marry.[29] In the middle of the nineteenth century, however, one Dalslander (Dean Anders Lignell) criticized parents who offered their daughter to a man who had come to propose and immediately allowed him to spend the night with her. More than 50 percent of brides were pregnant at the wedding ceremony.[30] Social pressure in Dalsland was such, however, that it forced a pregnant bride to marry quickly.

On the other hand, the increasing gap between landless and landed created different courting systems and sharpened the landed farmers' interest in controlling their children's choices. The higher up in the social pyramid, the greater the risk of unsuitable matches. In southern Sweden, parental supervision was rigorous, courtship was highly formalized, and marriage often the result of long planning. Dalsland had at least two different patterns of courtship, one in the northwestern part (night courting) and another in the southern part, (parental supervision). Here the future partner had a rather passive role in the matchmaking. Parents surveyed appropriate suitors in the neighborhood, and the discussions over marriage were sometimes restricted to the two sets of parents. Emma Åttingsberg described how her grandmother got married in southeastern Dalsland in 1855. She had never seen her future husband before the engagement. He had a private meeting with her brother and mother, and they simply called her into the room to give her consent to the marriage.[31]

In landed families where children were raised in a strict Lutheran atmosphere, arranged marriages occurred frequently. In such families, daughters received very little information about sexuality, preg-

---

[29]Ann-Sofie Kälvemark (Ohlander), "Illegitimacy and Marriage in Three Swedish Parishes in the 19th Century," in Peter Laslett, Karla Oosterveen, and Richard M. Smith, eds., *Bastardy and Its Comparative History* (London, 1980), 330–331; see also Jon Gjerde, *From Peasants to Farmers: The Migration from Balestrand, Norway, to the Upper Middle West* (Cambridge, 1982), 88–89.

[30]Lignell, *Beskrifning öfver grefskapet Dal*, 412.

[31]Åttingsberg, *Seder och Språkbruk*, 15–16.

nancy, and married life. The topics were taboo, and premarital sexual experiences were condemned. These behavioral standards were not always adopted by young people: premarital sexual activity not only was common, but it also took place outdoors. The erotic sphere was alluded to at harvest time, when young people came together at work and exchanged lewd jokes. This behavior was very open, but at the same time the youth group exerted social control.

Premarital sexual relations frequently resulted in pregnancy, of course—and social sanctions. The stigma of illegitimacy was placed totally on the mother, who was condemned by the church and by law. A man could deny paternity by swearing an oath, but a woman who gave birth to a bastard child in rural Dalsland had to go through a purification ceremony after giving birth, similar to that of a married woman but with an added dose of humiliation: she was treated like a prostitute. Church sanctions varied from private confessions to withholding the sacraments.

In Dalsland, it was mainly daughters of unpropertied families, sometimes sexually exploited by employers or abandoned by their boyfriends, who bore illegitimate children.[32] They were women without dowries and with small chance of getting married. In the Slätt Dal region, they were fired when they became pregnant, and the only option was to go back to the parental home—if there was any. Otherwise, the life of an unmarried mother was a constant struggle for survival. Without help from her parents, she had to rely on poor relief, being taken into the poor house or working "for nothing" as pauper in different farm households. Isolation and desperation could drive an unmarried mother to suicide.

In Skogs Dal, however, where night courting was practiced, a more liberal attitude to premarital sex prevailed. Anna Gödecke tells about her home parish in western Dalsland where, in the 1890s, a large number of women gave birth to lösbarn (bastard children)—often having as many as four. Here the mother seldom thought of suicide; she perhaps felt ashamed for a while, but soon she got over her "accident" and joined her fellows and friends. On the other hand, the

---

[32]Frykman, "Sexual Intercourse," 141. From 1833 to 1933 in Sweden, there was a strong connection between the large rural proletariat and high extramarital birthrate.

Spring and autumn laundry was women's work, outdoors at the lake or stream.
Photograph courtesy Roland Olsson.

illegitimate children suffered much from lack of family and parental care. Sometimes they were auctioned off as laborers to farmers or foster parents, who received very little money for taking care of them.[33]

The fate of an illegitimate child was always hard, and emigration was a way out. Such was the case with Anna Fredriksdotter, who emigrated to Chicago in 1889. Her skill as a laundress made her a wealthy and respected city woman. Her good fortune did not last, however. When she returned home after ten years to take care of her parents, she found out she had been defrauded of the savings that she had sent to her home parish, Tisselskog.[34]

---

[33]Anna Gödecke, *Bondfolk. Skisser från Dal* ([1898] Hembygden, 1964), 50.
[34]Olle Enbågen (neighbor of Anna Fredriksdotter), interview by Elsa Larsson, 1981. *Tisselskog* (Munkedal, 1990), 163–65.

Married Life, Work, and Crises

After marriage, a woman entered a new stage of life, in which she was related socially and economically to the position of her husband. If he was a landed farmer, her obligation as a wife was to organize household work. If he was a tenant farmer, however, she had to perform a certain amount of day labor for the landowner. She and her husband also had to manage their own farm work without any help from servants. At the turn of the century, the day-labor duties for many tenant farmers changed into cash payments. The tenant farmer and his wife had to save enough money to be able to pay for the use of the house and land.

A married woman could make use of everything she had learned in childhood and as a servant maid. Since women in Dalsland married rather late, they normally had about ten years of work experience from different households. Mothers, daughters, sisters, other female relatives, and female servants worked together. The tasks of a married woman varied according to season and childbearing. It was her responsibility to nurse and care for her children and to supervise their upbringing. Frequent births isolated a farmer's wife, since she was unable to participate in outdoor work.

On many occasions, women came together for collective work. Twice a year, in spring and fall, there were washing days. There were also two baking days, one in May when all the women came together to bake the local thin, hard bread which their families ate for the whole year, and another just before Christmas. In the fall, all women came together for cheese making, which lasted for a couple of days and was followed by a party in which fresh cheese was served. Another party was held after the main slaughtering in October; women came to help one another with the heavy work, often bringing coffee, bread, and cakes, exchanging news, and enjoying themselves. It was hard and skilled work to prepare the meat for the coming year, and a woman had to know exactly what to do with the butchered animal.

The day of a farm wife started at three or four o'clock in the morning, when she prepared the first meal for her husband and his hired men before they left for work. Oat porridge, milk, bread and butter, some cheese, and coffee were served to them, often with brandy. After the morning meal, the dairy maid or the wife milked the cows, fed them, carried water, and cleaned the barn. It was the women's task to look after and feed goats, sheep, pigs, and chickens. At nine o'clock, *dageln* (a second morning meal) was served, usually consisting of a soup made of oats, bread, and milk. At twelve o'clock, dinner was eaten, usually a soup of potatoes or turnips with salt herring, bread, and milk. The farmer's wife supervised all the domestic chores, textile production, food preservation, and flax cultivation.

During the early mornings and late evenings, women and girls sat together spinning, weaving, straw plaiting, and talking, sometimes singing, while the children tended the light. A special spinning wheel was used for linen yarn, another for wool. The sex segregation at work was sometimes flexible: when women were baking bread or preparing linen yarn, men could assist.[35] There was often cooperation, but there were tasks that men never performed. When it came to milking and washing, tradition was stronger than reason. Making butter was considered women's "magic," and men were not permitted to be present; similar ideas about men's dangerous influence on washing kept them away from that task as well.

In spring, the growing season demanded that all men and women be in the fields. Plowing and sowing were normally men's work, but in northern Dalsland the married women customarily sowed the first seed in early spring. Spring and summer were the busiest times, with preparation of the fields in spring, the harvesting of hay in June, and the harvesting of other crops in July and August. At harvest, men cut the hay and women raked; men built the hayricks, and women assisted. Women often worked longer than men, since they did not get breaks during the day. They had to bring food and serve at dinner time while the men were resting.

Late summer became even more hectic. The last meal of the day was served after milking, when everybody came home from work. After that, as in Mecklenburg, the women started to spin or weave, sometimes until midnight. The flax harvest started in August, and the women spent the following several months outdoors preparing the flax for linen yarn. These seasonal duties were added to their daily tasks.

[35] Åttingsberg, *Seder och Språkbruk*, 37, and same, *Så var det på farmors tid* (Uddevalla, 1978), 16.

Historical sources rarely give information about married women's private lives and even less so about crises. The Swedish law of 1734 prescribed that married women had to obey their husbands. Wives were expected to do their duties without complaint. Divorces were extremely rare in Dalsland: as late as 1910, there were only thirteen divorced individuals in the whole Vedbo district, which had a population of 23,151.[36]

Divorce was only one crisis in marriage, however. Farmers' wives were used to being left alone with their children for long periods of time while their husbands were working away from home in Sweden, Norway, or America. Deserted wives existed, of course, but they were few compared to all the wives working alone on their farms waiting for their husbands to return. "American widows" were numerous in Dalsland, and they took over the role of breadwinners. Some of them lived off the money sent home from America; others lived by their own work and helped support children, old parents, or other relatives. Some hired themselves and their children out to landed farmers as day laborers. Hulda Olsson's father lived in America for six years, and her mother and grandmother took over the tenant farm, digging ditches and clearing new land as well as tending the grazing cattle.[37]

Many marital crises were clearly related to alcohol abuse. The problem was a topic of frequent discussion. As Dean Anders Lignell remarked, "The drunkards are leaving their wives and children crying for bread." He also describes the misery caused at home by the local brandy (made of potatoes or grain) called *brännvin*. Alcohol abuse, according to him, was widespread among men and resulted in noise, quarrels, fights, crimes, and immorality. Parents actually taught their children to drink, for drinking was part of the male culture and a way to gain acceptance by the male group.

Before 1810, adultery and desertion were the only legal reasons for divorce in Sweden. Then the law was liberalized, and women could get a divorce on the grounds of certain crimes, drunkenness, madness, and asocial behavior. In the case of alcohol abuse by her husband, a woman had to apply to the king's court. The procedure

---

[36]*Swedish Population Census,* 1910, Table 1, 78.
[37]Olsson interview.

for getting a divorce was time-consuming, complicated, and expensive.[38] For example, in 1874 a wife from Steneby parish emigrated to America, leaving her husband and two children behind and never returning.[39] Her husband was noted as a vagrant in the church records. Another woman, Laura Elfrida Hellgren, filed for divorce from an irresponsible husband and, together with her five-year old son Fritiof, left for Chicago in 1893.[40]

In Dalsland, many women never married. These unmarried women had to find a way to support themselves, and many worked for farmers and their wives; they sometimes specialized in spinning, weaving, sewing, or other kinds of skilled work. Several of the women who were neighbors of Hulda Olsson's grandmother lived alone and had work specialties. One was an expert on fodder gathering for the winter and was often employed by farmers. She was also the best at picking blueberries and often packed her horse cart full of the fruit and drove to Norway, where she sold all the berries. Another old widow was an expert in herbal medicines. Hulda's own grandmother was known as a medical "doctor," curing all sorts of illnesses with garlic, wormwood and brandy, *Achillea millefolium,* and tea from elder flowers.[41]

Olsson describes a world of women: widows; married mothers; unmarried mothers; American widows; sick or handicapped women; women with sick parents or siblings; single female entrepreneurs who spun and wove, plaited straw, knitted, embroidered, carded wool and linen; and women who worked in households as cooks and food preservers. There were also wise old women said to be clairvoyants and fortune tellers. Hulda's own mother was one of those female breadwinners who had found her own niche: the preparation of dinner parties for weddings and burials. She went around to the households and took care of the heavy work involved in brewing, meat preparation, baking, and cooking.

---

[38]Beata Losman, "Förtryck eller jämställdhet? Kvinnorna och Äktenskapet i Västsverige omkring 1840," *Historisk Tidskrift* 3 (1982): 316–317.

[39]Household lists for Signebyn, Steneby parish, 1891–1895. Microfiche, Emigrant Register no. 024/1893 in Bengtsfors.

[40]Information given to the author by Elsa Sjödal (letters and interview, 1992), who has researched the Hellgren family from Dalsland.

[41]Olsson interview.

Single working women supporting themselves were found every-where in Dalsland, and according to Emma Åttingsberg these women did not have a bad life.[42] But there were also women who appeared in the household lists as *inhyse* paupers or farm hands. They were often old and sick, mentally disturbed, or mothers of illegitimate children.

Family and Kin

Family relations in Dalsland followed a tradition of gender segrega-tion and social prestige according to age. At home, the husband was the decision maker and ruler, while his wife was his assistant. He was the head of the family, which gave him the right to control as well as punish all family members and servants. He alone administered the property of the family. The dowry was inheritance in advance and came directly under the husband's administration after marriage. The husband's guardianship over his wife (legally until 1921) and lord-ship over the household (until 1865) tended to reinforce each other, limiting the married woman's freedom of action. The wife was given the power of lock and key, which meant responsibility for the home and the property but no right to buy or sell without the approval of her husband.

In a landless household, the rigid gender-based division of labor could not always be maintained. Many wives of tenant farmers and farm workers took over the main responsibilities for land and live-stock when their husbands were absent. There were consequences for the marriage: the wives gained more self-confidence and eco-nomic independence. In the landless households where women worked in profitable handicrafts, the husbands engaged in tradition-ally female tasks to an extent unthinkable among landed farmers.

The bilateral kinship system in Dalsland, as elsewhere in Swe-den, ranked motherhood and fatherhood as equally important. Kin-ship was reckoned through both sexes but in a patrilinear direction: a woman never got the family name of her husband. This practice lasted into the beginning of the twentieth century. Although sons were important to the family as heirs, daughters were welcome

---

[42]Emma Åttingsberg, *Bygden berättar* (Uddevalla, 1977), 81.

because they were diligent and hardworking. It was no disaster for a farmer to have only daughters. One of the daughters would inherit the farm, and a son-in-law would eventually take over. Often the bridegroom was a hired farm hand who had shown himself to be an efficient worker.[43]

Old Age

Dalslanders planned early for old age. The goal was to retire in dignity with sufficient economic means for a life in the place where they were born. Different strategies were used: marriage within the kin group, lifelong celibacy, or emigration to save money toward investments. There were rules for retiring parents about when the younger generation was to take over, however. Where impartible inheritance was practiced, the parents selected one heir among their children. They then set up a retirement contract with the chosen main heir, giving him or her rights to the farm in exchange for ample provision during their old age. Retirement contracts served a two-fold function: security for the aging parents and transfer of ownership while the heir was still in his or her most active years. Retirement contracts detailed which capital goods were to remain the property of the retired couple, what quantities of food were to be provided during the year, what transportation services were to be expected and, as a final condition, an "honorable burial." The contract was a legal safeguard in case of conflicts and a barrier against the new heir's selling the farm. If the farm changed hands later on, the new owner had to assume the responsibilities of the existing retirement stipulations. A farm with a retired couple that were to continue as residents usually had a low market value.[44]

The demands of the old couple varied according to the wealth of the farm. In wealthier households, the retired couple might have a separate residence, such as a small house of their own or a part of the big house. On small farms, the old couple usually remained fully inte-

---

[43]Beata Losman, "Kvinnor, män och barn på 1800-talets svenska landbygd," *Göteborg Women's Studies* I (Göteborg, 1986): 169–170.

[44]Orvar Löfgren, "Family and Household among Scandinavian Peasants: An Exploratory Essay," *Ethnologia Scandinavia* (1974): 40–43.

grated into the household, sharing the living quarters with the new owners and working side by side with them. Often old parents could do important work and were hardly an economic burden on the household. They often cared for small children and became responsible for much of the children's socialization. The contractual system led to three-generation families, which were mainly found among well-to-do farmers who had established an impartible inheritance.

With partible inheritance, the situation of old parents was more insecure, since responsibility was carried by all the children, who all had the same rights to the farm. Many aging farmers postponed retirement and thus had unmarried children working at home. The children sometimes got tired of "waiting out" their parents and left home, either emigrating or moving to industrial areas within Sweden. In this case, retirement meant selling the farm or dividing it into equal shares. The question then was where the aging parents were going to live. Sometimes they circulated from one child to another. If a farmer died, his widow might lose her social status as a married woman. And if the children pressured their widowed mother to sell the farm, she would lose her home and be forced to rent a small house or a room for herself.

Retirement contracts concerned only landed farmers, however. The landless could rarely afford to support aging parents in their cottages. Here retirement often meant taking up lodging with relatives or with people of the village. Widows of tenant farmers and soldiers were the worst off, since they often had to find employment as day laborers or *inhyse* servants. They lived a mobile life, sometimes with children and sometimes on their own, trying to find an economic niche for survival. Olsson's grandmother worked and lived with her daughter for as long as her son-in-law was in America, and later moved in with her brother, a widower, who needed a housekeeper on his tenant farm. Children were the safeguard for parents, and in Dalsland the daughters felt an obligation toward their parents. Sometimes they even returned from America to take care of them.[45] For those who never married or who remained childless, old age, illness, and poverty could be disastrous.

---

[45]Hulda Olsson from Skoghem, Dalen, in Rölanda parish and Anna Fredriksdotter from Tisselskog parish returned home to take care of aging and sick parents.

Mor-Lina (mother Lina) from Toppesud, end of the nineteenth century.
Many women in Dalsland lived alone in their cottages.
Photographer unknown.

A man or woman growing old without relatives could rely only on help from the parish council, or be taken to the poorhouse. The parish council was responsible for organizing help for the poor, paying for school and parsonage, supporting soldiers on their tenant farms, and hunting dangerous beasts. Every parish was divided into units (*rotar*), each of which was responsible for common order, church discipline, morality, and money for the poor. The Swedish poor law of 1871 made the *rotar* responsible for arranging poverty relief, which normally consisted of a "circulation program" where poor people could stay one week in each farm household. Widows, orphans, sick or mentally disturbed people, whole families, and unmarried mothers with their babies thus circulated from one household to another.[46]

Bad health was feared most of all. Illness cost money, and it was very difficult to get a doctor. In the whole county of Älvsborg, with

---

[46]Sten Markendahl, "Emigrationen från Steneby socken till Amerika och Norge, 1865–1930," in Sten Markendahl, Jan Vegelins et al., eds., *Gamla Steneby* (Munkedal, 1990), 61.

an average population of 273,494 inhabitants during the years 1891 to 1895, there were only 30 doctors and two hospitals (both in cities). In rural Dalsland, health care was nearly nonexistent, with the exception of regular vaccination visits by doctors to prevent smallpox epidemics. Most of the rural population relied on traditional methods, going to *kloka gummor* (old wise women) who were experienced in herbal medicine. Tuberculosis was a great killer: primitive housing, bad hygiene, and a poor diet (especially among the unpropertied groups) resulted in poor resistance to illness. Overcrowded houses where people had to sleep in one room created ideal conditions for infectious diseases.

Living Conditions

Housing

When Hulda Olsson moved in with her grandmother in the beginning of the 1890s, her home was an old cottage that belonged to the croft Tjärnholmen. "It was a rather big cottage made of timber, and under the kitchen floor a small storage room was excavated. To go down into the room, you had to lift a trap door."[47]

During the nineteenth century, the *Dalsland-stuga* (Dalsland cottage) became prevalent. It had two rooms upstairs and one room and a kitchen downstairs. Often it was painted red and had a white accent on the corners. In the latter half of the century, buildings were modernized by adding chimneys and roofs of tile or slate. Handmade furniture was replaced with purchased modern furniture. The new wood-burning iron stove (imported from the United States) was the big revolution in the kitchen. The comfort it provided amazed Dalsland women. The open fireplace with hanging kettle was gradually disappearing, but the new stove was too expensive for anyone but the landed farmers.

A tenant farmer's home was usually a timber house with one room and kitchen, along with outbuildings for fuel and a barn. The

---

[47]Olsson interview.

houses were furnished with a table, some wooden chairs, a bed or a sofa, and a long bench for the family to sit on while eating, or for visitors. The sofa could be transformed into a bed with a mattress of straw, a pillow, and a quilted bedspread. All clothes and textiles were usually packed into a large chest. At the end of the nineteenth century, wallpaper and curtains appeared in some farmers' homes. Every Saturday, the house was cleaned; the floors were scrubbed with sand and moss. Carpets were never seen in tenant farmers' cottages but did appear in some landed farmers' homes, where towels were sometimes used for floor coverings as well. Cottagers, paupers, and day laborers lived in *Back-stuga* (cave-houses)—dwellings literally built into a hillside, with only one door and a small window providing light and ventilation.

Food and Festivals

The landless groups in northern Dalsland depended on their employers for food. There was constant fear of starvation. In several narratives from Dalsland, there are accounts of half-starving children and servant maids trying to find something to eat. The herders who worked in the forest were hungry all the time. They got very little food, and what they did get was of bad quality. They never saw white bread, eggs, meat, or sweets. According to Emma Åttingsberg, the girl herders got bread crumbs in sour milk for the morning meal and a quarter of rye cake with cold boiled potatoes and a piece of salt herring for dinner. For a beverage, they were given *blanna*, water mixed with milk.[48] Hulda Olsson's mother taught her how to use wild plants for food.

> Most frequently we used nettle and roots of dandelions. In 1859, we had a year of famine, and my mother told me that she plucked lots of thistles and how she used the leaves for making a soup. People went the long way from Dalen to Hindalby just to find thistles for food. In famine years, we also used the white inner bark of pine. It had to be boiled first and beaten and dried before it could

---

[48]Emma Åttingsberg, *Så var det på farmors tid*, 39.

be ground and mixed with flour. If there was no flour, we mixed it with husks and straw.

For landed farmers and well-to-do people there was butter (for spreading on bread) cream, cheese, and sometimes eggs used in pancakes. But meat was usually eaten only at Christmas or on special days like weddings, funerals, or birthdays.[49] On such occasions, men and women ate separately: the men drank a lot, and the women and female servants often ate after the men. Very likely, women got less food. The diet for the landless people was monotonous, dominated by porridge, milk, potatoes, *Tunn bröd* (a wafer-thin, very hard type of traditional bread, baked only twice a year), and salt herring. But in most households, it was frequently supplemented with coffee and, in landed households, sugar or special bread. For those who could afford it, coffee was considered a key to happiness. The poor were also able to enjoy it; they reduced its cost by mixing it with rye or peas that had been roasted. Drinking coffee was part of social life; men loved *kaffe-gök,* coffee mixed with brandy, and women sipped their coffee from the saucer after putting a lump of sugar on their tongue. In well-off households, women arranged special *kaffe-kalas,* when sweet breads and different sorts of cakes were served. These get-togethers had their own meaning for women as an opportunity for social contacts and the exchange of news. Women showed their social status by how the party was arranged, who was invited, what sort of china was used, and how many kinds of cakes were baked.

Baptisms, weddings, and funerals were all big events in the family, and for the women they meant a lot of work to prepare large quantities of food and beverage. The table offered in abundance various dishes such as steak, meatballs, ham, stewed pike, cheese, and cakes. Always present was the specialty of Dalsland, called *kleninger.* It was a sandwich made of fresh rye bread with thick butter and grated whey cheese on the top and a pancake as the final layer. A dinner could consist of fourteen dishes and took about three hours to eat. For drinking there were home-brewed *dricka* and large quantities of *brännvin.* Drinking *supar* (liquor) was a part of the male culture,

---

[49]Kristina Rosell-Åström, "Mat på Dal," in *Dalsland—ett himmelrike på jorden* (Älvsborgs läns landsting, 1982), 73–75.

an ancient way to participate in social life and be acknowledged as a "real man."

Much as in Galicia, a wedding in Dalsland involved many guests, along with music and dance. Church weddings also took place, but only if the bride was not pregnant. Otherwise, the vicar came to the house, and the ceremony was held at home. A wedding could last three to four days. Usually the female guests brought *förning* (a basket filled with food) to the party. The first day was reserved for relatives; the second day was for friends and neighbors; and on the third and final day, all servants, tenant farmers, and helping hands were invited. Much of the prestige of a family was demonstrated at a wedding, and often the costs were so great that the newlyweds had nothing left for household formation.

Other celebration days were connected with the seasonal and work cycle. The spring festival occurred in Dalsland around Ascension Day in May. It was the day of *holingarna,* when the young people took the cattle out to the forest for the first time. On this day, named *Köra middag* (bring home dinner), the boy and girl herders got especially rich food for a picnic in the forest. Midsummer Day, the 24th of June, involved many pagan customs, such as ritual dancing around the Maypole and *midsommar-vaka* (staying awake all night to watch for omens and signs and predict the future).[50] Unlimited drinking of alcohol and violence, ritual parts of Midsummer Day among Dalsland men, were criticized by clergymen.[51]

The greatest event, however, was Christmas. In Dalsland, it was celebrated with church going and the preparation of special foods, surrounded with rituals and superstition. For women, Christmas started early in December with a general housecleaning and the baking of Christmas breads. Meat had already been prepared, along with dried fish and salt pike. The home had to be well decorated with linen and straw items. Beer and brandy were made or bought. The preparations were launched on the 13th of December, Lucia Day, which also was called "little Christmas." It was one of those danger-

---

[50]William Widgery Thomas, Jr., *Sweden and the Swedes* (Chicago and New York, 1892), 294; Skoog/ Thedin, *Dalsland,* 322–323.

[51]Hilmar Marin, "Beskrifning öfver Steneby socken," in Markendahl/ Vegelius, *Gamla Steneby,* 107–108.

ous dark nights when people believed that demons and Lucifer walked about. In northern Dalsland, these fears were assuaged by a shared snack. Young girls served coffee and bread in the middle of the night to the household members and sometimes even to the neighbors. A large meal was eaten at four o'clock in the morning, when the Christmas cheese was tasted for the first time.

Christmas Eve was celebrated with a fire in the fireplace, and water was heated for the ritual Christmas bath. This was the only bath for many of the family members during the whole year. Everyone had to go into the water, from the household head to the serving maid; men went first and women last. No one changed the water, but this bath had less to do with cleanliness than with demonstrating patriarchal order and social prestige. Presents were sometimes exchanged between members of the household. The servant maids received their annual gift, which was considered a part of their salary: home-woven material for a dress and sometimes a pair of shoes.

Before 1870 in Dalsland, there was no Christmas tree and no Father Christmas or Santa Claus. For the Dalslanders, the *tomten* or *tomtegubben,* the spirit of the family and protector of the farm, cared for animals and people and helped them with their work. He was old and small, with long hair, a gray beard, and a red cap. He had to be treated with respect, and presented with gifts such as food on Christmas Eve.

Clothing and Cleanliness

For the daughter of a tenant farmer or cottager, clothing problems were acute. In winter, the daughters had to avoid freezing and at the same time be neatly dressed for the important church holidays and church going. In summer, they needed dressy clothes for parties and dances as well as for church. Material for dressmaking was produced at home from wool and linen, but homemade dresses were not highly appreciated. A young Dalslander remembered his sister and her problems. It was in the 1890s, she was 16 years old and she had decided to leave her parental home. "She had to leave home to seek employment to support herself, but especially to obtain clothes, which were impossible for Father to provide. The income of the farm only sufficed for food and the most necessary clothing."[52] Adult children living at home seldom had any money of their own. Their father would buy their clothes, infrequently and sometimes secondhand, at rural fairs in autumn or winter—usually without first consulting his children about their desires or even their sizes. Protests were not tolerated, and this state of affairs seems to be one reason why so many young women left to find work.

Dalsland women had no traditional folk costumes. For working days, they dressed simply in wool or linen, colored blue, gray, or brown. On Sundays, they wore their best clothes, made of cotton or fine purchased material, usually imported. A dress made from purchased black material or even a dress bought in the city was regarded as finer than any homemade dress. The wages of a servant maid from a landless family barely covered her expenses for new dresses or shoes.

One way to "save" shoes was to go barefoot. Normally, girls and young women went barefoot from May to at least September. Developing "hard feet" was necessary for the poor herders who worked in the forest and had to run, climb, and walk long distances. Dalsland maids had a special ritual to ward off wounds and sores: at the end of March, on the evening of the festival celebrating the arrival of the cranes (a holy bird in Swedish antiquity, whose advent signified the beginning of spring), children and teenagers took off their shoes and ran three times around the farmhouse—even if there was still snow on the ground.

Land-owning and tenant farmers distinguished the six ordinary working days from Sundays and holidays, when everyone could behave differently, dress differently, and eat different food. On Saturday evening the house was cleaned, and everyone had to wash themselves. In old times, the sauna bath house was heated, but by the end of the nineteenth century the sauna was seldom used, and only the arms, hands, feet, and face were washed. We know little about how women viewed the problem of cleanliness, but we do know that they had the jobs of fetching water, cleaning the house, and doing the laundry. The northern districts of Vedbo and Tössbo were

---

[52]Quoted in Florence E. Janson, *The Background of Swedish Immigration 1840–1930* (Chicago, 1931), 430.

known for clean and well-decorated houses in spite of poverty and primitive shelter. Women who worked as servants for upper-class urban families learned about personal hygiene and home cleanliness and were also taught how to bring up children. A maid who had learned about hand washing, good table manners, cleanliness in the kitchen, and her own personal hygiene had something new to bring home to her village. The bourgeois urban ideal of a warm, clean, and well-decorated home with the wife as the central figure influenced the homes of Dalsland land-owning and tenant farmers.

Migration

Migration Traditions

For many Dalslanders, particularly in the Vedbo district, the natural resources of the parish were just enough to meet basic needs. What the land could not supply was obtained through subsidiary activities, and Dalslanders relied heavily on the tradition of finding seasonal work outside the parish. Seasonal migration to western Sweden and the coast of Bohuslän was practiced in the eighteenth century. Very often Dalslanders found temporary employment in Norway, where the wages were much higher for a day laborer or a servant maid, and everything was cheaper.

Before the coming of the railroad in 1879, young Dalsland people wandered together in large groups in search of work. They started in spring and returned in fall. Often, mothers accompanied their daughters to Norway to help them find employment as servant maids. Since their husbands were usually working in Norway also, they had to return to the farm work waiting in Dalsland. Dalslander women were in great demand as housekeepers and domestics in Kristiania (Oslo) and Fredrikshald. The young women were able to save money and buy nice clothes and shoes. Women also found employment in the textile industry as weavers and seamstresses.

Dalsland's maids learned many useful and practical things in wealthy Norwegian households, and became familiar with urban life there. For many, Norway was only the first step in emigration: the next was a ticket to North America, where the maids' training in housekeeping was welcome. Migration was neither unusual nor dramatic. For both men and women, it was a common strategy for survival in times of crop failures and crisis. It was a way to improve their living situation and a way to learn something new and "see the world." Migration traditions in northern Dalsland also affected the rural gender system: geographic mobility diminished inequality within marriage, as did the loss of the husband's one-sided economic control.[53]

For the landless families in the Vedbo district, migration was a part of everyday life. People walked long distances to find harvest work in southern Dalsland, and often walked to Norway to find employment for weeks or months. A landless father could stay in Norway for years working as a lumberjack or factory worker. One of those landless farmers was Hulda Olsson's father. "My father, who was born in 1841, worked for a while at a glass work in Norway. He lived away from home the whole week and returned on Saturday evening, only to start the long way back to Norway again on Sunday evening."[54] In the meantime, Hulda's mother and grandmother took care of the croft. Other wives and children employed themselves as day laborers for local farmers. For the Dalslanders, a trip to Norway was always a way to solve economic problems. But very few planned to leave Dalsland for good. On the contrary, short-term migration was a strategy to make life in the home parish possible. At any rate, the rural society of Dalsland proved to be more mobile and flexible than has been expected of a backward, stagnating province.[55]

Migration from Dalsland

Dalsland saw a large percentage of its population emigrate to North America. (Only the province of Öland lost more.) From 1862 to 1930, about 33,400 Dalslanders emigrated, of whom approximately 25 percent returned to their home province.[56] Nearly every Dalslander had

---

[53]See Elizabeth Bott, *Family and Social Network* (London, 1971), 302–303.

[54]Olsson interview.

[55]Lundholm, *Vedbo och Nordmarks härader,* 296–298. For a discussion on the mobility of nineteenth-century rural Europe, see Leslie P. Moch, *Moving Europeans: Migration in Western Europe since 1650* (Bloomington, Ind., 1992).

[56]Lundholm, *Vedbo och Nordmarks härader,* 306.

a relative "over there," and many counted the United States as their second homeland. At the beginning of the twentieth century, going to America was not much more thrilling than a trip to Gothenburg or Kristiania in Norway. Before 1860, however, almost no one had heard about emigration to the United States, since for centuries the traditional migration region had been Norway.

During the last decades of the nineteenth century, the county of Älvsborg was heavily affected by out-migration. Official statistics for 1851 through 1910 show that 91,712 people left, of whom 73,544 emigrated to the United States.[57] The population of Dalsland even decreased, from 80,926 inhabitants in 1880 to 69,712 inhabitants by 1910. The stream of emigrants was largest in the 1880s and thereafter diminished. At the same time, the group of returning Dalslanders increased.

In the middle of the 1860s, Dalsland was overpopulated, and the number of unpropertied people lacking means of support increased rapidly. A large share of the population lived in reduced circumstances even in normal years, but the crop failure of 1868 had devastating consequences. Mortality rose, and the northern and western parts of Dalsland were especially hurt by the famine. During 1869, more than 700 Dalslanders emigrated to the United States, and about 400 went to Norway. During the 1870s, about 2,500 men and women went away, most of them to Norway. The next wave of emigration came in the 1880s, when Swedish oats in general and Dalsland oats in particular were crowded off the market by cheap American grain. The result was mass emigration from Slätt Dal, where some districts lost more than 32 percent of their population. During the period 1880–1893, emigration from Slätt Dal to the United States made up 27 percent of the province's average population. In the peak year, 1887, 2,500 Dalslanders left their home province. In total, 15,500 Dalslanders emigrated between 1880 and 1894, when an economic crisis in the U.S. put an end to the stream. The next wave came in 1900–1913 but was considerably weaker, amounting only to 8,500 emigrating men and women. This last wave was related to the growing kinship network between the U.S. and Dalsland.[58]

---

[57]*Historisk Statistik för Sverige* I, Befolkning 1720–1967 (Stockholm, 1969), Table 27, 127; Table 5, 51.

[58]Noreen, "Emigrationen från Dalsland," 301–305.

TABLE 3.7

Migration from and to Dalsland and the Vedbo district, 1881–1910

Year	Dalsland		Vedbo	
	Emigrants	Immigrants	Emigrants	Immigrants
1881–1890	14,655	1,720	3,970	629
1891–1900	9,283	3,059	2,847	888
1901–1910	8,125	3,299	2,806	1,166

Source: Kjell Sanne, *Dalsland's befolkning,* Table 7, 73; Table 6, 72.

More and more siblings, parents, and other relatives were "brought over" by their American kin. Returning Dalslander-Americans also played an important role. The many visitors from the United States, who often wore expensive clothes, golden chains, and huge hats, had a "pull effect" on those living at home. Women fitted out in the latest fashion told everybody who wanted to listen how easy it was to make money in the new country. Economic crisis, famine, and hardship forced many to emigrate, but at the turn of the century it is doubtful whether emigration was the only way out for young people. Moving became more a part of youth culture, and a trip to America was regarded as "modern."

All but three of Vedbo's fourteen parishes underwent a population decline: Ärtemark, Steneby, and Bäcke. These three parishes had established some new economic activities in forestry and crafts. Parishes that lacked such subsidiary activities had the largest population losses, since they depended solely on small-scale farming and cattle breeding. The official statistics do not include the proportion of men and women emigrating. To get better information, an in-depth study of the Steneby parish was made for the period 1890 through 1910. The Steneby parish did not suffer much from emigration because it had some new industries, including a paper mill that had been converted from an old foundry. In 1890, the parish had 2,631 residents (1286 men and 1345 women), which included 408 married men, 413 married women, 49 widowers, and 112 widows.[59] In the

[59] *Swedish Population Census,* 1890, Table 1, 34.

years 1890 to 1899, 71 women emigrated as opposed to only 51 men, which may show the restricting effect of the new military service ordinance.[60] In the next decade, the trend was reversed: 97 men and 46 women emigrated.[61]

Table 3.8 shows single emigrants according to household position. In the early 1890s, serving maids were dominant, together with "unidentified women." At the beginning of the twentieth century, however, the women and men apparently wanted to present themselves as living at home with their parents. This was more true for women than for men; the stigma attached to living away from home was such that the term for such women, *piga*, could also be construed to mean a woman having extramarital relations. Young women who lived at home with their parents had a significant amount of social status, for being able to live at home denoted a stable economic situation and the promise of an inheritance. Those

TABLE 3.8

Social status of single emigrants from Steneby parish, 1890–1910

Years	Sons	Daughters	farmhand	maid	Worker, nonfarm male	Worker, nonfarm female	House-keeper, nonfarm	Unidentified male	Unidentified female
	(at home)								
1890–94	—	—	4	12	—	—	—	38	21
1895–99	1	2	—	—	1	2	1	5	16
1900–04	2	2	—	—	4	—	—	34	12
1905–09	23	12	1	2	11	1	—	1	2
Total	26	16	5	14	16	3	2	78	51

Source: Monika Åhlund-Efraimsson, "Emigrationen," in Sten Markendahl et al., eds., *Gamla Steneby* (Munkedal, 1990), 139–143.

Note: Excluded from this study are 12 married women and 11 married men, 3 widows, and 1 widower, as well as 11 boys and 13 girls, 1 female pauper, and 2 unmarried mothers. Married and previously married individuals and children were excluded from this study, as it concerned only single persons, their occupations, and their living situations. The situations of the unmarried mothers and the pauper are unclear.

---

[60]Lundholm, *Vedbo och Nordmarks härader*, 48–49.

[61]Emigrant records published in Monika Åhlund-Efraimsson, "Emigrationen från Steneby," in Markendahl/Vegelius, *Gamla Steneby*, 139–143.

who worked away from home, conversely, risked being labeled as coming from a poor family, or worse, having no parents. The children of landed farmers wanted it known that they were not servants or wage workers living away from home.

The pattern of Steneby resembles Sweden in the late nineteenth century: the great mass of agricultural emigrants consisted of farmers' sons and daughters living at home or serving in other homes. Their future prospects in an overpopulated agrarian society were uncertain, and that made emigration figures rise much higher than the national average.[62] The emigrants were young unmarried men and women living at home—or at least they wanted to be regarded as such. In 1892, among the 25 emigrants from the neighboring parish of Ärtemark, there were only one married man and his son and one widower, but no married women. The same year in neighboring Laxarby, 34 men and 13 women emigrated, of whom only one woman was married. Men dominated among the emigrants and also among those who returned: 11 people (9 men and 2 women) returned to Ärtemark, and 17 people (15 men and 2 women) to Laxarby.

From Vedbo, a stream of young people left for the United States to *pröva lyckan*, "to make it over there." Many were in their teens, and they came from both landless and landed families. Few of them intended to stay away for the rest of their lives; rather, they wanted to remain only long enough to bring home a fortune. A minority of emigrants were married men who had left their wives at home, the so-called American widows. The wives had to survive with their children on money that the husbands were going to send or by working on farms or in other households. The pattern had many similarities with the seasonal migration and later permanent migration to Norway.

And what did they take with them? Their cultural baggage was heavy, but how much was of use? They had grown up in an environment where nature and seasons had structured their work; they had experienced an adolescence with both individual freedom and social control and with an understanding of very limited opportunities;

---

[62]Sten Carlsson, "Chronology and Composition of Swedish Emigrants to America," in Harald Runblom and Hans Norman, eds., *From Sweden to America: A History of Migration*, Studia Historica Upsaliensia 93 (Uppsala, 1976), 142–143.

girls had learned, working as herders in the forest or as maids in other people's households, that they had to rely on themselves, but they also had to succumb to parental authority that could prescribe not only husbands but also dress. The well-known rites and rituals related to childbirth were not always able to prevent stillbirths or other problems, but the familiar midwife offered assurance and protection. A housewife's work was diverse, and much of it was done collectively; and it was carried out with an understanding of its significance for the continuity of the family. Old age was no Eden, but it was provided for in one way or another. How could this cultural baggage be adapted to "modern" urban life?

4

Land and Loyalties: Contours of Polish Women's Lives

Maria Anna Knothe

The parish of Zaborów in Galicia was in many ways a typical emigration area at the turn of the century. It was a totally rural community, untouched by industrialization and urbanization. It was also culturally homogeneous: all its inhabitants were Roman Catholic and of Polish descent. The parish included the village proper as well as the four nearby villages: Dołęga Pojawie, Kwików, and Księże Kopacze. The parish attracted the attention of historians and ethnographers in the 1930s and again in the 1970s. Their studies as well as parish records enable us to analyze Zaborów and at the same time draw general conclusions about the rural society of Western Galicia.[1]

---

[1] See Kazimiera Zawistowicz Adamska, *Społeczność wiejska. Doświadczenia i rozważania z badań terenowych w Zaborowie* (Łódź, 1948); Jędrzej Cierniak, *Wieś Zaborów i Zaborowski dom ludowy* (Zaborów, 1936), and *Zaborowska nuta* (Warszawa, 1956); Maria Wieruszewska Adamczyk, *Przemiany społeczności wiejskiej. Zaborów po 35 latach* (Warszawa, 1978); Ryszard Kantor, "Kluby parafii Zaborów w Chicago. Geneza, dzieje i stan obecny," in *Studia nad organizacjami polonijnymi w Ameryce Północnej*, Biblioteka Polonijna nr.19. (Wrocław, Warszawa, 1988), and *Między Zaborowem a Chicago. Kulturowe konsekwencje istnienia zbiorowości imigrantów z parafii Zaborowskiej w Chicago i jej kontaktów z rodzinnymi wsiami* (Kraków, 1990). For books on Galician villages, see Franciszek Bujak, *Galicja* (Lwów, 1914); *Limanowa. Miasteczko powiatowe w Zachodniej Galicji. Stan społeczny i gospodarczy* (Kraków, 1902); *Maszkienice. Wieś powiatu brzeskiego. Stosunki gospodarcze i społeczne* (Kraków, 1901); *Maszkienice. Wieś powiatu brzeskiego. Rozwój od 1901 do 1911* (Kraków, 1915); *Żmiąca. Wieś powiatu limanowskiego. Stosunki gospodarcze i społeczne* (Kraków, 1903); Krystyna Duda Dziewierz, *Wieś małopolska a emigracja amerykańska. Studium wsi Babica powiatu rzeszowskiego* (Warszawa, 1908).

Political, Economic, and Social Conditions in Galicia

Politics

The political history of Poland is characterized by ever changing boundaries, forms of domination, dynastic relations, and loyalties. In 1795 Polish territory was finally divided among three neighboring empires, Russia, Prussia, and Austria, and lost its political independence for more than a century. After Austria had been defeated in the wars against France in 1859 and against Prussia in 1866, separatist tendencies among the various nationalities ruled by the multinational empire gained momentum.[2] Galician Poles ("Galicia" was the name of the Polish territory under Austrian rule) achieved only relative autonomy in the emerging Austro-Hungarian Dual Monarchy, and during the following ten years, there were continuing political struggles over the forms and functions of Galicia's autonomy. But the resulting system was stable enough to last for the next four decades.

Despite its shortcomings, this system of self-government was much more advantageous to the Polish population than those existing at that time under the Russian and Prussian governments. At least it allowed Poles to take administrative posts, and there was no language discrimination in education on the local level nor was there ethnic and religious oppression. The system was conducive to the development of a national culture and a local press, and it created favorable conditions for social and political life.

Economics

Galicia was the least economically developed of the three Polish territories under foreign rule. Gradual development of the railroad system, however, opened industrial trade; raw materials were transported from Galicia, and imports, especially from Austria-Hungary, increased. Galicia's young industries included salt mines in the cities

---

[2]The following section is based on Stefan Kieniewicz, *Historia Polski 1795–1918* (Warszawa, 1987); Andrzej Pilch, "Emigracja z ziem zaboru austriackiego (od połowy XIX w. do 1918r.)," in A. Pilch, ed., *Emigracja z ziem polskich w czasach nowożytnych i najnowszych* (Warszawa, 1984); Marian Kukiel, *Dzieje Polski porozbiorowe 1795–1921* (London, 1963).

of Wieliczka and Bochnia, coal mines in the Chrzanów Basin, and crude oil refineries in the Borysław Basin near the cities of Jasło and Krosno.

The agrarian reforms of 1848 had granted small farms to the peasants. But because the government had agreed to compensate the former owners, the peasants had to pay high taxes to the central government. Despite the reforms, many large estates still existed, and their noble owners controlled most of the forests and pastures. They also owned exclusive hunting rights and a monopoly on producing and selling alcohol. Few people worked permanently on the estates, and laborers were hired on daily work contracts to fulfill specific tasks. The workers received little compensation: they often did not earn more than the equivalent of two kilograms of potatoes and two kilograms of rye flour for a day's work, or they received only payment in kind, one of every 11 or 12 sheaves of grain from the field.

About 80 percent of the land in Galicia was composed of small farms of around five hectares.[3] Their small size, combined with the heavy tax burden, prevented farms from being self-sufficient. An already precarious economy worsened when overpopulation became a severe problem in the 1880s. Hundreds of thousands of Galicians were landless, and small farms needed little additional labor, resulting in significant unemployment. Out of 3.7 million people working in agriculture, about 2 million were family members doing marginal work.

Peasant farms were passed down from parents and in-laws. After the son of a peasant landholder married, he usually received a small plot of land from his parents and another from his wife as a dowry. The demand for land in Galicia was strong, but there was little contiguous land available for sale. As a result, an average-sized farm usually consisted of several plots of land in different places. Peasants often had to spend all their savings to enlarge their farms, with a healthy chunk of the cost going to a land agent in the form of interest.

Toward the end of the nineteenth century, Galician agriculture improved with the introduction of machinery and better-quality

---

[3]In 1902, about 44 percent of the farms had two hectares (a hectare is equal to 2.471 acres); 37 percent had 2 to 5 hectares; 18 percent had 5 to 20 hectares; and only 1 percent had more than 20 hectares. See Benedykt Zientara et al., *Dzieje gospodarcze Polski do 1939r.* (Warszawa, 1965), 425.

seed grain. Nevertheless, overall crop production expanded only slowly. There were also some changes in animal husbandry. Peasants phased out raising sheep, for example, in favor of raising more profitable hogs. Despite these improvements, an unfavorable balance of trade remained, and productivity in Galicia, the poorest region in Austria-Hungary, remained low.[4] The economic situation of lands under Prussian rule was significantly better, since the economic development of Prussia was considerably more advanced overall at the end of the nineteenth century than was the development of Austria-Hungary.

Social Relations

In most of Galicia, the traditional peasant community prevailed. The family, the household, and the farm were the basic units of the village socioeconomic system. People in general were considered elements of the larger structure and individualism was minimized. Thus, many aspects of women's lives were viewed in the context of the family, and their position was a very dependent one.

Wealth and social status were measured not by monetary income but by land holdings. The top of the hierarchy was occupied by well-off farmers, who owned on average about nine hectares of land. These farmers hired laborers from among the smallholders and landless families. The next group down comprised poorer farmers, who owned between 0.5 and five hectares of land. They were able to cultivate their own land without hired labor, sometimes exchanging services with neighbors. The cottagers were lower still in the village's social hierarchy. They did not own any land and earned their living working for their better-off neighbors. Those who owned neither house nor land held the most inferior status and were fully dependent on the community.[5] A woman's social position was defined by this system: the larger the farm, the higher her position.

The manor was still the most important single element in Galician rural society. Despite the abolition of serfdom, the manorial es-

---

[4]Kieniewicz, *Historia Polski*, 389.

[5]Zawistowicz Adamska, *Społeczność wiejska*, 86. During the middle of the nineteenth century, about 28 percent of the peasant population in Zaborów were well-off farmers, whereas 40 percent were cottagers.

tate remained the place of regular employment for most of the rural population. In addition, the village inn, the mill, and other village manufacturers belonged to the estate. Permanent conflicts between the landed nobles and the villagers arose over the right to use the manor's forests and pastures, to which the peasants were formally entitled. In cases of conflict between the lord and the villagers, the villagers usually displayed unity and solidarity, thus obscuring socio-economic hierarchies.

Galicia was multiethnic. In the rural eastern parts of the region, Ukrainians prevailed, and poorer Jews inhabited the small towns. In 1880, 6 million people lived in Galicia. By 1890, the population had grown to 6.6 million, with the percentage of the population living in urban areas remaining the same. At the end of the nineteenth century, the Galician population reached 7.3 million, 49.3 percent of whom were Poles. By 1910, the Galician population had risen to 8.5 million, and Poles made up 45.9 percent. Galician villages were overpopulated, and the surplus of labor further depressed wages. The region's economic distress triggered migration to nearby countries and overseas.

Country fair in Galicia.
Photograph, Muzeum Etnograficzne w Krakowie, Archives.

Political Movements

Political power remained in the hands of the landed nobility through the nineteenth century. Poles enjoyed relative political autonomy under Austro-Hungarian rule, and they were able to launch an agrarian movement—which included some women of the intelligentsia, in the 1870s. One aim of the movement was to promote peasant education. During the 1860s, 90 percent of the rural population was still illiterate. Through the agrarian movement, the rate slowly fell: in 1880, it was 80 percent; in 1890, 67 percent; and in 1900, it was down to 56 percent.[6] Although the percentages remained high compared to those of central and western Europe, they nevertheless indicate that the literary movement was succeeding.

In Galicia's local parliament, the political parties that represented the lords' interests had limited the number of peasant representatives by weighting votes. Nevertheless, the so-called peasant problem—a raised political consciousness—increasingly became a matter of public concern and debate among politicians. Some people tried to deal with the issue by editing popular periodicals "for common people," to increase their political involvement and (mainly) to improve agricultural techniques. Also, numerous societies and self-help associations were established, which became an important element of Polish social life. There were agricultural cooperatives and savings and loan banks, which aided the peasants in times of crisis or special need—for example, when buying land. The Society for Folk Education helped in promoting literacy in the countryside, and the "Sokół" (Falcon) advocated sports, to prepare Polish young men for an eventual (perhaps military) struggle for independence.

The Agrarian Party was founded in 1894 to fight for common voting rights for the peasantry. The party sought to reduce the peasants' dependency on the landowners, and it demanded fairer taxes. Although the party advocated a moderate program, it nonetheless raised strong objections from the owners as well as from the clergy. These groups feared the loss of their traditional privileges.

---

[6]Kukiel, *Dzieje Polski*, 469.

The Parish of Zaborów

The village of Zaborów lies in the fork between the river Wista (Vistula) and its tributaries Uszwica and Dunajec. The nearest railway station and the district's administrative center, Brzesko, is about 26 kilometers away; Kraków, the main city of the region, is about 60 kilometers away. In the second half of the nineteenth century, the village had market relations with several towns in the area: Bochnia, Tarnów, Dąbrowa, and Koszyce.

Zaborów was a long, narrow village, its farmsteads located along the main road. All the farm buildings were built close to the road to facilitate the unloading of carts. Farmhouses and cottages were situated a small distance from the road, all facing the sun to take the greatest advantage of light and warmth during the day. In front of the cottages were small gardens; barns, stalls and pigsties lay behind the farmhouse, to the north. The village's layout made sense to the villagers, and this meaning of space was necessarily lost after migration to the city.

A notable trend from 1819 to 1934 was the increase in family size: the village of Zaborów experienced a population growth of 80 percent during this period, yet the number of families had increased by only 25 percent. In 1819, there were on average 4.6 people living in a family; in 1934, the number was 5.2. In fact, the total population in the 1930s was much lower than at the turn of the century. (This indicates

TABLE 4.1

Population growth in Zaborów parish, 1809–1933

Year	Births	Average number of births per year	Deaths	Average number of deaths per year	Population increase	Average population increase per year
1809–33	674	27	549	22	125	5
1834–58	810	32	744	30	66	3
1859–83	842	34	703	28	139	6
1884–1908	884	35	553	22	331	13
1909–33	664	26	584	23	80	3

Source: Jędrzej Cierniak, *Wieś Zaborów i Zaborowski dom ludowy* (Zaborów, 1936), 87.

how much out-migration had affected the development of the village.)

The village economy was based completely on agriculture, even though the soil was too acid and the crops usually poor. The typically fragmented farms added to the difficulty of making a living off the land; meadows especially were scattered in remote places, sometimes several kilometers away from the farmstead. Peasant farmers grew mainly wheat, rye, barley, potatoes, flax, and hemp, and they kept some cattle. The limited variety of crops and livestock, along with unsuitable soil, contributed to a poor diet generation after generation.

The nearby village of Dołęga, also part of the Zaborów parish, was culturally similar but probably a little more sophisticated. It was dominated by the manor of Dołęga, which became a local center of culture and education and an attractive meeting place that was occasionally visited by famous Polish writers. Pojawie was a smaller village, and lay, as did Dołęga, east of Zaborów. The much smaller villages Kwików and Księże Kopacze were located to the west. All the villages in the parish had a rather similar social and economic structure.

At the end of the nineteenth century, a traditional local community culture dominated the lives of the peasants. The main elements of this culture were a closely knit system of family farms and local institutions. Kinship and neighborhood, as well as people from nearby villages who participated in the regular village fairs, made up the fabric of this social system. Church, school, the local inn, country fairs, and prominent local authorities shaped people's lives.

Church and School

Church and religion permeated almost every aspect of community and family life. Most of the traditional habits and customs had a religious background, be it the common greetings and farewells, various family habits, or village festivities. The basic substance of life and the character of family ties were viewed from a religious and magical point of view.[7] Religious ideology glorified the hard-

---

[7]About magical elements in Polish peasant culture, see William I. Thomas and Florian Znaniecki, *Chłop polski w Europie i Ameryce* (Warszawa, 1976), I: 174–228.

ships of manual labor and served to justify the patriarchal patterns of family life.

Women were usually more devout than men. For the village women, the activities of the church—its various rites, pilgrimages, choirs,—offered the only possibilities to participate in public life. The church was also a source of primary social—and romantic—relationships: according to oral tradition, about 40 percent of the married couples in Zaborów had first met in church. Thus the church was the guardian of the family, which gave women a feeling of security. Its influence was not confined to religious affairs but was evident in all social and ethical spheres of life. But women had to tolerate a double standard in religious devotion. Whereas men were permitted to skip an occasional mass, women could not do so without inviting disapproval from the village. As would be expected, this double standard extended to sexual conduct. Bachelors had a certain sexual freedom before marriage; girls had none.

Market.
Photograph, Muzeum Etnograficzne w Krakowie, Archives.

Old people were usually the most religious. Excessive religious behavior such as going to mass every day, on the other hand, was not appreciated by the community.[8]

The parish of Zaborów was founded in 1819, and the first entries in the parish chronicle (*liber memorabilum*) date back to 1861. The village itself was inhabited by nearly 600 people at that time. The parish church was initially built with donations made by a noblewoman, clergymen, and peasants (who were members of the choirs or rosary groups).

In 1843, the first one-class parish school was founded, with a priest and an organist as its teachers. Twenty-five years later, a country school with a professional teacher was organized under the direction of a new priest, Father Wolff. It served four village communities, and its first teacher was Józef Prelich, a charismatic figure who exerted a great influence on the young generation of Zaborów.

Local Inns and Fairs

The local inn was a meeting place for men where local news and information were exchanged and business transactions conducted. And it was also a polling place, where local elections for the village principal (similar to a mayor) were held. Above all, however, it was a place for drinking vodka. Though alcoholism was a major problem in many villages, it was not especially severe in Zaborów. Regular drinking in Zaborów was perceived as more of a personal and family affair than a social problem. Women did not have any equivalent place to meet, and they had to rely on church meetings, fairs, and chats with neighbors across the fence.

Fairs were an important part of the economic and social structure of the village. At a fair, people could sell and buy agricultural products and handcrafted goods. Coral beads, farm implements, barrels, baskets, festive clothes, imported goods—practically anything could be bought at a fair. For years, fairs were the only outlet for women to sell their dairy products and poultry. The money they earned at a fair was usually theirs to spend as they chose. Fairs also had a social function. Peasants had the chance to meet with friends

---

[8]Edward Ciupak, "Rodzina wiejska i jej życie religijne," *Wychowanie* 9 (1961): 18–22.

or distant relatives or get to know new people, and useful information was exchanged. Preparation for a fair, as well traveling to the fair (which was often quite far away, since Zaborów did not have its own fair) were usually great events, especially for young people. Unlike going to church, where men and women were separated, going to a fair entailed social interaction between the genders. So the fairs, much like the church parish, defined areas of social contact beyond the local village community.

Village Authorities

Zaborów was a village commune, the smallest administrative unit in the system of territorial self-government that was created after the abolishment of serfdom in 1848. The commune was governed by the *wójt* (principal), who was elected by the adult male members of the village. In addition, the Commune Council decided on financial affairs, such as the building of a school. There was also a communal granary, to store grain for emergencies. In 1872 the granary was sold and the money transferred to the local Communal Loan Society. In times of crisis, this loan society offered financial aid. Women could neither participate in local self-government nor borrow money from the society. They had to rely on kin and family when in need.

Associations, Societies, and Mutual Aid

In 1901, an agrarian cooperative was organized that focused on improved trade and organized a cooperative village store. In Zaborów, the store became a place where people came together for talk and reading newspapers. The cooperative also disseminated information on better farming methods and artificial fertilizers. In 1905, additional self-help associations were organized, including a volunteer fire brigade and the Raiffeisen loan society.

A good school in the village made it possible for some children to continue their education in high school. Some even went on to attend college. At the beginning of the twentieth century, native young people who had received a higher education started a social-educational movement; The local intelligentsia—teachers, priests, and noblemen from the neighboring manor at Dołęga—joined in this endeavor.

They organized public lectures, celebrations of historic events, and excursions to Kraków or surrounding towns, thus widening the horizons of the villagers—many of whom knew nothing about the large towns. A branch of the Society for Folk Education and a local library were established as well. In 1904, an amateur theater was organized (theatrical performances were to become important in Chicago years later). The intelligentsia of the manor at Dołęga had a strong impact on these cultural activities.

In the decade before World War I, social life in Zaborów was rather well developed, and in this respect people were somewhat better off than those in other parts of Galicia. The strong ties that linked this local community were maintained during emigration and became evident in the behavior of immigrants after they settled in America. After the war, immigrants began to send regular financial aid to Galicia. The aid was used to support the village church and other community institutions. New bells, for example, were funded by Zaborowians from Chicago. Zaborowian immigrants also provided money for new altars, organs, paintings, sculptures, and other religious artifacts.

This tradition of common work for public welfare was based on the strongly rooted custom of mutual aid, which was applied not only in emergencies such as fires and floods, but also in agricultural work or in the building of a house. In Zaborów, the connection between traditional elements of folk culture on the one hand, and the development of social institutions of self-help and self-government on the other, were conducive to the strengthening of local ties. People in Zaborów were familiar with the concept of social institutions, both formal and informal. This enabled emigrant Zaborowians to forge new social and cultural institutions in their adopted country, even though the urban surroundings were alien to them.

Women's Lives in the Village

Marriage and the Family

The fundamental unit of the village was the household, understood as a general economic and social form of family existence. The farm was at the heart of family life; it provided the family's subsistence, determined its social status, and served to build the family's social ties within the village through the many social interactions it generated. Socialization of children in peasant households included their unceasing exposure to their parents' extremely hard work, and appreciation of what that work contributed to the children's future. There was little leisure time. Family members were either engaged in work or about to begin another task. In material terms, the lesson was austerity; the family was barely able to produce what it needed for survival.[9]

The peasant household and farm were so closely connected, that the household was thought of in utilitarian terms. The well-known Polish ethnographer Kazimierz Dobrowolski characterized the traditional peasant family as follows:

▲ The family was the unit of production and consumption;
▲ The family's interests coincided with the interests and needs of the farm;
▲ All the basic functions of the family focused on economic needs;
▲ The family was based on indissoluble marriage arranged by the kin group, and marriage was conceived as a sacred institution whose aim was to produce offspring and achieve economic goals;
▲ The family was not independent but had multilateral connections with the kinship and neighborhood system;
▲ Family life functioned according to a uniform rhythm set by seasons and farm work;
▲ Cultural norms, which included little personal freedom, determined the social roles of particular family members.[10]

At the end of the nineteenth century, the dominant type of rural family in Galicia was an extended family consisting of grandparents, their married and unmarried children, and grandchildren. It was a

---

[9]See Dyzma Gałaj, "Gospodarstwo chłopskie i kwestia chłopska w Polsce," in *Młode pokolenie wsi Polski Ludowej,* vol 5: *Gospodarstwo i rodzina* (Warszawa, 1968), 5–28.

[10]Kazimierz Dobrowolski, "Chłopska kultura tradycyjna. (Próba teoretycznego zarysu na podstawie materiałów źródłowych XIX i XX w. z południowej Małopolski)," *Etnografia Polska* 1 (1958): 19–51.

patriarchal family ruled by the father and husband, who was the formal owner of the land and the farm. Families were usually patrilocal; married women settled into their husbands' households and lived together with their parents-in-law.

Relatives took precedence over nonrelatives in all sorts of considerations, especially when it came to buying and selling land. Close relatives had rights and obligations. Helpful kinds of information were exchanged among kin, and relatives were obliged to render mutual aid in case of trouble. Relatives and neighbors alike exchanged services, however, and usually anyone afflicted by disaster was sure of his or her neighbor's helping hand. In the peak periods of agricultural work, the villagers regularly helped one another. A single woman (usually a widow) could always count on her neighbors' assistance when it came to harvesting, threshing, and digging potatoes.

The marriage laws in Galicia were regulated by the Austrian civil code of 1811, which was later amended. Only church marriages were legal. The husband had total priority and dominance over his wife in all economic and family matters. He was to be addressed first; he was the one who could go to court or get a loan; and he decided the future of the children—what education they were to get and whom they were to marry. Marriage was not a matter of individual choice. As in most rural communities, it was a union of the representatives of two families and reinforced local ties. It provided the possibility that the farm, through inheritance or dowry, would remain in the family.

Since marriage was the norm, single men and women were treated differently from "normal" people. The status of single people in the household depended on why they were single. The aged widow who headed a household was much esteemed, especially if she still was the owner of property. (Family uneasiness also accompanied widowhood, however. From the children's point of view, there was always the impending danger of a second marriage and loss of inheritance.) Old bachelors or old maids were disapproved of unless their single status was clearly the result of disability. The woman's main duty was to marry and bear children, who soon would became additional unpaid labor for the family farm.

A match with a partner from a family of more or less the same social status was considered to be the most proper. At the same time, this system made upward mobility through marriage impossible. The marriages were usually arranged by parents, and the father had the final word. It was sufficient if the future spouse fulfilled all the requirements of his or her social and economic position. Some additional qualities were also welcomed, however. An ideal woman was tidy, industrious, dignified, obedient, wealthy, and good looking. An ideal man would not beat his wife (violence against wives was widespread) and would be a good father. Candidates living in the same village or within the same parish were preferred.

Arranged marriages led to stable marriage patterns and a high degree of endogamy. Analysis of marriage registers in Zaborów parish between 1890 and 1914 (with figures on 491 women) shows that

- 59 percent of women married men from the same village;
- 17.2 percent of women married men from other villages within the parish;
- 15.8 percent of women married men from neighboring villages outside the parish;
- 7 percent of women married men from other villages in Austrian Galicia;
- 0.6 percent of women married men from the Russian portion of Poland; and
- 0.3 percent of women married men from the Prussian portion of Poland.[11]

Thus, more than three-quarters of the marriages involved partners from the same parish. If a circle with a radius of 10 kilometers were drawn around Zaborów, the number of marriage partners drawn from that region would be as high as 92 percent.

Negotiations over dowry and inheritance were important in a rural marriage. During the years 1848 to 1868, Galician civil law made male primogeniture obligatory; only the first-born son could inherit the property. After 1869, all the children, including daughters, were entitled to inherit. To avoid subdivision, however, property was usually passed on to only one of the children, most often the son. The

---

[11]All statistical data on marriages within the study area are based on an analysis of church records in Zaborów.

inheriting child was obliged to pay the other siblings compensation in cash. In this subsistence economy, cash was short. Inheriting owners who could not make a profit faced relinquishing the farm to siblings or watching it subdivided among strangers. Many were pushed to emigration because it was the only possible way to obtain money. Thus, not only people without property had to consider emigration but also those who owned property and had to pay off their brothers' and sisters' shares.

Although a girl could inherit land, her dowry usually consisted of money in cash, livestock (usually a cow), home equipment, bedclothes, good Sunday attire, and the like. Boys usually received a piece of land and a horse. Both families would strive to make the dowries of their marrying children complementary, especially if the young couple might start a farm household of their own. Arranging a good marriage for a daughter was a serious economic burden for the family, and the provision of money for a dowry became another factor that forced people—daughters as well as parents—to emigrate.

The difficulties involved in setting up a new household resulted in a high average marriage age for both men and women. During the years 1890–1914, the average age at marriage was 27.4 for women and 30.6 for men. If marriages of widows and widowers are excluded, the average age at first marriage was 25.5 for women and 27.6 for men. In 21.5 percent of all the marriages in the parish during this period, at least one of the partners was a widow or a widower. Of that group, 12 percent were widows, and 17 percent widowers. Kwików, which had the highest percentage of remarriages, also had the highest degree of endogamy; that is, most husbands came from the same village. In the case of a second marriage, it was easier to find a husband nearby, where people knew one another well and local ties were strong.

The average age at marriage, however, obscures the broad range of ages. More than 10 percent of the women were 19 years of age and younger, and more than 2 percent were older than 56. The largest group was composed of women who married between 20 and 25 years of age (43.6 percent). Another large group (21.1 percent) was those who married between 26 and 30, and the smallest group (12 percent) was those who married after 40. In Kwików, half of the women who married between ages 31 and 35 were widows. In Zaborów, one-third of the women between 35 and 45 were widows. (Two thirds of the women in this age group in Zaborów were marrying for the first time.) In Księże Kopacze, every widow who married was between 46 and 55. If nothing else, this suggests a tight marriage market.

In 71 percent of all marriages in Zaborów parish during the years 1890–1914, the husband was older than the wife, and in 25 percent the wife was older. If the man was older, the average difference was 7.3 years; if the woman was, it was 6.4 years. The age difference was lower for first marriages: 77 percent of the women were not more than five years older; and 11 percent were older by more than ten years.[12] Of men who were older than the women at first marriage, 9 percent were older by more than six years; 36 percent by three to five years; and 18 percent by one or two years.[13] Fifty-seven percent of the marriages (including second marriages) involved age-peer partners (within five years).

The following features characterized the marriage market in Zaborów parish around the turn of the century: the marriage age of both men and women was high (almost half of the women were older than 25 when they first married); a second marriage after the death of a spouse was almost a necessity (a farmstead always needed male and female labor) and thus occurred frequently; about half of the marriages involved partners close in age.

As these statistics show, the marriage market in Zaborów parish offered various combinations and choices. There were no prejudices other than those against an economic gap between the marriage candidates. But with a growing number of men emigrating or serving their obligatory three to four years in the military, the chances for a woman to find a proper husband, or any husband, became slimmer—especially for those with small dowries. Some thought their prospects might be better in the United States.

Procreation was one of the main functions of marriage, and children were much desired as hands on the farms and in the households. Large families also received the blessings of the Catholic

---

[12]The total number of women was 91.
[13]The total number of men was 269.

Church. Catholic principles banned any kind of birth control. Child-lessness, for which mainly women were blamed, was considered a divine punishment. At the beginning of the twentieth century, the average number of children borne by a woman up to the age of 50 was 9.4. The infant mortality rate was high, however, nearly 25 per-cent.[14] The village people came to consider the death of a baby or young child almost as natural as birth. A popular phrase of consola-tion was, "God gave it, God took it."

During the years 1890–1914, 491 women married and 2,700 chil-dren were born in Zaborów parish.[15] In 1905, the birth rate began to decline because of increasing emigration of women.

The parish records also give information on illegitimate children. Since the moral norms advocated by the Catholic Church did not allow for extramarital sex, the relatively high number of children born out of wedlock arouses interest. The five villages vary consid-erably in this regard: in Księże Kopacze there was not a single case of illegitimacy throughout the whole period under investigation, whereas in Dołęga the rate was as high as 32 percent (1894). Perhaps this can be attributed to the influence of the Dołęga manor, which employed many villagers, or the influence of the intellectuals and artists who often visited the manor. There are two features that all five villages have in common: the years 1890–1898 show the highest percentage of illegitimate children (9 percent); and the number dropped to its lowest point, 3.3 percent, during the period 1899–1914. A general improvement in the marriage market, owing to the growing number of unmarried women who emigrated, may account for this.

The months of birth tell us something about the sexual behavior of Zaborowian peasants.[16] Religious norms suggested sexual tem-perance during two periods of the year (Advent and Lent); the data reveal that these periods were not strictly observed, however. The month of March, which falls during Lent, showed a very high num-ber of conceptions. January and February were the months of carni-

---

[14]Danuta Markowska, *Rodzina w społeczności wiejskiej–ciągłość i zmiana* (Warszawa, 1976), 19.

[15]No data on childbearing age are available. No data are available for Księże Kopacze before 1905.

[16]Time of conception: January, 10.5%; February, 9.9%; March, 9.4%; April, 9.7%; May, 7.6%; June, 7.4%; July, 7.9%; August, 7.6%; September, 6.6%; October, 6.8%; November, 8.4%; Decem-ber, 8.1%.

TABLE 4.2

Children born in Zaborów parish, 1890–1914

Year	Total births	Illegitimate births	Percentage of illegitimate births
1890	108	8	7.4
1891	100	8	8.0
1892	103	8	7.8
1893	91	9	9.9
1894	91	10	11.0
1895	123	9	7.3
1896	121	12	9.9
1897	100	12	12.0
1898	120	10	8.3
1899	109	4	3.7
1900	128	6	4.7
1901	124	9	7.3
1902	141	5	3.5
1903	95	5	5.3
1904	106	1	0.9
1905	123	3	2.4
1906	117	5	4.3
1907	113	6	5.3
1908	117	1	0.8
1909	110	3	2.7
1910	93	3	3.2
1911	84	1	1.2
1912	94	3	3.2
1913	92	3	3.3
1914	97	1	1.0
Total	2,700	145	5.4

Source: Zaborów church records.

val, and the winter months of November and December were the main time when life and work on the farm allowed for some leisure. September and October, on the other hand, had the lowest rates of conception. These were the months when the many children conceived in the beginning of the year were born and also the time when every hand on the farm was needed to dig potatoes. Thus it was the seasonal cycle of farm work more than religious mores that influenced the sexual behavior of peasants.

The young took part in the family's everyday routines as well as in the celebrations and festivities. They naturally observed and imitated adult activities. The cultural patterns determining the division of labor and competence within the domestic group, which prescribed a specific role model for each member of the family, were repeated in the educational patterns.

The superior position of the father meant that he was to show endurance and skill and to maintain obedience. He was expected to be industrious, thrifty, full of respect for his wife, and just and strict toward his children. An ideal mother also had to be industrious, in addition to being thrifty and tender toward her children. Her task was to teach the young to respect their father and to be religious, and to train them in all the household and farm skills. Children were required to obey and to work hard. In a large extended family, the youngsters were taught to work properly, to respect their elders, to take care of the younger children and the disabled, and to get on well with their peers. Their personalities were formed according to the community's norms and demands.

Daughters were to help their mothers, sons their fathers. Young children were looked after as often by their grandparents and siblings as by their mothers. Usually the mothers were busy working in the fields or in the household. Everyday contact with grandparents guaranteed the transmission and continuity of the various traditional cultural patterns, family traditions, and practical skills. The mother could pay only limited attention to infants and young children; she nursed them for four to five months and saw to it that they were kept warm. Diapers were not used, and toddlers often went naked or wore only linen shirts. During the cold season little children had to stay in the house. At the age of five or six, children started to help on the farm, first herding geese, and later herding the cows and horses. The children's playground was the pasture, where peer-group contacts and competitions took place; but it was also the place of loneliness, severe cold, and discomfort.[17]

---

[17]Helena Bittner-Szewczykówna, "Dziecko wiejskie," *Rocznik Muzeum Etnograficznego w Krakowie* vol. 9 (1984), passim.

Grandparents held an important position as long as they were the formal owners of the farm. Once they could no longer manage the farm and handed it over to their son, however, they were no longer the primary decision makers, and they often moved to separate quarters in the house or even a small hut adjoining the family house. In the traditional peasant culture, however, much authority was attached to old age. Although the retired grandparents were not in charge of the farm, their opinions were highly regarded.

A close, extended family was valued, and young women who chose to stay on their family's farm were respected. Service was not a common occupation for young Polish women, nor did it function as a transitory stage between childhood and marriage. There were only few manors nearby, and they were not large. Workers, if needed, were hired for temporary contracts to do specific tasks. Families were usually large, and enough daughters provided the necessary services. Being a servant was not considered desirable. It did not provide enough cash for a dowry, nor did it improve one's social status within the village. Emigration, either seasonal or longer, was a much better solution for Zaborowian girls who wished to marry or otherwise improve their lot.

Rituals of the Life Cycle and the Yearly Cycle

Traditional peasant culture attached great meaning to ceremonies and rites. The whole universe was believed to be ruled by supernatural powers. People needed to control those powers, and magic and religion performed these functions. The ideological and behavioral order based on such a worldview provided sanctions for breaking the rules or disturbing the integrity of the community. Migration, which became so much a part of rural Polish culture, required these ceremonies and rituals to change. These changes may help us understand the amount of adjustment necessary in the process.

Traditional rituals included the rites of the yearly cycle and those of the life cycle. The annual cycles of folk rituals and Catholic feasts were closely connected with the natural rhythm of agriculture. These rituals marked crucial moments of the year, such as Christmas, Easter, or the end of winter.

Life-cycle ceremonies focused on moments of passage such as birth, marriage, and death. People were most vulnerable then to supernatural powers—not just the individuals involved, but the whole community. Thus the main task of the rituals was to protect against evil and to gain supernatural favor. The rural people were usually not fully conscious of the symbolic meaning of the rituals. They observed them simply because it was traditional to do so.

The woman was the subject as well as the object of many of these rituals. As a subject, she took an active role in preparing the ritualistic meals, customs, and ornaments. As also the main object of these rituals—she symbolized nature and life and was the giver of life—she had to be especially protected against evil influences. Severe social sanctions, including a marred reputation, followed the breaking of these rules. A woman who had lost her good reputation—which was as important as a dowry—was not greeted in the village, was not invited to the various village activities, and was not asked to become a godmother.

The most important initiation rite in a woman's life centered on marriage. The first ceremony, the proposal (*swaty*), took place after the proper match had been made by the young man's family. The future bridegroom visited the girl's family in the company of the *swat*, or matchmaker. About one-third of all marriages at the time were arranged by a matchmaker, usually an elderly man or woman.[18] Someone always acted as mediator. The proposal usually concerned both families, who negotiated the arrangements of the future marriage. The young people concerned did not take an active part. After the parents had reached a basic agreement, they discussed the economic aspects of the marriage, especially the dowries. Here the future couple participated. The negotiations were concluded with a glass of vodka. Drinking from one glass in turn was a symbolic gesture of consent. If the girl's parents wanted to express their refusal, they pretended not to see the glass.

The next step was an engagement or betrothal party, to which most neighbors and relatives were invited. The high point of the ceremony was when the matchmaker tied together the hands of the couple. From then on, the couple was considered engaged. The following day, the couple went to church to declare their intention to the priest, and on the four subsequent Sundays the banns were

---

[18]Markowska, *Rodzina w społeczności*, 83.

called. In the meantime, the couple exchanged gifts: the girl often received a colorful scarf, and the boy was presented with a shirt that the girl had embroidered herself. In the home of the maid of honor on the evening before the wedding, the girls' evening, *dobranocka*, (the "good night party") took place. It was a dancing party for the young only, and a farewell to carefree, unmarried life.

On the wedding day, the groom arrived at the bride's house early in the morning, and they both awaited their guests. Then they received the parents' blessing. Afterward, the whole party went to church in horse carriages or carts; a strict ceremonial order was followed about who preceded whom. The carts and the horses were decorated with green branches and colorful paper ribbons. The bride was expected to weep the whole way home to show that she mourned over her lost freedom. In some places, the road was barred with logs and ropes, and the village boys waited for guests to "ransom a free passage" (usually with vodka, tobacco, or sweets). The newlyweds were welcomed in the doorway of the bride's house by her parents, who had not been in church. The young couple was greeted with bread and salt.

Following a sumptuous dinner at the bride's house, dancing and singing began. But again the merrymaking followed a traditional ritual scheme. Special songs, related to the particular ceremony, were sung. (These songs were also sung later in Chicago, and in the 1930s they became available on record.) Earlier in the nineteenth century, additional ceremonies centered around the woman as ritual object. The ritual of *pokładziny* symbolized the consummation of marriage by publicly demonstrating the bloodstained sheet as proof of the bride's virginity. By the end of the nineteenth century, this ritual had disappeared. The *oczepiny* or "cap putting" ceremony was an even older ritual. Caps were the common head covering for married women; unmarried girls wore scarves or did not cover their heads at all. During the ceremony, the bride's braids were cut, and married women put a cap on her head. This act symbolized admittance to the social group of wives. This, the most "feminine" episode of the wedding, was the one most observed by emigrants, even if only in symbolic form.

The final ritual was the *przenosiny*, the (dowry) removal and housewarming. Usually the bride moved into the husband's household, and the richer the bride, the more elaborate the removal ceremony. The cart was loaded with all the objects of the dowry, including the dowry chest. The loaded cart was driven to the house of the bridegroom, and the husband's parents welcomed the young married couple with bread and salt. This was the definite moment of admission of the young woman into her husband's household, and her new life began.

The church marriage ritual was one small element in the tradition. Since the wedding party displayed the social position of both families, ceremonies had to be extravagant and showy. They usually lasted for several days. The high expenses were diminished because guests were expected to bring flour, butter, or eggs as gifts. Sometimes a wedding held in Chicago was followed by an extra ceremony in Zaborów, for the rest of the relatives and friends. The young couple sent money for this celebration from America to the home village.

The woman usually became pregnant soon after the wedding. Since pregnancy was a period of ritual impurity, the expectant mother was excluded from many activities. She was forbidden to draw water from the well or to plant cabbage or to gather fruit and vegetables, because her impurity could affect the crops. A popular superstition ordered people to fulfill all the pregnant woman's "fancies"—otherwise the child would be harmed. Other dangers threatened the future child. If the expectant mother looked at a big fire, the baby would be born with a red skin stigma. A gray or black spot on the baby, called a "mouse," was thought to be caused by a mother's having been frightened by a mouse. If a pregnant woman looked at a handicapped person, the deformity could be transferred to the fetus.

Babies were delivered by self-educated village midwives. The midwife's duties were not restricted to medical care but included some ritual acts as well. She welcomed the newborn baby by uttering special formulas and making the sign of the cross over it.

Much as in Dalsland, women in Zaborów were confined after childbirth. A period of "impurity" gave a new mother the chance to regain her physical strength. Following the rest, she underwent wywód, a church-held purification rite in which the priest blessed the woman so that she could return to full participation in community life. Until then, she was usually accompanied only by women, who helped her take care of the baby.

The christening ceremony closed the postnatal period. To be chosen godfather or godmother was an honor, but it carried considerable obligations. Godparents were responsible for their godchildren for the rest of their lives and were expected to give many gifts to their godchildren. In Zaborów, the villagers sometimes chose the noble landowners or priests as godparents, and these authorities rarely refused. After the baptism in church, guests were invited to a feast. The godparents presented their gifts to the baby, often a piece of linen cloth for a shirt or a sum of money. The participants in the feast contributed to the meal by bringing flour, eggs, sausage, and beer.

Rituals and superstitions were of course also associated with death. The dog's howling and the owl's hoot were believed to foretell someone's death. When someone was dying, *gromnica* (a candle consecrated on Candlemas, February 2) was lit, and the priest was called. In the home of the dying, the mirrors were covered and the clocks were stopped. Once death had occurred, all the people at the deathbed said rosary prayers. From the moment of death until the funeral, the mourners sat up day and night by the body, praying and keening; they never left the deceased alone.

Unmarried women were buried in their wedding dresses, which they had prepared in early adolescence. Married women were buried in their best attire, always with their caps on their heads. Thus, the social status of women was declared even at death.[19] The house of the bereaved was marked with small flags that hung outside, and wooden shavings from the coffin were strewn in front of the door. When the coffin was carried out of the house, the bearers knocked it three times against the threshold—the dead person's farewell to home. Most of the villagers attended the funeral ceremony. When the procession passed the village boundaries it stopped, and one of the elders delivered a valedictory speech. After the funeral, a meal was prepared at the home of the bereaved. The guests recalled the life of the deceased and comforted the mourning family, and sometimes inheritance matters were settled.

These rituals helped to organize local society and guided people's behavior. But rituals also caused social stagnation, especially for women. If a woman did not follow these rules, she was disapproved

---

[19]Wieruszewska Adamczyk, *Przemiany,* 90.

of by the village community. (Many of these customs would not survive the emigration process as later chapters discuss, and their transfiguration was to help liberate women.) Life in the urban environment hardly left any room for extensive celebrations. No employer would give leave for a three-day wedding, and no tenement apartment could accommodate so many wedding guests. Thus people had to adjust. Elements which could be integrated more easily—the food, the songs, the dances in saloons or halls—became part of the culture of the Polish-American community.

Living Conditions

Cottages were used for storing farm implements and food supplies; sometimes young calves, sheep, or poultry were also housed there. Pestles for grits and coarse flour, hand mills, cheese presses, and looms were kept in the hallway and the kitchen, (which also served as a living room). The cottage was the center of production for the peasant family unit.

The better-off inhabitants of Zaborów lived in cottages with walls constructed of pinewood logs, whereas the poorer ones inhabited houses of brushwood daubed with clay.[20] The roofs were thatched with straw, and the windows were covered with thin leather films, which were later replaced by glass panes. Usually the people had earth floors in their houses; only wealthier peasants could afford wooden floors. During the second half of the nineteenth century, chimneys and kitchen stoves with burners began to appear, replacing the ancient open fireplaces. The cottages usually consisted of two rooms, a hallway, and a storage room. Some cottages even had three rooms, but one-room cottages were not uncommon.

People slept on top of the stove, on long benches, or on simple homemade plank beds. Modern beds began to appear in the middle of the nineteenth century. At about the same time, pillows and down coverlets came into use. They were much valued and not for everyday use. Piled high on the beds and covered with ornamental bed-

---

[20]See Maria Ignatowicz (Knothe), "Materialne warunki bytu ludności," in *Encyklopedia Historii Gospodarczej Polski do roku 1945*, vol. 1 (Warszawa, 1981); Cierniak, *Wieś Zaborów*; Zawistowicz Adamska, *Społeczność wiejska*.

Ulaciej Nycz's house in a Galician village. He remigrated.
Photograph, Muzeum Etnograficzne w Krakowie, Archives.

clothes, they were displayed as a status symbol. Clothes were kept in richly decorated chests. Each young girl had a dowry chest in which she collected her trousseau. Everyday clothes were hung on rods.

If there were two rooms in the house, usually only one had a stove, which was used for heating and cooking. Another room, "the white room," served as a bedroom and for festive occasions as living room. Since the bedroom remained unheated, all members of the family—usually there were many—slept together in the kitchen-living room, which was the center of family life. In the corner opposite the stove, a table served as a home altar. Religious pictures decorated the walls above the altar. On the altar itself stood carved wooden figures of the saints, Christ, or the Virgin Mary, called *świątki*. The furniture was lined up along the walls, leaving the center empty.

The family ate meals while sitting on small stools or a low bench. Not until World War I were meals eaten at a table. The various courses of a meal were served in a single bowl for everyone to use.

Earthenware was used for kitchen cooking utensils. To add a decorative touch to the kitchen, flower-pattern mugs and plates were placed on shelves (or, in richer households, in a special sideboard).

The rural diet at the end of the nineteenth century relied on products of the domestic economy; only a few food items, such as salt, sugar, and sometimes vegetable fat, were purchased.[21] The everyday diet was monotonous, and the eating patterns were suited to the seasons of the agricultural cycle. People ate richer meals during the seasons of hard work in the fields; the last weeks before harvest, on the other hand, often meant undernourishment, sometimes almost starvation. Numerous fasting periods, in accordance with religious beliefs, were strictly observed.

The cereal products used were mainly coarse rye flour and different kinds of grits, such as rye, barley, buckwheat, or millet. Wheat, the most luxurious crop, was usually sold; only on festive occasions was wheat flour used for baking. The everyday bread was rye, and it was baked at home. Many foods were preserved through pickling, salting, or drying. Potatoes, cabbage, and peas were the main vegetables, and they were served cooked or pickled. Salads were unknown. Dairy products and eggs were the only sources of protein in the carbohydrate-dominated diet of the peasants. Meats were only served on special occasions, and the most valued were processed ham and pork sausages. Lard, which kept for several months, was used for everyday cooking to enrich dishes; oil or milk could be added if lard was unavailable. The usual beverages were milk or coffee made from burned grains; tea was saved for festive occasions. Since the peasants rarely had orchards, fruit was not plentiful.[22] Sometimes an apple, pear, or plum tree grew beside the cottages. Although the forest was several kilometers away, villagers went there to pick blackberries, raspberries, and mushrooms.

Typical peasant dishes were sour soup made of rye flour, *żur*, and red beet soup, *barszcz*. Pies and dumplings (*pierogi*), stuffed with cheese, potatoes, and cabbage and mushrooms were also very popular. Flat bread was often baked in ashes or on the kitchen stove.

---

[21] Anna Kowalska Lewicka, ed., *Pożywienie ludności wiejskiej, Praca zbiorowa* (Kraków, 1973).

[22] Józef Prelich, a village teacher from 1878 to 1898, worked diligently but rather unsuccessfully to spread the knowledge of fruit cultivation among the peasants.

Three meals a day were standard. Earlier in the century, breakfast was the largest meal of the day, later, lunch became the main repast.

There were many reasons to celebrate, and therefore feasts occurred rather often. Guests had to be entertained, and festive meals were luxurious: wheat cakes were baked; meat was processed into sausages and headcheese; and sometimes roast meat was served. Some special dishes were closely connected with particular rituals. For the Christmas Eve supper, a particular series of dishes was obligatory: potatoes, mushrooms, dried fruit, millet grits, dumplings in the form of fingers, and pies filled with cabbage. There was no wedding party without a *kołacz,* a cake richly decorated with "magical" ornaments. For Easter, there was the traditional Easter cake, *baba,* made from yeast dough. The characteristic Easter custom was and still is the *święcone:* a loaf of bread, a little salt, sausages, cakes, and colored eggs (*pisanki*) were put into a basket and carried to church to be blessed on Holy Saturday.

On many social occasions it was obligatory to serve meals to guests. Treats were expected, for example, when neighbors helped each other working in the fields—that was the customary form of repaying neighborly service. But immediate equal reciprocity was not an expected response to a sumptuous feast, which was held in part to show off the host's social position.

The consumption of alcohol among rural people was very high. After the middle of the nineteenth century, when rye vodka was replaced by much cheaper alcohol distilled from potatoes, consumption amounted to twelve liters per person per year. Both the church and various temperance organizations fought against excessive drinking. Alcoholism caused many family tragedies, the victims of which were usually women.

Clothing conveyed information about one's social status. As with food, there were great differences between everyday and festive clothing. On ordinary days, women wore shirt-like blouses made of thick linen, sleeveless bodices laced or buttoned in the front, and pleated skirts, sometimes two or more over each other. The skirts were covered with aprons. Women wore different kinds of outer clothing: doublets of various cuts, russet coats (similar ones were worn by men), and sheepskin coats. The large scarf covering shoulders and sometimes head was an important element in women's clothing. A married woman covered her head with a cap. Her attire was more modest and quieter in color, whereas girls were allowed to draw attention to their attractiveness. On cold days, women wore home-knit stockings. The usual footwear, although not worn every day, was shoes or high-laced boots. Underwear was not commonly worn.

The Sunday-best clothes were of better quality—the pattern more elaborate, the dress decorated, and some fineries added. These clothes in Zaborów resembled the traditional folk costumes of the Kraków region and could also serve as wedding dresses: a white linen blouse, a woolen bodice of black velvet embroidered with tiny beads, a colorful pleated skirt with a flower pattern, and a white apron. A necklace of coral beads often provided the finishing touch.[23]

Work

The work cycle began in early spring, usually in the middle of March with the first sowing of grain. This was a man's task, and women rarely participated. Sowing was followed by potato planting, collective work performed mostly by women and young people. It was work people were fond of because it was done in groups. Then came a few weeks relatively free of field work.

During the spring cleaning, the farmyard was swept, the rooms whitewashed, and all the wooden parts of the house and furniture scrubbed. The housewives aired clothes and sheepskin coats. The outer walls of the cottages were either whitewashed or scrubbed with soap and water. The dry wood was rubbed with oil mixed with kerosene, and the chinks between adjoining logs and edges were painted blue. Three or four women working together usually took a whole day to perform this work. If there were enough women in the family, they could manage this work without help from neighbors.

At the beginning of May, the peasant families began working in the fields again. The women planted cabbage and peas. At the end of

---

[23]Ryszard Kantor, *Ubiór–strój–kostium: funkcje odzienia w tradycyjnej społeczności wiejskiej w XIXw. i w początkach XXw. na obszarze Polski* (Kraków, 1982).

After the harvest.
Photograph, Muzeum Etnograficzne w Krakowie, Archives.

May, men and women worked together weeding the potato plants and hoeing cabbage and peas. Weeding millet and flax was next, and this work was done by women only. Haymaking came at the end of June. Men mowed the fields, and women raked and dried the hay, sometimes with help from the men. After haymaking came the grain harvest, the most demanding work. As with hay, men cut the grain and women sheaved it. Scythes used for reaping were considered men's tools. When reaping with a sickle could be handled, which was

smaller than a scythe, women did the job. After the crop was harvested and stored away in the barns at the beginning of September,
there was a second round of haymaking. Soon afterward, it was time
to dig potatoes. Women, elderly men, and youngsters did this work,
while younger men were occupied with the fall plowing. Fall also required another thorough cleaning of the home and farmyard.

In October, women began the tasks connected with flax, such as
hackling (cutting), drying, and soaking. These were arduous opera-
tions. The processing of hemp required almost the same amount of
labor. Spinning the yarn would wait until winter. (These women's
tasks were very common until the 1930s. Although ready-made products could be purchased at fairs, homespun linen was still much in
use for bedclothes and simpler dresses.) The threshing belonged to
men, but if able-bodied men were unavailable, women took the flails
and were usually proud of it. Several other tasks had to be performed
before the coming of winter. The house and the farm buildings were
insulated. Wood, which was hard to come by, had to be stored.
Zaborów had no communal forest, nor were there private forests belonging to particular farms. Some wood had to be purchased, and
people supplemented the wood with brushwood, dry twigs and
leaves, and fir and pine cones. Gathering these kept women busy.
Sometimes women also helped to saw wood.

For women, winter was no time for leisure. Spinning was done
collectively, and women met in neighbors' houses in turns. They
used spinning wheels as well as spindle whorls. The yarn was given
to weavers living in the nearby villages, who would weave it into
linen cloth for sheets and sacks. Plucking feathers was another job
that kept women and girls busy throughout the winter. Like spinning, it was done communally.

In addition to the women's annual working cycle, there were
many everyday tasks that were exclusively female. The housewife's
day began early, usually at six o'clock in the winter and at five o'clock
during the summer. First she had to feed the cattle, the pigs, and the
poultry. Then she cleaned the cow shed, milked the cows, lit a fire in
the kitchen stove, and cooked food (usually enough for the whole
day). In the afternoon, when there was no field work to be done, she
shelled peas, sorted grain, or sewed. All the simple clothes of the

family were made at home; only Sunday clothes were ordered from tailors or dressmakers. Later in the afternoon, fodder had to be chopped for the livestock. The animals were fed again and the cows milked. Then the woman peeled potatoes for the next day, built the fire again, and cooked supper or warmed up what was left from the midday meal. When the day came to an end, the woman tidied the kitchen, washed the dishes, and prepared for the next day.

If there were several women in the household, the housewife was the chief of this team. Daughters and often daughters-in-law had to obey her orders, do the hardest work, and, at the same time, learn complex tasks such as sewing and embroidering. This was a period of apprenticeship. Grinding grain in the hand mill also was a female task. Bread was baked once every three weeks, and the supply of bread was kept in the storage room or in the "better" room. Once a week, clothes were washed at the house. If the weather allowed for it, women washed the clothes outside, close to the well. Clothes and linens drying on fences were a familiar feature of the village landscape. The peasant woman's day was brimful with work. No wonder that women always preferred to have daughters than sons, since girls were taught to help their mothers from very early on.

Exchanging services among neighbors reinforced the community social ties. Planting and digging potatoes, spinning flax and hemp, and plucking feathers were usually done collectively. The work was performed in different households by turns. After the job was completed, the neighbors who had helped were treated to a substantial meal. It was a matter of honor to entertain the helpers properly. In the evening when the potato digging was finished, the hostess prepared the so-called *wykopek*, the potato-digging party. A good and plentiful meal was served; musicians were hired; and a dancing party followed. During the potato digging season, such parties took place one after the other in different households. Similar was the *wyskubek*, the feather-plucking party. For such parties, the wealthier villagers even prepared *kołacze*, the cake otherwise baked only for weddings.

The traditional peasant farms lacked economic self-sufficiency, and most households had some debt in money, food products, or services. The customary way of liquidating debt was to work it off; this system was called *odrobek*. During the last weeks before the new harvest, the poorer villagers had to borrow foodstuffs, grain for sowing, or money, from the better-off neighbors or from the manor. The wealthier farmer, for whom debtors were working off debt, had to treat them to a common ceremonial meal. Working-off was also the usual form of paying the local craftsmen. The only women paid in this way were dressmakers. This system of cooperation reinforced social ties in the village. *Odrobek* was the most popular form of selling one's labor.

Hired labor paid with money was not very popular in the parish of Zaborów. The demand for manpower was covered almost entirely through the exchange of services and working-off. Villagers in need of extra income could find employment for several months or for a year on the lord's estate nearby, or farther away in Russian Poland. Sometimes they also worked for wealthy peasants in the area. Both men and women were employed. The manor recruited the hired labor for seasonal work, such as haymaking and harvesting, by sending special agents to the villages. The laborers received daily wages and returned home after the season. Some villagers were employed for a year or two as domain servants. They were given accommodation and wages, paid partly in products and partly in cash, and after the contract ran out they returned home. The most popular form of employment for cash, however, was to migrate to Prussia or overseas.

The Culture of Migration

As elsewhere in Galicia, people from Zaborów parish emigrated mainly for economic reasons.[24] Other motives included aversion to military service, striving for personal freedom, or the desire for a new life experience and adventure. Personal or family motives were also very common. As migration became a regular phenomenon in village life, there were also such factors as imitation of others, fol-

---

[24]See Zawistowicz Adamska, *Społeczność wiejska;* Wieruszewska Adamczyk, *Przemiany społeczności wiejskiej;* Kantor, *Między Zaborowem a Chicago.*

lowing an invitation from people already abroad, or the wish to join family members.

In the village, women outnumbered men. The number of men declined because of military service (which usually produced only a temporary absence) and emigration. Women found it harder to find mates and achieve the status of a married woman. For unmarried women, emigration offered the chance to earn money for a dowry, which in turn provided better marriage prospects upon their return. They could also hope to find a husband while abroad. Married women, on the other hand, usually had the family prospects and the farm's needs in mind when they decided to emigrate.

Zaborów parish had a tradition of migration abroad that had its roots in the system of hired work at farms of wealthy peasants and lands belonging to manors. These farmsteads were often far away the native village, sometimes across the national border. Sea- migration to Germany started in the 1880s. According to local , one young man learned by chance about work in Ger- did not own a farm and had a wife and children to support. d to go together. During the next 13 years, he and his here every year. He worked not only as a seasonal la- s *auzjer*, that is, as a man who recruited seasonal tioned as their foreman. After his death, his wife, continued to go to Germany for the next 17

to Germany became so popular that hardly a t have at least one member participating. eople, old people, and even children. Al- mploy children under the age of 14, this en and women from Zaborów also nts. Women found employment in arries as well as in road and rail- etter paid than employment in seasonal.

id not have a significant im- l in Germany helped peo- he most necessary pur- n enough money for new investments in their farms, and the work abroad did not give them many cultural advantages. Having only short work contracts, they mostly worked very hard to earn as much money as possible. Nevertheless, the seasonal migrations helped create the attitude that it was possible to leave the local community temporarily without doing any harm to the family or farm. Seasonal migration made future decisions to emigrate to the United States easier.

Around 1900, a man who had heard about the possibility of getting work in Denmark recruited a group of workers, and for the next 16 years he acted as an *auzjer* and foreman. Many women migrated to Denmark seasonally, where they were hired to work mainly in dairy production and the processing of sugar beets. Women from the same village usually lived together in small groups. They were reasonably well paid, food was provided, and living conditions were good. The work day began at 6 A.M. and ended at 6 P.M., with a half-hour break for breakfast and a one-hour break for lunch. Sunday was a holiday. Because of better living and working conditions Denmark was a much more attractive country for migration than Germany. Work was hard to find in Denmark, however. Some people from Zaborów also went to Sweden, but there is little information about them.

Emigration to the United States opened a new chapter in the l[ife] of the village. Again, individual initiative set it all in motion. In 18[__] a forty-year-old married man, the father of three children and ow[ner] of a small farm, borrowed some money and went to Chicago.[25] [The] lender took a portion of the crops from the farmer's fields as in[terest] on the loan. The farmer's wife and children stayed behind. [During] his five-year stay in Chicago, this pioneer worked at railw[ay con-]struction. He returned to Zaborów but after six years wen[t to] Chicago. He could not find work in Chicago and ret[urned to] Zaborów after one year, this time to stay. He had not made [a fortune,] but he had paid all his debts and current expenses; part o[f which] he wasted on drink. His example, although financially n[ot a success,] stimulated others in Zaborów.

Most of the emigrants to the United States, main[ly men,] planned to earn money and return after a few years. T[hey]

---

[25]Zawistowicz Adamska, *Społeczność wiejska.*

improve their living conditions in Zaborów; they wanted to buy more land and to build new houses. Some went several times, usually spending an average of three to five years in the United States.

Mass migration to the United States began in the last decade of the nineteenth century and peaked in the first decade of the twentieth. During the period 1890–1919 about 75 women from Zaborów left for the United States. About 50 women remained in the United States permanently, so every third or fourth family in Zaborów had a female member living in America. Since many families were related, nearly every family in Zaborów had a female relative in Chicago.[26] Thus, emigration to Chicago was of a typical chain character, resulting from strong social links within the village community. These links were preserved in the new urban environment.

Emigration to the United States also had an indirect impact on the welfare of the parish. Those who stayed abroad sold their farms usually to relatives and neighbors, who enjoyed priority in such transactions. Land was extremely scarce, so emigrants' sale of farms increased the supply.

The Folk Culture of Emigrants

Emigration created its own folklore and found expression in songs, anecdotes, and stories. The folk character of these stories lies in their embellishment: the stories were only loosely related to real persons, places, and times.[27] The stories became the common property of all. Even tales with the least semblance of truth helped potential emigrants to prepare for the unfamiliar world, particularly its dangers. The local inn was the favorite gathering place for trading stories about emigration, although the stories were told everywhere. Some stories actually began at the inn: one popular story told about a farm hand who never returned home after getting drunk. Encouraged by neighbors and aided by an emigration agent, he went directly to America.

---

[26]There are no similar data available for the other villages in the Zaborów parish. The number of emigrants and percentage of women differed widely from village to village. On the basis of Chicago's parish records, however, one can estimate that no more than 200 women left the parish and moved to Chicago.

[27]Many examples were gathered in Zaborów by R. Kantor in the 1980s. See *Między Zaborowem.*

The main characters in many stories were return migrants, who created sensations in the home village. A suit, a straw hat, sometimes even a bowler hat or top hat and a walking stick—such were the accessories commonly associated with return migrants. "City ways" were remembered and always present in these folk stories. Another story tells about a man who, at the end of the nineteenth century, returned home from America dressed in a white dress coat and a straw hat. He paraded around the village, often stopping for a moment to pour vodka from a bottle into a steel mug and hopping on one leg while drinking. As this example shows, emigration produced "characters." Women, however, were afraid of being different. The village community would not have forgiven them for showing any eccentric behavior.

Some stories told about the various dangers one could encounter while traveling; others focused on language problems and misunderstandings. Bad behavior and drunkenness were stigmatized in a moralizing way. The theme of emigration often appeared in songs or in improvised wedding couplets. They related to actual situations or persons to whom the authors wanted to show respect or malice. This rich oral folklore about emigration is evidence of its significance in the local community.

In the rural society of Poland at the turn of the century, in a well-organized local community, a woman played many different roles. In the family she was daughter, sister, wife, mother, or grandmother. In the household, she was responsible for specific tasks and helped others in their tasks as well. In the village, she was a member of a close peer group, a potential wife, an experienced authority on ritual etiquette, and a neighbor. In the parish, she was the warden of Catholic values.

The social and cultural structure defined women's place in this community, and there was no room for deviation from the defined way of life. The woman was obliged to play these roles under the sanction of disapproval. If for some reason she was not able or did not want to fulfill these demands, she could try to achieve success through emigration, a choice approved of by the community. Emigration was often a modern way of achieving conservative patterns of life. With the money earned in Chicago, the farm could be enlarged after return to the village—and a larger farm improved a woman's position within Zaborowian society. In the United States, marriage prospects were better, and a young woman could be married soon after emigration. Many Zaborowian women chose emigration as the route to achieving their life goals.

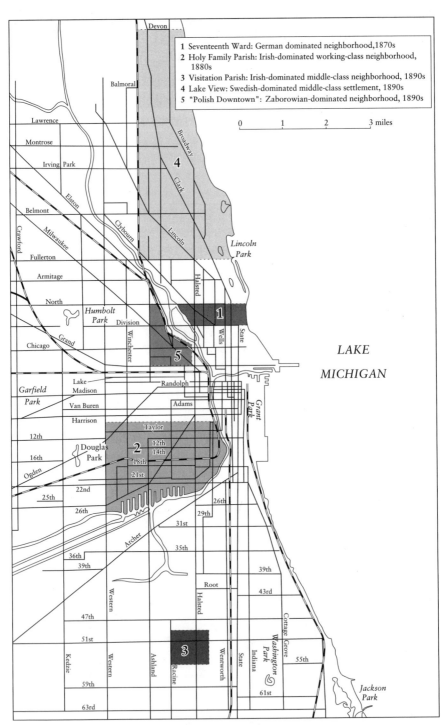

1 Seventeenth Ward: German dominated neighborhood, 1870s
2 Holy Family Parish: Irish-dominated working-class neighborhood, 1880s
3 Visitation Parish: Irish-dominated middle-class neighborhood, 1890s
4 Lake View: Swedish-dominated middle-class settlement, 1890s
5 "Polish Downtown": Zaborowian-dominated neighborhood, 1890s

0   1   2   3 miles

Chicago: Neighborhoods of settlement

PART II

Urban Life

5

Creating a Community: German-American Women in Chicago

Christiane Harzig

When Mecklenburgers began to arrive in Chicago in the 1850s, they encountered a city in the making, both physically and socially. The loose social structure of the city must have been astonishing to them: they had come from a society that wielded near-total control over individuals from birth to death. This new, urban life was radically different from the one they had known. In Chicago, they were able to build the urban social structures, institutions, and associations which created the texture of the German-American community. This community in turn shaped their lives and mental horizons, serving important daily needs and affecting their acculturation as well as their material well-being.

Class, ethnicity, gender, and generation all played a part in the ways in which change was incorporated into the lives of the immigrants. New opportunities and new demands meant that gender relations had to be renegotiated. This reshaping of roles was an ongoing process which took place in all aspects of life: in the family, in the public sphere of the ethnic community, in church, and in front of the welfare agent. "Labor" also took on new meanings for men and women, as well as for children. For men, labor became industrial work structured by a time clock, potential unemployment, and greater responsibility for the family income. For women, it became running a household under the constraints of the amount of cash at hand and the availability (or unavailability) of urban services. Children, whose work had been integral to the running of a farm, had to renegotiate their responsibilities to the family.

German-Americans in Chicago

Coming to the City

The 1870 census lists immigrants from Germany by their region of origin. In Chicago, people from Mecklenburg were overrepresented by 269 points (compared to 75 for people from Hannover and 52 for those from Württemberg).[1]

Chicago was not necessarily a neatly planned destination. Most Mecklenburgers whose initial stop, after departing from Hamburg, was New York, headed for areas that they thought offered them the best chance to settle. They traveled by train or ship to the Midwest, where they sought homes in rural Michigan and Iowa, as well as in Milwaukee and Chicago. Many Mecklenburg farm hands, maids and small farmers who at first settled in an urban area most likely planned to move on. They sought jobs in order to save for a piece of land. This step of joining the urban proletariat could last a couple of months or a decade, or it could remain permanent.[2]

Passenger records provide some clues about Mecklenburg immigrants. On board the *Freitag* arriving in New York from Hamburg in May 1848 was Christian Blank, a 40-year-old draper, his 37-year-old wife, and their five children, one of whom had been born at sea. They were joined by three other Mecklenburgers, a 17-year-old single servant maid, a 30-year-old laborer, and a 32-year-old ship's carpenter. Their destination was Illinois.[3] Some years later, in 1856, another group of Mecklenburgers embarked for Chicago. The *Guten-*

---

[1]The figure 100 would represent proportionally adequate distribution. See Walter D. Kamphoefner, *The Westfalians: From Germany to Missouri* (Princeton, 1987), 76. We should, however, be aware that Mecklenburgers did not comprise the majority of Germans in Chicago; in fact, most came from Prussia.

[2]We know little about the transition from rural to urban to rural living in the process of migration. See, for example, Horst Rössler, "The Dream of Independence: The 'America' of England's North Staffordshire Potters," in Dirk Hoerder and Rössler, eds., *Distant Magnets: Expectations and Realities in the Immigrant Experience, 1840–1930* (New York, 1993), 128–159.

[3]Illinois State Genealogical Society, *Quarterly* 17 (1985): 89–97.

berg carried 39 people: 15 men, 13 women (all of them in their 20s and 30s) and 11 children under the age of 14. There were five families, including grown children, but also six single men and five single women. All except two of the men were laborers; all of the women were servants.

Two Mecklenburg men made the trip in the late 1840s and wrote about their experience for others who might wish to follow. They recommended, for instance, a steamboat ride from New York to Albany on the Hudson River. In Albany, one of the men boarded a train to Buffalo, a ride which lasted about 24 hours. In Buffalo, they were impressed by the sight of Niagara Falls. The last part of the trip was a five- to six-day voyage by steamboat across the Great Lakes to Milwaukee and Chicago. The whole trip cost about $14, food not included. The authors of the travel guide advised their follow immigrants to bring their own provisions.[4]

What awaited Mecklenburgers coming to the city? Opportunity—for the prepared. At least until the 1870s, the city's industrial production was mainly based on craftsmanship and skilled labor. For those who had learned a trade in the old country, the dream of owning their own business could still come true.[5] Toward the turn of the century, industrial expansion and mass production opened other opportunities. But modern production also reduced the need for some skills and brought disappointment to many skilled German workers.

At first, however, opportunity prevailed. An example is Ludwig Wolff, who by the 1890s was one of the most successful German-American entrepreneurs in Chicago. In 1854 at the age of 18, he had come from the port city of Rostock, one of the major cities in Mecklenburg, together with his brothers and sisters. They had originally planned to buy a farm in Missouri. Shortly after his arrival, however, his parents died. As the oldest son, Wolff found himself responsible for his siblings. Working at odd jobs during the first year while he was learning to speak English, he finally found a well-paying job in his trade as a coppersmith. Shortly afterward, he invented a device used in the distillation of schnapps and opened his own business. By

---

[4]Franz and Rudolph Meier, *Gruß aus Wisconsin's Urwäldern in Nord-America an ihre Mecklenburger Landsleute* (Malchin, 1847), 28–39.

[5]For an account of early industrial development in Chicago, see Homer Hoyt, *One Hundred Years of Land Values in Chicago* ([1933] New York, 1970), 59.

1898, he owned two factories, employed 1,500 workers, and was worth $2.5 million. The bourgeois *Illinois Staats-Zeitung* featured his life story in its anniversary issue but noted that few Germans had careers as successful.[6]

Very few immigrants from Mecklenburg had a skill so highly in demand. Men typically found work as unskilled laborers in the lumber and brickyards, in the grain-processing industries, or on the truck farms at the city fringes. The neighborhood businesses, such as bakeries, dry-goods stores, tobacco stores, and tailor shops also needed employees, many of whom were German women. The never ending demand for servant labor also meant employment for many.

The German-American Community

By the 1870s, there was a well-developed German-American community. More than 50,000 German-born people were living in the city, 17.5 percent of the total population.[7] Churches, schools, orphanages, old people's homes, and hospitals were organized by Germans for Germans; singing and gymnastics associations, cultural organizations, and mutual aid societies served immigrants' social and practical needs; theaters and music halls catered to the Germans, as well as to the city at large; and last but not least, a thriving German-language press brought news to the immigrants.

The first German churches were founded in the early 1840s, and in 1849 the first lodges were organized. Other associations were soon to follow: the German Society in 1853, which primarily assisted newly arrived immigrants; the Deutsches Haus in 1856; and the Germania Club in 1865. A number of German men, especially the Forty-Eighters, had become active in politics. They helped organize the Republican Party and rallied support for the Civil War. Some became influential in local politics. One Forty-Eighter, journalist Lorence Brentano, helped establish German language teaching in the Chicago public schools. Beginning in 1848, the *Illinois Staats-Zeitung* covered daily affairs of interest to the German-American community,

[6]*Illinois Staats-Zeitung*, 21 April 1898, 69.
[7]Hartmut Keil and John B. Jentz, *German Workers in Industrial Chicago 1850–1910: A Comparative Perspective* (DeKalb, Ill., 1983), 21.

Bismarck Garden, Chicago. On Halsted and Grace in Lake View.

ran news on the politics of the home country, and interpreted the society and culture of the new homeland. Other newspapers followed suit. Through job advertisements, meeting announcements, wedding and anniversary announcements, and obituaries, the German-American newspapers created a sense of ethnic identity.[8]

As the German community became established, it grew in complexity. Class distinctions, religious affiliations, and regional origins served to differentiate the immigrant community as much as generation and gender. People organized along class lines and religious denominations. Associations based on regional origin became the vogue in the 1890s. Lodges carrying the name of Fritz Reuter, Mecklenburg's best-known literary figure, as well as the numerous branches of the Plattdütsche Guilde (a club for speakers of the Low German dialect), indicate the many German immigrants from the northern and northeastern parts of Germany. To show Americans what Germans were able to do when acting in unity, in May 1871 the

[8]In 1870, there were ten German weekly and monthly magazines; by 1890, the number had grown to 70. Almost every association, church congregation, or lodge had its own publication. In the 1890s, the daily newspapers reached a combined circulation of 159,000. See Annelie Edelmann, "Das Verhältnis der Deutschamerikaner zum Deutschen Reich (vom deutsch-französischen Krieg bis zur Samoa Krise, 1870–1900) anhand ausgewählter Beispiele aus der deutsch-amerikanischen Presse" (unpublished M.A. thesis, Free University, Berlin, 1982).

German-American community staged a large festival in celebration of the victory of the Prussian army and the subsequent founding of the German Empire. The *Illinois Staats-Zeitung* failed to report, however, that German workers stayed aloof from this celebration of German militarism. In later years, German workers chose to commemorate the days of the Paris Commune.[9]

Work and Family in a Mecklenburg Immigrant Neighborhood

By the 1860s and 1870s, Chicago was already clearly divided into neighborhoods, rendering ethnic and class distinctions visible. Some older German neighborhoods were on the Southwest Side and a few newer ones in the Northwest. The concentrations between Chicago and North Avenues on the lower North Side, however, were the strongest. Later, this district spread as far as Fullerton Avenue. Here in "the Old German Neighborhood," many businesses and institutions catered mainly to the German-American community.[10]

The census of 1870 revealed a large Mecklenburg population between Division Street and North Avenue (between the Chicago River and the lake shore), which at that time constituted the 17th ward. This area was first settled in the late 1840s, when German truck farmers provided fruit and vegetables for the city population. In the late 1850s, these pioneers were followed by people who wanted to escape the congestion of the central business district and the adjacent vice and slum area. The 1860s brought many Germans who were wealthy enough to afford houses into the area. Church buildings followed their congregations: the First St. Paul's Lutheran Church opened its fourth building on Superior and Franklin Streets; the St. James Lutheran Church and the Catholic St. Michael's Church, among others, served the German people north of North Avenue.

---

[9]Hartmut Keil and John B. Jentz, eds., *German Workers in Chicago: A Documentary History of Working-Class Culture from 1850 to World War I* (Chicago, 1988), 264–269.

[10]See Christiane Harzig, *Familie, Arbeit und weibliche Öffentlichkeit in einer Einwanderungsstadt: Deutschamerikanerinnen in Chicago um die Jahrhundertwende* (St. Katharinen, 1991), 295; Dominic A. Pacyga and Ellen Skerret, *Chicago: City of Neighborhoods: History and Tours* (Chicago, 1986), 37–87.

During the 1850s, the area along Lasalle Street and east toward the lake had become the neighborhood for elite German businessmen, most of whom had made their fortunes through the breweries (originally established along the lake shore). Many German professionals also lived there. They could freely associate with Chicago's elite and at the same time entertain in their own ethnically exclusive circles. But the wealthy German-Americans were not truly part of the super-rich, the super-fashionable clique. In the 1850s Lasalle and Dearborn Streets, with their beautiful large trees, had attracted fashionable residents, and land value was high. By the 1870s, however, the boulevards and avenues of the South Side had caught the tycoons' eyes. The appeal of the North Side had been limited by its poor access to the central business district. No streetcar yet crossed the river, and rising traffic made crossing the bridges an ordeal. Moreover, the North Side's fashionable residential area was hemmed in by factories. But this apparent disadvantage turned out to be a blessing for the maintenance of a stable German-American neighborhood. Property values had stabilized, allowing people to hold on to their houses and their small businesses.

Throughout the second half of the nineteenth century, the North Side remained an area where working and living intermingled. There was a clear east-west distinction, however. The lower-income and working-class families lived in the vicinity of the river, west and just east of Larrabee Street. This area was adjacent to the many wood, coal, and lumber yards, the brickyards, grain elevators, breweries, planing mills, and countless machine shops. The middle-class families lived in somewhat larger homes between Larrabee and Clark streets. Their property was worth $60 a front foot (a foot measured along the front of a lot), whereas the working-class property brought only $20 a front foot.[11] In the working-class neighborhoods, there were bakeries, tailor shops, shoe stores, furniture shops, wagon-making businesses, dairies, and grocery stores, not to mention a large number of saloons. All of these businesses supplied the daily needs of the residents and also offered employment.

In 1870, the census taker counted 18,155 people and a total of 3,891 households in the 17th ward. In this ward, 386 households (9.9 percent) included people from Mecklenburg (including servants and

[11]Hoyt, One Hundred Years, 97.

Band concert, Lincoln Park, Chicago.

boarders). A total of 1,620 Mecklenburgers were counted, or 8.9 percent of the total ward population. These people constitute the sample population for the following analysis of work and family life.

Almost half of the sample population had been born in Mecklenburg; 65 percent of the households were still headed by a person from Mecklenburg, and in almost 70 percent, a Mecklenburg woman kept house. After those born in Mecklenburg, the next largest group in our sample was children born in Illinois. The 1870 census does not provide precise information on when the immigrants entered the United States. One way to estimate time of arrival is the age of the first child born in the United States. (This method tells us nothing, however, about the period after arrival but prior to the birth of the immigrants' first American child.) According to this estimate, 41 percent of the people had arrived after the Civil War. A surprisingly high proportion (27 percent) might have arrived during the war; these immigrants' American-born children were between five and nine years of age in 1870. Another 26 percent of the immigrants arrived during the years 1856–1860, when emigration from Mecklenburg began to gain momentum. Five percent of the Mecklenburgers in this sample were Chicago pioneers: their children, born in Illinois, were more than 15 years old. Almost 90 percent seem to have come directly to

TABLE 5.1

17th ward: Places of origin (sample)

Origin	N	Percent
Mecklenburg	737	45.5
Prussia	144	8.9
Holstein, Hanover, Hamburg	46	2.8
Germany (other regions)	77	4.8
Illinois	543	33.5
U.S., other	50	3.1
Other and unknown	23	1.4
Total	1,620	100.0

Source: Analysis of the 1870 Census Manuscript.

Illinois. In very rare cases, some had migrated initially inside Germany, mostly to Prussia, and others had spent time in other places in the United States, such as New York or Wisconsin. Although families with children were willing to migrate, they were reluctant to look around before settling down.

The occupational structure of heads of household in the sample reflects the working-class and lower-middle-class background typical for this area. It also shows that the neighborhood provided its residents with both living space and work opportunity; houses, shops, and small industries were all located together, instead of being segregated by area.

Clearly, the skilled crafts and lower white-collar occupations (in trades and transportation) prevailed among the men of the sample population. Thus there were slightly fewer laborers living in this particular 1870 neighborhood than was true of Chicago German-American neighborhoods in 1850 (36 percent) and 1880 (34.7 percent). Among the crafts, the building trades dominated: brick masons, carpenters, and plasterers were in high demand in the booming city. Ten years later, this had not changed; in 1880, 13.1 percent of the Chicago German-Americans still worked in these trades.[12] Tailors increased

[12]See Hartmut Keil, "Chicago's German Working-Class in 1900," in Keil and Jentz, *German Workers in Industrial Chicago,* 19–36.

TABLE 5.2

17th ward: Occupational structure (sample), 1870

Occupation	Heads		Men		Women	
Professionals	4	1.1%	4	0.8%	—	—%
Public service	4	1.1	4	0.8	—	—
Trade and transportation	85	22.7	94	19.7	—	—
Proprietors	30	8.0	31	6.5	—	—
Store employees	12	3.2	28	5.9	5	8.9
Agents	3	0.8	5	1.0	—	—
Others	6	1.6	5	1.0	—	—
Transportation	34	9.1	44	9.22	—	
Crafts	152	40.5	201	42.0	—	
Food	9	2.4	15	3.1	—	
Building trades	53	14.1	68	14.2	—	
Metal	20	5.3	28	5.8	1	1.8
Wood	20	5.3	25	5.2	—	—
Clothing	43	11.6	47	9.8	16	28.6
Printing/publications	2	0.5	8	1.6	—	—
Others	6	1.6	10	2.9	—	—
Services	3	0.8	—	—	27	48.2
Washerwomen	3	0.8	—		4	7.1
Domestic servants	—	—	—	—	20	35.7
Midwives/nurses	—	—	—	—	3	5.4
Laborers	121	32.3	151	31.6	6	10.7
Others	6	1.6	5	1.1	—	—
Total	375	100	478	100	56	100

Source: Analysis of the 1870 Census Manuscript.

in number during the 1880s, when (with the help of Germans) the clothing industry began to settle on the North Side. Store owners, teamsters, and house movers were also numerous. Store proprietors usually were heads of household; store employees were often the proprieters' relatives or boarders.

Household heads from Mecklenburg were at the lower end of the economic scale. Although they comprised 65 percent of the sample, they held 80 percent of the laborer jobs. This high percentage reflects the pre-emigration occupations of immigrants from Mecklenburg. The large number of skilled craftsmen is a surprise, however. Perhaps men who had learned a trade in Mecklenburg were more likely to settle in the city, whereas Mecklenburg farm hands preferred rural areas.

The "professions" and "public services" are strikingly underrepresented in our sample; in the professional category, there are only three doctors and one banker. The banker exemplifies the well-to-do German bourgeoisie of that time. His name was Conrad Niehoff, and he was born in Prussia; in 1870, he was 44 years old. His wife, age 28 (most likely his second) was born to Prussian parents in New York. There were five children, ranging in age from one to fourteen years. A 25-year-old servant maid from Mecklenburg helped in the household, and a 20-year-old nurse from Prussia took care of the younger children. Conrad Niehoff owned $75,000 worth of real estate and held $25,000 in "value of personal estate." He lived at 569 North Clark Street, in the "Schwalben" neighborhood.[13] Niehoff was a well-known and active member of the German-American community. Among his civic activities was helping to organize an old people's home, including providing financial guidance.

Niehoff was by far the richest person in the sample, but others had also acquired both real estate and personal wealth. For 47.4 percent of the households, at least one of the two is listed. Primarily craftsmen and proprietors had accumulated some wealth; only 22 percent of laborers had done so. The amounts range from $150 to $25,000 in personal wealth and from $200 to $75,000 in real estate.

Although we are not able to say where all the laborers went to work, we can account for where the craftsmen and the lower white-collar workers did. They literally constructed their neighborhood and ward, and they produced what the people needed. They built houses and furniture, and they moved old houses to backyards to make room for new ones in the front. They baked bread, butchered meat, and sold groceries and dry goods; they made shoes and sewed suits and dresses; and they sold beer in the saloons. Many of these

---

[13]So called because of the "swallowtail" dress suits popular there. Vivien Palmer, "Study of the Development of Chicago's Northside" (unpublished manuscript, Chicago Historical Society, 1932), 78–79.

small businesses could only be profitable because the whole family, especially the wives and older daughters, worked in them. Few of the immigrants seem to have participated in Chicago's great businesses such as the grain trade or the iron and steel industries. The small neighborhood craft enterprises and businesses suffered severely after the fire of 1871, but most people could start over because their skills were needed to rebuild the city. The skills of the 1870s, however, rapidly became obsolete as industrial, technological, and commercial development picked up speed. The sons and daughters of Mecklenburg immigrants had to seek other employment opportunities.

In 1870, only 56 women in our sample were employed outside the home—6.9 percent of the female population.[14] Working women in the nineteenth and early twentieth centuries were mainly single and young. So to get a better picture of the labor force participation of German immigrant women, it is more informative to relate their number to this group. Counting only women ages fifteen and older and subtracting all those who "kept house," we get the number of women who were potentially part of the labor force. Of those, 55 percent had paying jobs. In 1900, with an aging first generation of German immigrants and a growing second generation, the employment rate of German-American women of that age group

TABLE 5.3

17th ward: The nonemployed (sample), 1870

Position	Men	Percent	Women	Percent
No data	192	23.8	214	26.3
At school	117	14.5	119	14.6
At home	19	2.4	56	6.9
Keeps house	—	—	369	45.3
Employed	478	59.3	56	6.9
Total	806	100	814	100

Source: Analysis of the 1870 Census Manuscript.

[14]For males, the figure was 59.3 percent.

was 63 percent.[15] In 1870, domestic service clearly dominated (35.7 percent), followed by the clothing industry (28.5 percent). The 1880 and 1900 census data register a sharp change, with the clothing industry dominating in the 1880s and clerical work gaining momentum in 1900.[16]

Family Cycle and the Life Course in Chicago

In Mecklenburg, people's lives were constrained by regulations imposed by nobles, landlords and village authorities. Lives took shape within these many confines and women were subject to them in greater degree than men were. As we have seen in Chapter 1, the stage in the life course determined the outlook, pattern, and content of females' lives. Whether they were children, young girls, married women, or grandmothers, the life stage defined the boundaries of their activities and prescribed what was expected of them. How were social relations affected by migration and life in an urban environment?

The Mecklenburg-American population differed from the population at home in a significant way: people were either very young or middle-aged. Children ages 14 and younger represented the largest group. There were only a few teenagers older than 14. In the middle-aged group, there were more men, especially between ages 40 and 50. And there was only a small percentage of elderly people. Migration was responsible for this demographic pattern. Most Mecklenburgers had emigrated as singles in their 20s. After settling down, they married, had children, and started a new family cycle. Seldom did people emigrate in the middle of their family cycle, that is, in their late 30s and 40s, taking half-grown children along. Therefore there were very few immigrants ages 15 to 24. The larger number of men in their 40s and 50s indicates the greater mobility of single men in their search for employment, and the higher number of females between 20 and 24 shows how necessary it was for these

---

[15]The figures are taken from my sample of the 1900 Chicago Census Manuscripts: 5,060 total female sample population; 1,903 girls ages 14 and younger; 1,734 wives; 1,423 potentially working women; 896 women employed (63 percent).

[16]See Christiane Harzig, "Chicago's German North Side, 1880–1900: The Structure of a Gilded Age Ethnic Neighborhood," in Keil and Jentz, German Workers in Industrial Chicago, 137.

young women to seek marriage partners in the emerging German-American communities abroad.

Childhood and Adolescence

Although most of the people in our sample were born in Germany, only a few of the children could have had strong memories of the old country. The vast majority of the children had an American childhood. Three-quarters of those (73.6 percent) under 25 years of age had been born in Illinois. Of those, 46 percent were of school age (ages 5 through 14). As far as can be judged from the census, families sent their children to school, although only for the minimum time required by law. By the age of six, 50 percent of the Illinois-born children were in school, and from ages seven to twelve the figure was almost 85 percent. Of those born in Mecklenburg, almost all of the 7-12-year-olds went to school (or at least told the census taker they did). There were complaints about the school attendance of German-American children. At a board meeting of the Missouri Synod school of St. John's on the West Side, for example, the board members were not willing to tolerate ten-year-olds being taken out of school and put to work.[17]

Most Mecklenburgh children most likely attended neighborhood religious schools, which enjoyed rising enrollments in the 1870s and 1880s. New buildings were erected, new classes were created, and more teachers were hired. The congregation usually saw to it that the children of its church members attended the religious school; however, "non-believers" were accepted as well. Parents had to pay a small tuition fee. These schools more closely resembled Mecklenburger than American schools: religion and obedience were emphasized. Pupils were taught in German, and the faculty was usually male (unlike in the American public school system). Whether the religious schools encouraged higher education other than study for the ministry is doubtful. As late as 1944, the pupils of St. James's Evangelical Lutheran School showed a strong orientation toward engineering and crafts for the boys, and marriage and secretarial work for the girls.

---

[17] *First St. John's Evangelical Lutheran Church Commemorative Newsletter* (1942), 5.

In Chicago, adolescence, the time between age 13 and marriage, was vastly different from adolescence in Mecklenburg, where almost every young boy and girl would leave home at the age of 12 to serve on the local estate or work for another peasant household. Life in the city offered a variety of choices. Young people could continue to go to school through high school graduation, an option chosen by only 18 percent of these teenagers. By the age of 15, all of them had left school. They had the option of pursuing gainful employment (57 percent), or remaining at home to participate in household labor (25 percent); the latter option was taken up mainly by girls.

Why did so few girls and young women enter the paid workforce? Many were needed to help in the family business. For example, one father was a saloon keeper and employed his three daughters, ages 11–17, at no salary. Most of the other parents who supported non-wage-earning grown children were laborers (and they did not even have particularly large families, so help with housework would not have been an issue). Were these young women, half of them born in Mecklenburg, reluctant to enter the urban labor market or did their mothers and fathers keep them from doing so? The concept of the slatternly and flirtatious working girl in the urban factory may not have reached Mecklenburg yet, but it was as widespread in urban Germany as it was in urban America. Early social reformers tirelessly warned of the negative impact factory work had on the morals of young women. Rumor had it that factories were hot and men and women dressed sparsely to stay cool. Thus, women's purity was in constant jeopardy. Although the image was shown to be false by the turn of the century, parents in Chicago may have remembered the alleged dangers of factory work and been reluctant to allow their daughters to enter the labor market.[18]

Marriage and Married Life

Married women made up the largest group among the female sample population in the Mecklenburgers' neighborhood. They were

---

[18]See the debate between Paul Göhre, *Drei Monate Fabrikarbeiter und Handwerksbursche. Eine Praktische Studie* (Leipzig, 1891) and Minna Wettstein-Adelt, *Dreieinhalb Monate Fabrik-Arbeiterin* (Berlin, 1893); I thank Eva Schöck-Quinteros for this information.

most likely to be Mecklenburg natives. Three-fourths of all wives (75.2 percent) were born there, as opposed to 67.3 percent of all male heads of households; 61 percent of families had both marriage partners born in Mecklenburg. What marriage patterns were to develop in Chicago? The church registers of St. James's Evangelical Lutheran Church tell us when people from Mecklenburg married and whom they chose as mates. Through the years 1870–1875, 25–30 percent of the marriages at St. James's involved people from Mecklenburg. This percentage dropped markedly after 1880. From 1884 to 1886, Mecklenburgers constituted only 6 percent of the annual weddings, and from 1887 on, 10 percent. Most likely, there were fewer Mecklenburgers coming to Chicago and wanting to get married. Alternatively, they may have moved away to other parts of the city or lost interest in church weddings. Nevertheless, between 1870 and 1890, 305 Mecklenburg weddings took place in that church, 116 (38 percent) in the first five years.

Despite the high degree of endogamy which had existed in their native province, Mecklenburgers were willing to consider marriage partners from other parts of Germany. Most marriage partners came from Prussia, Pomerania, and Holstein, the Protestant areas of Germany. Between 1870 and 1875 only a third of marriages in our sample involved two marriage partners from Mecklenburg; in another third, the wife was born in Mecklenburg and the husband in another area in Germany; in the final third the husband was born in Mecklenburg and the wife in another area of Germans. Thus, for two-thirds of the Mecklenburger men and women marrying in Chicago it was not of vital importance to find a partner from their home province. This trend became even stronger as time went on. However, it remained important to marry another German; far into the 1880s, Mecklenburgers had very few non-German-born partners. Even second-generation Germans did not choose partners from other ethnic groups.

The average marriage age for the men during 1870–1875 was 27.4 years and for the women 23.2 (three years lower for both men and women than that of their peers in Mecklenburg). Eight percent of the men and 7 percent of the women, (many of them widows) were 40 years old and older. (These marriages were not included in the average.) Ten years later, the average marriage age had dropped still further (26.2 for men, 22.3 for women). Many of the women now married at the age of 18 or 19, and many of the men were only 22. The lowered marriage was the result of urbanization rather than acculturation, since the women and men were first-generation immigrants.

Another aspect of urbanization was the growing tendency toward peer group marriages. During the early 1870s, there were still women marrying younger men, a pattern preserved from rural societies, where property was a prerequisite for marriage and a widow with property could often count on finding a younger partner. By the 1880s in Chicago, such marriages had disappeared. Sometimes the groom who went to the pastor to have his marriage registered did not even know the date of birth of his bride; one gets the impression that age was not a very important consideration anymore.[19]

Once married, the Mecklenburg women in Chicago kept their family size under control. Unlike the German families of 1900 who lived in inner-city Chicago neighborhoods and who had an average family size of 5.7, these earlier German-American families were much smaller, with just over four to a household.[20] Women were obviously able to control the timing of their first child and decide how many children they wanted to bear. Eighteen percent of all households consisted only of husband and wife. These were not all "empty nests," nor were all the women very young: although the wives in 46 percent of these households were younger than 29, in 20 percent of the households they were between 30 and 39. Only a quarter of the women were older than 50, and therefore could fall into the "empty nest" category. Among nuclear families with children, in 1870, 56 percent had one or two children; 31 percent had three or four; and only 13 percent had five or more.

Tracing the daily activities of a married woman in Chicago is less easy than doing the same for her counterpart in Mecklenburg. We do have a rather well-founded historical sense of the development of American housework—the changes in its form, content and demands.[21] Yet it is difficult to connect these histories to the everyday

---

[19]Figures taken from church registers of St. James's Evangelical-Lutheran Church, 1870 to 1884) (microfilm collection, Newberry Library, Chicago).

[20]Harzig, *Familie, Arbeit und weibliche Öffentlichkeit*, 126f.

[21]See Susan Strasser, *Never Done: A History of American Housework 1870–1907* (Pittsburgh, 1989).

TABLE 5.4

17th ward: Household structure (sample), 1870

Household	N	Percent	N	Percent
Husband and wife families			71	18.6
Nuclear families			213	55.5
1–2 children	118	55.4		30.9
3–4 children	68	31.9		17.8
>5 children	27	12.7		7.1
Non-nuclear households			98	25.7
With servants	14	14.3		3.7
With elderly parents	25	25.5		6.5
With relatives and boarders	43	43.8		11.6
Single mother with child	10	10.2		2.6
Roommate households	3	3.1		0.8
Singles	3	3.1		0.8
Total			382	

Source: Analysis of the 1870 Census Manuscript.

lives of Mecklenburg women in Chicago in 1870. A few clues will have to suffice.

A family living in Chicago in the 1870s and 1880s was confronted with the dominant urban ideology that the husband should be the sole provider of the family income. It was completely up to him to support his wife and children and to provide for old age and times of crisis, illness, or unemployment. This situation was totally unfamiliar to people from peasant cultures. In Mecklenburg, the work of married men was only a portion of family labor. Old age was provided for by the employer, and unemployment did not occur in a society which had a specific place for everybody (and caused people to leave if it did not have a place for them or employment to give them).

Equally unfamiliar to Mecklenburg families was the American notion that "the employment of wives otherwise than in their domestic duties and the placing at labor of children of school age, must be subversive of the best interests of the family, as well as of doubtful expediency as a measure of economy."[22] In rural regions, children were expected to provide help to the family by working during harvest time and caring for the animals year round. Whenever a conflict between school and work arose, work took priority. Children had obligations to the family. How was the Mecklenburg immigrant family to resolve these conflicts between traditional rural culture and American middle-class urban society? Was the husband's income sufficient to provide adequately for the family? Did he need to make use of family resources to provide for the family's survival, or was the family to do without the wife's and children's labor to submit to prevailing ideology—and thus perhaps forgo the dream of owning their own property?

Only three of the 356 wives in our sample informed the census taker about gainful employment; two wives worked as milliners, and one was a washerwoman. In each case, the women had only one or two children to care for. Their husbands earned livings as a milliner, a butcher, and a tobacconist. Were other households able to go without an additional source of income?

Family Budget and Household Labor

In 1884, the Illinois Bureau of Labor conducted a study to find out whether Illinois families required the earnings of wives and children as much as families in other areas did. They compared Illinois statistics with those of England and Massachusetts, and found conditions in Illinois to be "gratifying as compared with conditions elsewhere." In Chicago, 26 percent of families had to rely in part on the earnings of family members other than men.[23] Native-born American men, only 19 percent of whose families relied on such income, were "more successfully providing for their own by their individual efforts than any other race." German-American families were next, with 21 percent.

Laborers, 36 percent of the Illinois work force, needed support from family members more often than did other workers. In 11 percent of laborers' families, the wife contributed additional income of

---

[22]Illinois Bureau of Labor Statistics, *Third Report* (1884), 268.

[23]Ibid., 268, 270. The figure was 27 percent for Irish families in Chicago and 32 percent for Scandinavian families.

$103 per year, and in 25 percent of the families, the children provided an average of $229 per year. Altogether, the average earnings of a laborer's family in 1884 amounted to $414.02. With yearly expenses of $388.38, there were potential savings of $25.64 per year. Obviously the average laborer himself, with a yearly income of $344.59, was unable to provide sufficient income for his average family size of 4.57.[24]

We know how superficial statistics can be. Figures on yearly average incomes never adequately reflect weekly income or reveal the problems involved in making ends meet. Unemployment, layoffs or strikes, sickness, or unexpected expenses could always wreck a carefully balanced family budget. At least these statistics make us realize how important the woman's household labor was. As in Mecklenburg, the more a woman could produce herself and the less she had to rely on cash and the market, the further she could stretch her husband's income. On the North Side in the 1870s, houses could still have a patch of garden, and families could keep some animals in a shed in the back of the lot. It may have been a matter of close calculation whether a woman should go out to work for a meager income or stay at home and wash, sew, cook, bake, and raise and preserve fruit and vegetables. Her labor also may have been needed in the family business, to raise young children, or to provide services for the "singles" in the community.

Few people in the sample community lived by themselves. Three people, two men and a seamstress, lived alone. In three other households, working people roomed together; and there were ten mothers who were heads of household. These nontraditional households made up 3.4 percent of all the households in the sample. All the other single men and women, younger sisters, single men with children, orphans, elderly aunts (and some uncles), and sisters who had no husband but who had children to care for resided in a household where a wife kept house.

For a woman "keeping house" often meant caring not only for her husband and offspring but also for members of her extended family and community who had no immediate family of their own. Of nonnuclear households (which included extended and augmented households as well as singles and mothers with children) 44

[24]Ibid., 274.

percent included other than immediate family members (not including servants), and 26 percent contained elderly fathers and mothers.
As for augmented households, the census does not reveal the precise
status of household members. Boarders could be anybody: sisters,
brothers, in-laws, nieces and nephews, fellow countrymen, employees. As long as the boarders contributed to the household budget and
made use of the wife's housekeeping services, the wife did not need
to distinguish between those who were relatives and those who had a
purely pecuniary relationship to the family. Families did not always
take in boarders for additional income. They felt obliged to provide
for extended family members or to give fellow Mecklenburg immigrants a temporary place to stay.

Most of these women were in what industry would call their
prime working age: between 20 and 40. Many women had three or
more children to care for in addition to relatives and boarders. Few
had babies, however, and only 19 percent had one or two children under the age of five. Of the households without children, half were
composed of couples who were at the beginning of their family cycle (wife younger than 29), and the other half of those at the end
(wife older than 40).

To German-American women, housework was important for female and ethnic identity. Toward the end of the century, feature writers for the women's page of a German-American bourgeois newspaper demanded better recognition for women's household labor.[25]
These women journalists advocated a healthy lifestyle with clean water, lots of fresh air and exercise, and the preparation of nutritious
food. In contrast to what they considered "American" attitudes, the
writers insisted that the housewife should take full responsibility for
the management of the household and the education of the children. They were distressed that American women were having fewer
and fewer children. The German-American woman as guardian of
her family was, across socioeconomic lines, a central aspect of ethnic
identity.[26]

---

[25]Harzig, *Familie, Arbeit und weibliche Öffentlichkeit*, 234–254.

[26]Christiane Harzig, "The Role of German Women in the German-American Working-Class
Movement in Late Nineteenth-Century New York," *Journal of American Ethnic History* 8 (1989):
87–107.

Old Age

During the nineteenth century, when the retirement age was not yet nationally prescribed, transition into old age was a process which occurred over some length of time rather than a stage that began with one's 60th or 65th birthday. Thus any attempt to determine transition into old age from the census manuscripts, which capture only one moment in time, is arbitrary. Nevertheless, some conclusions may be drawn, and the ability to uphold one's own household can serve as one indicator. Husbands and wives tried to maintain their own household as long as possible. From age 60 onward and at the latest when they turned 65, men gave over responsibility to their married sons and daughters or moved into other households as boarders. For women, the age of 61 seems to have been the date of transition. From that point on they did not "keep house" but "stayed home," as the census taker noted. They more often moved into their children's households. Of the 25 families who sheltered elderly parents, 18 (72 percent) had the household head's mother or mother-in-law living with them. In five cases it was the father or father-in-law, and in only two cases both parents were part of the son's household. But elderly widows not only moved into the household of their married children—they could also keep house for unmarried sons and daughters. By doing so, they maintained status as heads of households.

Of the ten households in our sample in which a single mother lived together with her children, only two contained young children. These women had to earn a living as washerwomen. In the remaining eight households, the women were 50 years of age and older, and all of their children were grown and working.

The loss of a man's status as head of household did not coincide with the loss of his ability to work. Though the men 66 years and older remained "at home," the 55-65-year-old men were still working.[27] Much like their younger countrymen, they were laborers or craftsmen, working as gardeners, carpenters, house movers, and shoemakers. Very likely they had established their own small busi-

[27]All of these figures are taken from my analysis of the 1900 census manuscript. See fn. 15.

nesses. Unlike the men in the Pittsburgh steel mills at the turn of the century, who were forced out of work when their physical strength declined, elderly German-Americans in the 1870s may have been sheltered from economic pressure by their relatively independent source of income.[28]

The building and maintenance of homes for elderly people became one of the most important issues among church congregations and nonreligious community groups during the last two decades of the nineteenth century. The homes provided a place to live for those old people who had no family to care for them and not enough savings to pay for private services.

Immigration and Family Crises

The census, perhaps because it captures just one moment in time, conveys a rather orderly family life. Household members seem to undergo an unhindered sequence in the life course. Deviations seldom occur in the families, and a sense of strong family cohesion comes across. Charity records, on the other hand, point to many domestic conflicts and crises. (How many families had to rely on charity for temporary help or long-term assistance is unclear, because no systematic account of the charity cases exists.)

The Chicago Relief and Aid Society, as close as any agency to a united charity organization, annually reported the number of cases treated over the years and the ethnic groups involved. The society was founded in 1857 to provide temporary aid to help people get back on their feet. People who needed long-term help, such as the elderly poor and disabled and permanently ill people, were sent to other institutions. The society made it a point to help people help themselves, and to prove its success it pointed out the declining number of cases over the years. The number of cases dropped from 9,700 in 1874 to 3,300 in 1879 and 1,600 in 1884. The many people who received aid

---

[28]Stefanie Kleinberg, *The Shadow of the Mills* (Pittsburgh: University of Pittsburgh Press, 1989), 237f.

in 1874 were most likely victims of the economic depression of 1873, in addition to the cases "left over" by the fire of 1871.[29]

During the years 1877-1895, the Irish, Germans, and Americans were most likely to receive aid from the society, accounting for three-fourths of their cases. Scandinavians were next most likely to receive aid. During the early 1890s, the number of Germans asking for help for the first time surpassed the number of Irish, reflecting the last great wave of German newcomers to the city. By the mid-1890s, Germans, Irish, and Americans accounted for only half of aid recipients.

There was supposedly a clear division of function between the Chicago Relief and Aid Society and another private charity, the German (Aid) Society. The first was responsible for all individuals regardless of ethnicity, and the second only for German newcomers. The German Society became the main point of contact for many Germans who needed support, however, whatever the length of time they had spent in the city. From 1883 to about 1910, the records indicate more than 10,000 support cases.[30] The main applicants for help during the years 1883 and 1884 were single men (31.4 percent) and married couples (41.5 percent). Large numbers of men asked for travel money either to return to Germany or to go to other places in the United States. Many had just arrived and probably met the agent of the society at the train station. They needed shelter for the night and a train ticket to move on. Others asked for more general support—money to buy food, fuel, clothing, or working tools or to pay a hospital bill. Very few single women requested aid, because their numbers were small: a mere two percent of women were not married, and only nine percent of them were widows. Some of these women also wanted to move on, a few to return home but most to

---

[29] *Twenty-Seventh Annual Report of the Chicago Relief and Aid Society to the Common Council of the City of Chicago: From October 31, 1883 to October 31, 1884* (Chicago, 1884). The society had been the major agency authorized to distribute immediate relief to victims of the fire of 1871 and to manage outside donations. In 1873, during labor protests against layoffs, the society was criticized because it refused to distribute the remaining Fire Relief Fund to needy working-class families. Bessie L. Pierce, *A History of Chicago* ([1938] New York, 1957) 3:241–242.

[30] On the German Society, see Keil and Jentz, *German Workers in Chicago*, 115–124; John B. Jentz and Hartmut Keil, "From Immigrants to Urban Workers: Chicago's German Poor in the Gilded Age and Progressive Era, 1883–1908," *Vierteljahresschrift für Sozial- und Wirtschaftsgeschichte* 68 (1981): 52–97.

visit or stay with relatives in northern Illinois and Wisconsin. Most of them needed family support if they were to survive.

One typical Mecklenburg couple, Carl P. and Fredericke B., had just arrived on October 3, 1884 with their three children, who were between one and five years old. All had been born in Letzteren (?).[31] They wanted to move on to another town in Illinois, and asked the German Society for some travel money.[32] Also in October 1884, a laborer from Mecklenburg-Schwerin asked the society for help in reclaiming his two children, ages eleven and fifteen, from the "Home of the Friendless." The children had been brought there two years before but had since been given to another family by the institution, and the father was denied further information about the whereabouts of his children. The German Society promised legal assistance.[33]

The agency's policy was to provide short-term help. People who needed long-term charity (orphans, the disabled, the aged) were sent to appropriate institutions, often those also supported by the German community. The cases involving women for the years 1883–1884 provide a glimpse of crises and conflicts in German immigrant families. Because the number of Mecklenburg cases is small, our analysis extends to all cases involving German women.

The illness of a family member very quickly exposed the financial precariousness of a working-class household. Case records reveal that it did not matter much whether it was the husband, the wife, or a child who became ill: medical bills always broke the family budget. If the man was unemployed, it was generally assumed that the wife or the older children took over financial responsibility for the household. The woman usually worked as a washerwoman or seamstress, either at home or in a sweatshop. In one family of eight in which the youngest child was three months old, the father, a laborer, had been sick for more than five years; the mother and oldest daughter were maintaining the family by sewing pants for 75 cents a day. The family

---

[31]Illegible in the document. There is a small town in Mecklenburg by the name of Letzentin, to which the entry might be referring.

[32]German Aid Society, case number 662, Special Collections, University of Illinois, Chicago Circle.

[33]Case number 661.

asked the German Society for financial aid to move their house.[34] If a mother were to burn her hands, not recover from her last pregnancy confinement, or be prevented by rheumatism from taking in more washing, rent was often unpaid, and eviction usually followed immediately. These families turned to the German Society for help, and most received a small amount of money after convincing the agent that the mother would resume work as soon as she was able.

Desertion was the leading problem which forced women to ask the help of the society. According to the case reports, many husbands left their wives maliciously, often stealing what little property was left or taking the last savings along. In these cases, physical abuse and excessive drinking were often involved. Some husbands left to search for employment. They would leave for a week, a few months, or years, to seek work in other parts of the country or to work on the railroad. Some of them disappeared without a trace. Others kept in contact with their families and sent money. Then suddenly the payments would stop, and the wife would have no idea where her husband was. In some of the cases, women could not or would not explain to the agent why their husbands had left.

The common denominator of these cases was that the men had left when a family crisis was imminent. Long periods of unemployment, alcohol abuse, an unwanted pregnancy, or the illness of a family member had made it difficult to maintain a decent family life. There was a fine line between willful desertion and provident abandonment. But whether the men left because of violent family quarrels, with the good intention of finding better ways of caring for their families, or to escape from depressing and crushing responsibility, the result was the same: the family was left in even worse shape. Many deserted women were pregnant and had to ask for support and a place to live. Others wanted a temporary shelter for their children, intending to take them back when their circumstances improved. Here the German community could help, and the children were usually sent to Ulich's Children's Home (a Protestant institution). Some women needed help because of sheer physical exhaustion.

Whether deserted or widowed, a mother had to provide for her family. In general, women who had been widowed for a long time

---

[34]Case number 101.

were working women, even if they had to care for many young children. They usually earned money by washing and sewing, and when they applied for help it was because some additional calamity such as illness had disrupted their precarious but manageable existence. Others needed emergency support because their husbands had died suddenly—often in an accident at work—and they were deprived of all support. They needed help to tide them over until they could provide for themselves and their children.

Society records give some idea of the problems faced by single women on the move. Anna I., a widely traveled teacher born in Vienna who had just arrived from New Zealand, needed money to buy decent clothing before she could apply for a position. She was sure to get a good job because she could teach English, German, French, and piano. She had been recommended to the society by Amalie von Ende, the renowned editor of the women's page of the *Illinois Staats-Zeitung;* von Ende had given her shelter.[35] This highly qualified but temporarily indisposed middle-class woman was the exception; other clients were less singular. A milliner who claimed she had learned her trade in Paris was now looking for a job. She had expected to meet friends in Chicago, but they had moved on. She needed some money to claim her luggage at the station and to tide her over.[36] Minna B. lost her job as a servant because she had felt ill and unable to work on that one day. The mistress of the household at least had the decency to recommend her to the society.[37] Kathy Z. was laid off from her job as a cigar maker and consequently was unable to continue to pay for room and board for her daughter and herself. The agent suggested that she seek shelter in the poorhouse until she could find work again.[38]

All of these working women were temporarily unable to support themselves. All convinced the agent of their worthiness (though some were pregnant with illegitimate children). Two other women, however, failed to qualify: one apparently had loafed around for two weeks without attempting to find work, another was judged by the agent as "finding little pleasure in working."[39]

---

[35] Case number 199.
[36] Case number 640.
[37] Case number 114.
[38] Case number 115.
[39] Case numbers 606, 697a.

Times of acute crisis show us how fragile existence was for German-American working-class families. Unemployment, unwanted pregnancy, illness, death, desertion, and alcohol abuse could plunge a family into destitution. These misfortunes were not specific to any ethnic group, nor to the urban environment. Alcohol abuse, family violence, and desertion were familiar to rural societies as well. The urban environment, however, did alter the manifestations and contexts of these problems. Moreover, the lack of extended family and community support systems left the victims more helpless and made them more dependent on public institutions. Though some could receive support from neighbors, in a working-class area, resources were slim. In this respect, all ethnic groups experienced similar problems.

The ways that ethnically organized charity institutions reacted, however, and the kinds of remedies they had to offer were often culturally specific. The German Society, like the many German-American women's groups that regarded charity work as one of their main functions, was discriminating about who was eligible for support. People had to be deserving, which meant showing no sign of social disorder and having come on hard times through no fault of their own. Irish (Catholic) institutions were less discriminating in distributing charity.

Women in Community Organizations

As the German-American community in Chicago expanded in the second half of the nineteenth century, so did German-American associations. In the 1880s and early 1890s, women contributed to the community in many different ways. Sometimes they participated with men in social organizations, benevolent and mutual support groups, and lodges. Seldom were they presidents or secretaries for these organizations, however. They also organized subgroups, such as the gymnastics societies and choirs, or they formed their own associations. Establishing their own sphere of influence and activities, separate from men, was the main incentive. The institutions, however, provided different levels of involvement for women. What follows are examples for a narrowly defined women's sphere on the one hand and a lively female public sphere on the other.

Churches

One of the most important but least studied institutions of community building among Germans in Chicago was the church. For immigrants from Protestant regions, the German Protestant denominations in the city provided the opportunity to attend religious service in a familiar atmosphere. The institution itself offered anything but continuity to the people who participated in it, however. Rather, it demanded constant adaptation to the American culture.

For more than 200 years, the two Grand Duchies of Mecklenburg had been Protestant, and since the unification of the Lutheran and the Reformed Church in 1817, the people had been raised in the Evangelical-Lutheran faith and had grown up under a state church. (Church and state had been de facto separated during the first years of the nineteenth century, but the Duke still remained head of the Protestant church in Mecklenburg.) Because the church was so closely intertwined with the power of the state—and therefore an element of oppression—many Mecklenburgers may have developed an indifferent if not negative attitude toward the church.

In the old country, church taxes were collected from everyone, and the churches and pastors were provided for by the state and the nobles, whether the people liked it or not. Without the church, life could not take its course because the pastor baptized, confirmed, married, and buried. The church was also responsible for the education of the village children, and often pastor and teacher were the same person. Mecklenburgers thus depended on the church. In Chicago, participating in a church congregation and living a religious life were wholly voluntary and entailed positive involvement.

The history of the German Protestant church in Chicago dates back to the late 1830s, but it was not until 1843 that the first Evangelical Reformed church building was constructed (at the corner of Ohio and Lasalle Streets).[40] It housed St. Paul's Evangelical Church. After a transition period, during which migrating pastors served the small congregation, Pastor C. August Selle from Ohio was hired in

---

[40]"Die protestantischen Gemeinden von Chicago," *Illinois Staats-Zeitung*, 21 April 1898, 41–48. On the history of German Protestant churches in Chicago see Sharvy Greiner Umbeck, "The Social Adaptations of a Selected Group of German-background Protestant Churches in Chicago" (Ph.D., diss., University of Chicago, 1940), chapters 1–3.

1846. By that time the congregation numbered 76 families. Upon the arrival of the pastor, a parochial school for 26 children was organized. In 1847, St. Paul's hosted the convention that was to form the "German Evangelical-Lutheran Synod of Missouri, Ohio and Other States." Although many Mecklenburgers were married and buried by Missouri Synod churches, they were not bound to these churches. In fact, they also joined the Evangelical Synod congregations, which more resembled the Prussian State Church. But the Missouri Synod became by far the largest Protestant denomination in Chicago; its churches spread all over the city.

Pastor Heinrich Wunder dominated the affairs of first St. Paul's Church for many years, and on December 12, 1909, he celebrated his 60th anniversary. Under his auspices, mission work aimed at the newly arriving immigrants became one of the main tasks of the congregation. Most of the work centered on organizing parochial schools. And between 1854 and 1870, six "daughter" congregations were founded.[41]

The establishment of new congregations as the city and the number of Germans grew always followed the same pattern. First, members of a congregation decided to erect a school building on the fringes of their geographical sphere of influence, giving members who lived farther away the opportunity to send their children to a German religious school. The building then provided a place for services during the week. German schools clearly served as an effective missionary device, attracting new members to the Missouri Synod

---

[41]Immanuel Church on the West Side came into being in 1854, and it was followed by Trinity Church on the Southwest Side in 1865. Another church on the West Side, St. John's (a congregation with a strong working-class clientele), dedicated its building in 1868. Most of these congregations published their history in commemoration of a special anniversary. The following account is based on these chronicles: First St. Paul's Evangelical Lutheran Church, *In the Service of Our Lord, 1846–1946* (Chicago), *Das sechzigjährige Amtsjubiläum des Herrn Pastors Heinrich Wunder. Prediger und Seelsorger der Ersten Evangelisch-Lutherischen St. Paulus Gemeinde zu Chicago, Illinois. Gefeiert am 12 Dezember 1909* (Chicago); *Kurze Chronik der Evangelisch-Lutherischen Immanuels-Gemeinde U.A.C. zu Chicago, Illinois 1854–1904. Zur Feier ihres Fünfzigjährigen Jubiläums am 25. September 1904.* (Chicago, 1904); *St. Martini Evangelical Lutheran Church 1884–1934* (including the origins of Trinity Church) (Chicago, 1934); *Einiges aus der Geschichte der Evangelisch-Lutherischen Zions-Gemeinde U.A.C. zu Chicago, Illinois, 1868–1918 zur Feier ihres Fünfzigjährigen Jubiläums am 13. Oktober 1918. Im Auftrag des Komitee verfasst von A. Kuring.* (Chicago); *First St. John's Evangelical Lutheran Church* (no place, 1942); *Geschichte der Evangelisch-Lutherischen St. Jakobi-Gemeide in Chicago, Ill. Auf Anordnung der Gemeinde zur Feier ihres fünfzigjährigen Jubiläums am Sonntag den 8. Februar 1920. Verfaßt von Karl Schmidt, Pastor der Gemeinde.*

congregations. When the congregation grew too large, members could vote officially to dismiss some member families so that the families could found a new congregation. Sometimes the new congregation was provided with generous gifts in the form of property or it received financial support during its first years.

It took an instinct for real estate development to determine the location of a new church. Often the building was erected not among houses but among the truck farms and fields. Only years later did the church steeple stand in the center of a neighborhood.[42] Then church members who were real estate agents steered fellow congregation members toward the newly developing neighborhoods. New congregations sprang up as the city expanded into the prairie, and old congregations often relocated their churches—a reflection of ethnic succession and the upward mobility of their members.

The development of St. James's was also dominated by the personality of a gentle and able pastor, W. Bartling, who served the congregation for 27 years. Starting with only 31 member families, the congregation began to build a church in 1871 on the corner of Fremont and Garfield avenues. That same year, it (barely) escaped the Fire and was able to give shelter to many who had lost their homes. The congregation also profited from the Fire because it expedited the settlement of the area north of North Avenue. In the 1880s, the congregation had grown large enough to hire an assistant to the pastor; a youth group had developed; and a meeting hall was built, housing a gymnasium and a library. Once again, members were released to form St. Luke's Church farther north.

School enrollment kept increasing at St. James's Church, and by 1883 nine male and two female teachers were teaching eleven classes. School tuition even brought a profit. In 1895, however, the congregation was almost crushed when the fraud of an accountant left the members with $25,000 in debts. It took twenty years for the congregation to recover financially and it was not until 1917 that they were able to replace the old building with a new and larger one. According to the congregation historian, the whole congregation competed in providing for the church's construction and furnishings. Well-to-do members donated parts of the altar, and the church women's group

---

[42]First St. John's, 4.

pledged to sponsor the interior decoration. In 1920, when the congregation celebrated its fiftieth anniversary and published its history, it had 306 voting members. During those years, its pastors had baptized 18,636 babies, married 4,307 couples and presided over 7,243 funerals. The congregation sponsored a male choir and a mixed choir, a youth group, and a women's group. Its school committee was responsible for two buildings, five teachers, and 310 pupils.

Many church constitutions of the Missouri Synod prescribed German as the exclusive language in which faith could be expressed. In the 1930s, the historian of St. John's Church on the West Side, considered this rule "shortsighted."[43] Shortly after the turn of the century, language became the subject of vehement argument. The first English-language services in the Missouri Synod were conducted in 1901, at first once every other Sunday, early in the morning or late in the afternoon; the main service remained in German. By the 1920s, the German service was pushed to the sidelines. The pace of language change was determined by church location and changes in the neighborhood, as well as by the appointment of pastors. Although every pastor was required to know German, if an Anglo-American pastor was hired, English was on its way in.[44] For St. James's, this process started very late: it published its history in 1920 (in German and set in Gothic type), and language was not yet an issue.

As this brief history of St. James's Church suggests, being a pious Protestant in Chicago differed immensely from being a Protestant under the state church in Mecklenburg. Committees for governing church affairs were unheard of in Mecklenburg. In Chicago, a body of voting lay members, respectable men who had to apply for membership and who were accepted only after careful selection, oversaw the congregation. The development of the congregation was directly related to the financial capacities of its members. Constant fundraising drives were necessary, a distinctly American trait to which members had to adapt. The Synod, the large unifying body that a congregation was a part of, was far away and seldom seems to have meddled in community affairs.

---

[43] First St. John's, 4.

[44] In 1875, St. John's hired the Canadian pastor Henry Succop. This church was the first to introduce English-language services.

Women in the Church

For women, the church also took on a new meaning. Although they still had very little say in church affairs and could not become voting members, they could influence church development.[45] In church histories, women appear as members of women's groups, as teachers, or as daughters of pastors. St. James's had one women's group that, as we have seen, aided in the construction of the new church. Nothing more is known of this group. In the St. Paul's congregation, they formed the Mary-Martha Guild, which supported male students who went to Concordia College and studied to become pastors.[46] Other congregations offered even more opportunities. St. Martin's, at 48th and Frazier Streets, had a "Ladies Aid" group whose main duty was to raise money; a *Jungfrauenverein,* whose membership was confined to single women and whose sole responsibility was to decorate the altar; and a sewing circle. Members pledged one full day per week to the service of the Lord. All of these women's groups came into being in the 1890s. After the turn of the century, there were also some mixed-gender groups.

Female teachers always had a precarious position in Lutheran schools. They were always the first to be fired, and they received a much lower salary than their male colleagues. In 1867, St. John's hired a woman "since no male teacher was available." She received $20 per month, whereas a skilled male worker earned $1.75–$2.50 per day. (A seamstress could earn 75 cents per day, or $22.50 for a full month's work.) A month later, when "the classes proved too large for a lady teacher," a much younger man was hired at $35 per month.[47] St. James's was no more enlightened about female teachers. The church hired women when the budget would not allow for a more expensive male teacher, and even then it preferred cheaper male students to a fully qualified female teacher. These women were fired immediately when the number of pupils decreased and two classes were combined. The school, solely supported by the

---

[45]Until 1940, women could not vote in Missouri Synod churches. Sharvy Greiner Umbeck, "The Social Adaptations," 163.

[46]First St. Paul's Evangelical Church, *Dedication Book* (Chicago, 1942), 19.

[47]*First St. John's,* 4.

voting and paying members of the congregation and by tuition fees had to be profitable.

Some daughters of pastors, it seems, gained a key function. The Missouri Synod selected its ministers and teachers carefully, and its congregations were by and large spared the negative effects of incompetent and fraudulent ministers. So, like the daughters of established craft masters under the guild system, the daughters of pastors were supposed to ensure the continuity of the trade. They often married men who became school headmasters or assistant pastors in a branch congregation. Influential pastors, besides installing their sons as pastors or teachers, thus constructed an extensive network of family relations. In placing relatives in influential positions, they could broaden their range of power and also help guarantee the integrity of personnel.

Granted, the church, and especially the German churches of the Missouri Synod, offered limited opportunities for women's involvement. Women's tasks were reduced to support, aid, and last-resort substitution. They were given complete freedom only to decorate, beautify, and raise money. And since the Missouri Synod showed very little interest in social reform and charity work, this important area of activity for women was not open to them. Women were barred from any kind of decision making about the congregation. Sometimes they were not even in full control of their own group. Although the St. James's women's group had a female president and vice president, it was often the pastor who first addressed their meetings and who suggested possible activities. Nevertheless, women came together to talk, and to get involved in community affairs, thereby transcending the confinement of the household. For some, spending one night a week away from home on their own may have been liberty they had to fight for. For women, church groups could be the first step outside the home.

Women's Groups

In other areas of German-American life, women were not only visible but also actively shaped community affairs. In 1898, for example, there were five female choirs, four women's gymnastics associations, 28 social groups and charity organizations, and 21 lodges with an exclusively German-American female membership.[48] Because women were as much divided by class and political leaning as the German-American community at large, this list is only an estimate. The bourgeois *Chicago Freie Presse* as well as the working-class *Chicagoer Arbeiter-Zeitung* would each list different names and numbers.

Women typically organized for social causes, including female advancement. For example, as members of women's auxiliaries in gymnastics societies, they were responsible for the social life of the group. They organized fund-raising parties and festivities to celebrate the victorious gymnasts when they returned from an out-of-town competition. They taught the sport to the young, and they fought for the organization of a girls' gymnastics group. For most women's groups, some aspect of charity work was the main reason for being, and often the groups wanted to combine the desire for social entertainment with work for a good cause. There were various ways to promote both, and the women had to be creative and inventive to convince the well-to-do to give. They organized evening entertainments, "Kaffeekränzchen," balls and dances, fairs, picnics, and excursions. The women's groups decided for themselves what charity cause they wanted to promote, and they found various ways to do so. The women of the "Gesellschaft Erholung" decided to support "very old women who were denied the privilege of being admitted to an old people's home because of lack of funds and who still had to work to earn their living despite their old age." The poor women often received a monthly subsidy for their rent. Widows and children were supported, as well as those families "who had temporarily lost their breadwinner because of illness."[49] Only the "deserving poor" received the benefit of the women's attention.

Members of the "Frauenverein Altenheim," on the other hand, were reluctant to distribute piecemeal alms to needy families. Rather, they wanted to create one great lasting charitable institution. This idea was considered a revolution in charity work by contemporary observers. As the name indicates, the women decided on an old people's home. This women's group had originated as a women's auxiliary to the German Society in 1878 and in the early 1880s became

---

[48]Jubiläumsausgabe der *Illinois Staats-Zeitung*, 21 April 1898, 63–64, 67.
[49]*Der Westen* (Sunday edition of the *Illinois Staats-Zeitung*), 21 March 1897.

an independent organization. Frauenverein Altenheim was so successful that, only four years after it was founded, the association had 500 members. In July 1885, the foundation stone was laid for the German Old People's Home in Harlem, a Chicago suburb. This institution became one of the most successful German-American charity endeavors and is still in existence today.

But German-American women did not only come together to do tangible good. In 1893, the "Columbia Damen Club" was organized. The founding members claimed they were "the first and only German women's association which promoted purely intellectual aims."[50] Originally these women had met to invite a representative of the bourgeois German women's movement—they had Helene Lange (the leading figure in the conservative bourgeois women's movement in Germany) in mind—to the Women's Temple of the Columbia Exhibition. They remained together and organized "literary, musical and declamatory performances." The club was exclusive: to become a member, one needed at least two references. The two female editors of the *Chicagoer Freie Presse*—one of them Dorothea Boettcher, an emancipated poetess from Mecklenburg—were among the club's leading figures. Thus, the women's page of that paper reported extensively on the club's activities. The club is still in existence.

Being an officer of the Frauenverein was a full-time job. The officers organized fund-raising events; set rules and regulations; developed an elaborate system of financial checks and balances; and organized a men's auxiliary—which was to report to them. Time and again, the women had to solve new problems and confront unfamiliar challenges. Even "ordinary" members had to deal with factionalism and in-group fighting and compete for funds with other organizations. And they had to accept work discipline. The club imposed a fine on any member who was late for a meeting. Through the daily activities of the organization, the women effectively learned to participate in the public sphere.

These women's groups were of great value not only to the women who participated but also to the community. They offered

---

[50]*Chicagoer Freie Presse*, "Der Columbia Damen Club," 18 March 1894.

opportunities for involvement and for leisure and entertainment. The great charity ball, for instance, originally organized in support of the old people's home, became one of the major social events for the German-American upper-middle class. German-American choirs could sing for the benefit of a charity cause; young ladies could demonstrate their artistic education; and businessmen could use their generosity for promotion and advertisement. In organizing charity work, the women's groups took over important social functions for all those who needed care and help, and they also offered points of contact where all Germans, whether they participated in the associational life or not, could meet and get involved beyond their own narrow interests.

Chicago's novel urban culture offered vastly different opportunities from Mecklenburg's. And it confronted Mecklenburg women not only with other ethnic groups but also with different images of women's roles. German immigrant women made hesitant and careful use of what the urban culture had to offer. They sent their children to school but also made use of the children's labor. Young women chose whether to work outside the home, and if they did, they relied on skills and jobs familiar to them. And they had greater choice in when to marry. Since no manorial lord governed their love lives, they married earlier. They seem to have postponed childbearing until later, however, possibly waiting until they could afford it. The wives, much as they had done at home, used their household labor to care for aging parents and siblings but now also took in employees of the family business and fellow German immigrants. Running a household in a city and within a cash economy demanded new skills. Sometimes hardship forced women to rely on institutional help. More often than not, they provided help to others. They actively shaped the social life of the German-American community. They started with the carefully controlled "women's room" of the church and later, participated in women's social organizations, where they exerted wide social influence.

The urban environment expanded opportunities, but it also narrowed activities and experiences. Managing a rural household required, for example, a knowledge of food processing and animal care, and it often demanded creativity to make use of meager resources.

Not all of these skills could be applied in the urban household. Life in the village was much less wearisome than has commonly been assumed. The city could not always make up for the pleasures, including immersion in nature, and the fun.

German women neither clung to tradition and drowned in the urban environment nor became flaming feminists. They chose what they felt was appropriate for them. If we perceive the peasant woman who decided to emigrate as a resourceful person who made use of her traditional knowledge, skills, and talents to organize life in the new environment, we will understand why acculturation in the urban environment was, despite problems and setbacks, often quite successful.

6

Making Sense
and Providing Structure:
Irish-American Women in
the Parish Neighborhood

Deirdre Mageean

From the 1830s onward, Chicago attracted Irish emigrants and quickly became a center of Irish immigration. Like emigrants from Mecklenburg, Dalsland, and Zaborów, women from Munster made not only a physical passage from rural society to a fast-growing city but also a psychological one.

By focusing on life in the parish community, we have been able to open a window on the lives of Irish women. We begin with the communities that helped define the women's worlds. Within these worlds we focus on marriage and family life; the work realities of the single women; and opportunities for educational, and hence social and economic, advancement. The extent to which these small worlds interacted with the larger public world is explored in sections on social problems and charitable work and the involvement of Irish women in labor unions. Finally, we see the ways in which Irish women adapted to the new urban culture.

The Irish Community

At the beginning of the twentieth century, the number of Irish-born in Chicago was 73,912—an increase of 34,000 (or 85 percent) from

1870. Although the Irish community was growing steadily, it was not increasing as rapidly as were other ethnic groups. In 1900, the Irish constituted 12.6 percent of the foreign-born population and 4.3 percent of the total. The Irish were outnumbered by the Germans, and the Scandinavians and Poles, although less numerous, were growing faster. As Michael Funchion has pointed out; "A minority in the city as a whole, the Irish were also a minority in most of the neighborhoods where they lived. In the decades following the Great Fire, most Irish lived on the South and West Sides; except for a small area on the near North Side, they were only sparsely settled in the northern sections of the city."[1] From settlements in the neighborhoods of Bridgeport, Canaryville, and Goose Island, the Irish spread throughout the southwestern part of the city. Very few Irish could be said to live in real ethnic ghettos: the 1889 school census revealed that the Irish were the most dispersed of ten major ethnic groups.

Nevertheless, distinct communities derived their sense of identity and unity from a common ethnic and religious heritage and from institutions such as church, schools, and politics. Of these three institutions, the Catholic Church was the most important in maintaining a separate Irish identity, and it was the parish that provided the basis for the community.

The Church that the immigrant knew was not an abstract community—it was local and concrete.[2] The parish served the needs of a particular neighborhood, and in Chicago the parishes of the Catholic Church were defined both by geography and language. Church services in territorial parishes were held in English, whereas those in national parishes were conducted in the immigrants' native languages.[3] The Irish constituted the vast majority of English-speaking Catholics and came to dominate the territorial parishes. The parish became the closest thing to an ethnic village for Chicago's Irish: they retained

---

[1]Michael Funchion, "Irish Chicago: Church, Homeland, Politics and Class—The Shaping of an Ethnic Group, 1870–1900," in Peter d'A. Jones and Melvin G. Holli, eds., *Ethnic Chicago* (Grand Rapids, Mich., 1981), 17.

[2]Jay P. Dolan, *The Immigrant Church: New York's Irish and German Catholics, 1815–1865* (Baltimore, 1975), 4.

[3]Of the 119 parishes that were established in the archdiocese between 1880 and 1902, 63 were national parishes, of which 24 were German and 18 were Polish. Fifty-six territorial parishes served the English-speaking Catholics, the majority of whom were Irish. See Rev. Monseigneur Harry Koenig, ed., *A History of the Parishes of the Archdiocese of Chicago* (Chicago, 1980), xv.

TABLE 6.1

Index of dissimilarity by wards, 1898

Russian (Jews)	67
Bohemian	64
Italian	61
"Colored"	60
Polish	59
Norwegian	55
Danish	43
Swedish	34
German	29
Irish	27

Source: Peter d'A. Jones and Melvin G. Holli, eds., *Ethnic Chicago* (Grand Rapids, Mich., 1981), 217; the Index of Dissimilarity measures similarity in the patterns of different birthplaces or ethnic groups. The derived index ranges from 0 to 100. The closer the value is to 100, the greater the degree of segregation or ghettoization.

their ethnic identity through the parish structure, and the parish became the center of community. As in Ireland, it served not just religious needs but, through schools and social and charitable societies, social needs as well. It also served their political needs, for Irish politicians established their power bases in the parishes. Over time, most Irish communities became parish centered.

Most important, the Church in general, and the parish in particular, provided a familiar structure and organization. Amid the array of bewildering experiences, the parish was a common link between old country and new. It also served to break down divisions within the community, be they factionalism from the Old World or political conflicts in the New World, and to impose a sense of unity. Finally, the church was instrumental in "Americanizing" the Irish and in facilitating their mobility.

Thus I use the parish as a basis to study the destinations of Irish women emigrants. Two parishes, different in location, history, and socioeconomic composition, were chosen: Holy Family parish, founded in 1857 in the 19th ward on Chicago's West Side and Visitation parish, founded in 1886 in the 30th ward of the South Side. Civil and religious records were used to put together a picture of the lives of first- and second-generation Irish women.[4] These records provide considerable insight into the socioeconomic conditions faced by many Irish female migrants. They also provide details on how both lay and religious women of the Irish communities organized to help their fellow countrywomen. These local records provide us with a "micro-picture"—the everyday lives of Irish women in their Chicago communities. Records and secondary data on political organizations, labor unions, and public movements, and the newspapers that served the Irish communities yield a "macro-picture"—the framework within which their lives were acted out.

Holy Family Parish

Holy Family parish, established in 1857 by the Jesuits, quickly became the largest English-speaking parish in Chicago. It also became what has been called "the single great Irish workingman's parish."[5] The parish was immense: original boundaries were Polk Street on the north, the south branch of the Chicago River on the east and south, and what was effectively prairie to the west (see map). The first pastor, the Reverend Arnold Damen, understood the connection between church and community, and he anticipated more emigrants would be attracted to the parish. He was correct: in the first three years of the parish's existence, there were 151 marriages and 1,462 baptisms. By 1867, the schools of the parish had 4,000 students enrolled.[6]

---

[4]The census enumerators' schedules from the 1900 census were used to derive information on household size and composition, occupation, literacy, infant mortality, and house ownership. Sacramental (i.e., baptism and marriage) records were used to establish marriage patterns and age at marriage. Other records, such as parish histories and the histories of voluntary societies, were used to obtain information on schooling, the general levels of education attained by the girls, and the number and type of societies contributing to the community life of the area. Of particular importance were the records of the charitable societies and institutions that helped the Irish migrants adjust to their new lives and cope with the many problems and misfortunes that befell them and their families.

[5]James S. Sanders, *The Education of an Urban Minority: Catholics in Chicago, 1833–1965* (New York, 1977), 91.

[6]Thomas Mulkerins, *Holy Family Parish—Priests and People* (Chicago, 1923), 26.

When the parish was established, the Irish immigrants who constituted the vast majority of the parishioners were poor. Most were
laborers and lived in frame shanties and cottages without running
water, plumbing, or heat. Irish Catholics were among the poorest
people in Chicago. Yet they managed to erect a church that cost
more than $100,000. The building of ornate churches was frequently
criticized in city newspapers, but church building actually created co-
hesive communities. Efforts at fund raising brought together members of a church. "Damen and his poor Irish congregation believed
that the building of the church was a matter of pride for Catholics
who lived in frame shanties. . . . Perhaps because of their poverty, the
parishioners were particularly sensitive to the need to create sacred
space."[7]

Much of the parish territory was swampland, with barely pass-
able roads. But people were drawn to the area by its church and
schools. Within a short time, numerous families lived in the vicinity
of the church. Property prices began to rise, and businesses grew.
Lumberyards and sawmills, railroad yards and grain elevators were
built and provided jobs for parish residents. Later, big industries—the
canneries of the Wilson Company, Libby, McNeill and Libby, and
P. D. Armour—developed. The packing houses provided benefits beyond employment to poorer families. For instance, the Cullerton
Packing House, located on the west side of 18th Street on the river,
used to place a large box outside the yard that contained low-grade
cuts of meat. Spare ribs cost as little as two cents a pound. One hundred pigs' feet (cruibeens, they were called in Ireland) could be purchased for fifteen cents. Many a poor family's table was supplied by
these "rejects."

As the community expanded, shops and small businesses, grocery, butcher, tobacco, dry goods, and furniture stores, appeared.
They were small family businesses, what we would now term "mom
and pop stores." Many grocery stores were a combination of saloon
and food outlets, like those of the small towns in Ireland. The saloon
was usually in the rear, and liquor, wine, and beer were served.

---

[7]Ellen Skerrett, "Whose Church Is It Anyway? The Battle for Holy Family, Chicago," *Com-
monweal*, 18 November 1988, 623; see also Skerrett, "Bricks and Mortar: Creating Sacred Space,"
Chicago Architecture Foundation (Chicago, 1989), 2–3.

These businesses, generally located on the corners of blocks, were centers for socializing and gossip. An example is the grocery business of Thomas and Mary McEnery. The McEnerys came to Chicago after the Famine from County Limerick in the province of Munster. Their store was a meeting place for the neighbors and a stopping place for Irish emigrants. Contemporary accounts note that the McEnerys influenced many emigrants from Limerick to come to Chicago and make their home in Holy Family parish. Upon arrival, immigrants were advised by the McEnerys how to make a start in life. Help was not limited to advice: many of the newcomers were assisted financially. The store also was a meeting place for the politicians of the district, and it was headquarters for the United Sons of Erin, a fraternal society.

Local retail services meant that the people of the area rarely had occasion to travel beyond the immediate neighborhood, which served to strengthen the sense of community. Not all shopkeepers were Irish; some were German, a few Jewish. Their success depended on how the store was managed and stocked and on what attention was given to the customers. Important, too, were the owners' contributions to community efforts, such as fund-raising activities, bazaars, plays, and concerts.

Toward the close of the nineteenth century, the area had become densely populated, and the value of the property had increased considerably. By 1881, a parish census counted 20,320 residents. This population consisted of 4,267 families, for an average family size of 4.76.[8]

Visitation Parish

The South Side of Chicago was settled early and heavily by Irish emigrants. Many had been attracted by the stockyards, and parishes quickly grew around Bridgeport and Canaryville. By the 1880s, the Irish had pushed further south, and considerable numbers were living south of 49th Street and west of Halstead Street. In the summer of 1886, the new parish of Visitation was founded in the territory bounded by 49th Street on the north, 55th Street on the south, Wal-

---

[8]"Our Religious Orders, The Jesuits in Chicago," 27 March 1875, St. Ignatius College Preparatory Archives, quoted by Ellen Skerrett in "Whose Church Is It Anyway?" 623–624.

lace Street on the east, and Center (now Racine) Avenue on the west. A major part of the area was swampland, and transportation was difficult.

Originally the church was built on Carpenter Street close to 51st Street, where most of the Irish had built their small cottages. This was in the vicinity of the stockyards, where the majority of the Irish earned their living. But the neighborhood expanded toward the south, contrary to expectation. The church was relocated, to the corner of 53rd Street and Sangamon. Much of the building work on the church and the parochial hall was done by the parishioners—again, a community effort that further strengthened the bonds of neighborhood. In the late 1880s, many young families moved into the area, some of them first generation but a significant number second generation.

During the next twenty years, the area grew rapidly. The World's Fair held in Chicago in 1893 attracted new residents, and some settled in the Visitation area. The establishment of schools in the mid 1890s added to the attraction of the parish. Over time the swamps, cabbage patches, and prairie land disappeared, and comfortable homes sprang up. The composition of the parish also gradually changed, becoming more middle class. As the parish historical record noted, "The people, industrious and hard working, were fast gaining a place in the commercial and civic life of the city."[9] Development along the boulevards provided improved housing, and the parishioners were reinforced by those Irish who exchanged cold-water tenements for steam-heated "flats."

By the last quarter of the nineteenth century, the Irish were becoming physically and socially mobile as newer ethnic groups began to replace them in unskilled jobs. Older, working-class Irish parishes were losing members. In the 1890s, for example, when Finley Peter Dunne was writing about life in the immigrant working-class area of Bridgeport, a significant number of the Irish had moved out and up.[10]

---

[9]Anonymous, *History of Visitation Parish, 1886–1936* (Des Plaines, Ill., 1936), 73.

[10]Finley Peter Dunne, the son of Irish immigrants, was born in Chicago in 1867. A journalist for Chicago's *Evening Post*, he created the fictional character of Mr. Martin Dooley, an aging barkeeper-cum-philosopher in the South Side Irish neighborhood of Bridgeport. In all, three hundred weekly Dooley columns appeared over the years, documenting for the first time in literature what life was like in an Irish ethnic neighborhood. See Charles Fanning, "The Literary Dimension," in Lawrence S. McCaffrey, *The Irish in Chicago* (Chicago, 1987), 98–145. The Bridgeport area, where the Illinois Michigan Canal began, was the first area in Chicago to be settled by the Irish.

Conditions in Bridgeport had ameliorated over the years, but it was still a poor area. Those who had improved their lot in life moved to places like Visitation.

> Going there was "moving to the Boulevard" and moving to the Boulevard was always seen as meaning you had "made it." You still were south of the stockyards, but you were in the two-flat areas, and you had trees. It wasn't immigrant housing. You could say to someone "I'm from Vis" and they knew exactly where you were coming from.[11]

Like Holy Family, Visitation was a parish and community built from scratch on the edge of the prairie. Both ranked among the largest English-speaking parishes in the city and were "success stories" in terms of pastoral and social organization, community spirit, and achievements of their schools. The differences between them lay in their communities. Although Holy Family did contain some well-off families, the majority of the residents were working-class, first-generation Irish. Visitation had a greater mix of first- and second-generation Irish, as well as from the lower middle and middle classes. By 1900, Holy Family had begun to decline, whereas Visitation was continuing to grow.

Marriage and Family Life

Economic changes in Ireland after the Famine were characterized by a deterioration in the status and condition of married women. Many young women rejected those conditions. What motivated Irish women to emigrate to the United States? If the reason for going to Chicago was to find a marriage partner, then the rational plan would have been to work hard and amass an attractive dowry and return home.[12] In fact, however, very few did. What they did do was replicate many of the features of married life that were prevalent in Ire-

---

[11]Ellen Skerrett, cited in Robert Cross, "Chicago's Irish: Swimming in the Mainstream," *Chicago Tribune,* 17 September 1978, 43.

[12]Hasia Diner, *Erin's Daughters in America* (Baltimore, 1983), 50.

land: high rates of nonmarriage, high age at marriage, and high fertility within marriage.

Marriage registers and the census enumerators' schedules provide some, though incomplete, information.[13] The parish registers were neither consistent nor comprehensive. (In this respect they contrast sharply with the rich registers for the Polish parishes.) Information on marriage partners was minimal until 1908. After 1908, more detailed information is available on place of origin (derived from place and parish of baptism), age, and whether both partners were Catholic (a dispensation had to be acquired for a Catholic to marry a non-Catholic in a Catholic church). After 1908, the registers of both parishes recorded place of baptism, although sometimes merely as "Ireland." Only Visitation's register consistently recorded age.

A sample of fifty-six marriages in which at least one partner was Irish born was extracted from the register for the years 1908 through 1911. The median age for women is 25, for men 28. Only one woman was under 20 and only one over 35. For men, the age range was 22–41. These ages at marriage are lower than ages in Ireland at the time but higher than the American average.[14] The age at marriage found here may suggest some adaptation to the urban American norm, but it may also reflect the greater opportunities of the Chicago marriage market.

Both registers reveal high endogamy—a pattern as typical for the Irish as for any other ethnic group in the United States. Part of the reason may have been religious, but cultural factors were probably more important. After all, an Irish woman could have chosen from among the many Germans and the increasing numbers of Poles and Italians. But lack of social intercourse with these groups and language difficulties, as well as distrust or distaste for intermarriage, seem to have kept exogamy to a minimum. All but one of the cases of intermarriage involved non-Catholics, and of these intermarriages, only

---

[13]The marriage registers are held at the Archives and Record Center of the Archdiocese of Chicago. I am grateful to John J. Trainer, archivist, for permission to have access to the registers and to Timothy Slavin, associate archivist, for his help.

[14]In 1861, the mean age at marriage in Munster was 31.6 for men and 27.6 for women. James Donnelly notes that by 1891, only 5 percent of married women in Cork were under 25. See *The Land and People of Nineteenth Century Cork* (London, 1975), 221. Janet Nolan cites a marriage age of over 29 for women in Ireland during the 1880s. Janet Nolan, *Ourselves Alone: Women's Emigration from Ireland 1885–1920* (Lexington, Ky., 1989), 13.

one involved a non-English speaker (a German). The other partners were English, Scottish, and Canadian. In all cases (1 of 59 marriages in Visitation and 4 of 68 in Holy Family), the woman married outside the group—again, a characteristic exhibited by Irish women throughout the United States.

Even more striking, partners were from the same county and even the same parish in Ireland. In Visitation, just under a quarter of the fifty-nine marriages were between people from the same county, and half of these involved people from the same parish. In Holy Family, the rate was lower, 13 percent from the same county and 8 percent from the same parish. There is evidence of similar behavior in other communities.[15] As people from certain Irish counties became concentrated in certain neighborhoods and as the extent of chain migration from towns and villages in Ireland increased, men and women from the same area would meet in the Irish neighborhoods of Chicago.

Although the sample is small, it does provide us with some insights into marriage patterns among first-generation Irish women in the city. It seems safe to assume that the majority of Irish women married within the Catholic Church. For one reason or another, however, some married outside the church. Evidence comes from the register of another parish in the north of the city, where several pages document marriages of couples who had originally married outside the church to non-Catholics or who married in civil ceremonies. In some cases, the couples had been married for ten years or more. These entries may have been the result of the parish mission to return to the fold those who had left, or no longer attended, the Church because of marriage outside the Church.

Sacramental records give us details on selected vital events, but a more comprehensive picture of family life comes from the census enumerators' schedules. The following results are from a sample of 334 households drawn from wards 19, 23, 24, and 30 of the 1900 census.[16] As Table 6.2 shows, the majority of households in the sample

---

[15]Nolan, *Ourselves Alone*, 76.

[16]A sample of one in every five Irish households was drawn from the schedules of the 1900 census for wards 19, 23, 24, and 30, which broadly covered the territories of the respective parishes. The sample of 334 households contained 1,715 people: 856 females and 859 males.

TABLE 6.2

Household type, 1900

	N	Percent
Individual	6	1.8
One-parent family	43	12.9
Married couple, no children	22	6.9
Nuclear	201	60.4
Extended, with kin	47	14.1
Boarding house	14	4.2
Total	333	100

Source: Census Manuscripts, 1900, wards 19, 23, 24, 30 (sample based on one in every five Irish households).

(60.5 percent) were nuclear families. The remainder is composed largely of variants, most notably extended or multiple-kin households and households where only one parent is present. In the latter cases, the households are largely headed by widows. Overall, female-headed households constituted 16.5 percent of all households, a high figure compared to figures for other ethnic groups but comparable to those for the Irish in Philadelphia and Buffalo.[17] These figures are testimony to the high incidence of widowhood (13.8 percent) and desertion among Irish women.

Several households (13.8 percent) contained boarders, which may help account for the somewhat large mean household size of 5.08.[18] Represented in the households is a mix of first- and second-generation women. Of the 260 wives, 56.15 percent were born in Ireland, 18.46 percent in Illinois, and 15.8 percent in other American states. Of 439 daughters, 82.7 percent were born in Illinois, 7.3 percent in Ireland, and 5.9 percent in various areas of the United States. The low numbers of daughters born somewhere other than in Ireland or Illinois indicates that step migration of families was rare. Among

---

[17]Diner (*Erin's Daughters*, 61) quotes figures of 16.9 percent among the Irish in Philadelphia and 18 percent among the Irish in Buffalo.

[18]The mean household size is 5.08. In the case of this sample, the mean was affected by a "tail" of large households. Both the median and modal household size was 4.0.

the most notable differences between first- and second-generation women is their pattern of fertility. The average household size of first-generation women was 5.65, compared to 4.77 for the second generation. First-generation women bore an average of 4.4 children, with 3.3 children surviving, compared to an average of 3.4 children with 2.5 surviving for second-generation women.[19] The average age at marriage, twenty six, was the same for both groups.

The census returns support the view that very few married women worked outside the home, although participation in the labor force was probably higher than was reported. No occupation was recorded for 93 percent of the wives. Five percent were recorded as engaged in housework, and only 1 percent as working outside the home. But these women were not economically inactive. Taking in boarders and lodgers was a common practice, and the income contributed to the viability of the household. The practice was particularly strong among widows, although census enumerators did not necessarily record their occupation as boarding-house keeper. Of the 55 female heads of household in the sample, no occupation is recorded in 74.5 percent of cases. Overall, the number of Irish working wives appears very low in Chicago.

The Irish discouraged married women from working outside the home. Beyond cultural constraints, there were also practical difficulties: what to do with children under school age was a major problem for working mothers. Many women resorted to locking their children in their homes during working hours. Often this resulted in tragic accidents, including fires. Partly in response, the Catholic Women's League set up some badly needed day-care centers, although none were in Irish neighborhoods. Around the turn of the century, the league sponsored three centers: St. Elizabeth's at 906 North Franklin Street, St. Mary's Settlement at 656 West 44th Street, and St. Anne's at 710 South Loomis Street. All had strong ties to other ethnic communities—St. Elizabeth's and St. Mary's to the Polish

---

[19]The 1900 census records both the number of children ever born to a woman and the number still living at the time of the census. Hence it is possible to compute a crude estimate of child mortality. Since the average age of first-generation women in the sample (37.6) is older than that of the second-generation (33.9) women, however, there is a greater probability of mortality among the children of the first-generation women.

community and St. Anne's to the Italian community. Even St. Columbkille's at North Paulina Street, despite its Irish name and the Irish nuns who operated it, catered mainly to non-English-speaking families.

The one day nursery that did cater to Irish working mothers, Benton House at Sullivan Court in the Bridgeport area, was non-Catholic. In this poor working-class neighborhood near the stockyards, just under half the clientele were Irish (the rest were Polish, Italian, and Lithuanian), testimony to the changing ethnic complexion of the area. The nursery was run by the Women's Auxiliary, under the auspices of the Board of Mission of the Episcopalian Church. During 1911, thirty-two families used the nursery regularly, and twenty-one used it occasionally. Most of the women worked in laundries, restaurants, and shops, and their average wage in 1911 was $6.66 a week. The nursery charged 5 or 10 cents a day depending on circumstances, but for many even 5 cents was too much. The nursery took pride in never turning a child away. The day was long: the nursery opened at 6:00 A.M. and closed at 7:00 P.M. The annual report of the nursery gives a good indication of the circumstances of the women who used its services:

TABLE 6.3

Women leaving their children at a nursery

	N	Percent
Widows	15	28.3
Deserted wives	13	24.5
Unmarried mothers	7	13.2
Divorced	1	1.9
Women whose husbands are ill	3	5.7
Women whose husbands are in prison	4	7.5
Women whose husbands are habitual drunkards	3	5.7
One case of man in prison, wife dead	1	1.9
Families partly supported by husbands	6	11.3
Total	53	100.0

Source: Report of Benton House Nursery, 1911–12, Chicago Historical Society.

Centers such as Benton House and those run by the Catholic Women's League provided more than a safe place for children during the working day. Many gave mothers advice on nutrition, hygiene, and housekeeping and also served as a medical referral and general counseling agency for mothers.

Low employment among married women, along with high widowhood and desertion, placed Irish women in a very vulnerable situation. For women who were widowed or abandoned or whose husbands were unemployed, sick, or in jail, working was a necessity. The alternative was to turn to charitable services—an option that many a widowed or deserted mother had to pursue. Records of the St. Vincent de Paul Society show that most cases of relief to families arose from the temporary or long-term unemployment of husbands, sometimes compounded by drunken and abusive behavior. Unemployment and desertion often accompanied each another. The husband would leave the city to look for work elsewhere, leaving the family destitute and facing eviction.[20] The Conference reports for 1915 are filled with such cases as the following:

> Br. _____ reported that Mrs. _____ called at the central office stating that her husband left with 6 other men for St. Louis looking for work and that she had no money. President K. reported that Fr. McDonald had phoned to say that Mrs. C. of E. Ohio Street had called at the rectory, and stated that her husband was away looking for work and her landlady was putting her out. One of the officers called and persuaded the landlady to keep her on, paid some rent and gave Mrs. C a grocery voucher.

Frequently such cases led to the splitting up of the family:

> President K. reported that 3 of the F. children were sent to St. Mary's training school and the Chicago industrial school through the Juvenile Court, and Mrs. F. and the two younger children were placed in St. Vincents. The last heard of Mr. F. was somewhere in the Dakotas.

---

[20]A good description of the situation faced by such women is given in the story of the Casey family in the novel by Clara E. McLaughlin, *Just Folks* (New York, 1910), which is set in the area of Holy Family parish.

The records refer to two other deserted mothers who were forced to place children in care while they worked (one at St. Elizabeth's Day Nursery, the other at the St. Francis of Rome House on Washington and State street). Other women had to resort to longer-term placement of their children: "Mrs. C. has received notice from her landlord several times to move. She has but a little furniture—wants to store it and place the children so she can go to work. She had been working in a restaurant in the Gas Building but had had to quit it."[21]

The difficulties facing these women were enormous. If they did not work, they and their children faced eviction and starvation; if they did find work, they faced the problem of what to do with small children. If the children were sick, the women faced the loss of wages or being laid off. Nor were the wages generous: working in a wholesale grocery store brought in $7 a week, and piece work such as putting labels on bottles paid $8 a week. It is easy to understand why many married women remained at home and earned income by taking in laundry or boarders.

Female Urban Culture

Single Women

For single women, the work situation was different. They had relative autonomy, and their employment decisions were not directly influenced by the needs of dependents. The employment of single Irish women in Chicago mirrored the national profile. The women were concentrated in and dominated professions such as domestic service, restaurant work, teaching, sales, clerical work, and textile manufacturing. By far the most important professions in Chicago at the beginning of the century were domestic service and waitressing.

In 1900, almost a third of female servants and waitresses of foreign parentage were Irish. Irish women led in total number, although other women of foreign descent (such as Swedish, Norwegian, and

---

[21]St. Vincent de Paul Society Collection, Archives of the Catholic Archdiocese of Chicago, Chicago.

Danish) had a higher percentage of female breadwinners employed as servants and waitresses.[22]

Domestic service was popular among Irish women because it was an extension of their traditional domestic skills. Prospective Irish migrants were able to hone these skills either in domestic service in Ireland or through the training offered by the national and vocational schools. Few Irishwomen had the culinary skills and experience, however, for upper-middle-class homes in America. American families could not afford to be choosy. Domestics were in short supply, which many domestics realized and used to their advantage. Native-born American women scorned domestic service, but Irish women took the jobs in preference to factory work. Domestic service paid reasonably well, provided accommodation and uniform, and gratified a taste for civilized living. It allowed women to send for their relatives in Ireland and to save sufficient capital for marriage.[23] Clearly, domestic service had its drawbacks: domestics had little time off from duties, and they were often isolated and lonely. For first-generation women, the main benefit was steady employment. As soon as they could leave the work, however, they did. Among first-generation women, widows and deserted wives sought employment not in domestic service but in the industrial sector. The latter group usually could not accept domestic work because they had care of children and because domestic workers were required to live with their employers. Factory work provided a manageable option.

Education

In contrast to the first generation, second-generation women made their way into professional occupations, such as teaching and nurs-

---

[22]U.S. Department of Commerce and Labor, Bureau of the Census, *Statistics of Women at Work, Based on Unpublished Information Derived from the Schedules of the Twelfth Census, 1900* (Washington, D.C., 1907), 47–48. Among female breadwinners 10 and older, 30.8 percent of Irish, 56.4 percent of Swedes, 47 percent of Norwegians, and 44.1 percent of Danes were employed as servants and waitresses.

[23]Kerby Miller argues that domestic service allowed Irish women in America to save the capital equivalents of dowries so that they could attract the most promising Irish immigrant males available and secure the status and authority of Irish-American homemakers. See Kerby Miller, "For Love and for Liberty: Irishwomen, Emigration, and Domesticity in Ireland and America, 1815–1920" (paper presented at New York University, 5 November 1992). Miller argues that Irish women wanted both economic opportunity and domestic bliss in America and that they viewed the successful appropriation of the former as the key to the latter.

ing, and into skilled office work and sales. Their social mobility was achieved through education, particularly through the parochial schools.

By the 1890s, approximately 95 percent of the Irish entering the United States were literate. The value placed on education in Ireland was amplified in America. The first priority of new parishes was to build a church, the second was to build schools. Pastors provided for schooling as best they could, which often meant crowded classes in church buildings and converted houses. As a result of inadequate space, many children attended public schools, even though the curricula contained specifically Protestant religious instruction. Catholic parents and clergy saw the curricula as nothing short of proselytizing; they worried that the children's faith would be undermined. Both parents and clergy wanted education for the children, but they wanted it conducted in an environment with which they were comfortable. "Parochial schools represented a means of preserving the past and of planning for the future."[24]

Some parishes, by dint of extraordinary organization, managed to build impressive school systems. The most successful example is Holy Family parish. To cope with the demand for schools, Reverend Damen managed to recruit teaching orders to supplement his own Jesuits. In 1860, the Ladies of the Sacred Heart opened their school for girls on West Taylor Street; the initial enrollment was two hundred. Holy Family School, a school for boys, was opened the same year. The school, which was run by lay teachers, educated an average of 1,500 pupils a year during 1865–1880. The Sisters of Charity of the Blessed Virgin Mary came in the 1860s, and in 1867 St. Aloysius School (for girls) opened. In 1868, St. Ignatius College was founded, and the first classes were held in 1870. In 1874, Guardian Angel School was opened for children under twelve, and in 1878 St. Joseph's School was completed.[25] Enrollment figures for 1877 indicate that just three of the five schools were educating 27 percent of all the children enrolled in Catholic schools in Chicago.[26]

---

[24]Timothy Walch, "Catholic Education in Chicago: The Formative Years 1840–1890," *Chicago History* 7, no. 2 (1978): 92.

[25]Mulkerins, *Holy Family Parish*, 151.

[26]Walch, "Catholic Education in Chicago," 90.

Few parishes could hope to succeed at the same level as Holy Family; still, the school became a model for other parishes to emulate. Parishes such as Visitation followed Reverend Damen's example of bringing in nuns from teaching orders, and many schools survived because the nuns received only room and board. Many of these religious orders included a majority of Irish-born women in their ranks. They were influential figures for young Irish-American girls; they also recruited future nuns from the parishes they operated in. They were responsible not only for the upward mobility of Irish women but also, in the long run, for Americanizing them. For Poles and Germans, parish schools were means of sustaining the language and cultural traditions of their homelands. In contrast, Irish nuns did not transmit Irish culture. Indeed, "they had difficulty distinguishing between the specifically Irish and specifically Catholic aspects of their lives."[27] As a result, the parochial schools in Irish parishes differed little in curriculum from the public schools, although they did include religious instruction and taught within a specifically Catholic tradition.

American Catholic nuns inherited a tradition of female education that was centuries old. Although they did not neglect the teaching of boys, they invested disproportionate effort in educating their own sex. Among the Irish, the nuns encouraged females to continue education and train for the professions. This promotion of female education does not appear to have been specific to the Chicago Irish, although it was in Chicago that the first girls' Catholic high school was founded.[28] The three study parishes had a disproportionate number of girls attending school.

The situation reflects not only differences in aspiration and encouragement between boys and girls (for instance, boys were sent to work at an earlier age) but also the costs of education. Whereas some schools for boys (such as St. Patrick's Academy) were instituted

---

[27]Thomas N. Brown, *Irish-American Nationalism, 1870–1890* (Philadelphia, 1966), 34.

[28]In the absence of comparative figures on the educational levels of Irish girls for different cities or regions of the United States, it is impossible to say how typical the situation in Chicago was. In 1900, the national figures show that school attendance among girls with Irish fathers surpassed that among daughters both of American-born and of all foreign-born fathers. See Nolan, *Ourselves Alone,* 81.

TABLE 6.4

School attendance in Catholic high schools

	Boys	Girls
Holy Family Parish, total	1,478	1,710
Holy Family	425	305
St. Agnes	231	253
St. Joseph	486	463
Sacred Heart	189	573
Guardian Angel	127	116
Visitation Parish, total	375	470

Source: *Annual Reports of Holy Family and Visitation Parishes, 1900–1903,* Local archives of the archdiocese, Chicago.

specifically for boys with little means, Catholic high schools for boys were expensive. For girls, however, convent academies (such as Sacred Heart in Holy Family parish) subsidized free schooling, through tuition paid by wealthy parents.

The nuns were able to adopt this strategy because non-Catholics, attracted by the good academic results and reputation, sent their children to the Catholic academies. The nuns instilled middle-class values and catered to increasingly middle-class aspirations. The success of their efforts can be seen in the number of pupils who later went into teaching and nursing. By the turn of the century, the majority of female teachers were graduates of Catholic high schools, and they formed the majority of teachers in the city's public schools. So great was their dominance that at one stage the superintendent of the Normal School, Ella Flagg Young, attempted unsuccessfully to limit their numbers. Nursing was similarly influenced. The Mercy Nuns, through their training and teaching hospital, Mercy Hospital, recruited large numbers of Irish-American girls to enter nursing.

Nuns' investment in the education of Irish women and their daughters was a major factor in the economic success of women compared to men. By 1900 in Chicago, 8.5 percent of first- and second-generation Irish women were in the professional occupations, compared to 4 percent of the men; and 25.2 percent of women were white-collar workers, compared to 16.6 percent of the men.[29] Education may have helped retain the Irish pattern of lower marriage rates and higher age at marriage. The higher educational and economic success of women may have made it more difficult for them to find suitable marriage partners within their own ethnic group.

Finally, the nuns recruited for their own ranks. The annual reports and histories of the parishes list with pride the number of vocations from their parishioners. They list impressive numbers of priests, but the number of nuns is even higher. At a time when Irish women were pursuing independence and rejecting what married life offered (including high rates of widowhood, desertion, and abuse), the religious life appeared attractive. As Eileen Brewer remarks: "Convents offered their members power, respect, and a significant occupation. . . . Religious life also freed women from the probability of subordination to men in marriage, the pain and danger of childbirth and the drudgeries of domestic duties required to maintain a family."[30]

By offering education, serving as role models of independence and power, and demonstrating the importance of women helping women, religious orders influenced generations of Irish-American women. That influence can be seen in the fraternal, benevolent, and union organizations run by Irish and Irish-American women to help their fellow countrywomen.

Social Problems and Sources of Help

The Famine emigrants of the 1840s were ill equipped to face such problems as poverty, poor health, unemployment, and homelessness. Thus, Catholic immigrants defined social reform as carrying out the corporal works of mercy to the poor, the hungry, and the homeless. They viewed these works as charity, not as social change.

---

[29]See Funchion, "Irish Chicago," 33. The Chicago figures are similar to the national figures for 1900, which show 6.6 percent of Irish women in the professional services, compared to 3 percent of the men. See Pauline Jackson, "Women in 19th Century Emigration," *International Migration Review* 18, no. 4 (1984): 1008.

[30]Eileen Brewer, *Nuns and the Education of American Women* (Chicago, 1987), 18.

Throughout most of Chicago's history, Catholic women—both lay and religious—were major figures in benevolent work. They cared for the poor and disadvantaged in general and for women in particular. Priests recognized the need for aid among their parishioners, but it was nuns who responded. As one contemporary has remarked, many priests were better at preaching about charity than doing anything about it.

Women's Religious and Charity Work

Outstanding among the religious orders were the Mercy nuns. In their institutions they looked after the sick, the disabled, the orphaned, the deserted, and the indigent. In addition, they trained other women as nurses, teachers, and (eventually) social workers. The founder was Catherine McAuley, an upper-middle-class Dublin woman who inherited a sizable fortune and, in the mid 1820s, founded a kind of social service center. The center operated as a school for poor and working girls and a refuge for orphans and unemployed servants. (McAuley's original intent was to establish a group of female Catholic social workers). Fortuitously, in 1846 the Sisters of Mercy came to Chicago at the request of a Bishop Quarter, and they laid the foundations for many charitable and educational institutions. These nuns took over operation of the center and expanded the kinds of aid offered. They adopted a rule by which to live and evolved into a religious order, which was formalized in 1831. They had no central government and instead were organized on a diocesan level; hence they were under the authority of the local bishop. This arrangement made the sisters attractive to bishops who needed help in their dioceses. The sisters visited the sick in their homes and prisoners in jail; they opened the first five parochial schools, the first night school for Catholic adults, the first convert class for adults, the first orphanage, and the first academy; they took over the care of the sick in Chicago's Alms House; and they erected and maintained Chicago's first permanent hospital. They also founded Catholic girls' high schools, the first working-girls' home, the first Catholic training school for nurses, the first Catholic women's college, and the first Magdalen asylum for troubled young women.

Not until 1856, ten years after its arrival, was the Sisters of Mercy joined by any other order of nuns. By 1896, when the sisters celebrated their golden anniversary in Chicago, they numbered approximately 225. The majority of the sisters were first- and second-generation Irish and they recruited within the Irish communities, where they were always visible through their schools and charitable organizations.

The second major group of nuns to work in Chicago was the Sisters of Charity of the Blessed Virgin Mary, an order that was founded in Dublin (as was the Sisters of Mercy). Four young women lived together as a community and opened a small school. They had come to America in 1843 in response to the need for religious instruction among the children of Irish immigrants in Philadelphia.[31] In 1844, Sister Eleanor Hurley entered the order, and in 1867 she was called to found a branch of the order in Chicago. By 1923, the nuns ran twenty-four grammar schools and two high schools. The nuns' arrival in Chicago was a direct result of a request from Reverend Damen, the pastor of Holy Family parish. His belief was that they would be ideal for teaching the children of Irish immigrants. In fact, their mission was not only to instruct girls in knowledge of religion but also to provide them with "useful knowledge" and to prepare them to be good members of society. They opened the first central Catholic high school for girls in the country, and like the other female teaching orders they encouraged girls to aspire to skilled and professional jobs.

Other orders contributed: the Little Sisters of the Poor opened a home for the indigent elderly, and the Sisters of the Good Shepherd ran both an industrial school for girls and a home for women who were delinquent or who had been sexually exploited. Freed from many of the traditional constraints on women, nuns could pursue active involvement in areas that at the time were considered unsuit-

---

[31]One year after the formalization of the order in 1843, the nuns responded to an appeal to establish a school in Dubuque. At that time, the diocese comprised the entire territory of Wisconsin and the northern part of Illinois. Dubuque eventually became the mother house of the order, and from there the order spread into Chicago and other parts of the Midwest. For more on these orders, see Deirdre M. Mageean, "Catholic Sisterhoods and the Immigrant Church," in Donna Gabbacia, ed., *Seeking Common Ground* (Westport, Conn., 1993), 89–100.

able for women. They could also carry out social works without being branded female busybodies who should be tending to their own homes.[32]

Although they cared for the community in general, they were particularly sensitive to the needs of female immigrants. They provided homes for working girls and offered them night classes, cared for sick and indigent women, and offered shelter to abused and deserted women and their children. They also provided much-needed maternity services for women with little or no means. They looked after unmarried pregnant women who came to the city, caring for them during their confinement, helping with the birth, placing the children in homes. To immigrant women, the nuns were familiar figures from the homeland. Because the nuns were Catholic no religious boundary was crossed, and because they were women no gender boundary was crossed.

Female support in Chicago was not confined to religious groups. Lay women, particularly in the middle classes, were active in charitable organizations and in caring for other women. The main lay Catholic charity in Chicago (as elsewhere in the United States) was the St. Vincent de Paul Society, which operated at a parish level and therefore was sensitive to particular community needs. It was, however, all male, and in fact did not admit women until the 1960s. It was oriented toward families but declared that widows were just as important as orphans. A fundamental rule of the society was that the poor and needy should be visited in their own homes. The records show that families, widows, and deserted and abused wives constituted the bulk of their cases. Many cases involving women were referred to services provided by the nuns. The society members were known and supported by the local community, and they did

---

[32]The phrase "female busybodies" was used by the Catholic archdiocesan newspaper, *The New World,* in an attack on the social reformers at Hull House (a settlement house in Chicago), whom it condemned as "feminine busybodies who neglect their own homes in order to indulge in a little sentiment and gain notoriety by attempting to pauperize whole neighborhoods." See Charles Shanabruch, *Chicago's Catholics—The Evolution of an American Identity* (South Bend, Ind., 1981), 134. Shanabruch also explores some of the tensions between Hull House and the Catholic archdiocese. See also Deirdre Mageean, "Irish Women and Catholic Charity Work in Chicago, 1840–1910" (paper presented at the annual meeting of the American Conference on Irish Studies, Galway, Ireland, July 1992).

much-needed work in the Irish communities. But many women argued that there was a need for more services specifically for women.[33] Not until 1893, however, did an organization of women appear, in the form of the Catholic Women's League.

The World Columbian Exposition of 1893 in Chicago featured a Parliament of Religions in which religious leaders and lay people discussed how Christians could best teach and serve in the modern world. The discussions convinced many Catholics that they should enter the field of social action. A small group of women became the Catholic Women's League. The members were mainly educated middle-class women with the time and energy to pursue social reform. The officers in 1896 were mainly Irish, although some were German.[34] Most were wives of successful merchants and lawyers, but another significant group was single teachers, including the teachers' union leader, Catherine Coogin. Their principal work was the operation of badly needed day-care centers. The league also conducted direct relief, protection of unmarried girls who were new to Chicago, and cultural and educational programs. The development and support of settlements was a concerted effort to duplicate the work of humanitarians at Hull House, the University of Chicago Settlement, the Northwestern University settlement, and various Protestant institutions in the ghettos. The first three settlements on the North Side, West Side, and South Side had a nursery, a kindergarten, a sewing school, a library, a savings bank, a mothers' club, and employment and relief bureaus. In succeeding years, other settlements were established, most of which served residents of Polish and Italian neighborhoods. None directly served Irish communities.

The Catholic Women's League also began a program (in 1911) called the Protectorate "to prevent when possible girls and young women from taking a false step"; that is, the league sought to prevent inexperienced young women from being lured into prostitution

---

[33]Some of the first-generation Irish women had been familiar with such charitable and voluntary societies in their homeland. During the latter half of the nineteenth and early twentieth centuries, there was considerable growth in the numbers of such societies in Ireland that, like their American counterparts, allowed women the opportunity to participate in public life. For more on this, see Maria Luddy, "Women and Charitable Organizations in Nineteenth Century Ireland," *Women's International Forum* II, no. 4 (1988): 301–305.

[34]*Fourth Annual Charity Ball Given Under the Auspices of the Catholic Women's League* (Chicago, 1896). Booklet in Newberry Library, Chicago.

or sweatshop employment. To publicize its work, the Protectorate sent letters to priests in Europe, in the hope that the priests would share information with girls coming to Chicago. Volunteers staffed information desks at the six Chicago railroad stations to contact single young women traveling alone. "Those who needed to change trains were steered to the appropriate station and train. Overnight accommodations were obtained for young women who needed them. Those staying in Chicago were directed to safe boarding houses or temporarily to a Catholic institution. Employment was found, if necessary."[35]

The work of the Protectorate was successful but labor intensive. In 1914, the Catholic Women's League combined with the YWCA and various Jewish societies in the development of the nonsectarian Travelers' Aid Society of Chicago. Thus the women helped create the first cross-religious charitable organization.

The Visitation and Aid Society, founded in 1887, initially established to visit Catholics who were inmates of public institutions, but it quickly expanded. Soon it was finding care for abandoned and dependent children, employment for those without work, and a Christian burial for the indigent. The society had both paid and voluntary members (by 1889, it had 350 members) and met its expenses through donations, membership dues, entertainment activities, and the generous support of benefactors such as Michael and John Cudahy, wealthy Chicago-Irish meatpackers. Like the St. Vincent de Paul Society, many of its cases involved women and children. Sample cases from the annual reports involve families who needed help to return home; mothers who died and left children behind; drunken mothers and fathers; and elderly, dependent people. Some cases involved single women who had fallen on hard times, but increasingly the society's work involved children.[36] Society members worked as volunteer probation officers in the city's juvenile courts and were instrumental in establishing the nation's first juvenile court in Chicago,

[35]Roger J. Coughlin and Cathryn A. Riplinger, *The Story of Charitable Care in the Archdiocese of Chicago 1844–1959* (Chicago, 1983), 178.

[36]The annual reports for the years 1888–1896 show that the society assisted 9,742 children, obtained employment for 1,250 individuals, paid 1,363 hospital bills, paid for 541 funerals, and otherwise assisted 19,768 people. See ibid., 130; and the *Annual Reports of the Visitation and Aid Society,* Newberry Library, Chicago.

in 1899. The society found it difficult to recruit members, and it became defunct in 1911. Eventually the vast spectrum of Catholic charitable organizations was reorganized as the Associated Catholic Charities, which were centrally organized. The reorganization brought many changes to charitable work in Chicago. Amidst these changes, however, women (both lay and religious) continued to give their time. Many parishes would not have been able to care for the welfare of their members without these women. Nuns in particular made personal sacrifices to keep the charities going. Certainly the schools, orphanages, hospitals, and homes would have been beyond the limited means of Chicago's Catholics had it not been for the thousands of nuns who lived at subsistence level and whose orders took on the big mortgages necessary to build major institutions. The Irish did not have the tradition of mutual-aid societies that the Slavic Catholics had, and so the nuns' help was indispensable. For immigrant women—single or married, widowed or deserted—and their children, the nuns provided a network of sisterly care: women helping women in their times of greatest need.

Labor Unions

The world of work outside the home was largely the domain of single women, and they were most active in labor unions. In Chicago as throughout America, Irish women provided much of the female tradeunion leadership. In Chicago, they found encouragement from the American Federation of Labor, encouragement that was notably absent from the union at the national level. John Fitzpatrick, organizer of the Chicago Federation of Labor, encouraged women to organize separate unions and "respected their toughness and executive ability."[37] In jobs where they were heavily represented, ranging from nursing and teaching to the occupations of waitresses and cleaning women, Irish women played a leading role. Not all were first generation, but for many the forces that had led them to America provided

[37]A. M. Wheeler and M. Stein-Wortman, *The Roads They Made: Women in Illinois History* (Chicago, 1977), 77. The authors note that at a national level, the American Federation of Labor protected the wages of men and helped to eliminate women from the work force by making it expensive for employers to hire them.

A meeting of Irish women in Chicago. Mother Jones is at center.
Photograph, Chicago Historical Society.

the drive for their union activity. Some, such as Mother Jones (surely the most famous female Munster migrant), Margaret Haley, Elizabeth Rodgers, Agnes Nestor, and Mary Kenny O'Sullivan achieved national prominence, whereas others, mainly first-generation and representing working-class jobs, were known mainly within the Chicago labor movement. Among such women were Mary McDermott of the Scrubwomen's Union, Josephine Casey of the Elevated Road Clerks, Margaret Duffy of the Telephone and Switchboard workers, Elizabeth Maloney of the Waitresses Union, and Hannah O'Day, the "Petticoat Butcher" who led strikes in Back of the Yards (a district behind the stockyards).[38] We know little about the rank-and-file members of these unions.

One of the earliest leaders in the movement to improve the working conditions of women was Elizabeth Flynn Rodgers, who organized the Chicago Working Women's Union in the mid-1870s.

---

[38]See entries for Mother Jones, Agnes Nestor, Mary Kenny O'Sullivan, and Elizabeth Rodgers in *Notable American Women, 1607–1950. Biographical Dictionary* (Cambridge, Mass., 1971); Dorothy Richardson, "Trades-Unions in Petticoats," *Leslie's Monthly Magazine* 57 (March 1904): 489–500.

Rodgers was unusual among the predominantly unmarried union leaders, since she was married and the mother of ten children. Rodgers, who had grown up in Holy Family parish, was a housewife who became a pioneer in many women's organizations. Her union activities began in the 1870s. Between 1870 and 1880, the female proportion of the labor force rose slightly, from 17 to 18.5 percent. In some industries, however, such as the garment industry, it soared. Despite their labor force participation, women were not welcome in the Knights of Labor union. Faced with exclusion, a small group of women led by Rodgers formed the Working Women's Union in September 1878. The organization grew in strength, and by the end of 1886, eight local assemblies of the Chicago Knights were either partly or wholly composed of women. Rodgers became a District Worthy Foreman and later Master Workman of District Assembly 24. Although politically conservative, she was a committed feminist. When her husband sought to persuade her to resign her post, she refused and commented that "knowing my duty to my sex, I thought it was an opportunity to show our brothers how false that theory is that women are not good for anything."[39]

Rodgers's abilities were not confined to union activities. In 1891, she helped found the Women's Catholic Order of Foresters (the Catholic Order of Foresters was all male), a life insurance company of which she later became the High Chief Ranger or president. At first, she and other women were interested in joining a branch of the existing national order, but the order suggested that they establish an organization of women—independent of the men. The women finally obtained a charter in 1894. The first "court," or local group, was Holy Family Court No. 1, and the first convention of six courts was held in the same year at the Palmer House in Chicago. By 1898, 251 courts represented a membership of 16,267. The order became well established, and it eventually spread throughout the United States as an important fraternal benefit society. Before its inception, very few Catholic women belonged to an insurance society. The society enabled many families to receive death benefits and thereby some measure of financial protection. Above and beyond its main

---

[39]Richard Schneirov, "The Knights of Labor in the Chicago Labor Movement and in Municipal Politics, 1877–87" (Ph. D. diss., Northern Illinois University, 1984), 451, 463, 494.

purpose, the society gave liberally to charity and helped poor women in parishes throughout Chicago.

The sense of unity, strength, and public presence that women derived from their membership in fraternal societies such as the Foresters provided a spur to action in other domains. As one other famous member of the order, Margaret Haley, testified:

> Someone has said that the fraternal beneficiary insurance organizations of women did more to pave the way for women toward public life than did the actual enactment of the Nineteenth Amendment. Possibly it's true. I made my own entrance into the courts and the newspapers through membership in one of these organizations, the Women's Catholic Order of Foresters.[40]

Margaret Haley, a schoolteacher, may have had interests similar to those of Rodgers in the Foresters, but she was considerably more radical in her politics, earning herself the name the "Lady Labor Slugger." Her partner in the struggle for the rights of teachers was Catherine Goggin, another Irish schoolteacher and also involved in the Catholic Women's League. The Chicago Teachers' Federation that they organized and led became an instrument not only for the reform of education policy and improvements in the wages and pensions of teachers but also for civic and social reform.

Increased educational opportunities for women and social mobility had resulted in the feminization of public-school teaching. Whereas the percentage of women teachers nationwide increased from 59 percent in 1870 to 70 percent in 1900, approximately 97 percent of elementary teachers in Chicago were women. They were not proportionately represented in the positions of power, however: significantly higher percentages of men were in high-school classrooms and administrative positions. Female teachers were expected to be subservient and receive lower wages. Haley and Goggin brought to their organization a militant social feminism that successfully fought for teacher involvement in the making of school policies. By 1903, the Chicago Teachers' Federation had 3,000 members who were teaching in the public schools of Chicago and had introduced female white-collar unionism into American life.

---

[40]R. L. Reid, *Battleground: The Autobiography of Margaret A. Haley* (Chicago, 1982), 29.

Two other Irish women who attained national prominence were Agnes Nestor and Mary Kenny O'Sullivan. Nestor moved to Chicago while a young girl and later began work in a glove factory, where she was dissatisfied with working conditions. Within a year of starting her job, she led fellow workers on a successful strike. She became president of her own local union and rose through the ranks, eventually becoming president of the International Gloveworkers' Union. At one time, she also served as chairwoman of the committee on women in industry of the National Council of Catholic Women.

Mary Kenny O'Sullivan was born of Irish parents in Montana but came to Chicago in search of work. She organized the Chicago bookbinders and became one of the most influential of the early trade-union leaders. She was actively involved with Hull House, where the bookbinders held their meetings. With Jane Addams, she helped organize a boarding club for working girls. In 1891, she became the first woman general organizer of the American Federation of Labor (AFL). Her work lasted only five months: her contract was not renewed by an AFL that was not yet interested in the organization of women.

The early 1900s saw many strikes and conflicts in which Irish union women were active. In March 1900, Hannah O'Day led a band of unorganized Irish women on strike against the working conditions in the meat-packing industry in the Back of the Yards district. The initial walkout failed, and O'Day and her fellow organizers were blacklisted. They went on to found the Maud Gonne Pleasure Club, however, which became a local of the Amalgamated Meat Cutters and Butcher Workmen of North America. Within a few years, they had 1,200 members, and in 1904 these "petticoat butchers" joined 22,000 others on strike.

Elizabeth Maloney, who organized the Waitresses Union in 1902, brought to her work an unusual blend of labor union principles and Catholic ideals of feminine purity. She demanded that waitresses be treated with appropriate respect, and she worked for years to win a reduction in working hours that would give working women time for rest, leisure, and the pursuit of culture. Maloney was later appointed to the Illinois Industrial Survey Commission, which was charged with recommending legislation on women's working hours and occupational safety and health.

With a few notable exceptions, such as Mother Jones, most of the Irish women who were successful union leaders were second generation. At a lower but often equally effective level, first-generation working-class Irishwomen strove to improve conditions. All were extremely dedicated to the well-being of women, children, and families; the majority remained unmarried.

Why this high level of participation? It cannot be prior experience in Ireland: employment there was not industrial and did not involve large numbers of workers. The answer probably lies in the women's reasons for leaving Ireland. Those who had left in the second half of the nineteenth century and the early twentieth century clearly wanted to improve their economic standing and worth. They had left a society in which the status of women had deteriorated. Their motivation for self-advancement was high, and their tolerance of unfairness, discrimination, and exploitation low.

Unlike most other female emigrants from Europe, Irishwomen tended to emigrate on their own, not with their families. In emigrating, they had opted for some degree of autonomy, and to make their way in America they had to be self-reliant and assertive. Because many Irish women were unmarried, they were dependent on their own resources and work. They were, therefore, less likely to tolerate wages and conditions that did not provide an adequate living. They were also women who remitted vast sums to help relatives in Ireland survive or emigrate. They knew the value of money and their own economic worth. They also spoke the language and knew the system and how to use it to best advantage.

The "New Woman"

Discussion of the New Woman and the proper role for women filled the newspapers of Irish Chicago. Some male members of the Catholic Church saw conflict between the duties of wife and mother and involvement in public movements. Nowhere can that tension be seen more clearly than in *The New World*, the newspaper of the Catholic diocese of Chicago, during the 1890s. This organ of middle-class Catholic respectability was concerned about the loss of traditional "feminine virtues" and "feminine honor" as women became more involved in, and hence exposed to, the ways of the world. One page, "Woman's World," concerned itself with fashions, household hints, gardening, and social gossip from Europe. It also featured gems of wisdom on such topics as motherhood and marriage. Typical is "The Mother," which relates how men reflected on the influence of their mothers:

> Oh! there is an enduring tenderness in the love of a mother to a son that transcends all other affections of the heart. . . . She will sacrifice every comfort to his convenience; she will surrender every pleasure to his enjoyment; she will glory in his fame and exult in his prosperity; and if misfortune overtake him he will be dearer to her from misfortune.[41]

Sons were perceived as the prime objects of a mother's affections. Similar devotion was expected toward husbands. Daughters learned womanly virtues of domestication from their mothers. Motherhood and marriage were noble callings, and woman the foundation of the family. The paper did see fit to remind husbands of *their* responsibilities and their role in creating a good family environment, but the main concern was wifely virtues.

The paper is suffused with a concern that involvement in public life would be to the detriment of home and marriage and that the institution of marriage itself would be threatened. Catholic marriage, the female reader was assured, was the highest ideal. The workplace and the public world represented threats to her virtue, and striving for equality in politics or the workplace would bring only discontent. Hence, "Christian women, when your husbands and sons return to you in the evening after buffeting with the waves of the world, let them find in your homes a haven of rest. . . . Be attached to your homes. Make them comfortable. Let peace and order and tranquility and temperance abound there."[42]

The paper was expressing conservative fears that the ideals of the New Woman would lead to a loss of traditional female roles within the family, particularly the teaching of religious values and the nurturing of children, and that the institution of the family itself would be

[41]*The New World,* 17 June 1899.
[42]"The Christian Matron," *The New World,* 11 November 1893, 3.

questioned. Woman's role in life was perceived as equal to but not identical with that of men, and intrusion into traditional male spheres would threaten the stability of the family. *The New World* perceived the women's suffrage movement as a threat to home and family, and it warned women from getting involved in the mire of the political game.

In contrast to the ponderous commentaries of *The New World*, the newspaper columns of journalist commentator Finley Peter Dunne and the world of his fictitious character, Mr. Dooley, give insight into working-class Catholic views of the New Woman. Dunne's writing pokes gentle fun at the "lace curtain Irish." His focus on the Donahue family of Bridgeport reveals the ever-present battle between Old World values and new American ways, a battle waged in numerous Irish families. In conversation with his friend, McKenna, Mr. Dooley remarks:

> Molly Donahue have up an' become a new woman! . . . . It's been a good thing fr ol' man Donahue, though Jawn. He shtud ivrything that mortal man cud stand. He seen her appearin' in th' road wearin' clothes that no lady shud wear an' ridin' a bicycle; he was humiliated whin she demanded to vote. . . . But he's got to th' end iv th' rope now. . . . He'd come home at night tired out, an' afther supper he was pullin' off his boots, whin Molly an' th' mother begun talkin' about th' rights iv females.

Molly and her mother are defeated, temporarily at least, by Donahue's remaining in bed the following day and telling his New Women to go out and earn money for the family. The mother is horrified at the prospect of working outside the home, "Ye wudden't have th' ol' woman wurrukin' in th' mills," she says. Molly, meanwhile, is dispatched to do her work around the house.[43]

Social Life and Customs

Finley Peter Dunne captured life in the old community of Bridgeport, and James T. Farrell's Studs Loningan and Danny O'Neill novels describe life in the aspiring lower-middle class on the Boulevards.

---

[43]C. Fanning, ed., *Mr. Dooley and the Chicago Irish* (New York, 1976), 210–211, 213.

Although separated by several decades, both share certain themes, notably aspirations to achieve respectability and economic security. The mothers and daughters try to introduce "culture" in the form of pictures, soft furnishings, and pianos—often resisted by the menfolk. The two are also connected to that life in Bridgeport as described by Mr. Dooley, from which the upwardly mobile Irish escape as they move to the Boulevards.

Bridgeport and neighboring Canaryville were strong, tightly knit communities. Men and women who grew up there paint a picture of a community in transition, one in which people worked in the meat-packing industry but still clung to their earlier rural life. The immigrants there only gradually adapted to American culture. They retained some Irish customs, such as holding dances in their homes, and they resisted such American practices as removing a deceased person to a funeral parlor and holding the wake outside the home.[44]

In many ways, the community was self-contained. Employment was available locally, first in the rolling mills, sawmills, and stone quarries and later in the packing houses. Within the confines of the neighborhood were the Drovers' National Bank and the Stock Yards National Bank, as well as drugstores, restaurants, hotels, and saloons. Economic and social life was thus centralized and unified.

Houses were mainly of the one-story cottage type—reminiscent of homes in Ireland—with some two- and three-story houses divided into apartments. The homes were heated with wood and in later years with coal. The main foods in the 1860s were salt pork and beef, cabbage, and potatoes. Cabbage gardens were common, and the produce was sold to local markets (sometimes to German sauerkraut factories in the neighborhood) or shipped out of state.

Large cabbage gardens could be twenty acres in size and required the whole family. Tasks were divided strictly by gender. The men prepared the fields, the women planted them, and the children cultivated and weeded them. As one woman recalled, "I used to take dinner over to my two brothers and before father would let us have any-

---

[44]In 1890, John Kenny opened Kenny Brothers Funeral Home on 54th and Halstead on the South Side. A commemorative history of the firm notes that there was not a great deal of trade initially because Irish people found it difficult to accept the idea of holding a wake outside one's own home. *Kenny Brothers—A Century of Service, 1890–1990*, Commemorative brochure, 1990.

thing to eat we had to weed a ridge."[45] Produce from these larger gardens was shipped to St. Louis or Memphis, whereas produce from smaller patches was sold at local markets, a task usually carried out by the women.

Social life revolved around church and community. The churches were the chief social and recreational centers, hosting fairs, dances, and outings. Dancing was also held in homes and in some stores, which had more floor space. One woman recalled how the local "ham house" was used: "It was a big square building and we used one part for dances. They had a violin, harp, and piano those days and we danced square dances."[46] Churches and stores were also the centers of news and information:

> We didn't hear the news very often. Now and then we got a letter at church. The priest called the names at the altar. There was a big rush and scramble for mail sometimes. . . . At that time there were no newspapers so when we wanted to hear the news we walked to Nolan's general store on the corner of Archer and Halstead. A reader stood on the north-west corner and read out from the *Chicago Times.*[47]

Another account recalls that dress for women was simple and homemade:

> We didn't dress in silks like the girls do now-a-days, but wore our little calico dresses. When it was cold, we put on cloths, wore our hoods, knitted stockings and capes. My father used to say, when he saw a piece of silk, that it would ruin us. There were no ready-made clothes in those days. Before a girl could get married she had to knit stockings and make a man's shirt. If she didn't know how the women folks taught her.[48]

As transportation links between Bridgeport and Canaryville and the city of Chicago grew, the sense of community declined, and

---

[45]Vivian Palmer, "Social Background of Chicago's Local Communities," University of Chicago, *History of Communities of Chicago,* Vol. 6, Part 1, Document 5, typescript manuscript, Documents Collection, Chicago Historical Society, 1930.

[46]Ibid., Document 5, p. 2.

[47]Ibid., Document 2, p. 2; Document 3, p. 2.

[48]Ibid., Document 2, p. 2; Document 5, p. 2.

recreation and employment were found elsewhere. At the same time, many older families moved south to better conditions. The cabbage gardens slowly lost out to building and development. Customs and habits also changed. One old woman lamented the change in the behavior of young girls and compared them unfavorably to her own girlhood. Clearly the New Woman was not to her liking:

> The girls were not like they are now-a-days. They are so pert and independent now. At night you can see mobs of them out on the streets and even going off to dances alone. We had clubs years ago and no girl came to a dance without an escort. It isn't like that now; if you go down to Kaiser's Dance Hall you'll find them dancing with all sorts of fellows they don't know.[49]

These oral histories give us rich information about a neighborhood with a strong sense of community, strengthened by the fact that so many came from the same localities in Ireland. Social and economic needs were provided for within the confines of the community. The area was not without problems: times were often difficult, and the area had its share of drunkenness and gambling. But the people pulled together, helping one another out in times of need—just as they would have done in Ireland. Bridgeport in the 1860s and 1870s was a community with one foot in Ireland and the other in America, even retaining semblances of a family economy from pre-Famine times.

Irish neighborhoods in Chicago were in constant transition, partly responding to the demands of urban life and partly adapting to the mobility of the city's Irish population. For thousands of Irish women, however, the neighborhood, with its parish base and identity, was the one permanent thing in their lives. It was a major force in helping immigrants adjust to the journey from rural Munster to urban Chicago. Here they found a network of relationships and institutions with which they were familiar: church, school, pub, store. Here too they found resources that helped them cope with poverty and other social problems.

---

[49]Ibid., Document 2, p. 2.

The parish was something of a paradox, for it both advanced and retarded the cultural and socioeconomic progress of its parishioners. This paradox was particularly acute for Irish female immigrants. Religion and religious organizations maintained the separate spheres of men and women and upheld the traditional virtues of motherhood and family. Low rates of marriage and high rates of permanent celibacy in Ireland had led to the development of a gender-segregated social structure. In Chicago, as elsewhere in the United States, the marriage rate increased (although it was still low compared to other groups), but same-sex spheres and traditional familial values endured. Perhaps the survival of the old ways was in some measure because the Irish tended to marry other Irish—witness the high rates of endogamy in Holy Family and Visitation parishes.

Yet the Catholic Church in Irish-American society also encouraged accommodation to American life. Unlike Polish and German Catholicism, the Irish religious were not transmitters of ethnic identity; indeed, parishes accelerated the assimilation of Irish immigrants into American life. For Irish women, this integration—and, later, economic success—was achieved through the schools. Nuns, the main educators in the parishes, were vital to the success of Irish-American women. They concentrated on their own gender and encouraged them to enter the professions. They also provided resources for many Irish women who were unable to cope with the exigencies of urban life.

Given the forces that drove so many Irish women out of Ireland and their fierce pursuit of economic independence, it is not surprising to find them overrepresented in the professions and in trade unions. Their entry into these worlds was facilitated by the fact that they were highly literate and English speaking. Voluntary organizations, many of them parish based, provided a springboard for educated, middle-class Irish women to enter public life. (That public life, however, still did not include politics.) Here too we find a paradoxical situation. Irish women recognized that in those days, marriage and economic success were mutually exclusive. They fought fiercely and competitively in the marketplace and for the improvement of women's position in the world of work. Yet they did not fight for suffrage. Irish Catholic women did not become involved in the reform movement with Protestant middle-class women.

Finally, the experience of the Irish in Chicago was different from that in the Eastern seaboard, where they encountered a more highly structured society.[50] Chicago offered room for economic and physical mobility. Its open and expanding economy provided economic opportunities that allowed the Irish to move into the skilled working and lower-middle classes and, later, the middle classes. Added to this was the success of the parochial school system in Chicago. Education was crucial to the lives of Irish women in Chicago. The city had the first Catholic girl's high school, and overall Chicago had more Catholic girls' high schools than did the entire East. As the Catholic archbishop of Chicago, George Mundelin, noted in 1920:

> It will always redound to the credit and glory of the Irish immigrants that ... they always gave their daughters the chance of a better education. The father may have been only a laborer in the trenches, the mother without any education, but where the daughter showed signs of ability and a desire to study, they brought any and every sacrifice that she might have intellectual advantages.[51]

Irish women in Chicago had a strong female culture, fueled by the forces that drove them to leave Ireland, the encouragement of their educators, and the special opportunities offered by Chicago in that era.

---

[50]McCaffrey, "The Irish-American Dimension," in McCaffrey, ed., *The Irish in Chicago*, 7.

[51]Charles Fanning, *Nineteenth Century Chicago Irish* (Chicago, 1980), 30.

7

Embracing a Middle-Class Life: Swedish-American Women in Lake View

Margareta Matovic

At the turn of the century, Swedes proudly claimed that Chicago was the biggest Swedish city after Stockholm. Although Swedish dominance in old "Swede Town" had in fact decreased considerably, it was still the largest Swedish settlement outside Scandinavia. "Daughter colonies" had sprung up and were successfully competing with the "mother colony": increasing numbers of Swedish immigrants were moving to Lake View and other suburbs of Chicago. According to the Chicago school census in 1908, more than every fifth Chicago Swede lived in Lake View. The prospect of building new homes in attractive neighborhoods proved to be a powerful incentive, and Swedes who moved northward also advanced from tenants to homeowners. Next to the Germans, the Swedes had become the largest foreign group in this part of the city.[1]

The Swedish population in Chicago started with explosive emigration from Sweden during the famine years of 1868–1870, when nearly 70,000 Swedes emigrated to the United States. By 1890, the second generation already outnumbered the first. This trend reversed in the following decades as new waves of immigrants arrived.

---

[1] See Ulf Beijbom, *Swedes in Chicago: A Demographic and Social Study of the 1846–1880 Immigration* (Stockholm and Chicago, 1971), 81–84.

In 1910, the Swedish-born numbered 63,035, compared to 46,321 second-generation immigrants. The Swedes comprised 3.1 percent of Chicago's population of 2.2 million. Swedish immigrants during the period 1890–1910 were mainly young unmarried men and women, many of whom knew somebody in the city—parents, siblings, friends, or former neighbors. Until the late nineteenth century, men were the primary emigrants, but during the 1890s the number of female emigrants from Sweden greatly increased, and in some years women even outnumbered men.[2] The Swedish community had a striking number of women in the age group 15–29 years (the ratio was 136 females to 100 males) whereas there was a heavy predominance of men in the age groups 30–39 (100 to 73) and 40–49 (100 to 74).[3] The large number of marriage-age women in the 1880s favored a high frequency of marriage which contributed to a high birth rate and a large second generation.

The Swedish Neighborhood in Lake View

In 1913, the Swedish scholar E. H. Thörnberg was sent to Chicago to study Swedish immigrants, and during his trip he also visited Lake View.[4] He considered Lake View a "higher type of settlement" than working-class Swede Town. Impressed by the high standard of living, he praised the housing conditions, hygiene, food, and clothing as well as the educational system. But he could not overlook the social problems, such as alcohol and its effect on family life. He also noted health problems among the Swedish population, high insurance costs, unemployment, and work insecurity.

Lake View was annexed to Chicago on June 29, 1889. Even before annexation, it was quickly becoming an urban center. Farms were transformed into housing subdivisions and small shopping centers

---

[2]*Historisk Statistik för Sverge, Befolkning 1720–1967* (Stockholm, 1969), Table 49, p. 129.

[3]Beijbom, *Swedes in Chicago*, Table 14, p. 121, and 125, 142.

[4]Thörnberg was sent by the Swedish National Association against Emigration to study the Swedish immigrants in Chicago. His primary task was to give a less glorified description of living conditions in the city. E. H. Thörnberg, *Lefnadsstandard och Sparkraft med särskild hänsyn till den svenska befolkningen i Chicago* (Stockholm, 1915).

were developed. The Lincoln, Belmont, and Ashland Street area had already become a center of commercial activity. An increasing number of musical societies, gymnastic halls, outdoor beer gardens, and picnic groves provided inhabitants with leisure-time diversion.

With improvements in transportation, roads, and job opportunities, and the ready availability of modest homes at a reasonable price, more people moved out to Lake View. About 43 percent of the houses in Lake View were built between 1880 and 1894.[5] The first residents to arrive were immigrants from Luxembourg and Germany, followed by the Swedes and later on by English, Irish, and some Scots. A sizable Swedish settlement rose up near Belmont Avenue and Clark Street. Lake View was now a well-organized community with a network of small businesses—pharmacies, florists, grocers, a meat market, and saloons. Unlike other suburbs (such as Austin, Morgan Park, and Hyde Park), which enforced strict ordinances against saloons, Lake View had its own saloon keepers' society.

Though not all Swedes attended church regularly, five Swedish churches were erected in Lake View, including the Elim Swedish Methodist Episcopal and Trinity Lutheran Church, founded in 1883, and the Lake View Mission Covenant, founded in 1886. The Swedish Trinity Lutheran Church, the largest Swedish church in Lake View, was an offshoot of Immanuel Lutheran Church in old Swede Town. The regular members of Immanuel Church's Sunday school mission laid the groundwork for the new church; in the early days of Trinity's organization, services were held in members' homes.

Many other churches benefited from the growing numbers of Swedish immigrants. The Mission Covenant Church, which started out meeting in people's homes, became large enough to build a church. By 1900, the attendance at Sunday school reached 1,200. This North Side church community became an important source of leadership for Mission Friends throughout the Midwest and played a prominent role in the formation of the Swedish Evangelical Mission Covenant Church of America in 1885. Some church members formed the Swedish Covenant Colony, (in conjunction with Covenant College) which became an important institution for the

[5]See Anita R. Olson, "The Community Created: Chicago Swedes 1880–1920," in Dag Blank and Harald Runblom, eds., *Swedish-American Life in Chicago* (Uppsala, 1991), 11.

general education of Swedish immigrant children. The school, which moved to Chicago in 1894 and became known as North Park College, still maintains a leading role in preserving Swedish culture and tradition.[6]

Lake View had a well-organized educational system. Since children accounted for a third of the population (12,828) in 1884, schools were a priority. The first public school was built in the 1860s, and during the period 1878–1900, six new schools opened. Lake View High School was opened in 1874 and in 1889 became part of the Chicago public school system.

Many Swedish congregations conducted their own schools, motivated by the belief that the American public school system did not give adequate religious instruction. The Swedes were also eager to provide an education that would give their children a chance to advance in America. The first Swedish school was organized by Immanuel Church in Swede Town. It was called *Hvardagsskolan* (weekday school), to differentiate it from Sunday school. Classes were given in Swedish and English. In addition to religious instruction, the curriculum eventually included mathematics, history, geography, nature study, music, and German. Sunday school concentrated on Bible reading and preparing for catechism instruction. Collision with the public schools was avoided by having the weekday school primarily during vacation time, and attendance was limited to younger children. Children ages eight and older were usually sent to a regular school. In 1880, there were 138 parochial schools and 244 Sunday schools.[7]

At the turn of the century, there were several public schools in the vicinity of Belmont and Clark Streets. The public school system covered eight grades and was free of charge, including books. Illinois state law forbade employment of children under the age of 14, which contributed to students' staying in school. Swedish families that could afford to do so kept their children in high school and sent them

---

[6]Anita R. Olson, "Swedish Chicago: The Extension and Transformation of an Immigrant Community, 1880–1920" (Ph.D. diss., Northwestern University, 1990), 128–141; Philip J. Anderson, "The Risberg School in Chicago: American Aid and Swedish Immigrant Ministerial Education, 1885–1916," in Ulf Beijbom, ed., *Swedes in America: Intercultural and Interethnic Perspectives on Contemporary Research* (Växjö, 1993), 180.

[7]Beijbom, *Swedes in Chicago*, 256.

to college. The families' ambition was that the children avoid menial work, as adults and, through attendance at business college or high school, get skilled jobs.

For some Swedish families, language had become a problem because children mixed both Swedish and English. And in terms of ethnic identity, Swedes led a double existence: Swedish was the language for home and church; English was used at school and work. Language preference affected the choice of school. Some parents, for example, wanted their children to speak English as fluently as Swedish and looked upon religious schools as backward.

During their leisure time, Swedes of all ages enjoyed going to Belmont and Clark Streets. Here, in shops and restaurants such as Belmont Hall, the Viking Temple, and the Temperance Café, "Idrott" Swedish was the dominant language. Not far from the café was the Svithiod Singing Club. The "Dalkullan" book store was situated at 1727 North Clark Street.[8] It offered all sorts of reading in Swedish, from fairy tales and cookbooks to the latest novel by August Strindberg. Dalkullan Publishing and Importing Co. was founded by Captain L. Löfström, an immigrant from southern Sweden. He started out selling tobacco and newspapers but was soon operating a steamship agency, a shop for imported gifts, and a publishing house specializing in pirated editions of books, plays, and poetry from Sweden. The bookstore carried a variety of periodicals, humorous and serious books, dice games, bookmarks and tags, including the extremely popular book "Svenska Sagoboken" for children, and the Swedish cookbook *Utan Kock* (Without Cook).

The City as Remembered
by a Young Swedish Immigrant Woman

In the spring of 1989, Marie Carlsson, a 90-year-old widow born in Sweden and living in the Swedish Retirement Home in Evanston, recalled her first encounter with Chicago in 1914. She was 15 years old when she arrived by train along with her mother and two younger brothers.

---

[8]Archives of North Park College, Dalkullan Publishing & Importing Company, Boxes 1–14.

Oh, it was rough. I felt disgusted. I expected something different. Saloons all over the town. Awful. I couldn't understand what I saw. I had been raised by my grandmother. When my mother remarried a Dalslander, she left me and my two brothers with my grandmother; now I was forced to leave my grandmother. I should never have left Sweden. . . . I cried for fourteen days.[9]

Marie's first impression stands in stark contrast to that of the 18-year-old heroine of Theodore Dreiser's novel *Sister Carrie,* who is so much more familiar to us. Her experience may serve as a foil to contrast the Swedish immigrant women's experience. Carrie, who arrived by train in August 1889, had great expectations of Chicago: "I shall soon be free. I shall be in the ways and the hosts of the merry. The streets, the lamps, the lighted chamber set for dining, are for me. The theater, the halls, the parties, the ways of rest and the paths of song—they are mine in the night."[10]

In reality, however, Sister Carrie had little in common with young Swedish women who arrived in Chicago at the turn of the century. There is no evidence that they intended to throw themselves into Chicago's night life. On the contrary, their arrivals were usually well planned, with relatives or friends waiting at the railway station.

Carlsson also noticed the negative side of Chicago (seldom commented on in her letters home). At the turn of the century, the public spotlight was turned on many of Chicago's social evils, not least alcohol abuse among men and its consequences for women and children. Broken homes, deserted wives, murders and other crimes, the disappearance of young girls, and gang wars were discussed in newspapers, reports, and books. Organized crime was also rampant. The news media continually attacked the unholy alliance between corrupt politicians and the lords of the underworld.

Many Swedes, unlike the Germans and Irish, were avowedly temperate and had moved to Lake View to escape the social evils of downtown Chicago. After 1900, nearly all newly arrived Swedish immigrants went directly to Lake View, as was the case for Carlsson

---

[9]Marie Carlsson, interview by author, 23 April 1989. Swedish Retirement Home, Evanston, Ill.
[10]Theodore Dreiser, *Sister Carrie* ([1900] Cleveland, 1927), 9.

and her family. Carlsson recalls, "It was in Lake View that all the people from Sweden lived. I can't forget the first evening. My mother lined us up along the kitchen wall to be introduced to the neighbors. We couldn't understand what they were saying. They talked about us."

Her language skills improved, however, when she started to work as a maid. But adjustment to life in Lake View was far from easy, and Carlsson is not nostalgic about the experience. There is an note of bitterness in her voice when she talks about her mother, who brought her to Chicago against her will. "I had to get along. My mother wanted to get rid of me. 'Go out and get yourself a job,' she said. I had to leave. You had to manage if you wanted something. I worked as a maid until 1920. Then I got married."

Her life story is in no sense unusual, for Swedish immigrant women in Chicago typically worked, married, and then settled down in homes of their own. She married the man she loved, but she lost her twin boys—one died in a street accident and the second of fever. She had no more children. Carlsson worked until she was 61 years old. "I have always worked. I worked as a housekeeper. I worked for small families, always alone. I loved to care for the children. But you had to work hard. You got little pay—$2.50 a week. It had to be so. It was no problem. I worked 15 years in one family, 17 years in another family, and 14 years in a third one."

Carlsson spent 46 years working as a housekeeper taking care of the children of others. She worked part time because she had her own household, and so she received little pay. It was natural to her and her husband that she work outside the home even after marriage, since this meant extra income.

Carlsson lived all her life in Lake View. Recalling life there, she remembers the popular meeting places, the restaurants, dancing halls, and theaters at Belmont and Clark where Swedish was spoken. Here the churches arranged events where young people could come together. Carlsson was one of the "Thursday girls," Swedish maids coming down to Belmont Avenue for their free afternoon. "I remember the popular Café Idrott—that was the meeting place for all of us—and the shop Dalkullan. It had a Swedish owner, a lot of Swedish newspapers and food. We all went there." She loved to dance and remembers how she first met her husband: "It was love at first sight.

He was so handsome. It happened at a dance. I was 18 and he 23. Our wedding was in 1921." Carlsson also loved parties and picnics or any other amusements the Swedish community had to offer. She adapted easily to the Swedish-American enclave. But except for the families she worked for, she had very little contact with American society or American people. Since her relationships with her employers were good, and since she had no ambition to work for wealthier households, she did not feel any need for contacts outside the Swedish community.

Life in the Swedish Community

At the turn of the century, Swedes constituted 54 and 57 percent of the total population in the most prominent Swedish enumeration districts.[11] The Swedish-American population was young. About 40 percent of the Swedes were children under 15, and the majority of the adult population was between 20 and 40. More than 30 percent of adults were married. Swedish women could be choosy when it came to marriage: men outnumbered women in the age group 30–45. Women, however, dominated among the widowed and older population. The number of divorced people was extremely low.

Lake View was a lower-middle-class district populated by skilled workers, artisans, small entrepreneurs, and lower officials (such as clerks, bookkeepers, postal workers, and stenographers). The area was known for job stability and good wages. Swedish men were among the best-paid foreign-born workers, and their wives as a rule, did not work outside the home. The average yearly income for a Swedish skilled worker in 1909 was $900–$1,000. During the building boom of the 1880s and 1890s, some Swedish contractors earned more than $1,500 per year (a tidy sum at the time), and they in turn

---

[11]To study the social and demographic structure of the Swedish-American settlement, the 12th U.S. Census of 1900 was used. Enumeration districts (ED) 763 and 765 in the 25th ward, where Swedish households dominated with 54 and 57 percent, were analyzed. The enumerators were both of Swedish origin, and in ED 765 a woman, Miss Sylvia Eckberg, had been appointed for this task.

employed carpenters, bricklayers, and painters of Swedish origin, who earned an average weekly income of $24–$30.

Artisans and skilled workers dominated among Swedish men, followed by service workers and clerical professionals. For women, the leading professions were needleworker and domestic worker, followed by service jobs such as waitress, saleswoman, or clerical worker. Women's employment was related to family status. Swedish daughters between 15 and 30 years of age were expected to work. They found employment as clerks, saleswomen, dressmakers, or stenographers. Only eleven married women were registered with an occupation: one teacher and one midwife, along with dressmakers, seamstresses, and washerwomen. The census concealed the true situation of those, especially of married or widowed women, who had "invisible" employment both inside and outside the home. Of the 60 widows in Lake View, nearly all of whom were heads of households, there were a few small entrepreneurs running a bakery, a boarding house, or a laundry, but others supported themselves through domestic service.

TABLE 7.1

Occupational structure in 1900 of men and women in enumeration districts 762 and 765, in percent of the population older than 15 years

Men	N	%	Women	N	%
High officials	6	1.2	Entrepreneurs	6	1.2
Large entrepreneurs	7	1.4	Domestic servants	22	4.4
Low officials, clerks	47	9.5	Laundresses	12	2.4
Small entrepreneurs	42	8.5	Saleswomen	11	2.2
Artisans	149	30.0	Needleworkers	43	8.6
Skilled workers	84	16.9	Clerical workers	14	2.8
Unskilled workers	44	8.9	Factory workers	2	0.4
Service workers	66	13.3	Nurses	6	1.2
No answer given	51	10.3	Boarding housekeepers	2	0.4
Total	496	100	Teachers	5	1.0
			Service workers	5	1.0
			No answer	373	74.5
			Total	501	100

Source: Analysis of the Census Manuscripts.

Marriage

Lake View was very attractive for young families who had moved from other parts of Chicago. During the first two decades of the twentieth century, more single men and women arrived in Lake View. They came in search of jobs, and many roomed or boarded in the neighborhood. Later, they married and remained in Lake View.

Swedish-American men and women maintained the marriage patterns of their home country, but did so selectively. The marriage records of Trinity Lutheran Church for the period 1897–1907 show that women tended to marry in their mid-twenties, which corresponded to age at marriage in Sweden. Swedish men and women in Lake View wanted to be certain about financial prospects. Even though the city offered greater economic opportunity than Sweden had, economic stability was still hard to achieve. In Sweden, men often married older women with property. That pattern continued at first in Chicago but became weaker. Only 11 percent of the newly married couples in Trinity Lutheran Church were composed of an older wife and a younger husband, compared with 20 percent of couples already living in the two enumeration districts and 47 percent in Stockholm in the 1880s. In Sweden, the preference for an older wife was rational if an unpropertied man was looking for an experienced housekeeper who had her own savings. An older wife was also less fertile, and the choice can be seen as a strategy for limiting family size.[12]

TABLE 7.2

Average age at marriage (first marriage) of Swedes in Chicago

Year	1897	1898	1899	1900	1902	1903	1904	1905	1906	1907
Men	32	29	29.9	28.3	30.5	28	31	28.7	30.6	28.7
Women	24.6	26.8	26	24.2	26.8	29	26.7	25	24.4	25.9
Number of marriages	23	30	31	29	11	11	30	48	62	58

Source: Marriage Records, Trinity Lutheran Church, Microfilm, Archives of the Emigrant Institute, Växjö, Sweden. No data are available for 1901.

[12]Cf. Margareta R. Matovic, *Stockholmsäktenskap. Familjebildning och partnerval i Stockholm 1850–1890* (Stockholm, 1984), 183–186.

TABLE 7.3

Average age at marriage in Sweden

	Men	Women	Widowers	Widows
1891–1900	28.8	26.8	45.8	40.9
1901–1910	28.7	26.4	45.3	40.4

Source: Historisk Statistik för Sverge, Befolkning 1720–1967 (Stockholm, 1969), Table 32, p. 103.

Marriage patterns reveal an endogamy rate of 95 percent. In the rare cases of intermarriage, the partner usually had been born elsewhere in Scandinavia or in Germany or America.[13] Dalsland women who married in Chicago preferred men from the same province, but some of the women married Norwegians. The thirteen single Dalsland women represented in the 1900 census reports who can be traced from their home province through the Emigrants' Register made discretionary use of the marriage market. They certainly did not rush into marriage. Only eight married and, like their Dalsland sisters, they were, on average, 26 when they did. Three who lived in Chicago for more than ten years remained unmarried for life.

For women, the options to marry in Lake View were clearly better than they had been in the home country. There was a surplus of single young men who lived under crowded conditions in the area of Clark and Belmont. To facilitate meetings between men and women, the Swedish community organized social events such as dances, concerts, and picnics. Popular dances were held by the gymnastic clubs or the Order of Vikings, the Swithiod Order, and the Good Templars Order. For those who did not dance, the congregations arranged activities such as church socials, bazaars, choirs, and picnics. Women formed the backbone of most Swedish churches in Chicago, and in some congregations, 70 percent of the members were women. Domestic servants constituted the majority of female church members. And church was an important place for meeting prospective spouses.

---

[13] According to the census reports of 1900, intermarriage was very rare for the Swedish-American population. Two Swedish-born parents were the norm (92.1 percent of Swedish-American households). That compares to 86.5 percent of Danish-American households in which both parents were of Danish origin and 86.9 percent of Norwegian-American households in which both parents were of Norwegian origin.

At least two Dalsland women found their future husbands in Swedish church congregations.[14]

Swedish immigrant men preferred to marry domestics—but domestics were disinclined to marry. A housemaid who was accustomed to a high standard of living in wealthy households was unlikely to marry unless she was sure to maintain the same, or obtain a higher, standard of living.[15] A maid who was employed in a more modest home, however, might consider marriage if the suitor was well off. Interest in marriage thus depended on the living conditions of Swedish immigrant women. The personal and financial freedom many single women obtained in Chicago also may have deterred marriage. To avoid marital exploitation, many self-supporting women chose celibacy or consensual unions without marriage licenses. Thus they made use of "cultural baggage" brought from Sweden, which contained survival strategies for self-supporting women.[16]

Swedish immigrant men also hesitated to marry. For many, the economic prerequisites were difficult to achieve. Besides, some of the men found Swedish women demanding, especially the maids who seemed to be spoiled by life in rich people's homes. In 1897, a Swedish-American newspaper featured a debate about "love and marriage."[17] In that article, a Swedish male worker from Rockford, Illinois, warned other men not to marry a domestic because she was not used to being frugal. A factory girl would be a better wife, he said, because she knew how to economize. Swedish women suggested that love was the most important aspect of marriage, whereas the men stressed money: "You can buy everything for money—even love." But another Swedish man stressed that only love brought happiness in marriage. After 29 years of marriage, he and his wife had the happiness and security they had dreamed of: a house of their own (big enough to rent rooms out to other families) and an income

---

[14]Hilma Lund, born in Ärtemark parish in 1885, emigrated to Chicago in 1909 and married in 1913. Selma Åhlund, born in Bäcke in 1885, arrived in 1905 and married in 1910.

[15]See Thörnberg, *Lefnadsstandard*, 41.

[16]Margareta Matovic, "Migration, Family Formation and Choice of Marriage Partners in Stockholm, 1860–1890," in Ad van Der Woude, Jan de Vries, and Akira Hayami, eds., *Urbanization in History* (Oxford, 1990), 230–231.

[17]*Svenska Amerikanaren Tribunen*, 12 October 1897.

large enough to save for old age. "Now I play my concertina, and my wife sings funny songs."

When 25-year-old Sofia Gustafsdotter from Tisselskog in Dalsland left for Chicago in 1896, marriage was not foremost on her mind. After her arrival, she worked as a maid for 18 years, saved her money, and invested in a house, farmland, and forest in Tisselskog. In 1914, when she was on a visit to Dalsland, World War I broke out. She had to stay, and only then did she decide to marry. At the age of forty-three, she married a Dalsland widower with five children.[18]

Newlyweds who moved into a house or apartment of their own could count on more comfort than in Sweden: indoor plumbing and running water, central heating, and two or three bedrooms. For many Swedish families, one goal in moving to Lake View was home-ownership, and in 1910 at least 30 percent of Swedish families had achieved that goal. In enumeration districts 765 and 762 in 1900, 22 and 13 percent (respectively) of Swedish household heads were homeowners, and by 1910 the number had risen to 30 percent. The majority of homeowners paid mortgages on their houses. Fifteen percent (9 out of 59) of homeowners with mortgages were women.

Newly built houses in Lake View were usually "cottages," a frame construction with two or three floors, including five to eight rooms. In 1897, a house in Ravenswood, a section of Lake View, with six rooms and two doors was offered for $2,200.[19] Ten years later, a house just outside Lake View, containing three floors and six to eight rooms, cost $6,000. For a household with a yearly income of $900–1,000, this was a very considerable amount. Lower housing costs were available in Lake View, where rents, on average, amounted to $14–$32 per month. For an unskilled worker earning a yearly average of $600–$700, a house was expensive. Many had to rent out a room or two to lower costs. Nevertheless, the housing standard of Chicago Swedes was high.[20] The desire to own a house in a nice neighborhood, away from the noise and squalor

---

[18]Information provided by people in Tisselskog, Dalsland: Robert Alfredsson in Björke, who is a great grandson of her brother, and Per Bohlin in Dals Långed, who is not a close relative. According to them, Sofia had intended to return to Chicago, but was prevented from doing so by World War I.

[19]Svenska Amerikanaren Tribunen, 16 March 1897.

[20]See Thörnberg, Lefnadsstandard, 49–91.

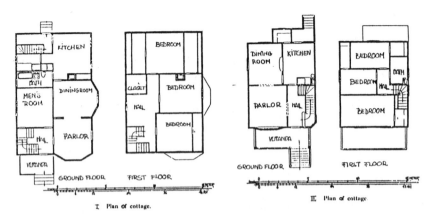

*Plans of cottages: The homes of Swedish workers in Lake View
at the turn of the century*

Source: A. Molin, "Hur Svenskamerikanarna bo," 39–40.

of the city, was an important incentive to save money. Realtors and urban developers laid out subdivisions specifically marketed to lower middle-class immigrant families.[21] Demand and supply met to shape the development of the city.

The household economy of a lower-middle-class family was fragile, vulnerable to unemployment and illness. Swedes chose to have few children and to take in lodgers for a measure of financial security. The higher the income group, the smaller the number of children. About 14 percent of the households were childless. In the two districts, 68 percent of Swedish households were composed of three to six members; families seldom had more than four children. Households consisting of only one person were as rare as three-generation families.

The census for the two districts shows that about 28 percent of families had lost one or more children to death. There are no statistics available for child mortality overall or illegitimacy. The U.S. Census does not separate illegitimate births; the inadequate system of birth registration in Illinois helped conceal the existence of these

---

[21] See Harold M. Mayer and Richard C. Wade, *Chicago, Growth of a Metropolis* (Chicago, 1969), 154–157.

TABLE 7.4

Family structure of Swedes, enumeration districts 762 and 765, 1900

	N	%
Nuclear families	240	69.8
Single-parent nuclear families	39	11.3
Three-generation families	41	11.9
Single-parent three-generation families	11	3.2
Single households	13	3.8
Total	344	100

Source: Analysis of the Census Manuscripts.

children. According to a 1909 study, however, the death rate among these children was twice as high as among legitimate children.[22]

American employers, doctors, pastors, and social workers knew that Swedish immigrant domestics frequently gave birth to illegitimate children. For the housemaid, single status was a prerequisite. Marriage normally meant the end of her career as a domestic. It seems likely that many women had stable relationships or secret engagements, primarily with Swedish men, and postponed marriage even in the case of unexpected pregnancy. This practice enabled them to keep their employment, but it also resulted in illegitimate births.

In Sweden, pregnancy was traditionally the first step toward marriage.[23] A liberal attitude toward premarital sex existed alongside an attitude that condemned premarital pregnancy. The moral condition of single Swedish women at the turn of the century was a topic of international discussion. According to Thörnberg, Swedish immigrant women were no more immoral than other women: they became pregnant more often only because they considered engagement as binding as marriage.[24] Another author was more critical,

[22]Louise de Koven-Bowen, *Safeguard for City Youth at Work and at Play* (New York, 1914), 131–132.
[23]Cf. David Gaunt, *Familjeliv i Norden* (Malmö, 1980), 79–83.
[24]Thörnberg, *Lefnadsstandard*, 42–43; Gerard Halfred von Koch, *Swenskarna i Förenta Staterna. Specialundersökning* (Emigrationsutredningen, Svenskarna i utlandet, Vol 20) (Stockholm, 1911), 131–132, 152–153.

claiming that Swedish immigrant women had a flagrant disregard for morals and were not ashamed of bearing illegitimate children.[25] Whatever the merits of the debate, the consequences of illegitimacy for a Swedish woman in Chicago could be disastrous. Unwed maids and factory workers with little or no savings rushed back to work after giving birth and placed their babies in an institution when the babies were about two weeks old. Illegitimate babies were then sold or given away.

The Swedish Pastor Peter Paul Waldenström visited Chicago and Lake View during the 1890s and described some destitute Swedish women, some of them pregnant or with their babies, who had been taken into the Home of Mercy in Bowmanville. The Home was run by the Swedish Covenant Church. It was not only an orphanage but also a home for old people and a hospital where some medical care was provided. In addition, it helped place unfortunate children in foster homes.[26]

Childbirth in a strange country frightened many Swedish immigrant women, especially the prospect of having a midwife who did not speak Swedish. We can imagine then that the medical practice opened by the Swedish doctor Ingeborg Tauström in January 1897 was welcomed by Swedish families in Lake View. A trained Swedish midwife, who arrived in Lake View in December 1897, was even more appreciated.[27] Most births took place at home, and women who assisted saw illness and frequent death. In their letters home, many women expressed their fears of having sick children or getting ill themselves. Illness was expensive in Chicago; doctor's were difficult to find, and might charge from $2 to $100. The two Swedish hospitals were often overcrowded because they were known for good, cheap treatment.

Lack of accurate knowledge about serious diseases like scarlet fever, diphtheria, measles, and bronchial pneumonia sometimes meant death for children. Albertina Andersson, a Dalsland woman living in Lake View, often wrote home to her brother Gustaf about

[25]Cecilia Millow, "Till frågan om det moraliska tillståndet bland svenska tjänsteflickor i Amerika," *Dagny,* Organ för Fredrika Bremer förbundet (Stockholm, 1904), 293–294.

[26]Peter Paul Waldenström, *Genom Norra Amerikas Förenta Stater. Reseskildringar* (Stockholm, 1890), 321–323.

[27]*Svenska Amerikanaren Tribunen,* 21 January 1897; 14 December 1897.

her bad health and her worries about her children. As she wrote in 1902 when she was working as a maid, "I feel far from well, but I hope to recover—otherwise I have to leave my employment. . . ."[28] The health situation among Swedish women in Chicago was bad, according to E. H. Thörnberg.[29] The women suffered from nervous diseases, uterine and stomach complaints, throat problems, and bronchitis. Thörnberg suggested that, even though frequent trips to Sweden were eating up women's savings, they were neverthe-less advisable because of the health benefits. Visits home served to cure women of different sorts of suffering—both physical and mental.

Married Life

To be a Swedish immigrant wife in Lake View at the turn of the cen-tury meant to negotiate a rising cost of living amid meager incomes. It meant that everything from household chores to family crises had to be handled in the context of an urban lifestyle. Since most married women had lived for some time in the United States and had worked in domestic service before marriage, they were familiar with the everyday life of American families.[30] Inevitably, they had made ad-justments to life in an American city. The life of a married woman, even if the woman was relatively well off, was a constant struggle to make ends meet. It was burdensome to pay rent and debts and at the same time save money for times of unemployment and illness. Daily tasks included preparing meals for family and boarders, supervising the children's schoolwork, and keeping an eye on husbands who too easily strayed to the saloon. The cost of food, housing, utilities, and clothing was high. Transportation, insurance costs, and fees to unions and churches also had to be paid.

---

[28]Information about Albertina Andersson was obtained from the church records of Håbol parish, household lists for the village Stenserud between 1886 and 1900, the emigrant register in the enumeration district, and a letter from Albertina Andersson to her brother Gustaf Spjut in Dalsland on 28 September 1902.

[29]Thörnberg, *Lefnadsstandard*, 48–49, 94–95.

[30]Of a total of 281 married women in enumeration districts 762 and 765, 42 percent had arrived in the United States in the 1880s and 27 percent in the 1890s, mainly between 1890 and 1895. Ac-cording to Thörnberg, *Lefnadsstandard* (44, 58), 70–75 percent of the Swedish housewives in Chicago had been employed in housework before marriage.

A young Dalsland couple in Chicago. Eric Johanson from Jarms parish became engaged to Anna in Chicago in the 1890s, and he sent this photograph home to Dalsland.

From Olof Ljung, *De for åt Amerika.*

No wonder Albertina Andersson was upset in a 1910 letter to her brother: "Rents and food and everything are getting more and more expensive every year, but they [employers] will not raise the wages without a fight. . . ."[31] Her husband was out of work, and they had just moved from Oak Street on Chicago's Northside to Sheffield Av-

---

[31]Letter from Albertina Andersson to her brother in Dalsland, 1 July 1910.

enue in Lake View with their children, Ruth (six years old) and Oscar (three years old). Albertina frequently wrote about money matters (mainly to have money of hers transferred from Dalsland to Chicago). Her husband intended to build a house on land they had already bought outside Lake View, and so the money problem was acute. Albertina was one of many Swedish housewives who continued clandestine work after marriage. She did not admit to her family what sort of work she did, only that she worked every evening.

Child care forced many women to remain at home, and some started to take in lodgers. In the two districts of our study, a fourth of households had boarders; most had one or two but one had five. In the district where Albertina and her family lived, a third of the families had lodgers. One of these families gives us an idea about women's activities.[32] John Johnson, a 52-year-old Swedish-born insurance agent, lived with his wife Hulda, who was 40 years old. They had no children, although they had been married for 20 years. Hulda took in lodgers and had sent for her mother Anna, a 79-year-old widow, to help her run the small boarding house. The Johnsons had one roomer (a 31-year-old-single Swedish carpenter) and four boarders, all women, three born in Sweden. Miss Gagen, a 22-year-old telegraph worker, was born in Illinois. Miss Davida Johnson a 27-year-old stenographer; Miss Clara Peterson (49 years old, no occupation given); and Miss J. Falke, a 37-year-old laundress, were born in Sweden. Hulda, like many Swedish landladies, preferred Swedish lodgers.

The Johnsons' lodgers belonged to a rapidly-growing group of self-supporting women that got the name "women adrift" at the end of the nineteenth century. The foreign-born contingent was significant: in 1880, more than two-thirds of these women came from Ireland, Germany, Sweden, or Norway. Among them were many single women but also divorced and widowed women, deserted wives, and unwed mothers. Most of them roomed or boarded in families like Hulda's. Living alone could be a problem. Chicago in the 1890s was a harsh environment, and lone status could be interpreted as sexual misbehavior. Landladies were often suspicious of women who had

---

[32]Information obtained from enumeration districts 762 and 765, Census Manuscripts, 1900.

lived on their own in an apartment, considering such behavior immoral.[33] In a family there was more security, and Swedish "women adrift" preferred household situations. A woman renter shared the bathroom with the landlady and with other lodgers, and if she boarded she would eat one or two meals prepared by the landlady.

No matter how simple the food was, it probably seemed rich and tasty. It usually consisted of white bread and butter, eggs or meat, and fruit or pie. For a former farm maid from Sweden, often half-starved by her employers, the American diet certainly could satisfy a yen for rich food. We do not know if Swedish landladies took up "Swedish cooking" and served porridge, potatoes, milk, and rye bread to keep down costs. At any rate, the food standard in Chicago was clearly higher than in Sweden.

The high standards for food and housing in the Chicago area meant that many Swedish families had difficulty saving money. There was little money left over for clothes and amusements. Married women were probably "less elegant" than single women in the Swedish enclave and less likely to buy a new outfit each year.

Clothing helped turn a peasant maid into a city woman. A Swedish domestic at the turn of the century usually spent $150–$160 per year on clothes for balls and parties; thriftier, more pious women spent $110–$125 per year. For everyday life and for work, a Swedish immigrant woman adopted the "Yankee style" and wore well-made but modest dresses. The trunk of a Swedish emigrant who was denied entry to the United States showed that even the work clothes the woman planned to wear were of high quality.[34] Women who decided to emigrate obtained information about clothing styles from "fashion plates" in magazines. The hat became the symbol of upward mobility and was worn to signal that a Swedish-American domestic maid was a "lady." Even a factory worker and unionist like Mary Anderson felt the need: "It was spring and we felt we had to have new hats. We had very little money, but that did not keep us

---

[33]See Joanne Meyerowitz, *Women Adrift: Independent Wage Earners in Chicago, 1880–1930* (Chicago, 1988), 10–11, 27.

[34]The trunk belonged to Anna Fredriksdotter, an emigrating Dalsland maid. When her papers revealed that she had been ill with a nervous disorder, she was denied entry into the United States. She returned home and never unpacked her trunk. The contents have been preserved in private ownership.

from getting hats. I paid four dollars for mine, a great big thing that turned up off the face. The next Sunday we took a walk in the park and people kept looking at us."[35]

Thrifty Swedish immigrant wives would not spend that much money on hats. Albertina Andersson never mentions clothing or hats in her letters, but she misses the sewing machine that she left in Dalsland.[36] Married life involved much more than clothing problems, however. Housekeeping was the central activity for married women. Cooking, cleaning, doing laundry, baking, and caring for children, husband, and relatives took up most of their time. Adjusting to the urban routine, which differed greatly from the demands of a peasant household, was also essential in becoming a city woman. As in the village, baking was a separate task, but in the city it traditionally was done on Thursday and was not a community affair. Fridays were reserved for cleaning. Monday was laundry day, which remained a heavy task. To do laundry every week was new for many Swedish maids, because they were used to two or three washing days per year: in spring, in autumn, and occasionally before midsummer. The young Dalsland maid Emelie, newly arrived in Chicago, complained in a letter to her cousin Hanna: "What a terrible lot of work they can make for you with the laundry. Perhaps you have heard that here they do the laundry every Monday all the year round. There is so much laundry for one week that you would really be afraid if you saw it."[37]

Married life in Chicago often brought insecurity and hardship. Crises occurred when the family head became unemployed, fell ill, or spent too much time in the saloons or beer gardens of Lake View. Alcohol abuse by husbands was at the core of most crises, often forcing wives to take over as breadwinners. Excessive drinking among Swedish men, both single and married, was, according to Thörnberg, a much bigger problem than illegitimate births. North Clark Street had a particularly bad reputation for drunk and disorderly men. Some Swedish women, such as Emelie Gustafsdotter, commented about

---

[35]Mary N. Winslow, *"Woman at Work": The Autobiography of Mary Anderson as Told to Mary N. Winslow* (Minneapolis, 1951), 19.

[36]Letter from Albertina Andersson, 16 September 1903.

[37]Letter from Emelie Gustafsdotter to her cousin Hanna in Tisselskog, Dalsland, 9 August 1900 (Private letter collection, Robert Alfredsson, Björke).

the evil of drunken men in the streets.[38] Fear of a drunkard husband may have made many women hesitant to marry.

If there was a family crisis, Swedish immigrant wives took on the role of breadwinner, and their children pitched in. They could expect more help from their daughters than from their sons, because daughters began to seek employment early and handed over their wages to their mothers.

Crisis in marriage seldom resulted in divorce. But when divorce did occur, it was announced in the Swedish newspapers: "Mrs. Anna Anderson wants a divorce from her husband Andrew, whom she accuses of cruelty and drunkenness." "Mary Johnson was divorced last week from her husband James, who had deserted her."[39] Alcohol abuse, desertion, gambling, adultery, and violence at home were the main reasons cited. Swedish men had a low rate of criminality in Chicago, but 84 percent of the crimes they committed were connected with drunkenness. Violence at home was probably a common occurrence for a drunkard's wife, but it was seldom reported. A newspaper item that appeared on New Year's Day in 1891 gives a glimpse of the problem: "E. M. Nordgren, living at 29 Hein Street, arrived home drunk late on New Year's Eve and mistreated his wife, forcing her and the two children to leave the house. The poor woman took refuge in a woodshed, where policeman Byrne took care of her and helped her into a [settlement] house."[40]

Childhood

What was it like to be a child in Swedish Lake View when trolleys and wagons were pulled by horses, and none of them went too fast; when on Mondays everyone did the family wash and hung it out in the fresh air to dry; when your mother made a pitcher of lemonade on a hot summer day; when times were (mostly) sane and clean?

One little girl, Gloria, was born in the neighborhood on March 27, 1899, at 341 Grace Street. Her father, Joseph Svensson, had come

---

[38]Ibid.; Thörnberg, *Lefnadsstandard*, 43–44.
[39]*Svenska Amerikanaren Tribunen*, 12 and 26 March 1891.
[40]*Svenska Amerikanaren Tribunen*, 8 January 1891.

to Chicago with his parents. Joseph was one of 14 children, and his strict Lutheran family went to church every Sunday. They did not allow their children to dance, drink, or play cards in the home. Later the Svenssons changed their name to Swanson. Joseph married a German-Polish woman, Adelaide Klanowski, and their only child was Gloria. She grew up in a mixed German-Swedish neighborhood. Recalls Gloria: "I was absolutely mad for dolls. I learned to walk by pushing a toy carriage with a baby doll in it. Later, my greatest pleasure was pushing a doll buggy through Lincoln Park and noisily playing Mommy."[41] Gloria Swanson had no idea then that she was to become a famous movie star. She was her mother's darling, always dressed in fancy clothes that her mother sewed for her.

Another girl, Ruth, was born in 1904 in Chicago to Albertina Andersson and her husband Charles. When the family moved to Lake View, Ruth was six years old. Her mother was born in 1876 in Dalsland, the youngest daughter of soldier Anders Spjut. Albertina had three brothers and two sisters, and when her brother Albert emigrated to Rockford, Illinois, in 1892 she decided to follow. As noted earlier in the chapter, she soon found employment as a housemaid. It was in Rockford that she met her future husband, Charles, a friend of Albert's. In 1902, Albertina and Charles moved to Chicago, where Charles got work in industry and Albertina in housework. They married in 1903 and moved into what Albertina described as a "nice little home" on Oak Street, where Ruth was born one year later. In her letters home, Albertina expresses her happiness over little Ruth, a strong and healthy baby girl.[42] She stayed home with her baby and seemed to enjoy motherhood, despite having health problems and feeling financially insecure. She kept her sister-in-law well informed about what Ruth was doing and sent some pictures of Ruth. Even when Ruth was joined by a little brother, Oscar, in 1906, she continued to talk mainly about Ruth. By 1909, Albertina had started working again (in the evenings, when her husband was home). He took care of the children when Albertina was busy. If it was at all possible, Swedish immigrant wives avoided work outside the home and stayed with the children, who remained at home

---

[41]Gloria Swanson, *Swanson on Swanson* (New York, 1980), 12, 13.
[42]Letter from Albertina Andersson, 31 July 1904.

longer than in Sweden.[43] But insufficient household incomes often forced them out into part-time work, mostly housework. Charles's participation in strikes as a union member had left him blacklisted and unemployed; Albertina had no choice but to work. Thus she had little time to entertain the ideas of "sacred home" and "cult of motherhood" prevalent in the American upper classes. Those concepts were familiar to immigrant women who had worked as domestics.

How many American child-rearing ideas and practices did Swedish maids adopt? Certainly there were concepts they frowned upon, but there were also aspects they liked. Images of the mother as the "light of the home" or "the educator and supervisor" hardly fit a working mother with low income and no child care. But the Swedish immigrant women shared the dream of education for their children. Many of them had been taught by grandmothers who had never gone to school. The women were anxious to create educational opportunities for their daughters. Lake View, with its well-organized school system, was the first step toward upward mobility. In this Swedish-American community, families tried to give their children the best education, and they treated sons and daughters equally. A good school education and professional training were considered the best dowry a girl could receive from her parents.

Boys or girls seldom left school before the age of 16, and many completed high school or a specialized business school. Girls remained at home while pursuing further studies to become teachers or government employees. American schools emphasized mathematics, writing, and foreign languages, as well as typing and stenography. Knowledge of foreign languages could enhance young people's eligibility for desirable jobs.

Family ties were significant in terms of both residence and obligation. The family as a source of social security was an aspect of the new life in an American city. When circumstances allowed, Swedish women adopted the American version of stay-at-home wife and mother, breaking with their traditional economic role of working mother. The women seemed to accept the role of housewife. (After

---

[43]Thörnberg, *Lefnadsstandard*, 29, 58. This has also been stressed by Janice L. Reiff in her study of Swedish immigrant women in Seattle: "Urbanization and Social Structure: Seattle, Washington, 1852–1910" (Ph. D. diss., University of Washington, 1981), 238–239.

all, many first-generation immigrant women had bitter experiences with exploitation by their employers.) Now daughters no longer left home after religious confirmation to find employment. The relationship between mothers and daughters became more Americanized: parental control increased, and daughters were expected to live in the parental home until marriage. There was little room left for them to be "on their own" or "to see the world." In that sense, freedom had diminished for young women.

Lack of physical security in the new life created a need for women to stay home with the children. Chicago was in many respects a dangerous city, and at the turn of the century prostitution and the established trade in kidnapped young girls—often immigrants—were social problems of urban life. Add to these the threat of murder, rape, and street accidents, and it is easy to see why Swedish women avoided leaving their children alone.

Despite the American emphasis on individualism, Swedish immigrant families grew even closer than was the custom in Sweden. It was still expected that children would contribute to the family economy, but children also enjoyed greater opportunities for individual development. In part because of urban dangers, however, parents felt more protective. When inadequate income mandated that a woman went out to work, she might choose to work part time rather than leave home all day.

Thus, the daily experience of a married woman—with children in public school and English spoken in her neighborhood—helped to make the American way of life more acceptable to her.

Community Activities

In the late nineteenth century, Swedish-American civic associations were dominated by males. The forty-odd associations that emerged before 1880 were for men (although some social gatherings included women), with only a few exceptions. The Svenska Fruntimmersföreningen (Swedish Women's Organization) was the most significant. The organization, founded by the wives of Episcopalian preachers Bredberg and Larsson, supported the Svea Society and the St. Ansgarius congregation. The church provided a meeting place for the 38 women, who supported the Svea Immigrant Hostel financially and took care of sick immigrants. This women's organization re-mained in existence until the 1880s.

Dalsland women were accustomed to local female networks and for a long time offered informal support to newcomers. In 1890 the all-female Fruntimmersföreningen, or Ingeborg Society, was founded. This charity association, whose focus was primarily on helping poor Swedish women, continued to function until its dis-bandment in 1958. The Induna Club and the Linnea Aid Society were also women's charity associations.[44] Still another society (this one for both men and women), Dalslands Vänner (Friends of Dalsland), was founded in 1925. A members' list from 1929 shows 260 people sup-porting the Colony of Mercy, a home in Bartlett, Illinois, for sick and handicapped people (primarily from Dalsland).[45]

Temperance organizations provided a social outlet for many Swedish immigrant women. The Good Templars in the U.S. were unique among the male organizations in welcoming women as members and leaders. Lodges in Chicago that were run by the soci-ety established youth residences and sport clubs as well as singing so-cieties to provide a nondrinking alternative for young people who wanted to socialize. In the fight against alcohol, Swedish women had more in common with American women than with women from other immigrant groups. A group whose mission the women agreed with, the Women's Christian Temperance Union, had its headquar-ters in Evanston (not far from the Swedish neighborhood). Some progress had been made in Evanston, a mainly "dry" town, and in Austin, a western suburb of Chicago. According to a letter written by Emelie Gustafsdotter in 1900, no saloons or drunkards could be seen in her neighborhood, which she liked much better than down-town Chicago.

Emelie and her sister Sofia Gustafsdotter were neither temper-ance activists nor club members. Their primary interest was church. "We usually go to church every Sunday and Thursday evening. We are going to the Lutheran Church. I like it better here than at home. Everything is freer. I do not know which church is the best. . . . There

---

[44]Manuscript Collections, Swedish American Archives of Greater Chicago. Manuscript series 1, box 13 and Manuscript series 12, box 1. Archives of North Park College, Chicago.
[45]*Dalslands Vänner*, member list, 1929. Archives of the Emigrant Institute, Växjö.

are so terribly many different sorts."[46] As would be expected, women's participation was greater in church societies than in social and welfare organizations. Church societies traditionally provided women with opportunities to socialize and to perform useful community services. When larger numbers of young single women made their way to Chicago, churches became surrogate families for them. The women supported their congregations generously, paying $15, $20, or even $30 yearly. Swedish congregations often received their best income from female domestics, who had few other forms of amusement and who saved most of their salaries.

Married women also participated in the social life of the congregation, as well as in organizations that had close ties to their church. One such organization was the Ingeborg Society, which provided financial aid to indigent Swedish-American women who needed medical care. The Linnea Aid Society, also conducted charity work for Scandinavians in cooperation with the Swedish Covenant Church. It enlisted women through a women's club, sewing circles, the Dorkas Society (a charitable organization), and a youth club.[47] At least three Dalsland women were active members of the Swedish Covenant Church.[48] Young Swedish women also took advantage of American organizations, such as night schools and sports clubs.[49]

After 1900, the pressure for women's societies grew, and in the 1910s, as women were pushing to gain suffrage, greater equality was reached in Swedish social organizations. Women created their own charity organizations at a brisk pace, and at least 25 women's lodges were formed between 1903 and 1916. The radical women's movement in the city was led by American middle-class wives and professionals. Well-educated American women were passionate in organizing; Swedish women were less active. The American-led Chicago Women's Club, founded in 1876, was often criticized for encouraging

---

[46]Letter from Emelie Gustafsdotter, 9 August 1900.

[47]Manuscript series 12, box 1, and Manuscript series 1, box 13 (the Linnea Aid Society), Archives of North Park College; parish records of the Swedish Covenant Church, Austin, Ill., 1910.

[48]Hilma Lund was born in 1885 in Ärtemark parish, Dalsland. Church records, Swedish Covenant Church in Austin, Ill., 1895–1910.

[49]Joy Lintelman, "'On My Own': Single, Swedish, and Female in Turn-of-the Century Chicago," in Philip Anderson and Dag Blank, eds., *Swedish-American Life in Chicago: Cultural and Urban Aspects of an Immigrant People, 1850–1930* (Urbana, Ill., 1992), 94.

women to work away from home. For many Swedish wives, the right to be home with one's children was novel and clearly attractive. Among the unmarried Swedish immigrant women, better working conditions than they had experienced in Sweden reduced their interest in fighting for women's rights, even though many of them sympathized with the movement.

Swedish Maids
and Other Female Workers

The large numbers of Swedish maids in Chicago were the result of mass emigration to the city among single young Swedish women in the early 20th century. Most of the women were in search of employment, and domestic service was readily available. At the turn of the century a fourth of all Chicago's domestic servants were of Swedish origin, and on the national level they were among the predominant groups in household labor, along with the Irish, Germans, and Norwegians.[50] A 1910 study of employers' preferences shows that American-born domestics were the first choice but next in order were Scandinavians.[51] Swedish housemaids were especially popular as live-in servants; they had a reputation for being honest, diligent, hardworking, willing to learn, and unlikely to complain.

The majority of domestics were first-generation immigrants. Second-generation Swedish women were three times less likely to work as live-in maids than the first generation. Such work offered both direct and indirect benefits to newly arrived immigrant women. Because room and board were provided, life was simplified, and the continual interactions with Americans enabled the maids to learn English quickly. And women who had been servants in Sweden found the wages excellent by comparison.

---

[50]David M. Katzman, *Seven Days a Week: Women and Domestic Service in Industrializing America* (New York, 1978), 49. In 1880 17 percent of Swedes were in domestic work, compared with 12 percent of the Irish, 5 percent of the Germans, and 8 percent of the native-born Americans. Beijbom, *Swedes in Chicago,* 167.

[51]Katzman, *Seven Days a Week,* 70.

Sweedie, the Maid

Sweedie, the "silly Swedish maid," hardly resembled the rational and frugal Dalsland woman. Nor was she a fearless and independent factory worker like Mary Anderson, who had also tried the profession of housemaid during her first years in America. "Sweedie" was the invention of the first generation of moviemakers in Chicago—to be precise, the Essanay Company on Argyle Street in Lake View. In their slapstick comedies, she was played by a man in woman's clothes. Wallace Beery, who played the role, talked in a stupid accent and wore a yellow wig as he-she indulged in kicking policemen and tripping roller skaters. Sweedie was a hit. The audience could not get enough, and the Essanay Studio produced "Sweedie" pictures twice a week. One young girl who visited a rehearsal in the studio did not think the pictures funny at all. In her memoirs, Gloria Swanson described the "Sweedie" series as insulting: "I thought it was vulgar, disgusting and stupid."[52]

"Sweedie" was a caricature of the hardworking Swedish domestic who was naive enough to be exploited. Sweedie behaved like a man, and she was dumb: she retained her Swedish culture totally, including working extremely hard (when it was no longer necessary). She was slow to Americanize, and she was a challenge to the American concept of womanhood. At the same time, she was "a woman adrift": she did not live with her kin, was economically independent, avoided marriage and, perhaps, gave birth to illegitimate children. Sweedie was a threat to the patriarchal order and the idea of women's submission. She was perceived as dangerous and had to be ridiculed.

Domestic Service as a Career Option

Did Swedish housemaids use emigration as a tool of emancipation? In 1907, Swedish women were questioned about their reasons for emigrating. Their answers revealed that crossing the ocean in search of work was a protest against bad treatment in their home country. They were well informed about working conditions and wages and

---

[52]Swanson, *Swanson on Swanson*, 26.

realized that their work could be easier and more valued "over there."[53] On the other hand, they behaved much as female servants did in Sweden, leaving employers they did not like and seeking better employment at higher wages.[54] Fifty years earlier, Swedish servant maids had left their rural provinces for magnet cities in Sweden such as Stockholm and Göteborg; for Dalsland women, however, the "way out" had always been Kristiania (Oslo) or Fredrikshald in Norway. Seeking employment with *fint folk* (wealthy people) was a reaction to exploitation by greedy Dalsland farmers. At the turn of the century, America was the place where decent jobs were waiting.

Although the Swedish immigrant domestics were still *pigor* doing similar work to that in the home country, they were rewarded by higher wages and greater esteem. Their success as domestic servants facilitated rapid upward mobility. They made a profession out of housework and used their knowledge and skills to specialize in their field. Swedish immigrant women were not ashamed to work in households, and the Swedish ethnic community viewed domestic service as a respectable and lucrative means of economic support.

For the Swedish maid, advancement was to a great extent a matter of mastering American customs and language. Knowledge of English was the key to all types of advancement and to higher self-esteem. For the newcomer, language problems were the main reasons for isolation, depression, and homesickness.[55] Dalsland-born Emelie Gustafsdotter, for instance, bitterly complained in a letter home that she could not speak English. The 22-year-old maid feared that she was too old and stupid to learn.[56] But many maids quickly learned the new language, often with the help of their mistress or the children they were looking after.[57] Once the language was mastered, the door was open to the "domestic career," in which positions were changed in search of better working and living conditions.

---

[53]See Ann-Sofie Kälvemark Ohlander, "Utvandring och självständigghet. Några synpunkter på denkvinnliga emigrationen fran Sverige," *Historisk Tidskrift* 2 (1983): 169–170.

[54]Ulf Beijbom, *Svensktamerikanskt. Människor och förhållanden i Svensk-Amerika* (Växjö: Emigrantinstitutets Vänners Skriftserie no. 3, 1990), 101–103; Gaunt, *Familjeliv i Norden*, 113–116.

[55]Dag M. Hermfeldt, "Svenska tjänsteflickor i Chicago under 1920-talet," unpublished paper, Institutet för Folklivsforskning, Stockholm University, 1984, 15, 19.

[56]Letter from Emelie Gustafsdotter, 1900.

[57]Winslow, *"Woman at Work,"* 15; Hermfeldt, "Svenska tjänsteflickor," 19.

For a maid, upward mobility could mean wealthier employers or another household occupation that brought better pay. The labor market on Chicago's North Shore drew thousands of Swedish immigrant women. North Shore families were "the upper crust"; they lived in spacious mansions and had from two to twenty live-in servants. The comfort level was high, and the employers were generally well educated.[58]

To be a live-in servant in a millionaire's home was the goal for many housemaids. Not only did they have a room of their own, often with a private bathroom, they also were surrounded by objects of beauty. Some maids were able to make full use of this cultural life. One such maid was Eva Nydahl-Wallström who, at the age of 15, worked for a childless upper-class family in Chicago. After a while, she was treated more like a daughter than a servant, and the couple introduced Eva to a new and fascinating world of art, music, theater, opera, and travel to foreign countries. "It was a blessing for a girl like me to come to such a home," Eva noted in her memoirs.[59] She continued working for this couple even after marriage, taking care of the husband and wife as long they lived. Indeed, if working conditions were good and pay acceptable, many Swedish maids became attached to certain wealthy families. For example, the five Wangman sisters worked at varying times for several branches of the same family. They benefited from the structure of domestic service that existed in wealthy households: a housemaid could be promoted by the employer to a higher level of professional skill. For instance, one sister was put through professional school by her employers to become a trained cook. Another sister was offered the opportunity to become a trained nurse.[60]

According to a report from the Illinois Free Employment Office in 1900, a qualified cook could earn $9–$10 a week, compared to $5 a week for a domestic with board.[61] In 1910, a trained cook could make $12–$15 a week, including board. Many live-in servants were able to save on their wages, and they were generous in the amount of

---

[58]Stina L. Hirsch, "The Swedish Maid, 1900–1915" (M.A. thesis, De Paul University, 1985), 38.

[59]Irma Wibling, "Eva Wallström berättar. Minnen från ett långt liv" (Härnösand, 1982), 34.

[60]Stina Hirsch, interview by author, 4 May 1989, Evanston, Ill.

[61]Illinois Free Employment Office, *Second Annual Report*, 1 October 1899 to 1 October 1900, Statistics of Labor, State Board of Labor Commissioners (Springfield, Ill., 1901), 40.

money they sent home. They also, as Dag M. Hermfelt points out, felt an obligation to those who had helped them find their first jobs.[62] They hurried to advance so that they could repay their debts.

Who were the Swedish maids in the households of the very rich? An index based on the 1900 census covering 1600–2100 Prairie Avenue and 1800–2100 South Calumet Avenue, among the most exclusive addresses in Chicago, provided information on all servants. A total of 344 servants, 269 females and 72 males, was recorded. The Irish were the largest group, constituting 26.7 percent, followed by the Swedes at 20.8 percent. There were also Germans, Danes, Finns, French, and Hungarians.[63] Among the 59 Swedish-born women, all except two were single, and most were between 23 and 35 years of age. The Swedes also constituted the largest number of male domestics, which indicates the high regard for domestic service in the Swedish-American community. Nine of the 15 Swedish men were married.

Since Sweden was hardly known for the high culinary skill of its people, the numerous Swedish cooks come as a surprise. Apparently many Swedish maids who wanted to advance showed interest in cooking and had a readiness to learn new dishes and the American style of food. In 1914, Eleanor Wangman wrote home to her mother: "The people I work for have many fancy dinner parties, and I am learning to cook fine foods."[64] The learning was mutual. Eva Nydahl-Wallström started to "help" in the kitchen shortly after being hired as a maid, and later introduced Swedish home cooking to the family that employed her, as did Mary Anderson when working as a maid. "[My mistress] did not do any cooking, so I had to do it all, but if we had something nice she always came out and told me how good it was."[65]

Several prominent families employed more than one Swedish domestic. The Keith family had two cooks and one lady's maid from Sweden as well as a laundress, a butler, and a coachman. A parlor maid, a chambermaid, and a laundress, all of them born in Sweden, worked for the Rotshild family. The majority of these women had

---

[62]Hermfeldt, "Svenska tjänsteflickor."

[63]See Thomas E. Golembowsky, "Prairie Avenue Servants: An Index Based on the 1900 U.S. Census," *Chicago Genealogist* 12, no. 2 (1988–1989): 40–46.

[64]Quoted in Ketty Johnson, *American Widow* (Sausalito, Calif., 1983), 171.

[65]Winslow, "Woman at Work," 15.

come to America between 1885 and 1895 and had taken about ten years to advance to a favorable position. Once she was associated with a prominent family and reputed to be honest and hardworking, the Swedish maid needed have little fear of unemployment.

Unlike in Sweden, however, there was no one-year contract (*städja*), only an agreement for one week at a time. That gave the employer the opportunity to fire the servant in case of illness or misbehavior. It also gave the servant the possibility of quitting without fanfare. But changing positions to improve working conditions was combined with insecurity, and many Swedish maids preferred stable work in good homes. If they found such a family, they gladly gave up the ambition to climb the status ladder to a millionaire's home.

Swedish immigrant women often relied on ethnic networks to locate new employment and to switch jobs. Fellow immigrants who spoke English provided them with detailed information. This lowered the risk of a position that was unsatisfactory. Albertina Andersson wrote how she had helped a female friend to find employment as a maid. Andersson also received letters from Sweden that informed her who was going to arrive and who needed help to find housing. Alma Jansdotter, who arrived in Chicago in 1892 at the age of 16, later became active in helping young people from Dalsland to find jobs and places to live.[66] The traditional support network of relatives, neighbors, and fellow parishioners continued in Chicago, where Dalsland women were important organizers and sources of information.

Mary Anderson and Ellen Lindström

Not all Swedish immigrant women became housemaids; some were determined to find something else to do. Mary Anderson was a farmer's daughter who frankly declared that she hated housework. She was born in 1873 in Västergötland (a neighboring province of Dalsland) and was brought up in an environment of pious religiosity, pragmatism, and a tradition-bound lifestyle. At the age of 16 she

---

[66]Letters from Albertina Andersson (1909–1910). According to information from Emma Åttingsberg in Uddevalla, the niece of Alma Jansdotter (telephone interview with author, 20 January 1990), Alma helped many young women and men from Dalsland with room and board.

emigrated to America with her sister Hilma, and the two joined their older sister, who was already working there as a maid. Mary also became a maid, but in 1893 she moved to Chicago and started to work in a factory. She was first a garment worker and then a shoe stitcher who was paid on a piecework basis; her wages were originally $3 a week and climbed to $12–$13 a week. She became a member of the International Boot and Shoeworkers' Union—and later an activist and organizer—and, through the Women's Trade Union League, a pioneer in industrial arbitration. In the 1920s, she was appointed director of the Women's Bureau in the U.S. Department of Labor in Washington, D.C.

In the mid-1890s, Swedish immigrant women found employment in the many sweatshops on Chicago's North Side, where 1,715 contractors employed 14,904 people. They also earned a reputation as excellent seamstresses for making pants and vests. But wages were low, and a Swedish vest finisher in 1892 did not earn more than $216 per year, which was about $127 less than a woman working in a shoe factory.[67] Wages improved, however, and even 15 years after their arrival, many Swedish immigrant women sought employment as vest finishers. In fact, a 25-year-old Swedish woman emigrating to Chicago in 1907 explained that she was leaving Sweden because she was a skilled vest finisher and could earn much more in Chicago than in her hometown of Stockholm. She had worked in Chicago before and had returned to Stockholm, but the high cost of living and low wages disappointed her. In Stockholm, she had earned $4–$5 a week making vests; in Chicago she could get at least $8 a week, and the cost of living was lower as well. Her long-term goal was to work in a factory as a dressmaker. She was proficient in English and felt at home in Chicago, where she had friends; in Stockholm, she felt "lost".[68]

In Chicago, work as a seamstress provided single Swedish women an adequate salary to support themselves. One seamstress in a coat shop not only supported herself but also saved enough money

---

[67]Illinois Bureau of Labor Statistics, *Working Women in Chicago, 7th Report, 1892,* I; and *The Sweating System: Descriptive Particulars, 4th Report, 1886,* II (Springfield, Ill., 1886), 404.

[68]*Emigrationsutredningen,* Bil VII, Utvandrarnas egna uppgifter, Kvinnliga utvandrare 1907 (Stockholm, 1908), no. 125.

to pay for tickets to the United States for her mother and siblings.[69] The irregular and seasonal character of work in the garment industry could, however, create financial insecurity.

One Swedish immigrant woman who arrived in Chicago in 1898 and found employment in a small North Side shop sewing men's pants found the conditions deplorable. Ellen Lindström had been teacher and governess in Sweden but finding no jobs available in her field after arriving in Chicago, she became a garment worker. She began to ask questions. Why were wages so low and hours so long? Why were the shops so narrow and hot during summer, and why were children allowed to work? In 1897, when the Scandinavian women in Chicago's garment industry asked the United Garment Workers to help them organize, the union did not respond. Lindström was undeterred, and she took the initiative in organizing. Observed Mary Anderson, "At that time, organizing women was very difficult. The Unions were unpopular because the girls were afraid they would lose their jobs if they joined, and their general attitude towards Unions was that only roughnecks belonged to them."[70]

Ellen Lindström succeeded despite knowing little about unions. In 1903, she organized 8,000 women in the garment industry. She won major concessions: a 40 percent increase in wages, a reduction in work hours to 10 a day, ample wages for overtime, and a half day off on Saturdays. Eventually, she became the business agent of the Garment Workers Union.[71] She was one of the female pioneers in the unions, devoting her life to the fight for better working conditions for women.

At the end of the nineteenth century, an increasing number of Dalsland women emigrated to the United States. About 80 percent of the women were single, and a majority of them were quite young. Official reports found their emigration alarming. Farmers and landowners complained about the shortage of female labor in Dalsland, and the maids who remained behind demanded higher wages and shorter working hours. The opening of a new labor market for

---

[69]Lintelman, "On My Own," 92.

[70]Winslow, "Woman at Work," 26.

[71]Dorothy Richardson, in *Leslies Monthly Magazine* 57 (March 1904): 489–500.

Swedish domestics in America made Dalsland women at home openly declare their dissatisfaction. They were well informed about wages and working conditions in the United States, where housework was truly confined to the house. That was in sharp contrast to the reality in Dalsland, where "housework" encompassed outdoor work, and women often had to perform men's work for half the pay.

Yet Dalsland maids were hardly rebels in the modern sense of trying to escape patriarchal control and submission. They were pragmatic and behaved as female servants usually did in Dalsland: they left employers who treated them badly, and they sought better employment at higher wages elsewhere. Decades earlier, servant maids had left their home villages for employment in regional cities or in Norway. At the turn of the century, however, it was not in Sweden or Norway but in America where jobs were waiting. And Chicago, a fast-growing city, was a magnet for emigration.

Emigrating Dalsland women were daughters of landless as well as landed farmers. They all had in common a high regard for wage work, a desire to become economically independent, and a network of relatives and friends already in Chicago. They relied on ethnic networks to locate employment and a place to live.

The goal of many Dalsland maids was a career in domestic service, which usually meant changing positions frequently in search of better working and living conditions. This upward mobility implied both the professionalization of housework and wealthier employers able to pay higher wages. Maids could save money to send home or to invest. A live-in servant in a millionaire's home was the top of the career latter, but it required single status, along with excellent health, self-discipline, diligence, and readiness to learn. Chicago employers were often ready to offer economic benefits and chances for promotion to excellent servants.

For those Dalsland maids who never found the very rich family's home to work in or who did not find a husband, a return to Dalsland was always under consideration. In fact, very few maids intended to stay permanently. Usually the stay in America was envisioned as lasting four or five years. Strong ties to the home province, the family, and friends caused several Dalsland women to return even in old age. For some single women, working in Chicago was simply a means to return to Dalsland and live in financial comfort.

Those who chose to marry and raise a family did so rather late in their life course and often rather reluctantly. The hesitation to marry may have been influenced by the hard lives of Swedish-American wives they witnessed in Chicago. Some of the women may have considered marriage inimical to personal and financial freedom.

Marriage patterns among Swedish-American women reveal an endogamy rate of about 95 percent. Dalsland women preferred to marry Swedish men from their home province or men from Norway. Although the "marriage market" was clearly more flexible than in Sweden, there was a decline in marriage rate among the Swedes in Chicago at the turn of the century.

To many Swedish immigrant women, the urban life of Chicago was a cultural shock. For rural Dalsland women the lack of fresh air, good drinking water, and green nature posed great problems. They suffered from the climate, which was too hot in summer. Chicago also had a harsh social environment, especially for single women. That was why so many Swedish single women who were not live-in servants chose to live as lodgers with a Swedish family. In a Swedish home, their native language was spoken, and they felt more secure.

For married Swedish immigrant women, the family dynamic changed. Mothers and fathers were expected to be more protective of children. After marriage, women avoided work outside the home if at all possible, adopting the American ideal of wife and mother. Abandoning their traditional dual roles as working women and mothers, Swedish immigrant women accepted a lifestyle that led to rapid acculturation. The Dalsland women who married in Chicago, combined traditional values about child raising and family economy with American ideas about the cult of motherhood.

Was there a specifically female experience of Swedish emigration to Chicago? At the most basic material level, they were freed from the extreme drudgery and austere living conditions that had been their lot in Dalsland. Socially, they were far freer as well. Liberation from patriarchal control and degradation yielded new self-esteem and such pleasures as being able to dress up "like a lady." When acculturation failed, however, the women's lives were characterized by short, unhappy stays in Chicago and frequent trips home to invest and prepare for old age in Dalsland.

8

Recent Arrivals: Polish Immigrant Women's Response to the City

Maria Anna Knothe

America was truly a new world for immigrants from Zaborów. One can easily imagine how different a dynamic, developing city like Chicago was from the quiet rural Galician village at the end of the nineteenth century. Immigrants from Zaborów had to adjust quickly to survive in a world that was so fast-paced, noisy, dirty, and dangerous. The structure of their everyday lives—their work habits, consumption patterns, living arrangements, and social relations—had to change in fundamental ways if the immigrants were to function in the urban environment.

Polish Downtown: A Zaborowian Neighborhood and Community

The Neighborhood and Its People

Emigrants from Zaborów parish began coming to Chicago in the 1890s and settled mainly in the so-called Polish Downtown on the Northwest Side, just west of the Goose Island industrial complex. By 1890, four other large Polish neighborhoods already existed in Chicago: the Lower West Side, adjacent to many factories along the Burlington Railroad and the Canal; Bridgeport and Back of the Yards, behind the Union Stock Yards; and South Chicago, next to the steel

mills. Many Germans and Bohemians, with whom Poles were familiar in the old country, also settled these areas.

The records of St. John Cantius parish, to which emigrants from
Zaborów mainly belonged, show that the highest concentrations of
Zaborowian immigrants were between Ohio Street to the south,
Cortez Street to the north, Ashland Avenue to the west, and Sanga-
mon Street to the east. Poles from Zaborów parish lived in the area
between house numbers 400-1400 north and 800–1800 west.

At the turn of the century, Polish Downtown was already a well-
developed neighborhood and community. In 1898, 86 percent of the
people who lived in eleven precincts of this neighborhood were of
Polish descent; 25 percent of all Poles in the city lived in this area, including many from Zaborów. It had originally been settled by Prussian Poles, and not long afterward, Germans moved in nearby
(around Noble and Division Streets). The first twenty years were
difficult for both groups, since for centuries they had been uneasy
neighbors in central Europe. But by the 1890s, most Germans had
moved northwest, and Poles from Prussian-ruled territories had become well established. Newcomers from Zaborów were eager to
move there. To them the crowded neighborhood offered help, protection, and essential information about life and work in the big city.

In less then forty years, the Polish population in Chicago had
grown more than tenfold, from 20,000 in 1873 to 97,496 in 1898 and
210,000 in 1910.[1] There was a higher percentage of women during the
earlier period of community formation than during the peak period.
In 1898, 36.6 percent of the Polish population was female, but by 1910 it
had declined to 28.9 percent.[2] Approximately 35,700 Polish-American
women lived in Chicago in 1898 and about 60,700 in 1910; 25 percent of
them (9,000 in 1898 and 15,000 in 1910) lived in Polish Downtown.

It is difficult to determine the exact number of women from
Zaborów parish who lived in Chicago, since Chicago municipal sta-

---

[1] M. Haiman, "The Poles in Chicago," in *Poles of Chicago 1837–1937: A History of One Century of Polish Contribution to the City of Chicago* (Chicago, 1937), 4; E. R. Kantowicz, "Polish Chicago Survival through Solidarity," in Melvin G. Holli and Peter d'A. Jones, eds., *Ethnic Chicago* (Grand Rapids, Mich., 1984), 216.

[2] Walter F. Willcox and Imre Ferenczi, eds., *International Migrations*, vol. 1, *Statistics* (New York, 1929), Table 9, 431, Table 10, 432–443.

tistics do not include village of origin. Some parish records, however, mainly those of St. John Cantius, indicate place of origin. And records of the oldest Polish parish in Chicago, St. Stanislaus Kostka, reveal that seven women from Zaborów parish lived in this parish during the years 1890–1913. Zaborowian women might have also lived in Holy Trinity, St. Josaphat, and St. Hedwig parishes, but the parishes' records do not specify the parishioners' village of origin. St. John Cantius was undoubtedly the parish with the largest number of emigrants from the parish of Zaborów.

Besides marriage records, St. John Cantius parish also preserved the banns books and baptism records. The banns books listed 176 women who were born in the five villages belonging to the parish of Zaborów and who married in 1893–1914. Another 192 women came from neighboring villages (the 176 will be called "Zaborowian" women, and the 192 will be called "neighbors") In the period 1893–1914, about 370 Zaborowian and "neighbor" women married in Chicago. Some had female relatives in Chicago, which was typical of Polish emigration to the United States. Because of increased transatlantic travel, Polish women came and went, and Polish-American women maintained links with their home country. Through their contacts, especially with other women, they preserved many aspects of traditional female roles.

The Parish and Its Institutions

Among Poles in Chicago, the desire for a Polish Catholic parish with a Polish-speaking priest was common. The Catholic Church had a central position in Poland, and immigrants felt a pressing need to recreate a Polish parish and a Polish church. Around 1865, some individuals had organized to promote the establishment of the first Polish parish, and in 1867 they founded the St. Stanislaus Kostka Church. The church was located on the corner of Noble and Bradley streets, several blocks north of St. Boniface, the German Catholic parish that up until then had served the entire multiethnic neighborhood. By the end of the nineteenth century, five more Polish parishes were established in the area.[3] Then in 1905, another parish was founded in Polish Downtown (The Holy Innocents, at 743 Armour Street).[4]

The basic unit of parish membership was the nuclear family, registered in the name of the male head of household or that of his widow. Adult children were entered under their parent's name until they established their own households. Unmarried adults who entered the parish without their families could register only as single members.[5] Each family received an account book and a family account number; single members did not receive an account book but did get a registration card with an account number. The church felt it necessary to differentiate between families and single people, but there were no further consequences as long as parish rules were followed. The family deposited parish dues and special contributions at the parish office; the amount was noted in the parish account books; and the receipt was noted in the family's book. The annual dues varied. In St. Hedwig parish, for example, they were $3.00 in 1911 and $5.00 in 1921.

If parish dues were in arrears for more than two years, the family was stricken from the parish registry. An unregistered family could not expect its children to be baptized and could not present them for first communion. Nor could family members be married in the church or attend as godparents during baptism there. The greatest threat of non-membership, however, was denial of last rites at death. This system of formal membership and strong institutionalization of parish life was unknown in Poland.

There were many parish societies. Some served only religious functions, whereas others were established to support the church, organize charity, or provide entertainment and preserve Polish national heritage. In St. John Cantius parish, these groups held prayer meetings and participated in processions. They also helped the pastors keep the church in order, which included mundane tasks such

---

[3] Holy Trinity, on Noble Street, south of Division, in 1873; St. Josaphat, at Lincoln Park, in 1884; St. Hedwig, at Logan Square, in 1888; St. John Cantius, at 825 N. Carpenter St., in 1893; and St. Mary of the Angels, at Logan Square, in 1897.

[4] Joseph John Parot, *Polish Catholics in Chicago, 1850–1920: A Religious History* (DeKalb, Ill., 1981), 234–237.

[5] See Mary Cygan, "Ethnic Parish as Compromise: The Spheres of Clerical and Lay Authority in a Polish American Parish, 1911–1930," *Working Papers Series 13*, no. 1 (spring 1983), 4–7.

as delivering coal for heat. The women usually provided fresh flowers for the altars, and the men helped with repairs or construction. The Society of St. Vincent de Paul operated in the Polish ethnic community, where it mainly conducted charity work. Parochial choirs earned money for the parish by giving public performances. St. John Cantius parish also had an amateur theater group (*Kółko Dramatyczne*), which organized performances and anniversary celebrations commemorating the Polish national heritage. Many groups preserved traditional Polish songs and poems, customs, and folk dress. The Society of St. Stanislaus Kostka had its own library, band, and theater group to provide both education and leisure-time activity.[6]

There were also parish societies that emphasized mutual aid, fraternal insurance, savings and loans, youth activities, sports, and even paramilitary activities. Almost all were segregated by gender, and as a result there were duplicate societies for men and women. Some organizations were also divided by marital status and age group. In this way, parish societies encouraged people to socialize rather than remain isolated at home.

This variety of church organizations had been unknown in a small village like Zaborów. The personal links that had formed the local community in Poland gave way in the urban environment of Chicago to parochially institutionalized social functions. In place of the system of casual volunteerism, voluntary financial contribution, and behavioral regulation through social disapproval which had existed in the village, the Zaborowian immigrant found formalized charity organizations, mandatory parish dues, and the threat of formal expulsion from the parochial structure.

Polish church and lay organizations played a vital role as preservers or even constructors of national sentiments and identity among the immigrants. The institutions established a public framework for the Polish language and folkways. Indeed, contact with Polish organizations in Chicago was the first opportunity for some immigrants to identify themselves as members of ethnic groups. (This was true even for those from Galicia, where oppression by Austro-Hungarian authorities was not as severe as in the territories under

---

[6]*Parafia Św. Jana Kantego. Złoty Jubileusz w Chicago* (Chicago, 1943).

Russian and Prussian rule.) There were no similar social institutions in Zaborów parish.

The parish thus had many religious and social functions. Almost as important, however, were its educational ones. Every church was accompanied by a school, and one of the most important aims of the Polish parochial school system was to preserve the ethnic identity of immigrants. The school of St. Stanislaus Kostka was founded in 1869, and five years later the Sisters of Notre Dame began to teach there. As the parish expanded, its educational institutions also grew. In 1890, St. Stanislaus College was founded, with the Rev. Joseph Halter, C.R., its first principal. Holy Family Academy opened in 1885 at 1444 W. Division Street, with Sisters of the Holy Family of Nazareth as teachers. Besides managing the day schools and boarding schools for girls and evening classes organized to teach young women sewing, embroidery, and music, the sisters also acted as business-women. They bought the two-story school building and the adjacent one-story frame structure, and a few years later they erected a new school. Another building, accommodating 600 students, was built in 1925. Holy Trinity High School opened in 1910 at 1110 Noble Street and moved two years later to the building formerly occupied by the Kosciuszko public school, on Division near Cleaver Street. The teachers and directors were teaching brothers of the Congregation of the Holy Cross, whose mother house was located in Notre Dame, Indiana.

Similar to the role of Irish nuns in the Irish-American Catholic school system, the Felician Sisters played an important part in the education of Poles throughout America. In 1874, they started a parochial school in Polonia, Wisconsin. They next established a convent in La Salle, Illinois, in 1877, where a school and later an orphanage were opened. In 1879, Felician Sisters were sent to Detroit to teach in the Polish school there, and in 1881 to Buffalo. A year later, they began to teach school in Bridgeport, South Chicago. The demand for Felician teachers was so great that 12- or 13-year-old novices were teaching, and the sisters organized a training and education program at their convent house in Detroit. At the turn of the century, there were Felician Sisters teaching in five schools in Chicago. They were actively involved in charity work. However, many paid for their sacrifice: the average age at death among Felician Sisters in the

United States was 27 years, compared with 47.5 years in Poland at the same time (1874–1932). The main cause of death was tuberculosis, which the sisters contracted through their extensive contact with the sick and needy.[7]

In 1886, there were 4 Polish parochial schools in Chicago; in 1900, 14; and in 1910, 18. In 1900, St. Stanislaus Kostka parish parochial school was the largest parochial school in the country, with 3,849 pupils. Holy Trinity parish school had 820 children in 1900 and 1,492 children in 1910. This rising interest in parochial education resulted from a combination of factors: the growing Polish population in the parish, American legal regulations regarding parochial schools, and Poles' belief that Polish ethnicity and Catholicism were inseparable.

School records often did not differentiate pupils by sex. The records at St. Mary of the Angels school at Logan Square, however, show that the proportions of girls and boys were fairly equal throughout the first years of the twentieth century.[8] The rules of the school also show us how a typical Polish parochial school was organized at the turn of the century:

- ▲ Only the children of parish members who paid their annual dues could be pupils.
- ▲ The pastor set the school's rules; parents were not allowed to interfere.
- ▲ A school fee was obligatory for all registered children, even if a child was ill.
- ▲ Children had to clean their classrooms themselves. If parents wanted to relieve their child of this duty, they had to pay a special fee.
- ▲ The monthly fee was 75 cents for each child in grades 1-5 and $1.00 in grades 6–8. If a family was not able to pay for all its children attending school, the pastor could waive the fee.
- ▲ Children were obliged to go to school from ages six to age fourteen; after that, they could receive a certificate and look for work. If they had not completed the sixth grade and had

---

[7]Computation made on the basis of data from *Historia Zgromadzenia SS. Felicjanek. Na podstawie rękopisów,* część III (Kraków, 1932).

[8]*1899–1924. Pamiątka srebrnego jubileuszu Parafii Najświętszej Marii Anielskiej* (Chicago, 1924), 31–33. The records cover the years mentioned in the title.

been absent from school for more than 130 days, however, the certificate was withheld.

▲ Parents were legally responsible for children 14-16 years old, who had to be at either school or work. Roving children under the age of 16 could be arrested and required to go to school.

▲ Parents whose children did not attend school had to pay a fine or went to jail. Their children could be taken away from them and forced to attend school.[9]

The parochial school was a fundamental element of ethnic identity and religious education. In 1920, 36,862 children attended Polish parochial schools in Chicago, accounting for almost 60 percent of the population ages 7–17 and constituting the highest rate of parochial school attendance among ethnic groups in Chicago.[10] Polish children seldom went beyond the parochial school, however; eighth grade usually meant the end of education. Among first- and second-generation Polish immigrants, there was little interest in education as a path to social advancement.

Home and Family

Household Structure and Family Cycle

To understand household structure and living conditions of Zaborowian emigrants, a sample of 106 households in 23 buildings was chosen from the Zaborowian neighborhood.[11] The inhabitants were highly homogeneous: 63 percent were Poles from Galicia; 15 percent, Poles from the Prussian-ruled territories, and 7.5 percent, Poles from the Russian-ruled territories. Poles thus accounted for 86 percent of the inhabitants. Some of their neighbors were Slovaks and Germans, and there were single families of Ruthenians, Hungarians, Bohemians, Danes, and American-born Poles.

---

[9]Ibid., 129–140.

[10]Kantowicz, "Polish Chicago Survival," 221.

[11]The following analysis is based mainly on the 1910 census manuscripts. The names and numbers of the streets are Holt, 844; Cornell, 1533, 1542, 1253, 1231; Augusta, 1545; Chicago, 1430, 1216; Fry, 1430, 1440, 1456, 1458, 1460, 1252, 1226; Noble, 1243; Will, 928; Cornelia, 1343, 1346, 1362, 1364; Milwaukee, 1024; and Center, 811.

The neighborhood was poor and ugly. Streets were full of manure and garbage in boxes, backyards were littered, and houses were unpainted. Most of the houses were two or three stories high, likely made of wood rather than brick (which was more expensive), and had external stairways. Only a few had front yards with grass and flowers growing. "A habitation whose horizon is bounded by a dreary rear tenement and a garbage-strewn alley is in no sense a home," wrote George Taylor Nemeth, who investigated the area in 1900.[12]

Toilets were located either in the basement or under the outside stairs. Their use was generally limited to three families or to one floor, whereas water faucets were one to a family. A spigot in the yard sometimes served entire buildings. Little daylight entered the rooms, and kerosene lamps were used even for daytime lighting. Houses sheltered more than thirty people in four to six households. One house had fifty inhabitants in nine households, including three female Zaborowian boarders. However, most Galicians were used to even worse conditions. The problem was not the number of people in a single building but rather overcrowding in the whole area.

Only fourteen houses had resident owners, among them six Poles from Galicia. Of the resident owners, five Poles came from the Prussian-ruled territories; one was a German; one was of unknown nationality; and one was an unspecified Pole. The other houses were likely owned by Germans and Poles who had already left for better neighborhoods. There was a total of 602 people living in this sample of 106 households. Among them were 197 children younger than 16 years (32.7 percent); 103 boarders (17.1 percent), of whom 30 were female (29 percent); 95 married women, of whom 80 had children (84.2 percent); 9 widows; and 2 widowers.

The average household (21.7 percent of the households) contained five or six people; 22.7 percent of the households, seven or eight members; 21.7 percent, three or four members; and 12.2 percent, one or two members. Although nuclear families with one or two children prevailed (55 percent of households), 13.2 percent of the

---

[12]George Taylor Nemeth, "The Housing of Wage-earners of the Sixteenth Ward of the City of Chicago" (unpublished manuscript, holding of the University of Chicago) (Chicago, 1900), 33. Nemeth investigated Polish Downtown, so his comments are generalizable.

families had three or four children and more than 18 percent of families had 5 to 9 children. Nearly 14 percent of the families had no children at all.

The mortality rate among children in Polish Downtown was very high: The average number of children per family was 5.8 during the 1890s, and by 1900, only 3.7 were still alive.[13] Even in an impoverished region such as Galicia before World War I, mortality was lower. Crowded living conditions were largely responsible. There was only one midwife in the sample neighborhood, and she served a large group of women. Most people lived in nuclear families, and neighbor women in Chicago could not substitute for the childbirth help offered by the extended family or local community in the Polish village. Qualified midwives advertised in local newspapers such as *Dziennik Chicagoski* (Chicago Daily), but until families became aware of these advertisements, many women had to give birth without the necessary attention.

The high infant mortality rate was not the only factor which accounted for the small family size. The mother's age and the migration cycle also played a role. The very young wives (30 percent were between 21 and 25) had arrived only a few years before the census was taken in 1910. They had come as young women looking for husbands, and thus were considered typical "immigrant girls." They had managed to marry and have children. Only a few mothers were in their early thirties, and they were considered "too old" for the typical life course of an immigrant girl. The older women (between 46 and 50) belonged to the earlier wave of emigration from Poland, coming from the Prussian regions rather than from Galicia.

Family size may have been relatively small for the time, but household size was not. About 30 percent of families had boarders; 16 percent had extended family members (siblings, nephews); 14 percent had both boarders and family members; and only 40 percent of families lived alone. The number of boarders tended to be low if family members also lived in the household. In the entire sample (106), there were only four cases of elderly parents living with a fam-

---

[13]Joseph Parot, "Praca imigranta polskiego i paradoks pluralizmu w amerykańskim społeczeństwie miejskim w latach 1860–1930," in Hieronim Kubiak, Eugene Kusielewicz, and Thaddeus Gromada, eds., *American Polonia: Past and Present* (Wrocław, 1988), 423.

ily. This pattern differs significantly from that among German immigrants in Chicago.

Almost 30 percent of boarders were young women. Most (51.6 percent) were between eighteen and twenty years of age. The proportion among female family members is nearly the same (52.9 percent in that age group). This high proportion of young female boarders indicates that it was common for young Polish women to emigrate without their families and live on their own in Chicago (though, often in a surrogate family). This was made possible because of the strong social links within the local community in the home country and fellow Poles in Chicago. Zaborowians perceived "their" community in Chicago as strong enough to protect "their" people.

Young Working Women

Most Polish women emigrating to Chicago were young and unmarried. The average age of Zaborowian and "neighbor" women arriving in Chicago was 18.[14] Together with their younger compatriots who had come as children, they formed a group of unskilled, inexperienced laborers. Young Polish women, or "working girls" as they were called by contemporaries, worked mainly in the service sector or in the garment industry in Polish Downtown. Dishwasher, restaurant helper, and waitress were the most common occupations. Fifty-two such working women lived in the sample neighborhood. They were either boarders or daughters of the heads of household (twenty females per group, at 38.5 percent each) and a smaller group (twelve females, 23 percent) were extended family members.[15] Girls or unmarried women who lived with their families tended to work in the garment industry, which offered opportunities for unskilled workers. Tasks such as basting, pulling out pins, making buttonholes, or sewing on buttons were easy to learn, even for girls only 13 to 15 years old. After acquiring some experience, a girl could start to work on the third, second, or first sewing machine (the last was the

---

[14]All data based on St. John Cantius parish records, if not otherwise specified.

[15]These data are not completely reliable because some of the handwritten census information is illegible.

highest position in this hierarchy). Another typical job was sorting rags. In 1890, for example, the newspaper *Dziennik Chicagoski* was full of job advertisements: two girls were sought for pulling pins; five girls for sewing; six girls for sewing-machine work; ten women for hand and machine sewing, and so on.

There was a great demand for the unskilled labor daughters in Polish families could provide. Female boarders and extended family members, on the other hand, were usually older and required more income than could be earned as an unskilled laborer in the garment industry. Work in a restaurant, for example, included the benefit of free meals. Many women were employed as laundresses or shirt pressers, either in private homes or in commercial laundries. Young women also took jobs, arranged by special agencies, as servants in large boarding houses. No families in the poor Polish neighborhood studied employed maids, and so the female family members were also responsible for domestic chores.

Polish parishes also offered some employment opportunities. A housekeeper, usually an older woman, cooked meals for the pastors and their assistants, did the shopping, and answered the door. Younger servants helped her with dish-washing, laundry, and cleaning. Other women found jobs in various industrial establishments as box makers in factories; tobacco packers; candy or cake makers; or bindery workers. Working conditions were bad: the work was long, hard, and poorly paid. But the girls were usually patient, because one month's wages in Chicago were equal to a season's earnings in Poland.

Marriage and Family Formation

Young Polish immigrant women usually married shortly after their arrival in Chicago. Forty-five percent of them found a husband during their first two years in Chicago, and another 36 percent married during the second two-year period. After only four years in the city, more than 80 percent of Polish immigrant women from the Zaborów area had married. The fact that 68.4 percent of the women in the neighborhood married within the first four years of their stay in the city is support for the assumption that many of them emigrated from Poland in order to leave the tight marriage market behind and find a husband in Chicago.

Chicago offered abundant opportunities for women to marry, since there were more young men than young women within the Polish immigrant group. As usual in chain migration, many cousins, friends, neighbors, and people from neighboring villages were living in close proximity and they were potential husbands. Young Polish-American women were not as burdened by the strict social and economic norms that had been prevalent in Poland and that had made marriage so difficult in the old country.

Although young people enjoyed more independence, the help or interference of friends and relatives was still significant. Either a man sent for a wife from the home parish, or the Polish community in Chicago made arrangements to find a suitable partner. If a man wanted a wife from Poland, he usually asked his friends back home to arrange everything. Often he would not know the woman. The man would send her a *szyfkarta,* a prepaid steamship ticket, and when she arrived in Chicago they were married. One woman recalled that she was invited to come to the United States and was sent a ticket. The invitation coincided with her own decision to emigrate because of difficulties at home. But she discovered she did not like the man. Her protest was weak, however; she was afraid of her relatives, and so married the man they had chosen. She was unhappy for the rest of her life.[16]

The city at least offered women the opportunity to choose their future husbands. Independent choice was not always successful either, however. One woman recalled that she was working in a restaurant as a waitress when she met a visitor to Chicago. After a short acquaintance, the man moved to the city, and she and he decided to marry. When they went to the pastor to make the necessary arrangements, the young woman thought the man's attitude toward the priest not humble enough. Only then did they speak about their expectations of each other. In his opinion, she wanted him to "wear a skirt" while she "wore the trousers."[17] They did not marry.

Ethnic community institutions also offered many opportunities, such as dances in the evening or amateur theater performances, to meet a future husband. Usually the prospective husband was chosen

---

[16]*Pamiętniki Emigrantów, Stany Zjednoczone* (Warszawa, 1977), 1:573–574.
[17]Ibid., 488.

from among men from the same village or parish in the old country. Marrying a person from the same region was widely perceived as a guarantee of a successful marriage. One girl preparing for emigration was given this advice by her mother: "Do not marry any stranger in America, only someone of our kind. . . . Being abroad one is looking for someone of one's own kind, not looking at difference of age, character, or other things."[18]

Zaborowian women took such advice seriously. In the years 1893–1914, a total of 176 Zaborowian women married in St. John Cantius parish.

Marriages with both partners from Zaborów parish accounted for 46.5 percent of marriages involving Zaborowians (76.2 percent in the old country) and marriages with partners from within a 10 kilometer circle around Zaborów for 72.1 percent (in the old country, 92 percent). Similar research on the Slovak community in Pittsburgh from 1880 to 1915 reveals an even higher degree of local-origin endogamy. There, 38.3 percent of partners were from the same village, and 84.3 percent were from villages less than 10 miles apart.[19] Thus, marriage was not only 100 percent homogeneous within the broad ethnic category but was also very high within local and regional culture.

TABLE 8.1

Geographic origins of husbands, 1893–1914

Origin	Percent
The same village	13.4
Another village within the parish	33.1
A neighboring village outside the parish	25.6
Other villages in Galicia	25.6
The United States (but of Polish origin)	1.1
The Russian part of Poland	1.1
The Prussian part of Poland	0.5

Source: Records of St. John Cantius parish.

[18]Ibid., 2:443.

[19]June G. Alexander, *The Immigrant Church and Community: Pittsburgh's Slovak Catholics and Lutherans, 1880–1915* (Pittsburgh, 1987), 103.

In Chicago, the desire to marry a husband from a familiar area in Poland remained strong. Having many friends and relatives from home, as well as many people who had emigrated from neighboring villages, living in the same neighborhood in Chicago made this an option. Immigrants could thus live in the United States without breaking ties with their home community. Since immigrants had to undergo major adjustments in Chicago, choosing a partner from home was one way to maintain a sense of continuity.

The marriage ages of Zaborowian women in Chicago differed significantly from those of Zaborowian women in Galicia. In Chicago, there were almost no marriages among widows—the group of immigrant women was too young. When the average age of marriage in Chicago is compared to the average age of *first* marriage in Zaborów, the difference is nearly four years. This was very important, since achieving the status of a married woman was highly desirable. For men, the difference was not so pronounced: in Chicago, they married 2.6 years earlier. This phenomenon, however, should be regarded less as a sign of assimilation than as a typical change provoked by emigration and the consequent easing of village restrictions on marriage.

According to the 1910 census, which covered a more diverse population, the group of Zaborowian women differed significantly from

TABLE 8.2

Marriage age of Zaborowian women in Chicago and in Galicia, 1893–1914

Age	In Chicago N = 368 %	In Poland N = 491 %
<19	22.0	10.5
20–25	69.1	43.6
26–30	7.6	21.1
31–35	0.7	7.0
36–40	0.0	5.4
>40	0.6	12.4

Source: Records of St. John Cantius parish.

the average female population in Polish Downtown. Zaborowian women married much younger: 91.1 percent of them were 25, and younger, whereas only 35.7 percent of the women overall in Polish Downtown married that young. In Zaborów parish, only 54.1 percent of the women married younger than 25, and nearly 25 percent were older than 30. In St. John Cantius parish, only about 1 percent of women were older than thirty when they married, whereas in Polish Downtown, 37.8 percent were older than thirty.

Among Zaborowian emigrants to Chicago, moreover, there was a stronger tendency toward peer-age marriages. According to St. John Cantius parish records, more than 84 percent of husbands in Chicago were older than their wives from Zaborów, as compared to 70.7 percent in Poland. In 5 percent of the cases, the wives were older than their husbands, in contrast to more than 24 percent in Poland. The average age difference between bride and groom was significantly lower in Chicago: if the man was older, the average difference was 4.3 years (in Poland 7.3); when the woman was older, it was 1.9 years (6.4 in Poland). In Chicago, the percentage of peer-age marriages (couples with less than five years of age difference) was 77.6, whereas in Poland it was 56.7.

Some people transplanted the old tradition of matchmaking to America, sometimes turning it into a business. A good opportunity for this activity was taking in male and female boarders. Shortly after arrival, the "girls" were "changed into Americans," given new dresses, brassieres, and shoes. When husbands were found, the matchmaking family made a profit. After the wedding, the husband had to reimburse the family for all of the money that had been spent on the girl.

When people decided to marry, they could go to church or to court. The first option was preferred, and dominated; the second was chosen mainly when the couple feared the marriage would not be fully accepted by their relatives and friends. A court ceremony was a completely new phenomenon for Polish immigrants. It was part of an urban secularization that affected many aspects of their lives, especially those related to customs and festivities.

Emigration totally changed marriage for Zaborowian women. Money and social status had become of minor importance, whereas age and region of origin assumed a new relevance. Since the dowry had nearly vanished and men outnumbered women, even a poor, not particularly pretty woman could easily find a husband. Whether a good husband could be found was another question. The age difference between them was small, which made it easier to have a family. And the resulting family was nuclear, since elderly parents had been left in Poland. Despite the strong desire to maintain tradition and to keep ties with the home community, family life for first-generation Zaborowian women in Chicago was structurally very different from that at home.

In 1895, the *Dziennik Chicagoski* presented a hypothetical correspondence (written by a man) between two Polish girls from the same village: Agata, who had left Poland three years earlier, and Maria, who was still in Poland.[20] The satirical character of the text captures the change in attitudes. In her first letter, Agata reports that she was busy working in the shop all day, but every evening she went out "to have fun." Having fun meant the opportunity to meet boys— that is, prospective husbands. She already had three candidates. The one she liked best had formerly worked as a mill laborer at the manor in a nearby village in Poland. In Chicago, he earned $11 a week and was "a gentleman." She wrote that "he had his own butcher shop and wore a high hat like that of the Mr. Doctor who used to visit the ladies at the manor." Agata imagined that she and the young man would wed as soon as they had saved enough money to buy furniture. She offered to send a *szyfkarta* (prepaid steamship ticket) for Maria so that she could get married, too. In her return letter, Maria talked about the condition of her family's cattle and who had married whom. She did not want to come to Chicago, because she was to marry a man "who had two sheepskin coats and a small piece of land behind the hill." Agata thought this answer showed that her friend lacked any interest in other than peasant ways. She, on the other hand, recommended America as a country where a woman, after marriage, could sleep until noon, do some shopping in the afternoon, and in the evening go to a show or dancing. She also informed Maria that in America a husband was obliged to support his wife, and that, under the sanction of jail, it was prohibited to beat women. She ended her letter by stating: "Do what you want, but I am not stupid."

---

[20] 21 January, 29 January, and 2 February 1895.

Children

Did the typical Polish woman continue to work outside the home after marriage until she bore her first child?[21] Our analysis of the census records shows that they stopped outside work at marriage. It was a rule almost without exception. Of the 95 wives in the study area in Chicago, only four worked outside the home. Of these 95 wives, 15 were childless, and all of them stayed at home.[22]

Children were born soon after marriage, and frequent pregnancies were the rule among Polish immigrant women.[23] The high mortality rate makes it difficult to determine the number of children a woman had while living in Chicago. Nevertheless, families with many children were standard: children were still regarded as an asset. The high birthrate was not simply the result of obeying Catholic rules and shunning contraception. In Chicago, as in Zaborów, children participated in the family economy. Schoolchildren often took their fathers' lunch to the factory, delivered to customers the clean linens washed by their mother, or helped at home

TABLE 8.3

Fertility of Zaborowian Women, 1893–1914

		Percent
1 child	after 2 years of marriage	92
2 children	3 years	56
3 children	5 years	41
4 children	7 years	24
5 children	8 years	10
6 children	9 years	5

Source: Records of St. John Cantius parish in Chicago for the years 1893–1914.

[21]So argues John J. Bukowczyk, *And My Children Did Not Know Me: A History of the Polish-Americans* (Bloomington, Ind., 1987), 25.

[22]1910 census records.

[23]The first child was born after one year of marriage in 81 percent of the cases and after two years in 11 percent; the second child was born after two years in 30 percent and after three years in 26 percent; the third child was born after three years in 6 percent, after four years in 17 percent, and after 5 years in 18 percent; and the fourth child was born after five years in 8 percent, after six years in 9 percent, and after seven years in 7 percent.

under their mother's supervision. Teenagers worked as helpers in family businesses, such as stores and restaurants, or as handy boys and girls to unskilled laborers. They were expected to contribute to the family budget and give their earnings to their parents. This was especially important if the family was trying to save to return home to Poland.

Baby care did not change much in America. Babies continued to be breast-fed for a long period, in part because parents believed that this practice served as a contraceptive. Simple pacifiers made from a lump of sugar or bread tied into a piece of cloth were common, although rubber pacifiers were also used. As had been true in Poland, mothers did not pay close attention to their babies. Although in the city mothers were free from the demands of farm work, they were still busy at home. Moreover, there were no grandmothers to help out.

In the late nineteenth and early twentieth centuries, illegitimacy was a severe problem in Poland. Although the average percentage in 1894–1914 was 5.4, it reached 7.5 in 1894–1902 and declined to 2.8 in 1903–1914. In Chicago, the illegitimacy rate plummeted. St. John Cantius parish records show that in the years 1894–1902, the proportion of illegitimate births was 0.9 percent, and in 1903–1914 it was 1.8 percent. High illegitimacy at the end of the nineteenth century in Poland was mainly the result of a very tight marriage market. Emigration to Chicago helped many young people fulfill their wish to get married, and the drop in illegitimacy was a visible effect of this. It is interesting to note that illegitimacy was always much lower in Chicago than in Zaborów Parish; legitimacy was highly esteemed for and among Polish immigrant women.[24]

The relationship between children and parents was also apt to change during migration: "Parental authority and discipline remained strict for a long time. . . . Children were taught to honor their elders, to address them respectfully, to kiss their hands at meetings or parting or in thanks for a favor, to obey their parents, to speak only when spoken to and in general to be quiet and not disturb their

---

[24]The low rate of illegitimacy was not peculiar to the Zaborowian women in Chicago. Cf. John William Mullally, "A Study of Marriage Patterns in a Rural Polish Roman-Catholic Parish [in Texas] from 1872 to 1959" (M.A. thesis, University of Texas, 1963), 86.

father when he wanted quiet and rest."[25] Physical punishment was a common child-rearing practice among Polish-American immigrants. Mothers' methods were not as severe as those of fathers, and they were the primary dispensers of punishment, since fathers were around mainly on Sundays. Childhood was not idyllic in other ways as well. Children had no choice but to contribute to the family economy, for example. A woman who had grown up in the Back of the Yards district recalled that her father used to tell the children, "If you don't work, you don't eat." This rule had force in the family.[26] In the years 1913 and 1914, the highest numbers of working children in Illinois were found among Polish-Americans.

The Work of Housewives

In our sample neighborhood, nearly 60 percent of the households included boarders, extended-family members, or both. Similar percentages are found elsewhere. In Johnstown, Pennsylvania, for example, 51.3 percent of all East Central European households kept boarders in 1900. "Keeping boarders did not just mean additional income, but also more crowding, less privacy, more drinking and fighting, and an exhausting seventeen hours a day of work for the wife who had to cook, clean, scrub, wash, iron, carry water, and do the shopping."[27]

The workday of the housewife began well before dawn. Ashes had to be emptied from the wood stove and the stove lit, and breakfast had to be cooked for all the males in the household. Then the women and children had to be fed. Next came cleaning, shopping at the corner store, hauling water for cooking and washing (if the house did not have indoor plumbing), and cooking lunch for the children and the husband. No sooner were these tasks done than the evening meal had to be prepared for the family and the boarders.[28]

[25]Eugene E. Obidinski and Helen Stankiewicz Zand, *Polish Folkways in America: Community and Family*, Polish Studies Series, (Lanham, Md., 1987), 1:108.

[26]Quoted in Adam Walaszek, *Polscy Robotnicy, Praca i Związki Zawodowe w Stanach Zjednoczonych Ameryki 1880–1922*, Biblioteka Polonijna (Wrocław, 1988), 20:58.

[27]Ewa Morawska, *For Bread with Butter: The Life-Worlds of East Central Europeans in Johnstown, Pennsylvania, 1890–1940* (Cambridge, 1985), 127.

[28]Mrs. Z. W., interview by author during field work in Poland, August 1979; see also Bukowczyk, *And My Children*, 24.

Backyard vegetable gardens were common, despite the yards' small size. Women picked and canned what they grew in their yards, and sometimes also raised chicken, ducks, or rabbits there for extra income. The garden was important not only as a source of fresh food but also as a symbol of a lost peasant environment. If no garden was available, the worker's wife could go to the farmer's market. Sometimes women went out to farms nearby to work, picking onions, for example, and then selling them.

Once a week they did the washing for the whole family, the boarders, and sometimes for others as well to provide additional income. One woman recalled how her mother took in laundry for $1.25 per (large) basket.[29] Washing laundry was a laborious effort. "[Women] scrubbed laundry by hand in a steaming tub set on a chair in the kitchen and ironed next to the crackling stove," writes Bukowczyk.[30] In the afternoon, there was time for mending or sewing, sometimes on a sewing machine. In the evening, the men came home from work dirty and hungry and had to be attended to. This aspect of housework routine resembled that of wives in Poland. Provided everything was going well, this was the normal day of a housewife.

All family members were expected to contribute to the family income. Sometimes a wife contributed a large share. An old woman who had grown up in Chicago remembers: "My father worked in a tannery, four of my brothers in factories, and my mother took care of four boarders. We lived off her income and saved my father's and brother's five salaries."[31]

How did emigration affect the family status of Polish women in Poland and America? In rural areas of Poland, after men emigrated, the women who stayed behind began to manage the farm and became more independent.[32] (But some men who emigrated maintained close contact with their families at home and managed the farm from a distance).[33] In America, housewives could play a prominent role in the

---

[29]Oral History Archives of Chicago Polonia, Adamic Series (ADA-036), 1 (tape), p. 2 (stenograph). Quoted by Parot, "Praca Imigranta," 428.

[30]Bukowczyk, *And My Children*, 24.

[31]Mrs. J. M., interview by the author, Poland, 1979.

[32]Helen Stankiewicz Zand, "Polish Family Folkways in the United States," *Polish American Studies* 13 (1956):77–88; Bukowczyk, *And My Children*, 25.

[33]Mary E. Cygan, "Polish Women and Emigrant Husbands," in Dirk Hoerder and Inge Blank, eds., *Roots of the Transplanted*, vol. 1 (New York, 1994), 359–376.

family. Unlike in Poland, men were usually at work and away from home during most of the day or night. Women worked, but at home. It was their space, and they were the strategists of the family's economy. They managed the savings and controlled or influenced consumption. It was owing to their abilities and ambitions that the status of the family rose. Thus a clear and sharp separation appeared between male and female fields of activity.

> The household was one of the few areas in which the average immigrant working-class person could enjoy much authority. In the home, migration seems to have affected basic relations between Polish men and women. This probably often caused substantial tensions ... but immigrant wives were gradually coming into their own.[34]

The Rituals of Peasant Culture Transformed

Rituals of the Annual Cycle

Although the annual rituals of Polish immigrant life were no longer based on the rhythm of agricultural work, they were still numerous. Many were connected with Catholic holy days. The cycle began at Advent with preparations for Christmas. The house had to be cleaned and decorated for Christmas and the tree and manger prepared. The nuns, with the help of the church organist, made Christmas wafers, a necessary part of the Polish Christmas Eve. Some of the wafers were sent to absent relatives, both to and from Zaborów. Sharing these special wafers during the Christmas Eve supper was the centerpiece of the family ceremony.

Christmas Eve and Christmas Eve supper were celebrated in nearly the same way as in the old country. Women prepared the festive meals according to such rules as serving an odd number of courses, having an even number of people at the table, putting straw or hay under the tablecloth, and leaving food on the table for poten-

---

[34]Bukowczyk, *And My Children*, 25.

tial visitors.[35] Nearly every house had a Christmas tree, along with Christmas decorations, such as an evergreen bough hanging from the ceiling (*podłaźnik*). The whole family sang carols after supper, and at midnight everybody went to church for a special mass (*pasterka*).

The custom of blessing chalk, gold, and myrrh in the church on Epiphany (January 6th) was celebrated as in Poland, as was writing "K+M+B" on doors with the sanctified chalk. The latter custom gradually disappeared in the United States.

Some Polish-American customs were adopted by Poles back home. Giving gifts at Christmas was one such import. A dance party on New Year's Eve, very popular in Chicago, was another. In the old country, New Year's Day had been observed more than New Year's Eve, and by older people rather than by the young. That tradition had changed in both countries. The Christmas season was for all Poles a time for visiting relatives and friends, eating festive foods, and wearing festive clothes. The period between Christmas and Epiphany was not free of work, however. In Chicago, because of work responsibilities, festivities had to be limited to two or three days.

February 2nd was another important day: Candlemas, the Purification of the Blessed Virgin Mary (*Matka Boska Gromniczna*). Special candles (*gromnice*) were blessed in the church; in Poland, they were lit and carried home. In America, usually only older women went to the church to bless candles. *Gromnice* were kept in the home, and people believed that they protected them against lightning during storms. This holy day was much more important in Zaborów than in Chicago.

The carnival time between Christmas and Lent was full of weddings and parties, as in Poland. But in Chicago, these festivities were held not in private homes but in the halls of various societies. They ended with *ostatki* or *zapusty*, special parties that were shortened from three days in Poland to one in the United States. Palms were blessed on Palm Sunday, a week before Easter. In Poland as in the United States, palms were eventually replaced with pussy willow branches. The latter were sometimes given to children as a treatment for sore throats, according to traditional beliefs.

---

[35]Obidinski and Zand, *Polish Folkways*, 62–63.

Holy Week celebrations resembled those in the old country, except that fasting was not observed as strictly. The religious character of these ceremonies dominated in both countries, and the Polish custom of *Święcone,* the blessing of food on Holy Saturday, was incorporated into the ritual canon by Polish immigrants. Small portions of festive Easter foods such as ham, sausage, bread, special cake (*baba*), salt, vinegar, and beautifully colored and decorated eggs (*pisanki*) were carried to church in large baskets. In the old country, the size and contents of the basket were a matter of womanly pride; in America, they were a tribute to tradition. Easter Monday was also a holiday. It was a custom to sprinkle girls with water on that day (*Śmigus Dyngus*). Easter was a time for eating large amounts of festive food, with a preponderance of meat meals.

Since an agricultural work cycle was irrelevant to Chicago's Poles, the customs connected with the beginning of spring (*Marzanna*) vanished. Another custom not transplanted was St. John's Eve (June 23rd and 24th). On that night in Poland, girls released wreaths into streams: the girl whose wreath was first "fished out" by a boy could expect to be married soon. In the old country, these celebrations symbolized the passage from spring to summer, which was important in a rural culture but not in the city. The harvest festival (*dożynki*) was not continued in America either, although it was a very important tradition in Poland. But August 15th, the Feast of the Assumption, known in Poland as Our Lady of the Herbs (*Matka Boska Zielna*), was celebrated with great enthusiasm in America. Women picked wild flowers, such as goldenrod and black-eyed Susan, and herbs for sale at the market. "Many of the women who took the bright yellow and orange bouquets to the church still wore their Old World kerchiefs, and the sight of them as they converged upon the church with the bouquets held stiffly before them made a colorful picture."[36] The bouquets were kept at home in a place reserved for blessed objects.

As far as possible rituals were continued, with an important role for the women, who were responsible for all aspects of the feast. The customs of Candlemas and Assumption Day also show that Polish-

---

[36]Ibid., 71.

Americans maintained a specifically Polish religiosity, with its strong cult of the Virgin Mary.

One significant factor accounted for many transatlantic differences in customs and festivities. Traditional celebrations that had other than religious functions were most likely to change in America. For example, in Chicago, wedding meals were not the lavish affairs they had been in Poland. They used to provide one of the few opportunities for people to get enough to eat, but now there was adequate food. Traditional meetings also fell by the wayside, because various institutions provided outlets for socializing. These changes were also related to secularization; they provoked a clearer distinction between *sacrum* and *profanum*, and they moved some situations from holiday to everyday reality.

Rituals of the Life Course

As in the old country, the traditional Polish wedding in Chicago took place in the Catholic Church. Three Sundays before the wedding, the first banns were published in the bride's parish. Quite often a house was rented for the couple before marriage, so they had their own place to go to after the ceremony. Sometimes a special party took place (a custom unknown in Poland) called *wybieranki*, a "choosing party." At this party, the bride's and groom's friends and relatives chose partners from among themselves as everybody was expected to attend the wedding ceremony as couples. Selecting the right partner was important, because the partners were often treated as prospective marriage candidates. Also, every guest couple was photographed separately (at its own expense), and no one wanted to be "immortalized" with a person they did not like. This custom was new for Zaborowian peasants; however, they were quick to pick it up in Chicago.

The wedding party was held in the home of the bride's parents or relatives or in the hall of a local society or a saloon, rented for the occasion. On the day of the ceremony, the groom was blessed by his parents. The bride, meanwhile, was attended to by friends, who helped her with the veil and other preparations. Some older women remembered traditional wedding songs from the old country. When the groom came to the bride's home just before the ceremony, he

A Polish wedding party in Chicago.
Photograph, Chicago Historical Society.

and the bride knelt before the bride's parents and were blessed. Then everybody went to church. Following the wedding, the couple was welcomed with bread and salt by the bride's mother, a custom traditional among Poles all over the world. Music was played, and everybody was invited for a festive meal. After the meal, all participants went to a photographer. Photos were often sent to the village as a form of correspondence about the American way of life. Upon returning from the photographer, everyone went to dance at a local society hall or saloon. If the wedding party was held in a saloon, it was the saloon keeper who provided the drinks, such as beer, vodka, or wine. In the evening the rest of the guests (those who had not attended because they did not want to lose a day at work) arrived. Late arrivers were given dinner and drinks, after which they joined the dancing. Weddings could take place on any day, though there was a preference for the carnival period. Using saloons to hold weddings and saloon keepers as the people responsible for drinks—a significant component of the ceremony—was a sign of sophistication.

The collection of money was a necessary component of the ceremony. It took different forms, but the idea was the same: to pay for the wedding expenses or help the newlyweds start their household. In a Chicago saloon, for example, at about 11 P.M. a table and two chairs were put in the middle of the hall. The bride sat on one chair, one of her relatives on the other. Special music was played as a cue, and every male guest had to dance with the bride, then put a few dollars on the table.[37] Another method was the throwing of silver dollars at heavy dinner plates until the plates were broken. "A stack of the plates was put in the middle of the floor and the men guests attempted to break the plates with silver dollars. A dollar once thrown could not be picked up for the second try. Since the plates were tough, many dollars were taken in."[38] The collection could also take the form of pinning dollar bills on the bride's dress or passing a plate "for a cap" during breakfast or dinner. The cap was part of the *oczepiny* ritual, the final stage of the wedding. Although the custom changed from putting a cap on the bride's head to taking off the veil, the symbolic meaning was the same: the passage from single woman to wife.

All essential wedding rituals remained intact in Chicago, although the ceremony was often limited to one day and not all "necessary" participants, (such as parents) could take part. The social, or community, meaning of the wedding was underscored by inviting many guests. Sometimes Zaborowian brides in Chicago would send money back to their villages so that friends and relatives at home could hold a wedding celebration on their behalf. This not only allowed those who could not be present for the festivities in Chicago to take part in absentia, but kept the emigrant couple's presence in their community alive—an important concern for those intending to return home.

The newlyweds did not live with the husband's parents, as in Poland. Usually they rented an apartment and began their new life on their own. A woman was not subordinate to her mother-in-law, and, because of her significant contribution to the family economy—

---

[37] *Pamiętniki Emigrantów,* 1:146. A similar description is given by a Mrs. B.S., interview by author, Poland, 1979.

[38] Obidinski and Zand, *Polish Folkways,* 92.

measurable in cash—her position in the family was stronger than in Poland.

Most superstitions connected with pregnant women were given up in Chicago, especially those that excluded pregnant women from specific jobs. Other beliefs prevailed. For example, birth defects were still attributed to certain experiences of the mother during pregnancy. When a woman gave birth in Chicago, if she received any help at all it was usually from a midwife, much as in Zaborów. These midwives, however, were more experienced and better trained than those in the village. Yet they were familiar with, and indulged, the traditional beliefs. There is an account of a grandmother who "buried the placenta in the cellar to have on hand in case the child had a birthmark, to rub on the affected part."[39]

As in Poland, the christening ceremony was held within two weeks after the child was born. The festivities surrounding the ceremony, however, were smaller. The guests no longer brought food, but gifts for the baby were always welcome. The social meaning of the ceremony was not as strong as in Poland, although it was still an important day in the neighborhood. There is an interesting change in the names that were given to girls at baptism. Traditional names given to daughters in Zaborów, usually a saint's name connected with the day of birth or a name connected with the village culture, were now in the minority. In Chicago, names were chosen more according to fashion. The ones that occurred most frequently in the baptism records of St. John Cantius parish were Anna, Maria, and Zofia.

Much as in Poland, the period of confinement after giving birth was regarded a time of female impurity. Thus the ceremony of "churching" (wywód) was also performed in Chicago. It was not connected with any festivity; there was only a blessing in church. In the church of St. Mary of the Angels, churching took place only on Mondays, Tuesdays, Wednesdays, and Thursdays between 7 and 9 A.M.[40]

Polish peasant beliefs and rituals connected with death were maintained in Chicago. As in Poland, the religious character of the moment was important. Yet the institutionalization of the ceremony

---

[39]Ibid., 97.
[40]1899–1924. Pamiątka srebrnego jubileuszu, 129.

in Chicago must have been shocking to the peasant from Poland. For example, deceased people could not have a church funeral if they had not been administered the sacrament of extreme unction at their deathbeds and if they had not made their Easter confessions—which could be accomplished only after paying the annual fee to the parish.

Living Conditions

From Boarding Houses to Homes

Even landless Polish peasants usually owned their own homes. Therefore, one of the main aspirations of Polish immigrants was home ownership. The desire motivated them to improve their economic lot. Around the turn of the century, home ownership was uncommon among Zaborowian immigrants and Galician immigrants in general. They typically rented apartments in one-and-a-half story houses with a grocery, saloon, or other business on the ground floor. Living conditions in the Polish countryside had always been very bad, so those in Chicago were not seen as worse, merely different. A man who came to Chicago in 1906 recalls his experience in a boarding house:

> It was a small house, almost worse than in our village. There were many boarders already living there, but the owner, a Polish woman, took me, too, to increase her earnings. . . . There were many quarrels when all the men came home from work, dirty and sticky, and ran to the one wash basin. Finally we decided to wait in line. . . . There was neither gas nor electricity. It often happened that someone ended up with someone else's shoes when he went out for his night work.[41]

There might be up to fifteen men living in a three- or four-room apartment in a boarding house. Sometimes "it was like a hospital when you looked at all the men sleeping on the floor or in narrow beds, wherever it was possible," recalls the same immigrant. When

---

[41] *Pamiętniki Emigrantów,* 2:300.

boarding houses had fewer boarders, living conditions naturally were better. One woman recalls that her family's rented apartment had its own large kitchen and one private bedroom.[42] The family had four boarders, and the girl did not remember the other rooms because they were always occupied.

When home ownership was finally realized, aspirations often were raised to an even higher level. If a family was well-off, the women expected a better house. One woman remembers her mother's attitudes. The mother did not like the house built by her husband because it was too small; it had four rooms, in addition to the kitchen and a bathroom, but there was no second floor. The father had to sell that house and build a new one. "The entrance to the new house was on the ground floor, and the kitchen was also there. On the second floor, there was a bathroom and four bedrooms. Two of the bedrooms were for boarders. I had a room for myself, and my parents slept with the other children in another bedroom."[43]

Whether people were renters or homeowners, certain aspects of housing were continually upgraded. Every year, utilities were expanded by the city. Gas, electricity, and indoor plumbing were more available to residents in 1908, for example, than in 1893.

Interior decoration of homes was usually the women's task. Although the furniture was manufactured in factories and lacked the individuality of handmade furniture, a new set of furniture was nevertheless the pride of a woman. Adoption of urban interiors did not mean a total abandonment of Zaborowian ways, however: pictures of saints were hung on the walls, and palms blessed on Palm Sunday and bouquets of herbs and flowers blessed on Assumption Day were stuck behind the picture frames. Sometimes a statuette of the Virgin Mary stood on a shelf. Religious items were abundant in Chicago and were often sold by Poles to Poles. For example, at 676 Noble Street, a J. Kowalska ran a shop selling prayer books, religious paintings, crucifixes, and scapulars. Underneath the holy pictures there was often a vigil light burning, and inside the door there was a small font for holy water for customers to cross themselves as they entered and left.

---

[42]Mrs. J. M., interview by author, Poland, August 1979.
[43]Mrs. Z. W., interview by author, Poland, August 1979.

Polish-American families retained many elements of rural Polish interiors in their Chicago homes: "While roomier and brighter because of more and larger windows and with well scrubbed wooden or linoleum-covered floor instead of the hard packed earth floor of the typical peasant cottage in Poland, the interior of the average Polish home of that early period presented a strongly Old World appearance."[44] Pillows and featherbeds were still piled high on the beds, as they had been in Poland. Flowers and pottery, which had been standard features of household decor in the old country, continued to brighten rooms in Chicago. A strong remembrance of Poland was provided every Saturday, when the time-thrifty housewife scrubbed the floor: to keep the floor clean until Sunday, she covered it with newspapers. Usually there were only Polish newspapers in the house, so many children retained their Polish culture through studying these "Polish carpets."

Food

Looking at the foodways of Polish-Americans enables us to assess the amount of immediate adaptation necessary in the city. Since the women were responsible for providing and processing food, they had to learn quickly in order to put dinner on the table. The changes that took place were due as much to urbanization as they were to assimilation. For Polish peasants from Zaborów, both the quantity and types of food represented a big change, and a mixture of peasant and urban diets appeared, enriched by tastes from different regions in Poland. As a result, Zaborowian women in Chicago learned to prepare many Polish dishes they had not eaten at home before.

The quantity of food obtainable was striking to the immigrants. Since meat and meat products were always the most desired foods, having an abundance of sausages and hams available was prized. Numerous Polish butchers were important features of the neighborhood. Vegetables, fresh and processed (mainly sauerkraut), and wheat flour were also plentiful. Thus immigrants concluded that living in America meant eating on a regular basis festive foods one could afford only on holy days in Poland. This perception of

---

[44]Obidinski and Zand, *Polish Folkways*, 22–23.

enhanced living conditions may well have made other shortcomings of urban life in the United States, such crowded apartments and difficult working conditions, bearable. On real festive days, Christmas, Easter, or weddings, the food was even more extravagant, with traditional dishes prepared in the Polish way. When migrants returned to their village, the general opinion was that they "looked better" and were better "nourished." For the most part this was true.

Clothing

Clothing in Chicago conveyed social status, as it had in Poland. Women coming to the city wanted to throw away their villager's "stigma" and change their way of dressing as soon as possible. But this attitude varied according to age, socioeconomic status, and time of arrival in the United States. Young women usually came to Chicago at the invitation of friends or relatives who already knew how a city girl "should" look. They immediately bought a new dress for the newcomer as well as a corset, shoes (often with high heels), a hat, and gloves. It did not make any difference whether the dress they wore on arrival was made especially "for America," nor did it matter that it was the best they had ever had. It was not suitable for the city—it was not fashionable. The standardization of clothing based on factory technology was the desired look, whereas in Poland each region had a specific way of dressing.

There was a strong determination among female newcomers not to be recognized as "greenhorns." Girls wore good dresses to work, a big switch from the village, where they wore their worst clothes to do (farm) work. However much conformity with urban fashion was desired, wearing high-heeled shoes was a real trial for a person used to walking barefoot. Corsets were also unknown to Polish village girls. Sometimes they bought one and went to more experienced women for advice on how to wear it. More positive feelings were connected with wearing underwear, which had not been popular in the Polish countryside. An old woman, still living in Chicago, remembered that for "the first time in my life I was warm."[45]

---

[45]Mrs. W. N., interview by author, Chicago, 1989.

Unmarried young women usually had an easier time adjusting to all these changes. Women who were already married when they arrived and who did not have the experience of working outside the household were usually more conservative. They were the ones who sat in the first row at church with scarves on their heads. If they were still young, they may have changed their way of dress, too, but not as rapidly. The great gap that had existed in Poland between everyday and festive clothing diminished. In the city, the Sunday dress that could be worn only to church in the home village now was worn to evening dances as well. But when women returned to the home village, the American dresses were quickly abandoned, sometimes put in the bottom of the chest as memorabilia. Changes in clothing patterns exemplify two phenomena. The first is a strong fear of being recognized as newcomers. The second is the equally strong desire "to be like a lady." In Poland, the living standards of the manor served as models: Polish peasants admired the lifestyle of the country nobles. Thus being able to dress like a Polish lady was considered a great success in America. In sociological terms, this reflects the process of urbanization more than that of assimilation.

The Female Public Sphere: The Polish Women's Alliance

Around the turn of the century, while Polish immigration into Chicago was still in its early phase, most ethnic institutions functioned at a strictly local, parochial level. Polish women, however, were able to organize on a national level. The Związek Polek w Ameryce, the Polish Women's Alliance in America (PWA), was founded in Chicago in 1898. Its consideration for the needs of working women, devotion to the family and, most of all, flaming Polish patriotism and love of the Polish language, made the organization attractive to Polish immigrant women.[46] The organization was

---

[46]Jadwiga Karłowiczowa, *Historia Związku Polek w Ameryce. Przyczynki do poznania Duszy Wychodźctwa Polskiego w Stanach Zjednoczonych Ameryki Północnej* (Chicago: 1938). See also William J. Galush, "Purity and Power: Chicago Polonian Feminists, 1880–1914," *Polish American Studies* 67 (1990): 5–24.

bourgeois, however, dominated by "Prussian-Polish" women. Therefore, newly arrived Zaborowian women had difficulty participating.

An early attempt to organize Polish women in Chicago into a social alliance was made in 1884, when a group called Grosz Polski[47] was founded. Since the first Polish emigrants came from the Prussian-dominated parts of Poland, the political situation in these territories was the main point of interest. Grosz Polski collected money to help Poles buy their land back from the Prussians, who had deprived Poles of their farm holdings. The "American" aim of Grosz Polski was to build a "House for Girls" in Chicago, where they could be taught sewing and housekeeping. After only a few months, however, Grosz Polski folded.

In 1887, two other groups were established in Chicago: Gwiazda Zwycięstwa (Victory's Star) and Towarzystwo Centralne Polek (the Central Society of Polish Women). The first group quickly disappeared, but the second was in existence until 1938. The latter group gave birth to ideas later implemented by the PWA. Its first president, Teofila Samolinska, noted that a woman could not obtain insurance in existing mutual-aid and insurance societies but only through her husband. The many single Polish women in Chicago, unmarried or widows, had to join the societies of other ethnic groups to obtain help. In 1895, another society addressed to insurance for women was founded: Klub Patriotycznych Polek, the Club of Polish Patriot Women.

All of these groups had two main aims: mutual aid and the preservation of Polish sentiments. After several unsuccessful attempts, the concept of a larger women's organization succeeded in the form of the PWA. Its aims were published in the Polish press in October 1898: to unite Polish-American women into one organization, to pay death benefits, and to preserve Polish culture.

Death benefits were simple: if a member died, the other members paid $1.00 each. The maximum benefit awarded was $500. Individuals and existing societies alike could be members of the PWA. For the individual woman, it was now possible to construct her own security net based on a nationwide insurance system (which also

---

[47]The *grosz* is the smallest Polish monetary unit, one hundredth of a zloty.

offered loans). For many local and parochial groups, the PWA represented a means for a unified Polish community.

The first president of the PWA Board of Administration was Stefania Chmielińska. Anastazja Borecka, Łucja Wołowska, and Maria Rokosz were the earliest members of the board. All of them were well established Polish-Americans from earlier waves of emigration, mainly from the Prussian-ruled parts of Poland. As a rule, these immigrants were better educated. Almost every year, beginning in 1900, a convention took place to decide policy. Members who participated in that first convention passed a resolution recommending to members that they speak only Polish to their children. At the third convention in 1902, the PWA launched its own journal, *Głos Polek* (The Voice of Polish Women). It was published monthly as part of a daily, *Dziennik Narodowy*. Also at that third convention, the role of education in upward mobility was emphasized, and a special educational department was created. During the first decade of the twentieth century, the PWA established contacts with the women's movement in Poland and supported various patriotic causes.

In 1908, at the seventh convention, participants protested the Russification and Germanization of Poles. They also protested the way the Chicago census was organized (the census defined nationality according to the state or region the person came from, not according to ethnic identity). The convention resolution stressed the necessity of retaining knowledge of Polish language, history, and literature.

The PWA set forth what it considered traits of the ideal Polish immigrant woman: sincerity, hospitality, enthusiasm, rationality, and social responsibility. A measure of the PWA's success is the switch in 1910 of the *Głos Polek* from a monthly insert to a separate weekly. The organization also expanded its community services. Summer vacations for poor children were organized for the first time in 1910. And the educational department of the PWA established classes in Polish language and literature and in handicrafts. In 1912, the PWA built a new headquarters at 1309-15 N. Ashland Ave. The organization was growing every year and at this point consisted of 143 groups with 10,930 members. Beyond its activities related to the old country, the "local" (that is, "American") activities included loans, death benefits, and insurance, and contacts with American societies. The beginning of the First World War opened a new chapter in the activities of PWA, but this moves us beyond the scope of this study.

There were no Zaborowian women among the active members of the PWA. Although they were arriving in Chicago at the time when other Polish women were beginning to become active, they had no political experience from the old country, and they were not educated enough. They were not yet acclimated enough to American culture to know how to act in such an institution. Only a few Zaborowian women had joined before 1914.

What Was New in America?

Material elements of urban American life such as buildings, furniture, clothing, and food were very different from those of the old country and required adjustment. The material sphere of life was not hard to adapt to, however. In social life, traditional ethnic culture coexisted in varying degrees of ease with modern urban American life. For Polish women, the high-profile public activity in the parish and civic organizations and workplace was a novel experience. In Poland, there had been neither reason nor room for such activity, because the parish was not organized around lay and volunteer activism. Chicago was different. Parishioners paid for the church and thereby had the right to influence it. Parishioners took this right seriously. In 1895, riots against an unpopular priest broke out in the parish of St. Hedwig (*Jadwigowo*), which was in the Zaborowian neighborhood. Women were the main participants. *Dziennik Chicagoski* (9 February, 1895) reported that, during a meeting of mostly women in the local society hall, a decision was made to demonstrate against the parsonage and the church. The idea came from local male activists who were in conflict with the pastor. Someone suggested that the women take along miscellaneous iron tools and pepper to throw into the policemen's eyes. At 7 A.M., a crowd of women mobbed the church. The pepper was used. One woman was bitten by a policeman. Fighting went on until 10 A.M., even though the day was very cold. Some women had their babies with them. The women's final act was to lock themselves in the church, and a policeman had to take them away by force. Although the initiative for this action came from outside the women's group, this event made it clear that women were to be reckoned with as a social force.

Industrial work offered even more opportunity for the liberation of gender roles. For example, Polish-American women participated in the 1909 strike in the Chicago garment industry. The Chicago Cloakmakers' Union, which was newly affiliated with the International Cloakmakers' Union, had four active sublocals. One of the sublocals was Polish and, wanting to reach the great number of Polish workers in the garment industry, asked the international union for leaflets printed in Polish.[48] Although the participation of women in such organizations was not large, for Polish village women it was a new sphere of life.

Charity organizations had been unknown to Polish village women. Here the difference between the village community and the urban neighborhood became most apparent. The material and emotional support that had been provided by the village community and families in Poland required an institutional and organizational framework in Chicago. The Polish Catholic church provided care for the sick (St. Mary's of Nazareth Hospital, founded and run by the Sisters of the Holy Family of Nazareth); for the aged (St. Joseph Home for the Aged, founded in 1894 and run by the Franciscan Sisters of the Blessed Kunegunda); for orphans (Holy Family Orphanage, operated by The School Sisters of Notre Dame, and St. Vincent's Orphanage, founded in 1899 and run by the Franciscan Sisters of the Blessed Kunegunda); and for the children of working mothers (St. Elizabeth's Day Nursery, founded in 1904, and the Guardian Angel Day Nursery, founded in 1912). There was also the Home for Working Girls, managed by Rev. Louis Grudzinski, which had room for fifty unemployed or homeless women. The home cared for newly arrived Polish immigrant girls as well. Polish charities were not as well developed as Irish or German charities in Chicago, and Poles often applied to institutions run by the other ethnic groups. Since it was primarily women who organized charities and women who needed help, charity work became a major vehicle for interethnic gender relations.

---

[48]Wilfred Carsel, *A History of the Chicago Ladies Garment Workers Union* (Chicago, 1940), 49.

Also new to Polish immigrants were laws pertaining to family life. In Polish villages family problems were never resolved by legal proceedings. Social rules, not laws, directed behavior. In Chicago, a deserted wife could try to find her husband or obtain money from him with the help of the court. Even the breach of a marriage proposal could be prosecuted. Polish immigrants were generally well informed about these possibilities.[49] Easy access to the legal system encouraged immigrants to make use of legal intervention. The Chicago Legal Aid Society received many complaints from Polish women about problems such as alcoholism and domestic violence. The availability of legal protection, a protection independent of personal attitudes and social relations, was important to immigrant women.

The many social changes Polish-American women experienced transformed gender relations and gender identities. Some of these changes were discussed in *Głos Polek,* the weekly of the Polish Women's Alliance. Women from all groups and walks of life were struggling for equal rights at the beginning of the twentieth century, but the struggle was even harder for those trying at the same time to adjust to a new country. *Głos Polek* championed women's equality and offered a forum for strategies on how to achieve it. The publication presented information from both the United States and Europe (particularly from the Polish territories). Not only the political aspects of equality were discussed but also the social implications. One article published in 1911, written by a man, argued that since the hardest industrial jobs could be done by machines, women's physical strength was no longer a valid reason to exclude women from industrial labor. The author noted that women have the same ability to operate machines as men do. He also pointed out that when women and men work for wages, they suffer the same problems: unemployment, low pay, and bad working conditions. Women, however, have an added burden: unlike men who are fighting for fairer work policies, they cannot forget their family duties. Women can count only on themselves. Therefore, the author concludes, education must be women's route to professions, which would bring them equal rights.

---

[49]William A. Thomas and Florian Znaniecki, *Chłop Polski w Europie i Ameryce,* vol. 5 (Warszawa, 1976).

The author also touched upon the second issue which was prominent in *Głos Polek:* patriotism. The writer called on Polish mothers to cultivate love for the old country in their children; like Hungarians and Bohemians who helped their countries get rid of occupiers, Poles could and should do the same.[50]

A month later the editor resumed the debate. She argued that the main reason for the exploitation of women is that women are not allowed to vote or legislate. Norway and Finland, where women could already enter parliaments, were depicted as positive examples for what could be achieved. A strong Polish women's association such as PWA, she argued, should lead the struggle for women's voting rights.[51] Other Polish female activists also picked up the suffrage cause. In 1911, with the support of the American suffragist Jessie Campbell, the Polish League of Political Equality was founded in Chicago.

Patriotism toward Poland and retention of Polish culture were frequent themes in *Głos Polek.* Feminist arguments and patriotic elements were always intertwined. A Polish immigrant woman always had to remember her motherland, to be responsible for the patriotic education of her children, and to preserve the mother tongue. She also had to be active in ethnic organizations, and the example of high-achieving patriotic Irish women was often cited. This mixture of traditional, patriotic attitudes and American feminist ideas was characteristic of this more advanced stage of acculturation.

One must remember, however, that the ideology of the PWA represented a degree of acculturation not yet acknowledged by most Zaborowian women. As noted earlier, they were not activists in this organization: rather, they were the addressees of the ideology. Their stage of assimilation was typical of immigrants who had only recently arrived. They could adjust quickly as part of a survival strategy, but they remained traditionalists. For many women, especially those who returned to Zaborów after living in Chicago for several years, emigration helped them to realize their life aims. Using money earned in America toward a dowry and an early marriage, they became well-to-do farmers' wives in Poland. Many other women who

---

[50]Julian Korski, *Głos Polek,* no. 5, 2 February 1911.

[51]*Głos Polek,* no. 9, 2 March 1911.

stayed in Chicago continued to dream about returning to the village. This attitude helps explain a rather slow and gradual acculturation, which occurred mainly in the material sphere of life and not in the sphere related to mentality. Not until Zaborowian women underwent further acculturation was there a significant shift in gender identity.

Index

Christiane Harzig is Assistant Professor of North American History at the University of Bremen. Maria Anna Knothe is president of the Center for the Advancement of Women in Warsaw, where she also serves on the City Council. Margareta Matovic is a historian and historical demographer working in Stockholm. Deirdre Mageean is Assistant Professor of Sociology at the University of Maine, Orono. Monika Blaschke has completed her dissertation at the University of Bremen on women in the German-American women's press.